DATE DUE

| | | | |
|---|---|---|---|
| | | | |
| | | | |
| | | | |
| | | | |
| | | | |
| | | | |
| | | | |
| | | | |
| | | | |
| | | | |
| | | | |
| | | | |
| | | | |
| | | | |
| | | | |
| | | | |
| | | | |

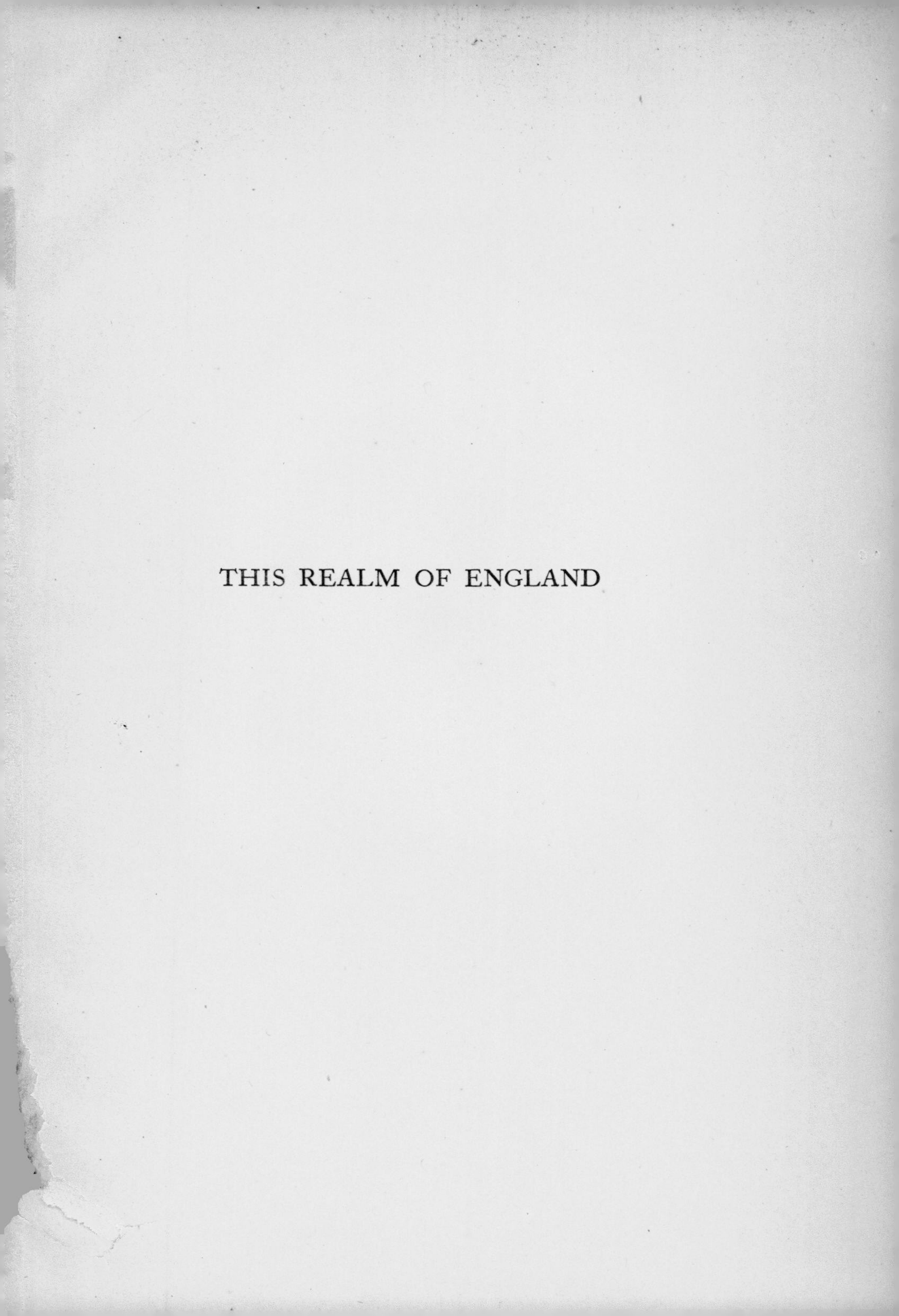

THIS REALM OF ENGLAND

# THIS REALM OF ENGLAND

## MONARCHY, ARISTOCRACY, DEMOCRACY

BY

SIR JOHN MARRIOTT

*Honorary Fellow (formerly Fellow and Lecturer in Modern History) of Worcester College, Oxford. Late M.P. for the City of York*

BLACKIE & SON LIMITED
LONDON AND GLASGOW

BLACKIE & SON LIMITED
50 *Old Bailey, London*
17 *Stanhope Street, Glasgow*

BLACKIE & SON (INDIA) LIMITED
*Warwick House, Fort Street, Bombay*

BLACKIE & SON (CANADA) LIMITED
*Toronto*

*First published, 1938*

*Printed in Great Britain by Blackie & Son, Ltd., Glasgow*

# PREFACE

THIS book has been written with a twofold purpose, and is addressed to two classes of readers. Primarily I have had in mind the general reader, the patriotic citizen who is proud of his country and its Constitution, but has no special knowledge of the process by which the Constitution has been evolved. He realizes that the noble inheritance which he enjoys as a life tenant, and administers as a trustee, is not the result of a sudden access of fortune, but that it has been gradually built up by the patient labours of successive generations. He is aware that his countrymen were the first to work out the peculiar type of government known as " Constitutional or Parliamentary Monarchy ", and he believes that (for himself at any rate) it is the best Constitution as yet evolved by the wit of man and the accidents of history.

It may be that he desires to know something more about the process by which this Polity has reached its present stage of development. But, although he is no specialist in History, he demands, and rightly, that the narrative designed to supply his need shall, without any ostentation of original research, take account of the conclusions reached by the most recent and most competent authorities.

Such is the modest purpose of this book.

An immense amount of valuable work has in the last thirty years been done on special aspects and periods of Constitutional History. But of the results achieved a large proportion can still be found only in monographs and in articles contributed to Technical Reviews and Journals.

To these the general reader is not likely to refer, nor are they always accessible to those who are only embarking on the study of the English Constitution.

Of this work I have, as far as possible, availed myself, and, though the narrative is based upon prolonged study of the "classical" historians, frequent reference will be found to more recent authorities such as the American Professors Dr. McElroy and Dr. Baldwin, Dr. Tout, Dr. Tanner, Dr. Pollard, Mr. Chrymer, Mr. K. Pickthorn, Miss Clarke, and many other specialists for whose contributions to the Technical Reviews every student must be grateful.

The mention of these authorities suggests the other class of readers I have had in mind, those who are beginning the serious study of Constitutional History and who need a single-volume work which, while embodying the results of recent research, covers the whole ground, rapidly yet without sacrifice of accuracy or lucidity. That need, I hope, this book will supply.

I ought, however, to warn all readers, experienced or immature, that this book has been written from an angle not hitherto adopted, as far as I know, by any Constitutional Historian. We have, of course, been accustomed, ever since our first introduction to *Little Arthur* and *Mrs. Markham*, to study English History in a series of "*Reigns*". But that fashion has not (for obvious reasons) been generally followed by the Constitutional Historian. I cannot but think, however, that it has become too much the fashion to write the History of our Constitution as though it were merely the History of Parliament. I yield to no man in my appreciation of the advantages of Parliamentary Government in this country and its Dependencies. But Parliament in England is a mushroom growth as compared with the Monarchy. Down to the sixteenth century at least, Parliament was not really important. Everything depended on the King. Perceiving this truth, some specialists have recently pursued their researches into the history of the King's Court and Council, and in other directions some reaction against the prevalent fashion of the nineteenth century is manifest.

I have gone further; and have frankly made the Crown—the Personal Monarchy down to 1714, the "Constitutional" or "Parliamentary" Monarchy since that date—the central point of my story. I believe that, regarding English History as a whole, this method brings us nearer to the truth of history than that which has hitherto prevailed.

I have inflicted on the reader as few footnotes as possible, but I must sincerely apologize if a good many of them refer to previous works of my own. This is because I am impaled on the horns of a cruel dilemma. This is my first book on English Constitutional History as a whole. But many aspects of the subject I have treated in previous works. Some repetition, then, is unavoidable—though I fear few readers will detect it! To reduce such repetitions to a minimum I have had recourse to a method from which my modesty recoils, and for which I crave forgiveness.

In a short bibliographical appendix I have, I hope, included all the works to which I am consciously indebted, and this general but grateful acknowledgment will, I trust, be accepted by their authors. No one can, however, teach a subject for long years without incurring innumerable debts which he cannot recall, still less acknowledge. For this also I crave pardon.

One special debt, at least, I can acknowledge. It is to my friend and former colleague, the Rev. M. W. Patterson, Fellow and Tutor of Trinity College, Oxford, who most kindly read in proof Chapters I–XI inclusive and made several useful suggestions, for which I am grateful.

That even with his help I have entirely avoided errors I can hardly hope; but in regard to large omissions I would remind readers that my purpose has been strictly limited. This is not a History of England. It represents merely a modest attempt to assess the value of the peculiar and characteristic contribution which England has made to the history of civilization. My assessment may be faulty; but the success or failure of my attempt can be judged fairly only by those who recognize the precise purpose of my book and the limitations its fulfilment has imposed.

J. A. R. MARRIOTT.

LONDON,
*16th May, 1938.*

# CONTENTS

## BOOK I. THE MAKING OF ENGLAND

### A.D. 43–1215

## BOOK II. THE MAKING OF THE CONSTITUTION

A.D. 1215–1485

## BOOK III. THE PARTING OF THE WAYS

A.D. 1485–1714

# CHAPTER I

## PROLOGUE

---

## The Achievement of England

"The lot is fallen unto me in a fair ground;
yea, I have a goodly heritage."

**At the Bar of History.**

IF England should some day be summoned to stand before the Judgment Seat of History, what is the account that she will make? If some future Gibbon should undertake to write *The Decline and Fall of the British Empire*, in what terms will he characterize its achievement, what value will he assign to the legacy it bequeathes to mankind?

We glibly assess the value of the Legacy of Greece and the Legacy of Rome. The Greeks, we say truly, set for all time a standard of beauty: they attained perfect proportion in plastic art and in literature; in poetry and drama, in philosophy and rhetoric, their achievements have never been surpassed. But in the Art, though not in the Science, of Politics, the verdict has gone against them. Politically, Greece is said to have failed. Difficult, indeed, it is to associate failure with Athens, which not only exhibited the City-State at its highest, but produced or sheltered Æschylus, Sophocles, Euripides and Aristophanes, Herodotus and Thucydides, Aeschines and Demosthenes, Pheidias and Praxiteles, Themistocles, Solon, Cleisthenes and Pericles. Yet Athens failed to found an Athenian Empire or even an Hellenic State, and so failing, disobeyed the primary law of political being. Hellenic culture survived: the Greek peoples were absorbed into alien empires.

Rome succeeded where Greece failed. Though imitative in Fine Art, and less original than Athens in literary production, in History and Philosophy, in Poetry and Drama, Rome taught the world the art of Government: she devised a code of laws, which laid the legal foundations on which a great part of the civilized world has been built.

And England? What will be accounted her characteristic achievement? Should her Empire fall, what legacy will she leave? Many claims may be made, and justly, on her behalf, in more than one sphere of human activity.

In the Arts, England, despite notable achievements, can claim no superiority. In painting, her landscape school has attained well-deserved renown, but in the department of Fine Art as a whole she must yield pride of place to other nations. In Music, she is the equal neither of Italy nor Germany. Her Literature, on the contrary, is in beauty, range and variety inferior to that of no other nation in the Ancient or Modern World. Chaucer and Shakespeare, Milton, Shelley, Keats, Wordsworth, Tennyson and Bridges—can any people since the decadence of the Greeks produce a bevy of poets equal to these? Is the comedy of Sheridan far behind that of Terence, Plautus or Molière? Clarendon, Gibbon and Froude need not fear the rivalry of Thucydides and Tacitus. In the art of the Novel, Great Britain is indisputably supreme. Science, theoretical and applied, is admittedly international; scientific progress is co-operative rather than competitive. Yet, in generous rivalry, Newton and Darwin may stand beside Archimedes and Galileo as men who have revolutionized the outlook of man upon his world; Watt and Stevenson wrought a change in the conditions of life comparable with that effected by the genius of Edison and Marconi.

In all these spheres of human ingenuity, however, England has rivals. In another sphere she has none. Her supreme achievement, her most characteristic contribution to the sum of human happiness, lies in the sphere of Politics. No other nation in world-history has excelled or equalled her in the art of Government, in the ordering of the Common-

England's Supreme Achievement.

wealth, in promoting the well-being and happiness of the many peoples committed to her charge. By prolonged and patient experiment England has gone nearer than any other nation towards a solution of the ultimate problem of Politics.

What is that problem? How has England solved it?

The problem, briefly and broadly stated, is, to reconcile Liberty and Order, to achieve Stability without retarding Progress.

**Parliamentary Monarchy.**

England has solved it by the curious, confusing, but characteristic compromise which, with unconscious arrogance, we describe as "Constitutional Monarchy". "Constitutional" is, indeed, a capricious and question-begging epithet. "Parliamentary Monarchy" might be accepted as a less invidious and more scientific classification.

At the outset of a work designed to trace the stages by which the goal has been reached, it may be convenient to indicate what Constitutional or Parliamentary Monarchy involves.

It involves (i) a *Monarchy*, at once hereditary and limited; (ii) a *Legislature*, "broad based upon the people's will". The primary function of every Legislature is to make laws, but the distinctive function of the English Parliament is to sustain in office an Executive Committee. (iii) This Committee, the Cabinet, or more properly the *Ministry*, is appointed from among the members of the Legislature, and is responsible both to the Legislature (of which the King forms part) and to the King as the sole and supreme Executive. The Ministers are "Ministers of the Crown"; they are appointed in theory, and to a limited extent in practice, by the Sovereign, who nevertheless acts, in all political affairs, on the corporate advice of a body of men who are still officially described as "His Majesty's Servants".

But (iv) both the Legislature and the Executive, the Legislature directly, the Executive indirectly, are responsible to an *Electorate*—now co-extensive with the whole adult population. The Electorate is thus politically Sovereign, though legal Sovereignty is vested in Parliament.

**Product of Evolution.**

It is essential to a comprehension of the Constitution, thus broadly outlined, to insist that it was not the product of a single brain. England never produced, or even invented, a Solon or a Cleisthenes. Nor was it, like the Constitution of the United States, or that of the Union of South Africa, the creation of a Convention sitting behind closed doors, and opening them only to present to the people a fully fledged Constitution. The English Constitution is the product of a prolonged process of evolution and adaptation. Nor has the process reached a term. *En Angleterre la Constitution peut changer sans cesse; ou plutôt elle n'existe pas.* De Tocqueville's oft-quoted aphorism expresses the precise truth. More picturesque is the image employed by De Tocqueville's brilliant countryman to describe this ever-changing Constitution. M. Émile Boutmy compares it to *un chemin qui marche*, or to " a river whose moving surface glides away at one's feet, meandering in and out in endless curves, now seeming to disappear in a whirlpool, now almost lost to sight in the verdure ".

The fluidity of English Political Institutions has been the despair both of the scientific commentator and of the practical copyist. The commentators are naturally baffled by the lack of authoritative texts. Some of them, however—M. Boutmy conspicuous among the number—are astute enough to perceive, and candid enough to acknowledge, the political advantages of a flexible and unwritten Constitution. " The English," he writes, " have left the different parts of their Constitution just where the wave of History had deposited them; they have not attempted to bring them together, to classify or complete them, or to make a consistent and coherent whole. This scattered Constitution gives no hold to sifters of texts and seekers after difficulties. It need not fear critics anxious to point out an omission, or theorists ready to denounce an antinomy. . . . By this means only can you preserve the happy incoherences, the useful incongruities, the protecting contradictions which have such good reason for existing in institutions, viz. that they exist in the nature of things, and which, while they allow free play to all social forces, never allow any one of these forces room to work out of its allotted line, or to shake the foundations and walls of the whole fabric. This is the result which the English flatter themselves they have arrived at by the extraordinary dispersion of their constitutional texts, and they have always taken good care not to compromise the result in any way by attempting to form a code." [1]

**Colonial Constitutions**

If commentators have found it difficult to understand and to interpret English Political Institutions, would-be imitators have found even more disheartening the attempt to reproduce them. To the failure of the copyists there has, however, been one notable exception—one of those exceptions which proves the logical rule. The system of government evolved in the island-home has been substantially reproduced in the new homes established by Britons in distant continents. But the secret of success is that the men who have to work these Colonial Constitutions are, for the most part, men of British blood and steeped in British traditions of self-government. Moreover, the British Colonies in Canada, Australasia and South Africa did not, at a single step, attain to the dignity of self-governing Dominions. That would have been entirely inconsistent with British methods. The young communities overseas had to go through a term of apprenticeship, though, for obvious reasons, the apprenticeship period was greatly curtailed in their favour. The process prolonged through six centuries in the homeland was completed in less than a hundred years by the Dominions. The result is that there are now, distributed over four continents, five Democratic communities, alike in structure, equal in status, completely autonomous, but united in common allegiance to our King. India stands at present in a class apart, no longer a mere Dependency, but not yet enjoying the full status of a Dominion. Besides the great Dominions and India there is a vast congeries of Colonies, Dependencies, Protectorates and Mandated States in various stages of political development.

The British Empire is, then, a unique phenomenon in the history of political formations, and it demands excep-

[1] *Studies in Constitutional Law*, pp. 4, 7.

tional qualifications in its administrators: it calls for a combination of strength and skill, of tact, courage, resourcefulness and adaptability, only to be found in men inheriting a long tradition of self-government, and endowed with a native genius for politics.

**Foreign Spectacles.**

That genius is by common consent attributed to Englishmen. *Securus judicat orbis terrarum.* The unanimous verdict of mankind cannot be mistaken. It is true that to minds more tidy and logical than our own the English Constitution may appear to be a cumbrous compromise, a hardly intelligible makeshift, at best a series of brilliant improvisations. Nevertheless it has, throughout the ages, excited the admiration—even if in admiration there be an admixture of perplexity—of foreign commentators and chroniclers.

***Perfide Albion.***

Foreign statesmen and diplomatists have, indeed, been less indulgent than philosophical observers towards the defects of the system as it has affected international relations. *Le Perfide Albion* has become a byword in the vernacular of diplomacy. As far back as the seventeenth century Peter the Great was complaining that England was "variable dans ses projets". "There is no country in Europe," said Torcy in 1715, "where maxims of Government change so often as in England."

Vergennes, the greatest of French diplomatists in the eighteenth century, declared in 1783 that "Nothing is so changeable as the policy of the Cabinet of St. James's, in relation to continental politics". Kaunitz, the great Austrian contemporary of Vergennes, held that upon "*si singulier gouvernement*" it was impossible to count. A century later Bismarck, though he would have liked to draw England into the orbit of the Triple Alliance, held that it was useless to make an alliance with a Power subject to the changes and chances of Parliamentary Government. Even Albert Sorel, not a politician but a great historian, is fain to admit that the caprice rightly or wrongly attributed to Party Government tends to make continuity difficult and alliances insecure.

Such accusations, even if unjust, are not unintelligible.

British Foreign Policy.

Nay more: on short views of policy, natural to the diplomatist living for the hour, they are justified by the facts. But the historian, taking longer views, should be able to perceive that ever since the European states-system emerged in the sixteenth century, England has pursued a consistent policy based upon fixed principles. There is no denying that those principles have compelled us to take different sides at different times. Wolsey, the first of our great Foreign Ministers, espoused the cause of the Emperor and the French King alternately. Queen Elizabeth, true to Wolsey's principles, but employing the methods appropriate to her own sex, held out hopes that she might bestow her virginal affections now on this suitor, now on that. She had, of course, no intention of marrying any of them, for she was "married to England"; marriage with a foreign prince would, therefore, have been for her an act of political adultery. Cromwell's war against Spain was superficially in accord with the Elizabethan tradition, but the Protector was not quick enough to perceive that conditions had changed, and that regard for the European equilibrium would have dictated alliance with decadent Spain against the rising power of France. Parliament brought Charles II back, perhaps unwillingly, on to traditional lines, with the result that neither Louis XIV nor William of Orange could be quite sure of him. William III and Marlborough committed England to war with France, but she was accused of perfidy when, at the close of the Spanish Succession War, she deserted her allies to conclude peace with France at Utrecht (1713). In the War of the Austrian Succession (1740–8) England fought on the side of Austria against Prussia and France, and ten years later on the side of Prussia against France and Austria. Frederick the Great never forgave us for deserting him in 1761, and in the War of American Independence the whole of Europe was against us. We never wavered, however, in our opposition to Napoleon when he threatened to dominate the Continent, nor, one hundred years later, did we fail France when a like danger threatened from the other side of the Rhine.

Perfidious! Variable! Inconstant! In detail, the charge is specious. But it would be greatly to the advantage of world-peace, if the world would realize that there are certain fixed maxims on which England has, with singular consistency, acted for the last four centuries.

**La Puissance médiatrice.**

(i) The first is that England has invariably been "*la puissance médiatrice*". Anxious to exercise a mediatorial influence, she has consistently opposed the domination of any single Power; she has laboured to maintain the equilibrium essential to the liberty of Europe as a whole, and particularly to the independence of the smaller and weaker countries.

**England and the Low Countries.**

(ii) The key position has for centuries been held by the country, variously designated at different times, situated on the delta of the Scheldt and the Rhine. In the independence of the Low Countries England has, therefore, always been profoundly interested. No great Power has ever, with England's concurrence, been allowed to dominate, still less to absorb them. Reluctantly Elizabeth fought Philip II on that issue. A century later Louis XIV's attempt to conquer the Low Countries brought England into the field against France. She remained in that field, as will presently appear, for another reason.

Another century passes. Pitt could not be induced to enter the war against the French Republic until the Republic attacked Belgium. Napoleon might, in 1814, have retained the throne of France, if he would have surrendered Antwerp, whence he could always (in his own phrase) "point a loaded pistol at the heart of England". Exactly a hundred years later the Germans might well have reached Paris had they marched through the gap of Belfort instead of violating the neutrality of Belgium.[1]

In all this it is not easy to discern the signs of inconstancy and variability. On the contrary there has been, in the foreign policy of England, a singular measure of consistency and continuity. England has maintained, not in her own interests alone, but in the interests of every country that

[1] For the historical relations of England and the Low Countries see Marriott: *European Commonwealth* (Oxford, 1918, Chap. VIII).

desires to preserve its independence, the European equilibrium. Wipe this little island off the map, and Europe will be at the mercy of the first Power that can command the biggest battalions.

(iii) In order to play the part she has assumed, England has for the most part relied on her superiority at sea. That superiority, though temporarily broken during part of the American War of Independence, has been generally maintained since the development of the Overseas Empire in the seventeenth century. To the maintenance of that Empire sea-power has been an indispensable condition.

For another reason it has become indispensable. After the industrialization and urbanization of England, and the deliberate subordination of agriculture to commerce, naval supremacy became essential to the existence of a population which could no longer sustain life on the produce of its own soil. That truth was in 1917 painfully driven home.

**Appreciations, English and Foreign.**

The charge of inconstancy must, then, be repudiated; but candour compels the admission that if foreign critics have been quick to discern the defects of English foreign policy, they have been, to an amazing extent, unanimous in concurring with native commentators as to the outstanding merits and achievements of the English system of government.

As early as the fifteenth century the famous French chronicler, Philippe de Comines (1445–1509), wrote: "Of all the kingdoms of the world, known to me, England is the one where public affairs are best conducted." Sir John Fortescue (*d.* 1476), Chief Justice of the King's Bench, who was almost contemporary with Comines, was the first Englishman to analyse the essential characteristics of the English Constitution. Sir Edward Coke declared that Fortescue's *De Laudibus Legum Angliae*, compiled for the instruction of a royal pupil, was worthy of being written in letters of gold. The Constitutional Monarchy of England appeared to Fortescue to combine the advantages of autocracy (*Dominium Regale*) and republicanism (*Dominium*

*Politicum*). The secret of English liberty he discovered in the fact that " A King of England cannot at his pleasure make any alteration in the laws of the land, for the nature of his government is not only legal but political ". The " subjects are not bound to obey any laws or pay any taxes to which they have not consented ". Consequently they " enjoy their properties securely and without the hazard of being deprived of them either by the King or any other ". About a hundred years after the death of Fortescue, Sir Thomas Smith published *The Commonwealth of England*. Sir Thomas was ambassador to France in the early part of Elizabeth's reign (1562–6), and his work is declared by Dr. Pollard to be " the most important description of the Constitution and Government of England written in the Tudor age ". It went through many editions, both in English and in Latin, and was translated into German and Dutch. Like Fortescue, Smith highly extolled the Parliament of England, " which representeth and hath the power of the whole realm, both the head and the body ".

In the seventeenth century we find the best commentators on the English Polity among the poets. Sir Henry Taylor, an admirable critic, went so far as to say that " the poetry of this country is its best storehouse of political wisdom ". There is, in truth, much political instruction to be drawn from the Chronicle Plays of Shakespeare, but his teaching is mostly, as good teaching frequently is, indirect. Yet no finer apostrophe to England was ever penned than that which Shakespeare put into the mouth of John of Gaunt. Milton's noble tribute to the characteristic excellence of the English Constitution, the perfect balance of political forces that maintains its equilibrium, was in prose: " There is no civil government that hath been known . . . more divinely and harmoniously tuned and more equally balanced as it were by the hand and scale of justice, than is the Commonwealth of England, where under a free and untutored monarch, the noblest, worthiest, and most prudent men, with full approbation and suffrage of the people, have in their power the supreme and final determination of highest affairs."[1] Dryden, as was proper to the laureate of the Restoration, dwelt on the virtues of moderation and the happy avoidance of extremes under the ægis of a Constitutional monarch:

> Such impious axioms foolishly they show,
> For in some soils republics will not grow;
> Our temperate isle will no extremes sustain
> Of popular sway or arbitrary reign;
> But slides between them both into the best,
> Secure in freedom in a monarch blest.

Tennyson perhaps had Dryden's verse in mind when he wrote:

> Turning to scorn with lips divine
> The falsehood of extremes.

In the eighteenth century we are again in an age of prose. To Sir William Blackstone, whose famous *Commentaries* were first published in 1765, belongs the credit of having been the first to analyse, systematically and adequately, the legal principles on which the British Constitution rested. Superbly did the great lawyer vindicate the "vigour of our free Constitution": the Executive power lodged in a single person; the legislative sovereignty of Parliament; the distribution of legislative power between King, Lords and Commons; the liberty of the subject and his free enjoyment of personal security and of private property; the regular administration and free course of justice in the Courts of Law; the delicate equilibrium of the several forces within the State—all this has become the commonplace of criticism and has been familiarized to our own generation by the expository skill of Albert Venn Dicey, and the genius of Walter Bagehot.

How foreign jurists must have envied England as they read Blackstone. The greatest of them, the Baron de Montesquieu (1689–1755), died, in fact, ten years before the *Commentaries* were published, but his admiration for that land of liberty was writ large over the face of his *Esprit des Lois*. Of Montesquieu, Madison, the great American jurist,

[1] *Of Reformation in England.*

wrote with just discernment: " The British Constitution was to Montesquieu what Homer was to the didactic writers on epic poetry. . . . [He] appears to have viewed the Constitution of England as the standard, or to use his own expression as the mirror of political liberty." That liberty he attributed to the separation of powers—legislative, executive and judicial, and he built up the main body of his argument on that thesis.

Just a century after Montesquieu's death Montalembert published *The Political Future of England* (1856), a work which well deserves to be recalled, and if necessary republished. Montalembert held up to ridicule the croakers who announced (to use his own words) " the near and inevitable ruin of this last asylum of modern liberty ". The price paid for liberty was sometimes, he admitted, rather high, but too much attention must not, he argued, be paid to occasional and noisy demonstrations, and with great good sense, added: " With all his affected modesty and with all these ugly appearances and alarming incidents, the Englishman is not a whit less persuaded that his country is the first country in the world; he does not say so until he is contradicted, but he believes it, and for doing so has some very good reasons, and it only rests with himself to make those reasons still better " (pp. 29–30). And there is every prospect that he will; for " no other form of government has ever given to man, more opportunities of accomplishing all that is just and reasonable, or more facilities for avoiding error and for correcting it ". Only one great danger did Montalembert discern in the political and social structure of England—the " increase of functionaries, and the deluge of officials ". And that was in 1856, when the total public expenditure in Great Britain fell far short of the Estimates for a single Department to-day!

The jump from Montesquieu to Montalembert has involved the omission of all mention of a number of commentators on the English Constitution, of De Lolme (1771), of the Whig writers of the early Victoria era, such as Lord Brougham, Lord Russell and Lord Grey, of Disraeli, and, greatest of all, of Edmund Burke. Two American commentators, Dr. Laurence Lowell and Dr. Woodrow Wilson, would call for inclusion did this catalogic enumeration aim at comprehensiveness, as would the great English jurists Sir Henry Sumner Maine and James, Viscount Bryce. Passing reference has already been made to Émile Boutmy, and if no mention is made of Dr. Joseph Redlich of Vienna and M. Ostrogorski, it is only because their valuable works were monographic, because they were specialists writing for specialists. But after the emphasis laid on the appreciations of many French writers it were invidious to neglect entirely, though the reference be wholly inadequate, two great German publicists.

**Rudolph von Gneist.**

The work of one of them, Rudolph von Gneist (1816–95), is well known in this country. The main purpose of his many books was to make English institutions better known and more widely appreciated among his own countrymen, and to lead them along the path of constitutional evolution so wisely trodden, as it seemed to him, by Englishmen. "During the eighteenth century, England," he wrote, "as the only great free State, stood alone amongst the other great European States. . . . It appeared as though this great Germanic people was destined by Providence to preserve to Europe during the eighteenth century the picture of a free State, in order that in the nineteenth century it might become the common property of the European world." But he added a timely warning that the English Constitution was "in no way capable of application to other nations in the absence of the previous conditions upon which it arose".[1]

Gneist's warning was unfortunately ignored. One country after another attempted to copy the English Constitution without submitting itself to the long disciplinary process essential to the successful handling of a singularly delicate mechanism. The breakdown of premature experiments in the field of Parliamentary Democracy must be held in part responsible for the prevalent reaction to Dictatorship, for

[1] *Constitutional History of England,* I, pp. 435, 437.

the exaltation of the totalitarian State. The reaction is doubtless to be deplored; but it is the part of wisdom, while deploring the results, to strive to apprehend the causes.[1]

Wilhelm Dibelius.

Much less comprehensive than Gneist's works, but more remarkable in view of the circumstances under which it was written, is the *England* of Wilhelm Dibelius. The original German edition was published in 1922, and an English translation in 1930. Gneist both loved England and admired her. Dibelius, it may be surmised, had no love for England, but he had an immense admiration for her achievement, and a very acute, if somewhat cynical, comprehension of the national characteristics which had conduced to it.

Here is a good illustration of his method. He is arguing that, though English policy is in reality far from disinterested, it has to the world the appearance of disinterestedness. How different from France! "While France, since Richelieu's day, has kept the world busy and excited by plans of expansion and perpetual flag-waving, England quietly grows, waving its flag as seldom as possible. . . . When it does hoist its flag, the place generally happens to be some sterile promontory or cape which represents no great loss to the Power that yields it up, but gives a most powerful position into the hands of a naval nation. . . . But the fact remains that Britain is the solitary great Power which has never injured the vital interest of another European people by annexation, and it is a fact of immeasurable moral effect in a period dominated by the principle of nationality" (pp. 102–3).

In his analysis of the causes of England's success Dibelius naturally attributes great importance to her Political Institutions, but the special achievement of English "Parliamentarism" he finds in the fact that "it has given a great people a political education and presented it with leaders of singular competency" (p. 230). Not that England has been particularly fertile in the production of leaders. On

[1] My *Dictatorship and Democracy* (2nd Ed., Oxford, 1937) is a modest attempt to supply a commentary on this text, and to that work the reader may be referred for details.

the contrary, "England can live without great men comparatively longer than any other country". Her achievement is "in the last analysis not the individual achievement of single statesmen, single legislators, single generals, or single thinkers, but the collective achievement of the Anglo-Saxon race". It is true that there have never been wanting, either in England itself or in the Colonies, simple men, of average endowment, who "quite naturally, good naturedly, and egotistically pushed with their elbows and went on making the world more and more English. . . . On such men rests England's greatness; because of them it has survived, without notable loss, periods when its statesmen were definitely mediocre, periods when the world was looking forward to England's downfall" (p. 504). If this is very acute criticism, more subtle is the remark that England's great achievement is to have made the State superfluous. "It is good for the world, and good for nations with other ideals, that the world contains a State such as has made the State wellnigh superfluous." It is true that the outside world feels as a danger England's dominant quality, her "lust for power", but the supreme good fortune of England consists in a circumstance which foreigners and even Englishmen have been slow to appreciate at its real significance. It is this: "England is the single country in the world that, looking after its own interest with meticulous care, has at the same time something to give to others; the single country where patriotism does not represent a threat or challenge to the rest of the world; the single country that invariably summons the most progressive, idealistic and efficient forces in other nations to co-operate with it. . . . Britain is the solitary great Power with a national programme which, while egotistic through and through, at the same time promises to the world as a whole something which the world passionately desires—order, progress and eternal peace" (pp. 103–9).

Order, Progress, Peace! What finer epitaph could a nation desire? If it be conceded that England has given to the world an example in this respect, she can go before the

Court of Historical Appeal with the confident assurance that its judgment will be given in her favour.

What are the special endowments of nature, what are the peculiar characteristics of her people, or the conditions of her historical development, that have given to England the opportunity of achieving this position, of enabling her to make the claim conceded to her by competent critics?

The purpose of this book is to attempt an answer to these questions.

It may be that the answer will be found in the fact that the people of this island have worked out for themselves a unique system of government, and have bestowed upon their daughter lands the Political Institutions which in the course of centuries they have themselves evolved. That system of government was unknown to the ancient world, and in the modern world was first developed by a prolonged, laborious but partly accidental process in this land. "Constitutional" or "Parliamentary" Monarchy happily combines the principles of Authority and Freedom, of Authority limited by law, of Freedom enjoyable only in obedience to the law.

That system has been extensively imitated, but with success only in those countries which, like ourselves, have served a long apprenticeship in self-government. In countries which have had no such opportunity, or have refused the indispensable discipline, imitation can only lead, and in some cases has led, to disaster.

Before we could approach the problem of constitutional liberty we had, however, to solve the problem of national unity. Parliamentary government presupposes the existence of a nation. English history has, indeed, too often been written as though it were the history of the English Parliament. That fashion has been superseded by another. Emphasis has now shifted to social and economic developments. Needless is it to insist that Parliamentary and social history are alike important; but, long before Parliament came into existence, the King was moulding the form of the English State: upon the social and economic life of the people the Monarchy exercised a profound influence. The making of a nation depends, at any rate in primitive times, on the existence of a strong Monarchy. Succeeding chapters will, therefore, record the genesis of kingship and will indicate the all-important part played by the Monarchy in the making of England. They will exhibit the Crown, now in conflict with the national Church, more often in alliance with it, and almost always steadily resistant to the intrusive claims of the Roman Curia. They will trace the conflict between the Monarchy and the magnates under the Norman and Angevin kings, the evolution of Parliament under the later Plantagenets, and the breakdown of a premature experiment under the Lancastrians and Yorkists. They will explain the circumstances which justified the Tudor dictatorship, and will show how the success of that dictatorship led inevitably to the crucial struggle between Crown and Parliament under the Stuarts. Later chapters will describe the relations between the kings of the Hanoverian dynasty and the " Revolution families " who from 1714 to 1832 ruled England, and will sketch the evolution during that period of the Cabinet system. Queen Victoria's reign was coincident with the political supremacy of the middle-classes, and an attempt will accordingly be made to estimate the place of that great Queen in the evolution of Parliamentary Monarchy. Not until after her death was the government of England a Democracy. The outstanding achievement of King George V was to reconcile the principles of Hereditary Monarchy and Parliamentary Democracy. Both principles were not only accepted in Great Britain but were applied in the British Dominions beyond the seas. A concluding chapter will, accordingly, attempt to demonstrate the importance of the Crown as the " golden link " of the Empire, as the apex of the constitutional structure of the British Commonwealth of Nations.

## CHAPTER II

# King and Nation
# The Making of England

NATIONAL unity, if not a condition precedent of Political Liberty, is an essential precursor of Representative Democracy. It was, therefore, logical that the nation which was the first to evolve a complete Parliamentary Constitution should have been the first also to develop a precocious sense of national unity.

For England's precocity, in this respect, there were many reasons, to be discussed in a later chapter. Enough for the present to say that the most powerful was the exceptional strength of the Monarchy at a relatively early stage of national development.

" War begat the King." So, in his incisive way, said J. R. Green. Bishop Stubbs agreed with him. But if war begat the King, the King begat the Nation-State. Thus it was that the Nation-State, the characteristic political formation of modern Europe, first emerged in England under a national Monarchy, and national unity ultimately found expression in the constitutional structure of the thirteenth century.

Fortunate in its kings, this country was fortunate also in its conquerors, who invaded Britain between the second and eleventh centuries. Their sequence is indicated with sufficient accuracy in the audacious doggerel of Daniel Defoe:

> The Romans first with Julius Cæsar came,
> Including all the nations of that name,
> Gauls, Greeks and Lombards and, by computation,
> Auxiliaries or slaves of every nation.

With Hengist, Saxons; Danes, with Sueno came
In search of plunder, not in search of fame.
Scots, Picts, and Irish from the Hibernian shore,
And conquering William brought the Normans o'er.

From this amphibious ill-born mob began
That vain ill-natured thing an Englishman.
The customs, surnames, languages and manners
Of all these nations are their own explainers:
Whose relics are so lasting and so strong
They ha' left a shibboleth upon our tongue,
By which with easy search you may distinguish
Your Roman-Saxon-Danish-Norman-English.[1]

With one exception the successive conquests were effected by men of kindred blood. Racial amalgamation was thus rendered easier, more rapid, and more complete, with the result that by the time of Henry II an English nation had emerged. It was, says a contemporary, hardly possible to distinguish (speaking only of freemen) between an Anglian and a Norman.[2]

**The Romans in Britain, A.D. c. 43–c. 410.**

To the rule of consanguinity among our conquerors the one exception was the Roman. Of the inhabitants of pre-Roman Britain a good deal has of late been written, but little is known. The literary history of this island begins with Julius Cæsar and Tacitus. Julius Cæsar made two expeditions into Britain (55 and 54 B.C.), but as Tacitus observes, " he seems rather to have drawn the attention of his successors to Britain than to have bequeathed it to them ".[3] Augustus may have had fleeting dreams of a conquest of Britain, but they never materialized: the official opinion at Rome in his time was that a conquest of Britain " would not pay ".

The Emperor Claudius (41–54) and his advisers took a different view. Roman capitalists were convinced that

[1] *The True Born Englishman.*

[2] Vix jam cohabitantibus Anglicis et Normannis et alterutum uxores ducentibus vel nubentibus, sic permixtae sunt nationes ut vix discerni possit hodie, de liberis loquor, quis Anglicus, quis Normannus sit genere.

[3] *Agricola* 13.

Britain was full of unexploited wealth—especially mineral wealth. Moreover, the increasing activity of the Britons in Northern Gaul made them irritating if not dangerous neighbours, while the death of Cunobelinus (the Cymbeline of Shakespeare), ruler of the Timobantes, the chief tribe of South-Eastern Britain, was followed by family feuds among his sons, and by an appeal to Rome for interference.

That appeal was welcomed by Claudius, who was all in favour of a "forward" foreign policy. Accordingly in 43 he dispatched to Britain a powerful army of 40,000–50,000 men which, under the command of Aulus Plautius, began the systematic conquest of the island. It was completed, if not under Julius Agricola (78–85), at least by the time of Hadrian's visit to Britain (121). The details of the conquest do not concern us. With the results of the ensuing occupation, which lasted roughly for four centuries, it is otherwise.

What permanent impress did that occupation leave upon the land and the people, upon their language, laws and institutions? Although that question involves us in the realm of controversy, certain features can be clearly discerned, and may be described without risk of contradiction. Part of the island was completely Romanized; in the rest of it the occupation was merely military, and its effects were evanescent.

Within a quadrilateral the lines of which may be drawn from Chester to Lincoln, from Lincoln to Canterbury, from Canterbury to Caerleon-on-Usk, and from Caerleon to Chester, the Romans permeated Britain, transforming not merely the face of the country, but the life of the people.[1] In the rest of the island, notably in the north and west, the occupation was superficial.

Agricola raided Scotland more than once (80–3) and planted posts on the line of the Forth and Clyde, but his victories over the Caledonians had no permanent effects. The attempt on Scotland was renewed by Antoninus Pius

[1] East Anglia, though cut off from the "Quadrilateral" by a broad strip of fen and forest, must be included in it.

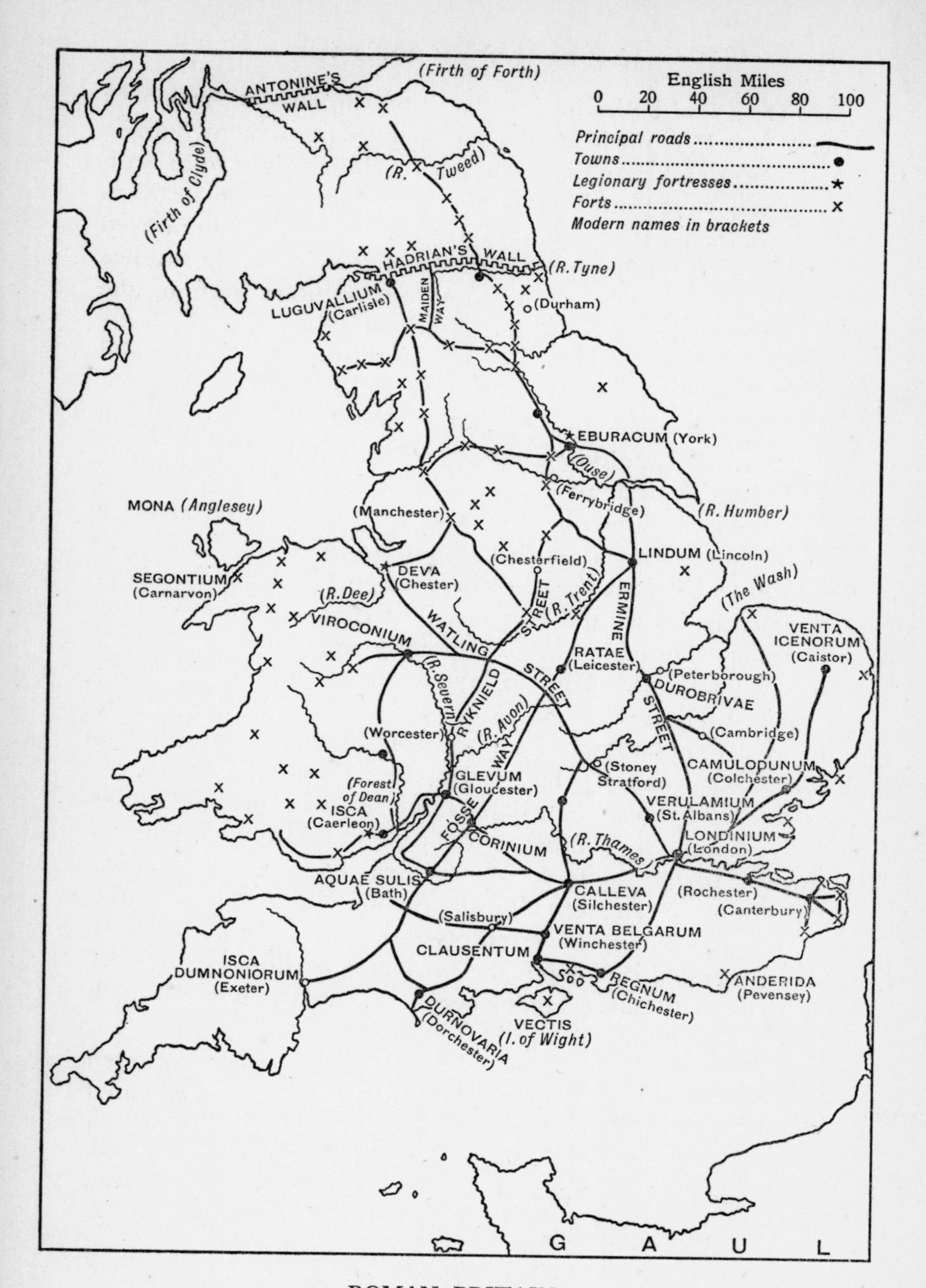


ROMAN BRITAIN

in 142–3, and he built a new wall on the line of Agricola's forts, but Pius made no deeper or more permanent impress upon Scotland than his predecessor. Hadrian's famous wall, built about 120 from Tyne to Solway, may, therefore, be taken to mark the northern limits of Roman Britain as an organized Province of the Empire. Of that Province York was at once the capital and the most important military station, the base-camp originally of the Ninth and later (120) of the Sixth Legion. Two other legions were stationed at Chester and Caerleon, the former to guard the estuaries of Mersey and Dee against Irish pirates, and both to protect the Welsh frontier. In addition to the three great garrison towns a large number of small forts were erected; each was garrisoned by auxiliary regiments, from 500–1000 strong, and all were interconnected by a network of military roads.

Quite different was the character of the Roman occupation to the south and east of a line drawn from Severn to Humber. Throughout that region the population as a whole was Romanized. Therein lay the great cities (*municipia* or *coloniae*)[1] Colchester, St. Albans, Gloucester and Lincoln, besides London and a number of smaller towns such as Canterbury and Rochester, Dorchester and Exeter, Cirencester, Silchester, and Bath. But Roman Britain, unlike Italy, Spain or Southern Gaul, never became a land of towns. In the main, as Mr. Collingwood has pointed out, "Britain was an agricultural country where towns served chiefly as administrative centres and markets for the country districts round them, and the work of agriculture was chiefly carried on by large landowners living in the houses which we call 'Roman villas'".[2]

**The Villae.**

The sites of some five hundred of these *villae*, scattered throughout southern and eastern England, have been located by archæologists. In some cases the villa was the home of a Roman immigrant, but the vast majority of villae were occupied by Romanized provincials, descendants, we may surmise, of the old Celtic nobility. The demesne, or home-

[1] There was, at this time, little distinction between them.

[2] Collingwood: *Roman Britain*, p. 79.

farm (the former term survives in Ireland), was cultivated by slaves, and the rest of the estate was let to *coloni*, who, like the villeins of the Norman manors, were semi-servile, being tied to the soil they cultivated, though in most other respects they were free men.

Throughout the third century, and the first half of the fourth, Roman Britain enjoyed a considerable measure of prosperity. A contemporary[1] writes in 296 of its wealth in corn, cattle, and metals; and the results of archæological research have generally confirmed the truth of his picture. Towards the end of the third century, however, the security of the island was threatened by pirates from North Germany. To defend the island against the Saxon raids a series of forts, distinguished by high thick walls, was built along the "Saxon Shore", from the Wash to the Solent, and put under the command of a special officer afterwards known as the "Count of the Saxon Shore". About the same time the Roman forts on the West Coast (e.g. at Carnarvon) were rebuilt, and new ones at Cardiff and elsewhere were built to guard the island against the raids of the Scots from Ireland.

For a time these precautions sufficed. But in 367 hordes of Saxons and Scots, in concert with Picts from Caledonia, swept over the whole land as far south as London. The military disaster was retrieved by Count Theodosius, but from the widespread devastation caused by these invaders Roman Britain never recovered. Fortified towns escaped the general destruction, but of the hundreds of Romano-British villas the Teutonic invaders of the fifth and sixth centuries found only the ruins; even the villages were largely waste. Plainly the way had been prepared for the next important stage in the making of England.

Meanwhile, one question demands an answer. Early in the fifth century the Roman troops were withdrawn from Britain; the Romanized inhabitants were left to look after themselves. How far did they hand on the Roman tradition to their Teutonic conquerors? What permanent impress

[1] Eumenius: *Panegyricus Constantio Caesari*, *ap.* Oman, p. 140.

did the Romans, after an occupation of four centuries, leave upon their remote Province?

**Roman v. Teuton.**

Half a century ago the "Teutonic School", represented by men like Bishop Stubbs and Kemble, J. R. Green and Freeman, were in full possession of the field of History. They answered the above question unequivocally: of everything Celtic and Roman the Teutonic invaders made a clean sweep.

"Were the evidences of intermixture of race much stronger and more general than they are, to the student of constitutional history they are," wrote Bishop Stubbs, "without significance. From the Briton and the Roman of the fifth century we have received nothing. Our whole internal history testifies unmistakably to our inheritance of Teutonic institutions from the first immigrants. The Teutonic element is the paternal element in our system, natural and political." [1]

To this challenge the Roman School retorted with a direct negative. They asserted that the origins of the English Constitution—our political institutions, the basis of our laws, the outlines of our land system—were traceable not to the *Germans* as seen by Tacitus but to Roman influence, and were handed on by Romanized Britons to the Teutonic barbarians by whom they were conquered, but not, as the Teutonic School aver, exterminated. The Roman apologists contended that many English towns owed their origin to Roman *municipia*; that the Anglo-Saxon *guilds* were directly descended from the Roman *collegia*; that the Roman *villa* was the lineal ancestor of the Norman *manor*, and so on. Scarth [2] identified the Roman *territoria* with the English *shires*, and the English *ealdorman* with the *comes civitatis*. Pearson turned the argument from language against the Teutons.[3]

The most serious assault upon the Teutonic theory was delivered from the side of Economic History, and was based upon the character of the mediæval land-system.

Von Maurer and Kemble, followed more cautiously by

[1] *Select Charters*, p. 3. [2] *Roman Britain*, p. 226. [3] *English History*, II, p. 102.

**Villa, Mark and Manor.**

Stubbs, had insisted that the *mark* was the "original basis upon which all Teutonic society rests" (Kemble). By the *mark* these writers understood "a voluntary association of freemen", governing themselves, owning no superior or "lord", owning and cultivating the land of the village in common. This, it was maintained, was the "normal" type, both before and after the migration, among our German ancestors. But it was conceded that from the first there would be exceptions. Here and there one of the greater men would organize a community with semi-servile cultivators on manorial lines. But the free community was the rule.

Then came Frederick Seebohm, who published his *English Village Community* (1883). Two years later, M. Fustel de Coulanges, still smarting under the defeat of his country in the Franco-German War, published his defiance of the Teutons in his *Recherches sur quelques Problèmes d'Histoire*. Coulanges roundly declared that the whole theory of the *mark* was "a figment of the Teutonic brain", while Seebohm contended that "English history begins with the serfdom of masses of the rural population . . . a serfdom from which it has taken a thousand years to set them free". The argument in support of this thesis must be sought in the works referred to. It may be admitted that even if the free village community furnished the prevalent type, there did exist, from the first, *some* village communities dependent upon a land cultivated by semi-servile labour and hardly to be distinguished from the later manor. Still less is it denied that between the Roman *villa* and the Norman *manor* there is a close resemblance: but resemblance does not prove derivation.

Descent implies continuity. Two questions then arise: Did the Romans impose their culture and institutions upon the Britons? If so, were the Britons in a position to hand them on to their barbarian conquerors? Evidently the latter question is vital, and the answer to it must depend on the view taken of the scope and character of the Teutonic conquest. Did that conquest involve virtual extermination, or did the conquered Britons settle down among and intermingle with their conquerors?

**The Teutonic Conquest.**

On these matters there has been abundant theorizing and conjecture; the ascertained facts are scanty. We know that in the year A.D. 410 Alaric and his Visigoths captured Rome and that the Emperor Honorius " sent letters to the communities of Britain bidding them defend themselves ". That was the end of the Roman Empire in Britain. We also know that in the year A.D. 597 St. Augustine, a Roman missionary, landed in Kent and entered on the task of converting the English. That was the beginning of Roman Christianity in England.

Between these two dates, however, there is a complete absence of contemporary records. Gildas provides us with a rhetorical account of the invasions of the fifth century, but he wrote in the middle of the sixth century and his reliability is gravely suspect. The *Anglo-Saxon Chronicle* narrates the events of the Teutonic conquest in chronological sequence, but the narrative was not composed until the end of the ninth century. The *Ecclesiastical History* of the Venerable Bede was written about 730, but for the earlier period he does little more than attempt to rationalize Gildas. For the details of what happened between the " departure of the Romans " and the arrival of St. Augustine we are accordingly thrown back upon oral traditions collected by the " authorities " just mentioned and upon conjecture.

Fortunately this narrative is concerned less with the actual course of events than with their effects. There is no doubt that by the end of the sixth century Britain was in a fair way to become England. There had then evidently been, during the dark interval, a migration or series of migrations on a large scale. The rise of the curtain reveals the migrants from the farther shores of the North Sea established in a number of petty kingdoms, stretching from the Straits of Dover to Morecambe Bay, from Somerset to Lothian, from the Norfolk coast to the Welsh border. Among these we can identify the kingdom of the Jutes in Kent, which preserved into the historic period institutions and customs which distinguish it from the rest of England; the kingdoms of the South Saxons (Sussex), of the West and East Saxons in Wessex and Essex respectively; the kingdoms of the Angles (East Anglia), and north of the Humber, of Deira and Bernicia, presently united in Northumbria. Immediately south of the Humber was the kingdom of Lindsay. The great kingdom of Mercia occupied what we know as the Midlands—roughly from the Thames to the Trent—while on the Severn the Hwicce had a kingdom co-extensive with Worcestershire, and between Mercia and East Anglia lay Middle Anglia. There were, perhaps, other kingdoms less certainly identified. The term "Heptarchy" represents a rough estimate.

**The English Kingdoms.**

A new word has crept into the preceding paragraph. "Kingdoms" imply kings. Whether the keels of the Teutonic invaders carried kings is a disputed question. Certain it is, however, the kings very soon made their appearance on British soil and began to rule over districts known as kingdoms. War, then, had begotten kings; but the important stage in the making of England is marked by the substitution of *a* king for kings.

**The Consolidation of England.**

The process was gradual. Between the petty but independent kingdoms there quickly and inevitably ensued a contest for supremacy. Ethelbert, King of Kent, may have exercised some sort of supremacy in the latter years of the sixth century. He is named as the 3rd Bretwalda (or Overlord), and his position is attested by the fact that in 575 he married Bertha, a daughter of Charibert, King of the Franks. That marriage was of high political as well as of great spiritual significance, for Bertha being a Christian, her marriage opened the way for the Augustine mission.

Throughout the greater part of the seventh century supremacy belonged to Northumbria. About the year 613 Ethelfrith, its king, won a notable victory over the Britons at Chester. Until that time there was a chance, perhaps remote but by no means negligible, that a powerful British kingdom extending from the south-western peninsula to the Firth of Clyde might have been established independent of the Saxon-Norse kingdoms to the east of it. Ethelfrith's victory shattered that possibility.

But the Northumbrian supremacy was short-lived. The victory of the Picts over King Egfrith (685) brought it to an end, and a contest then ensued between Mercia and Wessex. Under its great king, Offa (757–96), Mercia's supremacy was incontestable, but on the accession of Egbert to the kingship of Wessex, supremacy passed to the West Saxons. With the West Saxon kings it remained.

**Supremacy of Wessex.**

The growth of the West Saxon kingdom had been slower than that of its rivals, but its ultimate ascendancy was based on much stronger foundations. Absorbing as it did all the kingdoms south of the Thames, Wessex occupied a dominant geographical situation—handy for intercourse with the Continent yet removed from the first fierce impact of the Danish pirates. Racially it was far more homogeneous than Mercia or even Northumbria. The absorption of Kent gave it command over the ecclesiastical organization of the whole English land, while in the House of Egbert it found a succession of strong kings to whom all England began to look for leadership against the Danish invasions. It was indeed those invasions that gave to the West Saxons their permanent ascendancy, and to England a powerful impulse to political union.

**The Danish Invasions, *c.* 780–*c.* 850.**

For more than half a century the Danes were bent only on plundering raids. Advancing up the rivers they would land, sack monasteries, burn villages and slaughter the inhabitants, but, save in the rare cases where they were themselves overcome, they would regularly return home to spend the winter in enjoyment of their booty.

After the middle of the ninth century it is a different story. The Danes came no longer in small bands, whose sole object was plunder, but in a great army bent on conquest. In less than a quarter of a century they had conquered a large part of England—half Northumbria, most of Mercia and the whole of East Anglia. In 870 they invaded Wessex, but the House of Egbert was at that moment represented by one of its greatest sons.

As a boy of sixteen Alfred succeeded his brother in 871. For the next seven years the Danes carried all before them;

the West Saxon king was a fugitive, but in 878 he rallied the men of Wessex, and inflicted on the Danes a crushing defeat at Ethandun, near Chippenham, and dictated the Treaty of Wedmore. The Danes, with their leader Guthram, accepted Christianity and acknowledged the suzerainty of Alfred. But England was rent in twain. Alfred remained King of Wessex and South-Western Mercia; over the rest of England—the Danelaw—the Danes were sovereign, though even in the Danelaw the Danish penetration was less complete than some writers have supposed.

**The Partition of England.**

**Alfred.**

Alfred's work for England was of outstanding importance. His victory in the field saved Christianity from extinction; he gave an immense impetus to education and, by his example, encouraged literature; by fortifying towns, building a fleet and organizing a national militia (the *fyrd*) he provided for national defence; he codified the law and immensely improved the administration of justice.

Edward the Elder succeeded his father in 901, and with the help of his sister Ethelfleda, "The Lady of the Mercians", carried a stage further Alfred's work. He reconquered a great part of the Danelaw, and secured his conquest by fortifying towns ("timbering the burhs"[1]); he united all England south of the Humber under the House of Wessex, and over the rest of Britain established his suzerainty.

**The Unification of England.**

Edward's work was completed by his sons and grandsons (925–75), and in 959 the greatest of them, Edgar, known significantly as "the Peaceful", succeeded to a throne which commanded the allegiance of the whole of England. More than that. The legend that Edgar was rowed on the Dee by eight tributary kings from Wales and Scotland attests his Imperial position. King of all England, he was also Emperor of the whole island some day to be known as Great Britain.

That was the zenith of the Saxon monarchy. The seeds of disintegration had been already sown. Feudalism as a coherent system was, indeed, still far in the future, but the

[1] A *burh* was a stockaded fortress constructed on a mound, generally on the bank of a river. The "castle-mound" at Oxford is an excellent example of a *burh*.

elements of it are discernible long before it was systematized by the Norman kings. A weak king encourages the great men of the realm to insubordination and independence. In 979 there succeeded to the throne the first weakling in the House of Egbert, Ethelred the Redeless. Within a few months of his accession the Danish invasions recommenced, but under an entirely new aspect.

**Canute.**

If England had lately been consolidated, a Scandinavian Empire had also been established, and in many directions extended. Of that empire England, under Canute, formed part. The weakness of a king, vainly endeavouring to buy off by *Danegeld* an enemy he could not defeat; the disloyalty of a great magnate, Edric Streona, Ealdorman of Mercia; the help given to the invaders by the Danes of the Danelaw—all combined to facilitate the final Danish conquest of England. The Redeless king, after an ignominious flight to his "spiritual home" in Normandy, died in 1016. London, the centre of patriotic resistance to the Danes, elected his heroic son Edmund Ironsides as king; but in the same year Canute was elected king at Southampton. So stout, however, was the resistance offered by Edmund, that Canute concluded with him the Treaty of Olney, under the terms of which England was again partitioned, on the lines of the Treaty of Wedmore. Hardly, however, was the Treaty concluded when the murder of King Edmund rendered it void, and Canute reigned as undisputed king over all England (1016–35). He ruled well, and as a true English ruler; he married, as his second wife, Ethelred's widow, Emma of Normandy; he re-enacted the laws of Edgar; he encouraged learning, protected the Church, and gave an immense stimulus to English trade. In fine, he was as good an Englishman and almost as great a king as Alfred himself.

**The Great Earldoms.**

Canute's position was, however, personal: his empire was top-heavy; his sons (half-brothers) quarrelled; the old divisions reappeared; the Danelaw again emerged; above all, the disintegrating principle, held in check under strong kings like Edgar or Canute, but ever increasing in strength with the extension of the English kingdom and the expansion of the Danish Empire, reasserted itself. The forces thus released might well have retarded for centuries the unification of England. The triumph of feudalism was averted only by the Norman Conquest. On the eve of that conquest England was divided into great earldoms; but for the strong hand of William the Bastard these earldoms might well have developed if not into the Sovereign States of Germany, at least into the feudal principalities which were for long centuries fatal to national unity in France. Of the earls, Godwine and his sons were the most powerful, and it is significant that they led the English party which during the reign of Edward the Confessor (1041–66) resisted the pro-Norman policy of the king. But the earls represented the principle of feudal disintegration, and it was the lack of unity that ensured the ultimate victory of the Norman duke on Senlac Hill.

**The Norman Conquest.**

If that victory was conclusive, it was largely because the unification of England under the Saxon and Danish dynasties was superficial. A strong king like Edward the Elder or Edgar could impose upon the English kingdoms a semblance of unity, but the Danish invasions had a curiously contradictory effect. In their earlier stage, as marauding expeditions, they gave a powerful impulse to consolidation; their permanent settlement tended, on the contrary, to disintegration, and thus prepared the way for the triumph of the last Viking invader.

William the Bastard claimed, on more than one ground, to be the lawful successor to the English throne. His claims were, however, a mere pretext to justify deliberate aggression, and need not be discussed. Nor need the course of the conquest detain us. Beginning with a crushing victory over Harold Godwinson at Senlac, the Norman Conquest was completed by the surrender of Ely, where, under Hereward the Wake, the English made their final stand (1071).

The death of Harold and his two brothers on the field of Senlac wiped out the House of Godwine, and both in a military and constitutional sense immensely smoothed

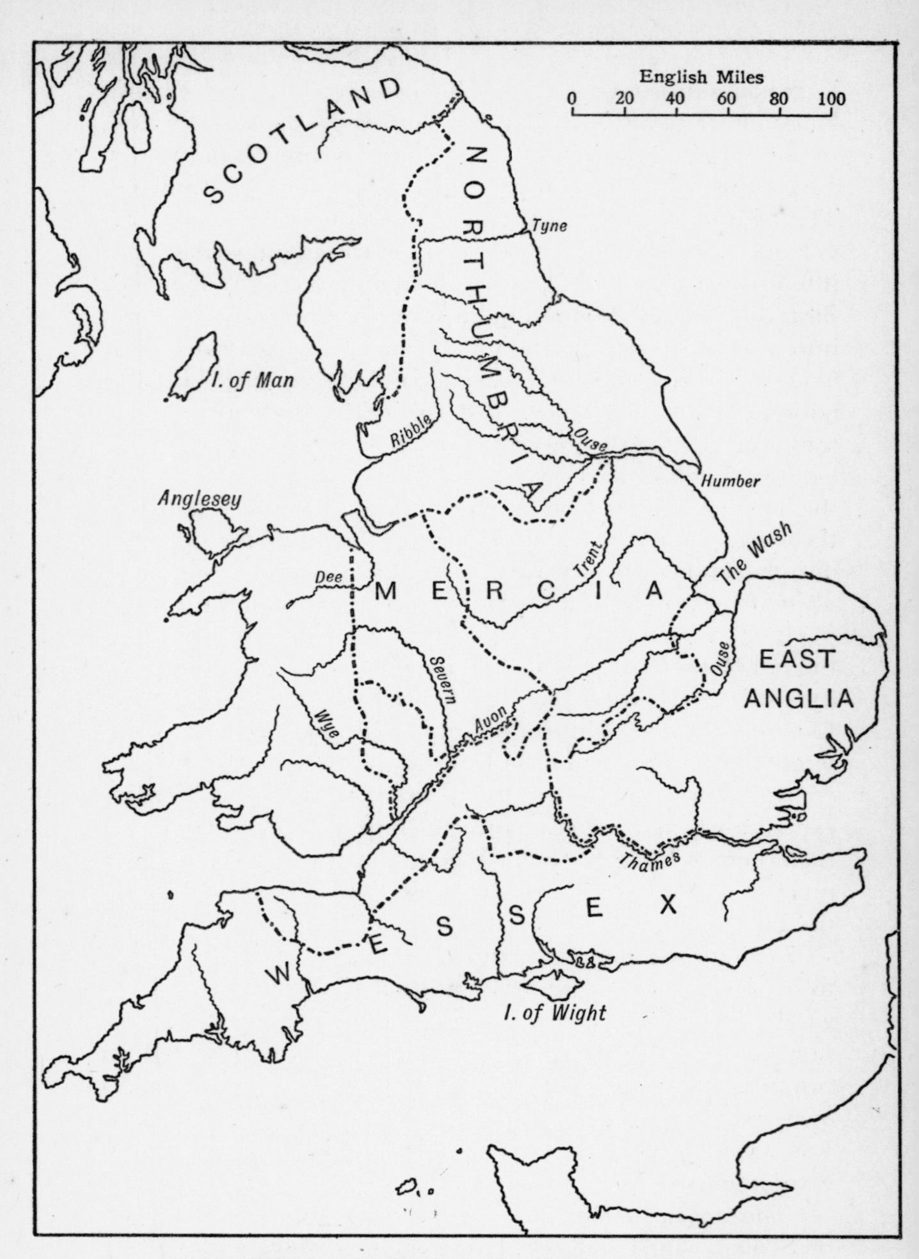


THE GREAT EARLDOMS ON THE EVE OF THE NORMAN CONQUEST

William's path. He marched on London, was elected king by the Witan, and at Christmas (1066) was crowned.

Risings there were, notably in the west and the north, during the next four years, but among the opponents of William there was no cohesion, and he crushed them one by one with merciless severity. The north of England, which gave him most trouble, he ravaged and laid waste. After the capture of Ely all resistance on the part of the English was at an end. The Norman duke had achieved his object. His work was final. Never again did England suffer invasion, nor accept the yoke of a conqueror.

There was still some way to go before England finally emerged as a Nation-State. But the Norman Conquest marked an exceptionally important stage in the gradual process. It profoundly affected the European position of this island, and this powerfully reacted upon the domestic situation; it opened a new chapter in the relations of Church and State; above all, it left a profound and permanent impress upon English political institutions. Of those institutions incomparably the most important was the monarchy.

CHAPTER III

# The English Kingship
## Monarchy and Local Government

FOR a thousand years the kingship was, in Maitland's phrase, "the centre of the centre"; the king was indisputably the most important person in the community; he not only reigned but ruled. A Theodore of Tarsus or a Dunstan might leave a deeper impress upon the history of England than most kings; a Godwine might temporarily overshadow the Confessor; Hubert Walter meant more to the English people than Richard I; a Warwick might make or unmake kings during the troubles and tumults of the fifteenth century; but down to the eighteenth century a good king meant a happy people, a bad king involved the country in misery; a weak king brought upon it national humiliation.

**The King.**

To the student of English institutions the character of the kingship is, therefore, of pre-eminent importance.

The kingship was not, at first, hereditary, but elective. Traces of the elective character of the English monarchy still survive in the Coronation service, but there was a persistent tendency for the kingship to be confined to a royal family even if the choice of the electors fell not on the eldest son of the late monarch, but on the kinsman most likely to make a competent ruler. The recommendation of the reigning king also counted for something; even Duke William of Normandy thought it worth while to cite among his claims to the English throne the nomination of the Confessor.

If the kingship was not at first hereditary, neither was it territorial; it was personal; the king was king of the people not of the country; the King of the English not of England.[1] But the growth of the feudal principle wrought, in this as in other respects, a notable and rapid change. Alfred is King of the West Saxons; Athelstan is King of the English; but Edgar is *Totius Angliae Imperator*. Moreover, the dignity and power of the king increased intensively with the expansion of his kingdom. This phenomenon was not peculiar to England; it is an almost universal law. Close proximity is inimical to that sense of mystery which, as Walter Bagehot insisted, is perhaps essential to monarchy. The heroic kingships of ancient Greece did not long survive the development of the City-State. A city is too contracted a sphere for monarchy; Louis Philippe, posing as a "citizen king", gave the *coup de grâce* to the Bourbon monarchy. Conversely in England, the extension of the area of the kingdom added not only to the actual power of the king, but to the reverence with which he was regarded by those who ceased to be his companions (*comites*) and became his subjects.

Other influences were working concurrently in the same direction. The Church inculcated the moral duty of obedience; the king became both the fountain of honour and the source of justice; offences against the law became offences against the king; the national or public peace (*frith*) was gradually superseded by the "King's peace" (*grith*). The king became in a special sense responsible not merely for the maintenance of peace and order at home, but for the defence of the realm against external enemies. The repeated attacks of the Danes tended to increase the power of the king both directly and indirectly: demanding a leader of the host in war and also driving the defenceless ceorl, the simple freeman, to seek by "commendation" the protection of a lord, thus bartering his personal freedom for personal safety. Commendation was, indeed, one of the customs making towards the feudal-

[1] The distinction is by no means obsolete. Louis Philippe was King of the French, Louis Napoleon was Emperor of the French, in contradistinction to their "legitimist" predecessors, and in 1871 the German princes were willing to recognize William I of Prussia as German Emperor but not as Emperor of Germany.

ization of England before the Norman Conquest. Every step towards the feudalization of land tenure evidently meant increased power for the supreme landlord, the apex of the feudal pyramid—the king.

**Reign of Edgar.**

The reign of Edgar marked the culmination of the Anglo-Saxon monarchy. Soon after his time it became apparent that there were two sides to Feudalism: if as a system of land tenure it tended to exalt the power of the king, as a method of government it tended to diminish it, to decentralize power, and to make the great vassal the rival of the king.

**Limitations**

Greatly as the king's power increased between the sixth century and the tenth it was at no time unlimited. "*Nec regibus infinita aut libera potestas*" was the comment of Tacitus upon kingship among the Germans.[1] The same author describes the king's power as circumscribed by a Council of the magnates (*Principes*), with whom rested the decision on matters of administrative detail ("*de minoribus principes consultant*"), and by a folkmoot, the whole body of freemen, to whom were submitted the larger issues ("*de majoribus omnes*"). This triple organization is common to primitive societies. The Homeric king had to convince by superior argument the elders of the Council, and by his commanding eloquence to commend his policy to the whole body of freemen assembled in the *Agora*, the host in arms.

**The Witenagemot.**

From early days the English kings had their *Witenagemot*—the meeting of the wise men of the realm. Around the question of the composition of the Witan—whether it was an aristocratic or a democratic body, a council of the wise (*sapientes*), or an assembly of the *folk*, open to all freemen—controversy has raged hotly, but the discussion is in truth academic. The Witan certainly included all the great men of the realm, archbishops and bishops, abbots, ealdormen and king's thegns (*ministri* or *gesiths*). Whether, in addition to these, every freeman had the right to attend is a point in dispute. If he had the right, certain it is that he rarely

[1] The description of the Germans given by Tacitus is immensely interesting and historically important, but the Germans known to the Romans were not those who conquered Britain, and between the date of the *Germania* and the earliest of the Teutonic invasions of Britain at least three centuries elapsed.

exercised it. Of the 140 meetings of the Witan said by Kemble [1] to have been held between 596 and 1066, only a few were meetings of the "folk", and they were concerned only with the election of kings and the promulgation of laws.

However composed, the Witan undeniably exercised real power, especially when the king was a weakling. It met at least three times a year, at Easter, Christmas and Whitsuntide, and at other times as occasion demanded. It elected the king, though within the limits, as a rule, of the royal family. It exercised also the right of deposition. At least three kings of Northumbria were deposed between 774 and 808 and, over a more extended period, five kings belonging to the West Saxon House. The functions of the Witan were legislative, executive and judicial. Laws were enacted with the counsel and consent of the Witan; it regulated ecclesiastical matters; it confirmed monastic charters, and sanctioned the transfer of land, and in particular the conversion of folkland into bocland; it co-operated with the king in imposing extraordinary taxation, such as the Danegeld; it summoned the host to arms; decided on war and peace and ratified treaties. It may, indeed, as Bishop Stubbs says, be "safely affirmed that no business of any importance could be transacted by the king in which (the Witan) had not, in theory at least, a consultative voice. Nor were the functions of the Witan merely legislative and executive, it acted also as a supreme court of justice both in civil and criminal cases."

This is an imposing enumeration of powers and functions, but we must take heed to the caution uttered by Maitland. Vast as were the powers of the Witan on paper, the area in which they were exercised was circumscribed. Extraordinary taxation was rarely called for, and few laws were made. That legislation is a primary function of the State is pre-eminently a modern idea; the happiness of the people depended, in olden days, upon administration, and in particular upon the character of the local government.

Local government was from the earliest times in England

[1] *Saxons in England*, I, pp. 203–30.

**Local Government.**

eminently popular—a matter for the people. "England alone among the nations of the earth," wrote Erskine May, "has maintained for centuries a constitutional policy, and her liberties may be ascribed above all to her free local institutions." That is true; but it is equally true, and in the present connexion even more important to observe, that nothing did more to give its special character to the English monarchy and to enhance the power of the king, than the close connexion persistently maintained between the king and his central court and the local "popular" courts.

Of these the most important was the court or *moot* of the shire.

**The Shires.**

The history of the shires is still wrapped in some obscurity. The word itself merely signified the division of a larger entity. Thus the city of York contained six "shires". But the historic shires date from different periods and derive from various origins. Perhaps the earliest to emerge were those which, like Ham-*ton*-shire and Will-*ton*-shire, were formed round a "tun". These West Saxon shires, with others such as Dorset and Somerset, represent the early settlements of the West Saxons. Kent, Sussex, Middlesex, Essex and Surrey were ancient kingdoms. Norfolk and Suffolk may represent the two divisions of the Norsemen of East Anglia, or perhaps the pre-Danish dioceses of Dunwich and Elmham.

Another batch of shires represents an artificial delimitation of the Danelaw after its reconquest by the West Saxons. These shires are designated by the name of the capital or county town—Oxford, Warwick, Derby, and so on—round which they were grouped. Other shires were formed still later. Lancashire was not formed into a shire until the twelfth century; Cumberland was the English shire of the old British kingdom of Strathclyde or Cumbria. Wales was finally carved up into shires in the sixteenth century.[1]

**The Shire-moot and the Sheriff.**

Every shire had its shire-moot, or county court, consisting partly of official and partly of representative members, each township being represented by its reeve and four

[1] Edward I began the process; Henry VIII completed it.

men. The constituting officer of the court was the shire-reeve, a royal official, nominated by the king, and specially charged, as the king's steward, to look after his interests financial and otherwise. With him sat the bishop and the ealdorman, a national official, appointed by the king, though in conjunction with the Witan.

**The Ealdorman.**

The ealdorman may in some cases have represented the reigning family of the original kingdom, or sub-kingdom, but his jurisdiction was not, like that of the sheriff, confined to a single shire. Wessex, for instance, had only two ealdormen, and the greater part of Mercia was under a single ealdorman. The ealdorman was also the *Dux* or heretoga, in military command of the whole district, or rather the leader of its host when called to arms. The shire-moot met twice a year; all lords of land were bound to attend it, and with the officials and representatives of the townships collectively formed the judges. For the functions of the shire-moot were not merely administrative but judicial. It was in Maitland's phrase " the great ordinary court of litigation for all the men of the shire ", and it was not wholly superseded in this function for a long time after the Norman Conquest. In the thirteenth century another and even more important function was, as we shall see later, thrust upon the shire-court.

The shires were subdivided into hundreds and townships.

**The Hundred.**

The origin of the hundred raises one of the many hotly disputed questions connected with the early history of political institutions in England. Whether the English hundred originated in the settlement of the hundred warriors of the Teutonic host; whether we must regard it as merely a unit for the assessment of taxation, or as an artificial subdivision of the shire created primarily for police purposes—these are matters for the specialist. But it is certain that the hundred was a territorial district dating from very early days, and was not confined to England. Nor was it of uniform size. There were sixty-four hundreds in Sussex, sixty-three in Kent, but only seventeen in Cambridgeshire, nine in Bedfordshire and five in Leicestershire. If the "hundred" represented the area originally occupied by one hundred warriors, this disparity would be accounted for. While the conquered area was circumscribed, the portion allotted to each hundred warriors would necessarily be small; as the tide of conquest advanced and larger areas were available, the distribution would be on a more generous scale. All this is hardly more than conjecture. But we do know that in later Saxon days the hundred moot or court was the ordinary resort of the men of the hundred for the administration of justice, civil and criminal; and that in the hundred court as in the shire court "all the suitors were the judges", though they acted through a jury of twelve. The court met monthly, and twice in the year the sheriff attended and held his "tourn" to see that the police regulations of the district were being faithfully observed. After the Norman Conquest the importance of the hundred court rapidly diminished. Its decay was due partly to the development of private jurisdictions in the manorial courts of the feudal lords, and partly to the increasing ubiquity of the king's judges and the growth of the royal courts.[1]

But even in the judicial and administrative system of the Angevin kings the hundred had still an important place. It was still the unit of the police system, of the military system for the arming of the people in the national militia; it was still responsible for the pursuit of malefactors, and for presenting, through its grand jury of twelve lawful men, the criminals of the district for trial before the king's judges of assize. Of this last function there are still lingering traces. Thus Manchester for assize purposes is still in the "hundred" of Salford; Liverpool in that of West Derby; Birmingham in that of Hemlingford. Down to 1886 the hundred was still responsible for damages due to riots. But long before that the hundred and its court had for all practical purposes ceased to exist, and to-day the interest which attaches to it is purely antiquarian.

It is otherwise with the township—the vill or tun, the

[1] For a detailed account of the Local Courts (here summarily treated) cf. Pollock and Maitland: *History of English Law*, I, Chap. III.

**The Township.**

unit of local self-government from time immemorial. Into townships the whole of England was exhaustively divided, and the township was, as Maitland points out, selected by the State as the "unit responsible for good order". As a unit for fiscal purposes the township, as we have seen, was represented in the court of the shire by the "reeve and four best men", and it is from the townships on the royal demesne that John first summoned representatives to the central assembly of the realm. Yet the name "township", still more "vill", has an antiquarian flavour. And for a simple reason. From the seventh century the "township" was captured by the Church as the unit of ecclesiastical organization, and for all practical purposes became henceforward known as the "parish". But the Church did not win its ultimate victory without a struggle. Another force was beginning to operate to the detriment of the free townships and, in less degree, to that of the ecclesiastical parish and its meeting in the vestry of the church.

**The Manor.**

Even before the Norman Conquest a very large number of "townships" had become dependent upon a "lord", or, in technical language, had become manors—a *manerium* being merely, in the first instance, the seat of a lord. But this development will demand attention later on. For the moment it must suffice to point out that for all practical purposes the legal township merged, from the eleventh century onwards, into a manor, and as a manor was regarded and organized until the decay of feudalism in the fourteenth century and the reorganization of local government under the Tudor sovereigns. When the township re-emerged from under the ruins of the feudal superstructure elaborately imposed thereon, it is as the "parish", which was selected by the Tudors to be the unit of their new administrative system.

Few things in the history of England are more remarkable than the persistence and continuity of local institutions. County, district, parish, each with its appropriate and elected council, reproduces to-day the administrative organization of our Saxon forefathers.

Two points must, however, be emphasized. The first is that, partly as a matter of practical convenience, partly in deference to philosophical theory, functions have been differentiated, powers have been separated. In early days legislative, executive and judicial functions were theoretically confused and practically concentrated. But, as the total area of operation was circumscribed, the menace to personal liberty was less noticeable and less serious than it is in the highly organized societies of the modern world.

A second point is that, despite the feudalization of society, Saxon institutions had taken such firm root in the national polity that, though in some cases renamed and even temporarily transformed, they re-emerged as the tide of feudalism receded. The villagers of to-day, though their designation recalls the Norman manor, still meet in the folk-moot of the parish, and still manage local affairs either personally or by elected representatives. In the smallest villages the principle of direct democracy prevails; in the larger villages democracy operates indirectly on the representative principle characteristic of the modern State. But transitory as was the period of feudal ascendancy, and partial as was (in England) the application of the feudal principle, English feudalism is sufficiently important to demand separate treatment.

## CHAPTER IV

# Church and State

THE history of the English monarchy is inextricably bound up with the history of the English Church. In combination they contributed to the making of the English nation, and not less conspicuously to the precocious evolution of a national polity. It is, then, with the Church in its *political* aspect that this chapter is exclusively concerned.

Whether Christianity was originally planted in this island by an apostolic hand; whether St. Paul himself found in Britain that " boundary of the west " to which St. Clement of Rome referred; whether, according to a beautiful legend, St. Joseph of Arimathea planted his staff at Glastonbury—these have long been matters of lively but, in the present connexion, of fruitless controversy. There is no reasonable doubt that Britain was originally Christianized by missionaries from Gaul, in the course of the second century. Whether Christianity ever obtained, during the Roman occupation, any hold upon the Britons is doubtful, but it is certain that the Britons did not communicate their Faith to their Teutonic conquerors. Consequently, the origins of the English Church must be sought elsewhere.

**The Anglian Mission.**

" In the year of our Lord 592 . . . Gregory, a man renowned for learning and behaviour, was promoted to the apostolical see of Rome. . . . He, being moved by Divine inspiration, in [596], and about the 150th year after the coming of the English into Britain, sent the servant of God, Augustine, and with him several other monks who feared the Lord, to preach the word of God to the English nation."

Thus did the Venerable Bede commemorate the foundation of Christianity in England. Many years before his elevation to the Papal chair the Deacon Gregory had, according to the well-known tale, been touched by the appearance of the fair-haired English slaves exposed for sale in the Roman Forum, and had resolved to bring the light of Christianity to these Angles with the angel-faces. The marriage of Ethelbert, King of Kent, with Bertha, the daughter of the Christian King of Paris, gave Pope Gregory his opportunity. The Augustine mission was the result. Early in 597 Augustine landed at Ebbsfleet, in April King Ethelbert consented to receive Christian baptism, and before Christmas more than 10,000 Kentishmen had followed the example of their king. From Kent Christianity was rapidly extended to the East Saxons and the people of East Anglia, and eventually to Northumbria. Augustine received episcopal ordination, and four years later the Pope sent him the Pall—the symbol of metropolitan authority. At the same time Pope Gregory forwarded to Augustine a scheme for the government of the infant Church. England was to be divided into two provinces—with archbishoprics at London and York, each archbishop being assisted by twelve suffragan bishops. It is significant of the ignorance prevalent at Rome about the northern island that Gregory's scheme of Church government was based upon the assumption that Teutonic England still retained the administrative divisions of the old Romano-British province.

Pope Gregory's solicitude for the infant Church was, unquestionably, sincere. Nevertheless, the Augustine mission was on the whole a failure. The authority of Ethelbert was sufficient to secure a superficial acceptance of Christianity in South-Eastern England; Edwin could do the same in Northumbria and its dependencies, but as yet Christianity had got no real hold upon the people at large. The consequence was that when a great wave of heathen reaction, emanating from Mercia, swept over the country, Christianity was on every side submerged. In Northumbria, in Mercia, in East Anglia, in Essex, even to some extent in Kent itself, the people fell away from Christianity and relapsed into worship of the pagan gods.

Thus the flame of Christianity, which for a moment had burnt brightly, was on the point of extinction when it was relighted by Celtic missionaries.

**The Celtic Mission.**

Christianity, almost extinct in England, was flourishing in Ireland; the Irish Church was aflame with evangelizing zeal, and about the year 560 Columba, an Irish monk, made his way to the Western Isles and founded his famous monastery on Iona. After the Mercian victory over Northumbria (633), Oswald and Oswy, two princes of the royal Bernician line, took refuge in Scotland and received Christian baptism at the hands of the monks of Iona. In 634 Oswald established himself on the throne of Northumbria, and in 635 St. Aidan was consecrated bishop and founded a monastery, modelled on that of Iona, on the island of Lindisfarne.

Lindisfarne, now rightly renamed Holy Island, was the cradle of Christianity in Northern England, the home of Aidan, Cuthbert, Cedd and Wilfrid, by whose devoted labours not only Northumbria and Mercia, but Essex and Sussex were converted or reconverted to Christianity. For Wessex similar work was done by an Italian missionary, Birinus, for East Anglia by Felix, a Burgundian monk.

Nevertheless, admirable as were the spiritual results of the Celtic mission, its success constituted a menace to the incipient political unity of England. In the middle of the seventh century there was real danger lest England should be divided in ecclesiastical allegiance between Iona and Rome. Between the disciples of St. Patrick and St. Peter there were differences, not only on matters comparatively trivial such as the date of Easter and the method of the tonsure, but on the question, vital politically if not spiritually, of ecclesiastical organization. The Irish Church was a missionary Church; its organization was based on the monasteries; it had no territorial system of dioceses and parishes. Consequently, its political influence was not centripetal but centrifugal. If Iona had prevailed over Rome, the unification of England might have been indefinitely deferred.

The danger was averted by the decision taken at a Synod held under the presidency of King Oswy in 664 at Whitby.

Bede (Bk. III, Chap. 25) gives a vivid description of the crucial debate at that famous Synod. Colman, St. Aidan's successor at Lindisfarne, championed (with Cedd and St. Hilda) the Celtic cause; Wilfrid, afterwards Archbishop of York, that of Rome. King Oswy, sorely distracted, ultimately decided in favour of St. Peter, on the ground that to him Christ had confided the keys of the Kingdom of Heaven. The Irish monks accepted defeat, and withdrew to Iona. Rome consecrated a Greek monk, Theodore of Tarsus, as Archbishop of Canterbury, and sent him to reap the fruits of the victory won at Whitby, and to reorganize the English Church (667).

**Theodore of Tarsus.**

Theodore reached Canterbury in 669, and he effected a work incomparably important not less for the English State than for the English Church. The whole Church in England was brought to recognize the metropolitan authority of Canterbury, and in 673 all the bishops met in a great council at Hertford. Ten canons were passed at the council, and their promulgation constituted, as Stubbs insisted, " the first constitutional measure of the English race ". Having thus asserted the authority of Canterbury, and secured conciliar unity, Theodore proceeded to reorganize the diocesan system. Pope Gregory's scheme, based on an unreal hypothesis, had never materialized, and the delimination of dioceses had in fact followed the lines of the " Heptarchic " kingdoms. Consequently, but for the relapse to paganism, the Church, instead of promoting unity, might well have perpetuated partition. Theodore broke up these unwieldy " Heptarchic " dioceses, and redivided the whole country into sixteen dioceses, all obedient to the metropolitan of Canterbury. This arrangement did not last long: York soon regained its metropolitan dignity, and for a short time (during the Bretwaldaship of Offa) Lichfield also was created into a third metropolitan. But in its main outlines Theodore's scheme still remains intact.

Nor can its political significance be overrated. An annual Synod representative of all England, obeying the summons of a single ruler, making laws, equally binding upon Wessex and Northumbria, East Anglia, Kent and Mercia—what is this but the anticipation of a national Parliament?

"The Church of England," wrote Bishop Stubbs, "is not only the agency by which Christianity is brought to a heathen people, a herald of spiritual blessings and glorious hopes in another life; it is not merely the tamer of cruel natures, the civilizer of the rude, the cultivator of the waste places, the educator, the guide and the protector, whose guardianship is the only safeguard of the woman, the child, and the slave against the tyranny of their lord and master. The Church is this in many other countries besides Britain, but here it is much more. The unity of the Church in England was the pattern of the unity of the State: the cohesion of the Church was for ages the substitute for the cohesion which the divided nation was unable otherwise to realize. Strong in its own conformation, it was more than a match for the despotic rule of such kings as Offa, and was the guardian of liberties as well as the defence of the oppressed. It was to an extraordinary degree a national Church; national in its comprehensiveness as well as in its exclusiveness." The Church which was to be the pattern for the State was the Church as organized by Archbishop Theodore.

That great prelate died in 690, and during the next two centuries there was reaction both in State and Church. The invading Danes wrought widespread havoc, especially to the monasteries, and the whole country was completely disorganized and finally partitioned. In 957, however, Edgar succeeded to the throne of Northumbria, and his first act was to recall from exile in Flanders the famous abbot of Glastonbury, Dunstan. Two years later, on becoming king of a reunited England, Edgar nominated Dunstan to the see of Worcester, and in 960 to the archbishopric of Canterbury.

**Edgar and Dunstan.**

For nearly twenty years the king and the archbishop—each truly great—worked in harmony so complete that it is difficult to apportion merit between them. Dunstan was the first of that long line of statesmen-ecclesiastics who until the sixteenth century, and even the seventeenth, acted virtually as Prime Ministers. Wolsey, or perhaps Laud, was the last of them.

An ardent reformer of ecclesiastical abuses, responsible for establishing in England the discipline of the Benedictine monks, Dunstan was no "cloistered saint". Emphatically he was a many-sided man. A good craftsman, working in metal and wood, he made bells and organs, and wisely insisted that every priest should learn a handicraft so as to be able to teach it to others. He was a zealous educationist: "the whole of England," says his biographer, "was filled with his light." The far-reaching influence of St. Dunstan is attested by the number and dispersion of the churches that were dedicated to him. Besides three in London, there were six in Middlesex, five in Kent, one in Sussex, another in distant Liverpool, and another in his reputed birthplace, Beltonsborough in Somerset. But, saint and ecclesiastic as he was, Dunstan was, above all, a great statesman who perceived the special need of the moment and set himself to supply it. The need was the elimination of racial antagonism, the union of all the inhabitants of this distracted island in the bond of peace. Cordially, therefore, he advocated a conciliatory policy towards the Danes, sparing no pains to promote the unity, as well political as ecclesiastical, of his master's kingdom. In the historian's simple but pregnant phrase, he "turned the men of the Daneland into Englishmen".

Dunstan, when crowning his king at Bath on Whitsunday, 973, invited Archbishop Oswald of York to participate and all the bishops of England to assist in the ceremony. Once again was the unified Church a pattern for a consolidated State.

Dunstan died in 988, and the eleventh century registered another reaction. To brightness there succeeded gloom; the hopes generated by Edgar and Dunstan, though sustained for a while by Canute, were dissipated by Edward the Confessor and Stigand. A schismatic at Canterbury was an appropriate archbishop for an England partitioned into earldoms.

**The Norman Conquest.**

The Norman Conquest arrested the process of disintegration in the State, and in the Church reaffirmed obedience to the Papacy. No sooner had Harold Godwinson been proclaimed king than Duke William of Normandy denounced him to the Papacy as guilty of sacrilege and perjury, and appealed for Papal assistance against him. In that appeal Hildebrand, then only archdeacon, but soon to become Pope as Gregory VII, saw the Church's opportunity. A Pontifical Bull, sanctioning his expedition to England, was forwarded to Duke William together with a consecrated banner. Under that banner the composite [1] host commanded by the Norman duke advanced to victory at Senlac.

[1] William's army consisted of volunteers collected mostly in France, but also from all parts of Europe—only one-third of the knights were Norman.

CHAPTER V

# The Crown and the Magnates England under the Normans and the Angevins (1066-1199)

"A MONARCHY powerful and well served, a baronage feeble in comparison, these are two important features which place England in sharp contrast to the other European nations."[1] M. Boutmy's shrewd comment may well serve as the text for the present chapter. Throughout the Middle Ages the forces of integration and disintegration, of consolidation and disruption, were in constant conflict. The centripetal force is represented by the Crown, the centrifugal tendency by the magnates—the feudal aristocracy. In England the Crown achieved a speedy and comparatively easy victory. In France the contest was prolonged until the final defeat of the English king—the most powerful of the feudal vassals—in 1453, perhaps until the wars of the Fronde (1648–53), or even until 1790, when the Constituent Assembly superseded the historic "Provinces" of France by the new-fangled and artificial "Departments". In Germany the confusion between the Holy Roman Empire and the German kingship combined with other causes to undermine the power of the monarchy and to exalt the magnates into the position of sovereign territorial princes. Had it not been for counteracting influences, an Earl of Wessex or an Earl of Northumbria might well have developed into a Duke of Burgundy or a Duke of Brittany, perhaps into a King of Saxony or a King of Prussia. The creation of the German Empire (1871) was the first effective

**Contrast with France and Germany.**

[1] Boutmy: *The English Constitution*, p. 14.

step towards a unification of Germany, but it was not until 1933 that the "Enabling Act" permitted the Führer to complete the process. The achievement of Italian unity was deferred until 1871; in Spain the process is still incomplete.

England's position was, then, among the Great Powers unique. She owed that position to a combination of causes: to her detached and insular location, outside the orbit of the Roman Empire, remote from the seat of the Roman Papacy; to suspicion and dislike of "foreigners"; to her manageable size and the absence of internal barriers to intercourse; to racial homogeneity; to the "nationalism" of the Church; to uniformity of customs and laws; above all, to an exceptionally powerful monarchy, and to the admirable administrative system devised by the Norman and Angevin kings, and worked by a "nobility of service".

**The Norman Conquest.**

A dictatorship can be justified only if it is not unduly prolonged, and if the discipline it enforces is educative. English dictatorships have all reacted to this test. The Norman and Angevin dictatorship lasted for about two centuries and, except when it degenerated into a tyranny under a Rufus or a John, was almost wholly beneficent.

**William I.**

After the completion of the conquest the Conqueror's first task was to arrest the development of the fissiparous tendencies so manifestly gaining ground in the preceding century. He could then establish on a firmer basis the authority of the Crown.

William's companions in arms had, indeed, to be rewarded. They were volunteers who had followed the adventurer in the hope of sharing the spoils of conquest. Domesday Book proves that the rewards were not niggardly, but they were bestowed with almost uncanny circumspection. The Norman barons were not to be allowed to become petty kings; their numerous manors were not consolidated but were distributed throughout the length and breadth of the conquered land.[1]

[1] This may have been due less to policy than to the circumstances of the Conquest. Contiguous estates are more common as the tide of conquest advanced from the south-east.

Of forty-one great vassals five held manors in seven counties, six in eight, two in nine, four in ten, four in eleven, three in twelve, one in thirteen, two in fourteen, one in twenty, and one in twenty-one. To this rule of distribution there were only a few exceptions. For purposes of defence great earldoms were set up—the Palatine earldoms—in Durham, Chester and Kent, and lesser earldoms in the border counties of Salop, Hereford and Cornwall. Moreover, the earldom of Durham was entrusted to a Churchman whose title and office could not become hereditary. For the rest, the Conqueror retained in his own hands the fiscal rights pertaining to an earl. Nor were the barons permitted to wage private wars, or to exercise exclusive jurisdiction even over their own vassals. To avert that danger William kept up the " popular " courts of the shire and the hundred and the old English system of police. He also maintained, as a further check upon the feudal forces, the old national militia, and insisted that all tenants by knight service owed that service to the king and not to their immediate feudal lords. Almost the last act of his reign was to summon to Salisbury (1086) the landowners of the kingdom and to extract from them an oath to be " faithful to him against all other men ". There was to be no division or conflict of allegiance.

**Crown and Church.**

Over the clergy, too, the Conqueror kept a tight hand. His friendly relations with Archbishop Lanfranc averted the conflict, soon to break out between Rufus and Anselm, but ecclesiastically not less than politically, William was determined to be master in his own house.[1] He was well served by officials; he selected them from the lesser baronage, and organized them into an embryonic civil service. Equally with the great barons these officials were summoned to the king's court (*Curia Regis*) and naturally attended it with much greater regularity. Without their skilled assistance the great survey of the land could not have been carried out, nor the results embodied in the " Book of Winchester ", afterwards known as " Domesday ".

[1] See *infra*, Chap. VI.

All this points to an orderly administration maintained to the great advantage of the common folk. Nor did the *Anglo-Saxon Chronicle* fail to recognize the debt the people owed to the Conqueror: " A man might go through his realm with his bosom full of gold unhurt." No greater tribute to a mediæval ruler could be found.

Rufus maintained his father's system, but in a different spirit. The Conqueror was ruthless but just. Rufus was a despot *sans phrase*. He tyrannized alike over the baronage, the Church and the people. But the monarchical principle suffered no declension at his hands.

**William Rufus.**

The tyranny of Rufus was quickly overpast. Henry I reverted to the methods of his father and, under auspices much happier, carried on his work.

**Henry I, 1100–1135.**

On the day of his coronation he offered an olive branch to the Church by the recall of Archbishop Anselm, and published to the nation a comprehensive Charter of Liberties. That charter, based upon the " Laws of Edward the Confessor ", formed the groundwork of the Great Charter of 1215. Thus in England is age linked to age and the continuity of our institutions maintained unbroken. The abuses practised by Rufus are abjured and forbidden. The Church is to enjoy its rightful privileges, the people to be freed from the oppressive exactions of the late reign. Special concessions are made to the king's vassals, but are not to be engrossed by them: the rights of the subtenants are safeguarded: " in like manner shall the men of my barons relieve their lands at the hand of their lords by a just and lawful relief ".[1] From the outset Henry made it clear that he meant to be king of the whole nation, of the English no less than the Normans. The goodwill of his English subjects was further evoked by the punishment of his brother's minister, Ranulf Flambard, the personification of foreign oppression; still more by the king's marriage with Matilda, daughter of Margaret of Scotland and niece of Edgar Aetheling of the royal house of Wessex. Henry's victory a

[1] Reliefs were succession dues paid by an incoming heir to the overlord, as an acknowledgment that his tenure was conditional.

Tenchebrai

few years later (1107) over his brother Duke Robert before the castle of Tenchebrai further enhanced his popularity with the English. Fought on the anniversary of the battle of Hastings against a Norman duke, and followed by the annexation of the Norman duchy to the English kingdom, Tenchebrai might well seem to have avenged the defeat suffered by Harold and his Englishmen at Hastings.

As the years went on, Henry I had need of all the store of popularity on which he could draw, for the social conditions were truly pitiable. To the heavy load of taxation necessitated by foreign wars, to grievous exactions levied under the name of "purveyance", to the debasement of the coinage and consequent rise in prices, were added visitations of nature: devastating floods, famine and pestilence. The contemporary Chronicles bear witness year after year to prevalent and persistent suffering. Thus in 1124: "In this year were many failures in England in corn and all fruit, so that between Christmas and Candlemas the acre seed of wheat was sold for six shillings; and that of barley, that is seedlips, for three shillings; the acre seed of oats for four shillings, because there was little corn and the penny was so bad that a man who had at market a pound could by no means buy therewith twelve pennyworth." In 1125 there are records of great destruction of crops and bridges by flood; in 1131 "there was so great a murrain of cattle as never was in the memory of man". Nor was nature only to blame. One chronicler found it "not easy to recount all the miseries the country suffered through various illegalities and imposts which never ceased, and ever as the king went there was plundering by his followers on his wretched people, and at the same time often burnings and murders". Such was the picture drawn by contemporaries. There is no reason to doubt its accuracy. But such pictures are apt to be partial. There was another side to them, similarly supported by contemporary evidence. Henry did all in his power to enforce order and bring malefactors to justice. "A good man he was," says the Saxon Chronicle, "and all men stood in awe of him; no man durst misdo against another in his time. . . . Whoso bare his burden of gold and silver, no man durst do him aught but good."

These words evidently point to a strong administration. This result was obtained partly by a tightening up of the pre-Norman system of police, centred on the local courts of the shire and the hundred, partly by the organization of a central administrative system, and not least by an ingenious device for connecting central and local administration by means of "itinerant justices". Of this administrative system the reign of Henry I saw only the beginning; for its full development we must await the reign of his grandson, Henry II.

**Anarchy under Stephen (1135-54).**

For the intervening period a brief reference will suffice.[1] Stephen's reign is only negatively important—as affording striking evidence of what might have been the fate of this country but for the strong hands of the post-Conquest kings. The reign, as Stubbs put it, exemplified "the working of causes and principles which had no other opportunity of exhibiting their real tendencies".[2] Feudalism of the continental type, for the first and only time in England, got its head. New earldoms were created and endowed out of Crown revenues; castles sprang up like mushrooms—nearly 1200 of them it was said—in every corner of the country; the barons issued each his own coinage, and administered each his own rough justice; baron was at war with baron, and all laid imposts on the towns. All classes suffered, as the Saxon Chronicle makes clear: "When the traitors perceived that Stephen was a mild man, and soft and good, and did no justice, then did they all wonder. . . . Every powerful lord made his castles and held them against him. . . . When the castles were made they filled them with devils and evil men. Then they took those men that they imagined had any property . . . and put them in prison for their gold and silver and tortured them with unutterable torture. . . . Many thousands they killed with hunger. . . . They laid imposts on the towns. . . . Nor

[1] And see also *infra*, Chap. VI.

[2] *Constitutional History*, I, p. 335.

forbear they a bishop's land, nor an abbot's, nor a priest's. . . . The bishops and clergy constantly cursed them but nothing came of it. . . . However a man tilled, the earth bore no corn; for the land was all foredone by such deeds, and they said openly that Christ and His Saints slept. Such and more than we can say we endured nineteen winters for our sins." Weakness, varied by occasional acts of violence, alienated all classes, barons, merchants, the people at large, and most fatally the clergy. Moreover, the arrest of Bishop Roger of Salisbury (1139) meant the paralysis of the whole administration of the country. The king's court ceased to function: no councils were held; the only law which reached the common folk was that which issued from the baronial castles; justice there was none; the police system was in abeyance. Only the Church, despoiled as it was, managed to emerge from this welter of disorder with its organization not merely intact but strengthened. And the Church it was that before the reign actually closed negotiated the compromise embodied in the Treaty of Wallingford (1153). Stephen was left undisturbed on the throne for the brief remainder of his reign, but had to acknowledge as his heir Henry of Anjou, the son of his rival, the Empress Matilda.

**Administrative Reformer.**

Henry II was, with the exception of Edward I, the greatest of our mediæval kings. And his great work was done in the face of difficulties, domestic, political, and ecclesiastical, far more harassing than those which confronted his great grandson. Territorially and dynastically he was ostensibly the most powerful prince in Christendom; yet the reign as a whole is a record of almost continuous struggle to maintain his position against a succession of enemies—largely of his own household. That record must be sought elsewhere: our concern is to indicate the importance of the reign as a stage in the evolution of the Constitution.

**Restoration of Order.**

Nothing could be done until order was restored. That was the first business to which Henry set his hand. The Flemish auxiliaries, who had flocked to England in the hope, not vain, of profiting from the civil war, were expelled; the "adulterine" castles were destroyed; the earldoms were reduced to the number permitted by the Conqueror; the royal castles and the royal demesne were resumed; private jurisdictions, whether baronial or ecclesiastical, were rigorously curtailed; and a single standard of coinage and measures was established. But the great work of the reign was to carry a stage, or several stages, further the organization begun by Henry I of his administrative financial and judicial system.

**Administrative Reforms.**

In describing the administrative system we must beware of two dangers: the tendency to over-precise definition and the temptation to clear-cut differentiation. The differentiation of functions is a modern idea; government in the Middle Ages meant the issuing of orders—embodied later on in statutory enactments; the enforcement of those orders; the defence of the realm against external dangers; the maintenance of the king's peace at home; the collection of his revenue; and the decision of disputes between his subjects. The functions of legislation, administration and justice were in fact combined if not confused.

**The Curia Regis.**

The core and centre of the whole machine was the king's court (*Curia Regis*). But Dr. Tout has justly reminded us that all the business of State was originally transacted in the *domus regis*, the chamber (*camera*) and the adjacent wardrobe, and that all the ministers of State began as servants of the household.[1] The Treasury, for example, was originally no more than the strong chests which formed the appropriate furniture of the king's *wardrobe*. Soon after the Norman Conquest the Treasury was located at Winchester, and early in the thirteenth century the Winchester Treasury passed under the control of the Exchequer at Westminster, into which it was presently absorbed.

In composition the *Curia Regis* closely resembled the old Saxon Witenagemot, and like it was exceedingly elastic. To it the king summoned the wise men of the realm: barons bishops, and, increasingly, officials—the heads of an em-

[1] T. F. Tout: *The Administrative History of Mediæval England.*

bryonic civil service whose functions, however, extended beyond the wildest ambitions of the modern bureaucrat. Thus, on one side, we may think of the *Curia Regis* as the child of the Witenagemot and the parent of the Great Council of the Realm, later to be known as Parliament. On the other side, it was the parent of the whole administrative, financial, and judicial organization.

Under Henry II these several functions were somewhat more clearly differentiated, though all the officials discharged them indifferently. Sitting as a small council (*Concilium Ordinerium* or *Secretum*), they advised the king in all matters pertaining to government. As judges, they decided suits in which the Crown was involved, as well as suits between subject and subject. Presently, the distinction resulted in the setting up of separate courts, the *King's Bench* to deal with the former; the *Court of Common Pleas* with the latter. Out of the *Curia*, too, there emerged the *Exchequer*, but the functions of the Exchequer were not originally confined to finance. The " barons of the Exchequer " were employed by Henry II in all kinds of business, administrative and judicial, as well as financial. From that time, however, the Exchequer, presided over by the Justiciar, was more and more clearly differentiated from the *Curia* and was permanently located at Westminster. Then, or soon thereafter, the Court of Common Pleas was also located at Westminster, but the King's Bench had to follow the king.

Another famous court—Chancery—derives from the same prolific parent, but the Chancery continued to be a part of the Household at least until the middle of the thirteenth century; the accounts of the Chancery were not " finally disentangled from those of the Household " until Edward II, and it was not until near the end of the fourteenth century that we can definitely describe the Chancery as a court of law. Until that time the duties of the Chancellor were not primarily, much less exclusively, judicial. Originally a household officer, the Chancellor had come to be, in Palgrave's phrase, " the Secretary of State for all Departments". In course of time, with the increasing importance of the Treasurer and the King's Secretary, the Chancellor became more and more of a judge, but he had never ceased to be one of the most important of the political advisers of the Crown.

**Itinerant Justices.**

The administrative reforms of Henry II, immensely important as they were, would have touched remotely the life of his subjects but for the development of the system of itinerant justices—more properly described as Commissioners on circuit. Thanks to these judges in eyre, the government of Henry II became truly national: an orderly, systematic, coherent and uniform system was extended to the whole kingdom. That system dealt the death-blow to feudalism. The Commissioners connected central and local administration, they brought Winchester and Westminster into touch with the remotest parts of the country.

**The Sheriff.**

The link was provided by the *sheriff*, whose functions steadily increased[1] in variety and importance as the reign of Henry II proceeded. Nor were the emoluments of the office —regular and irregular—inconsiderable. For irregularity there was plenty of scope, and in 1170, after four years' absence on the Continent, Henry II deemed it well to issue a special commission primarily to inquire into the truth of certain charges alleged against the sheriffs, and also to investigate the whole provincial administration of justice, alike in the popular courts and in those of the barons and clergy, not excluding the administration of the forests. As a result, almost all the sheriffs, most of them local magnates, were removed from their offices, and in their place the king instituted officers of the Exchequer. The new sheriffs not only introduced order and uniformity into local administration, where previously there had been great varieties of custom, but brought it into closer connexion with the central government at Westminster.

Of other reforms, directly anti-feudal in tendency, two were of special importance. By the institution of *scutage* (shield-money) the barons might be required to make

[1] Except in judicial matters which were committed to judges of assize.

money-payments instead of sending knights to serve under the banner of the king. By the *Assize of Arms* (1181) the ancient national militia, which had lately proved its worth by repelling at the battle of the Standard a formidable Scottish invasion, was reorganized and rearmed. Every freeman was required to furnish himself with arms commensurate with his means, his liability being ascertained by the justices on the sworn testimony of local jurors possessed of a high property qualification.

It remains a marvel how Henry II, compelled to repress baronial lawlessness, distracted by his quarrel with Becket and by continental complications, was able to make an impress so profound and permanent upon English political and legal institutions.

**Legal Reforms.**

How profound the impress can be adequately realized only by a survey of his legal reforms much more detailed than is consonant with the plan of the present work. Of two of his more comprehensive edicts mention must, however, be made. The *Assize of Clarendon*, issued with the assent of the Great Council in 1166, is of the first importance not merely as a contribution to legal reform, but in its bearing on the development of the Constitution. It prescribed new machinery for the administration of the criminal law. In each county and hundred inquiry was to be made by twelve " lawful " men of every hundred and four lawful men of each township, and they were to declare on oath that they will " speak the truth ", whether there were in their respective districts any persons accused or suspected of robbery, murder, brigandage or any harbourers of the same, and to make their report to the sheriff and also to the king's justices on circuit. The men accused or suspected were to go to the ordeal by water; if they failed they were to be punished by death or mutilation; if they survived the ordeal they were to abjure the realm. It was assumed that the grand jury (if we may anticipate the later appellation) would present only those persons of whose guilt they were practically certain. Thus the jurors were witnesses as well as jurors. Later on the grand jurors were allowed to summon to their assistance jurors who could bear witness to the facts, and the grand jurors, ceasing to be witnesses, gave judgment on the facts as presented in evidence. The judges declared the law. Of this system the beginnings are to be found in the Assize of Clarendon, and it was further developed by the Assize of Northampton (1176), which framed the instructions for the six commissions sent forth in that year to administer justice throughout the country. Thus for the first time the land secured both uniformity of law and uniformity in the mode of its administration.

**Political Significance.**

These great *Assizes* had a political as well as a legal significance. The machinery devised for the presentation of criminals could be, and was, adapted to wider purposes. An efficient system of judicature is a great thing: it is well that punishment, sure and swift, should wait on the commission of crime; but an efficient system of government is an even greater thing. Early in its political life England began to lisp the lessons of self-government. The germs of our parliamentary institutions are to be sought partly in the local, popular assemblies, but partly also in the decrees of our Plantagenet kings. "It is," wrote Stubbs in a notable passage, "in the new system of recognition, assizes and presentments by jury, that we find the most distinct traces of the growth of the principle of representation; and this in three ways. (i) The institution of the jury was itself based on the representative idea: the jurors, to whatever fact or in whatever capacity they swore, declared the report of the community to the fact in question. (ii) The method of inquest was in England brought into close connexion with the procedure of the shire-moot, and thus the inquisitorial process . . . was . . . carried on with the previously existing representative institutions, such as were the reeve and four best men, the twelve senior thegns. . . . (iii) The particular expedients adopted for the regulation of the inquests paved the way in a remarkable manner for the system of county representation . . . by two sworn knights in the national council." [1]

[1] *Constitutional History* (slightly abridged), I, pp. 608–9.

These are the outstanding points which—details apart—give special importance to the work of Henry II.

**Richard I.**

How sound was that work, how firm its foundations, is most strikingly illustrated by the reign of his successor. Except in the romances of Sir Walter Scott, Richard Cœur-de-lion counts for little in our history. Almost wholly an absentee, he touches the development of our Constitution only by his insistent demands for money and men. To the efficiency of the father's system of government there could be no higher testimony than the fact that it survived the absence, the avarice, and the reckless extravagance of his elder son, and the presence, the levity, and the wickedness of the younger.

**Longchamp.**

The survival owed a great deal to the ability of two ministers who virtually ruled the kingdom in the prolonged absence of Richard I. William Longchamp, Chancellor, Chief Justiciar and Papal Legate, was the chief minister from 1189–91. An alien, an upstart, vulgar in ostentation, Longchamp was exceedingly unpopular with all classes, but if unscrupulous and high-handed he was an honest and faithful servant to his master. In 1191 the cup of Longchamp's unpopularity overflowed, and his enemies, acting on a mandate from the king and headed by Prince John, Archbishop Geoffrey of York (the king's natural half-brother), and Hugh Puisset, the powerful Prince-Bishop of Durham, drove him into banishment.

**Hubert Walter.**

Longchamp had put to an excellent financial use the machinery devised by Henry II, but it was Hubert Walter, Archbishop of Canterbury (1193–1205), Chief Justiciar (1194–8) and Papal Legate, who developed and improved it. Hubert Walter was an admirable representative of the new official class; he had been trained in the administrative methods of the late reign in the household of the great Justiciar Ranulf Glanvil, and his rule was as orderly as it was strong.

His first duty, like that of his predecessor, was to raise money, but he raised it by methods which were of real constitutional significance, and incidentally gave a powerful impulse to the development of representative institutions. The famous Commission (the Judicial Visitation, or *Iter*) of 1194 is in this connexion particularly important. Rules were laid down for the constitution of the Grand Jury: four knights were to be elected in the shire-court; these were to select on oath two knights from each hundred, and these two, also on oath, were to co-opt ten more for the jury of the hundred. One very serious blow was dealt at the overgrowing power of the sheriffs, by forbidding them to act as justices in their own shires, and their power was further circumscribed by the election in each shire-court of three knights and a clerk to act as *custodes placitorum coronae*—to keep the pleas of the Crown, a provision which gave birth to a new official, the Coroner. The Assize of Northampton had deprived the sheriff of the duty, shared (under the Assize of Clarendon) with the justices, of receiving presentments from the hundreds and townships. Evidently the intention was to increase the power of the central authority at the expense of local administrators. The Commissioners of 1194 were further instructed to ascertain precisely the extent of the king's feudal claim in regard to wardships, escheats, and the royal demesne, to extract tallage from all cities, boroughs and demesnes of the king, and to carry out a scheme for preserving a record of all debts owing to the Jews.

In 1195 the Justiciar issued a Proclamation for the Preservation of the Peace, requiring all persons above the age of fifteen to abstain from crime and to take part in the hue and cry after criminals. The edict was to be enforced by specially appointed knights, in whose duties Stubbs finds the germ of the office of Conservator of the Peace, the lineal ancestor of the long line of descendants still known as Justices of the Peace.

Hubert Walter was evidently much more of a statesman than an ecclesiastic, and it was from a brother bishop, Hugh of Lincoln, that he encountered serious opposition, based on constitutional grounds.

In 1198 the Justiciar laid before a great council held at

**Opposition to Taxation.**

Oxford the king's demand for three hundred knights to serve for a year and to be paid by the barons at the rate of 3*s*. a day. Led by Hugh of Lincoln, the barons successfully resisted the demand on the ground that they were not obliged to provide such service except within the four seas. To discover here the first definite assertion of the right of the Great Council of the Realm to control taxation may be fanciful, but it is, at the lowest, an interesting anticipation of a principle of first-rate constitutional significance, and it resulted in the resignation of the minister.

Plainly, constitutional development was not arrested by the absence of the king. On the contrary, in Richard's absence, the country was thrown back upon itself: barons, clerics, and people became conscious of common interests and ready for united action in defence of them. Only a few years elapsed before the results of national self-consciousness were unmistakably revealed.

## CHAPTER VI

# Church and State under the Normans and Angevins

TO the absentee Richard Cœur-de-lion there succeeded his brother John Lackland. John, if not the least able, was the most deservedly detested of all English kings. " A tyrant rather than a king, a destroyer rather than a ruler." Thus wrote Matthew Paris; and truly.

Yet John's tyranny and rapacity contributed to the " making " of England hardly less directly than the high statesmanship and reforming activity of any of his predecessors. For that tyranny was exercised impartially over all classes, over the magnates, the people, and not least the Church.

His quarrel with the Church broke that " tacit Concordat " (to use Bishop Stubbs's phrase) which, despite occasional and serious quarrels, had been maintained between Church and Crown ever since William had fought, under the Papal banner, on the field of Senlac. The high significance of the rupture of the " Concordat " can be understood only by a retrospect which must needs be the lengthier because so long deferred.

**Church and State.**

To the Concordat there were three parties: the king, the National Church, and the Papacy. The relations of these three parties constitute that problem of Church and State which looms so large in mediæval history, and not least (if in a peculiar aspect) in the history of this realm.

Towards the Papacy William I was, though not obsequious, invariably respectful, and one of his first acts was to restore the legatine authority of the Papacy.

The legate promptly undertook a purge of the English

Church. The Archbishop Stigand, regarded as schismatic, was deprived, as were most of the bishops and abbots. The vacancies thus created were filled by foreigners. Of the new appointments the most important was that of Lanfranc to the archbishopric of Canterbury (1070).

**Lanfranc.**

A native of Pavia, a great scholar and jurist, Lanfranc had lately become Abbot of St. Stephen's at Caen, recently founded by Duke William. Reluctantly he was persuaded to follow the fortunes of his patron and accept the see of Canterbury. Cautious and resolute, scholar and saint, a devoted Churchman and a brilliant diplomatist, he filled the post with high distinction, and, on the whole, to the advantage of his adopted country and the satisfaction of the king.

William found in Lanfranc a wise counsellor, but cordial as were the relations between them, the king never allowed the counsellor to become the master. For the most part, however, the two strong men worked in complete harmony with a common purpose. A Church, strong, highly organized and efficient, was to provide spiritual sustenance for the people, and at the same time to strengthen the authority of the Crown.

**Ecclesiastical Reforms.**

The metropolitan authority of Canterbury was extended over the whole realm; national ecclesiastical synods were revived, and, subject to the assent of the king, were invested with the power of ecclesiastical legislation. At the same time, the bishops retained their place in the Great Council of the Realm, though they sat there, perhaps, as bishops rather than barons.[1] Their " temporalities " were regarded as baronies, held, like all other baronies, from the king, and to the king homage has been paid, for these temporalities, from that day to this. Another step significant of the change in the position of the bishops was the gradual removal of their sees from villages to cities, e.g. from Sherborne to Salisbury, from Wells to Bath, from Dorchester-on-Thames to Lincoln, and from Lichfield to Chester. The most important of all these changes was, however, the separation of secular and

[1] The point is disputed. The bishops were summoned *fide et dilectione* not—*homagio.*

ecclesiastical jurisdiction. Ecclesiastical causes were no longer to be heard in secular courts; but contempt of the ecclesiastical court was to be penal, and the king's officers were to enforce punishment.

The famous Ordinance by which the separation was effected [1] represented, beyond doubt, a triumph for "clericalism", but it was vaguely worded; it contained no definition of "ecclesiastical causes"; and consequently it sowed seeds of mischief which yielded an abundant harvest for future generations to reap.

So long, however, as William and Lanfranc lived there was no rupture in the good relations between Church and State. The English Church, as Stubbs insisted, was a "national" Church. William, though he imposed his will on a conquered people—as also, indeed, on those who had assisted him in the conquest—resolved to rule as a "national" king.

Nationalism does not admit of divided allegiance. If a national king could not suffer an *imperium in imperio* at home, still less could he permit a foreign bishop, even though wielding œcumenical authority from Rome, to exercise direct jurisdiction over the English realm.

**The Hildebrandine System.**

Despite good will on both sides, the situation was, therefore, intrinsically difficult, the more so as the rule of the Normans in England coincided with the remarkable revival of Papal authority effected by one of the greatest of the Popes—Gregory VII, better known as Hildebrand. Magnificent was Hildebrand's conception of the world-position and world-mission of the Church of Christ. World-wide, it was to be extra-national—independent of the secular arm, and supra-national—exercising supreme authority over emperors and kings. A celibate clergy, unembarrassed by human relationships, freed from the jurisdiction of secular courts, were to be members of a cosmopolitan association taking its orders from Rome. Clerics were not to accept investiture at the hands of laymen, still less pay homage to laymen or make to them simoniacal gifts.

[1] Text in Stubbs: *Charters*, p. 81.

If the Hildebrandine claims could be reasonably represented as involving a conflict between spiritual freedom and feudal slavery, between justice and injustice, between right and might, between enlightenment and ignorance, between purity and debauchery, between pure religion and moral anarchy, who would not be on the side of Hildebrand? But the question at issue is less simple. Nationalism is in these latter days (1937) temporarily suspect, owing to the extravagant claims put forward in its name. But for long centuries Nationalism enshrined a principle not less vital than Catholicism. For Italy and Germany the triumph of the Hildebrandine Papacy meant a retardation of national development, and for that retardation the world is paying a heavy penalty to-day. England, thanks largely to the National Church, was in a different position. By the time of the Norman Conquest she had advanced some way on the path of national development, and Pope Hildebrand was great enough to recognize in England's Norman king a foeman worthy of his steel or a friend worth conciliation. The Conqueror's respect for the Church was unfeigned, but, on receiving the Pope's demand for homage and Peter's Pence, he returned an answer which is historic.

**William I and Pope Gregory VII.**

"Thy legate, Hubert, Holy Father, hath called upon me in thy name, to take the oath of fealty to thee and to thy successors, and to exert myself in enforcing the more regular payment of the money which my predecessors were accustomed to remit to the Church of Rome. One request I have granted, the other I refuse. Homage to thee I have not chosen, nor do I choose to do. I never made a promise to that effect; neither do I find that it was ever performed by my predecessors to thine. The money in question, during the three years past, owing to my being frequently in France, has been negligently collected. Now, as I am by divine mercy returned to my kingdom, the money which has been collected is transmitted by the aforesaid legate. As for the rest, it shall be sent as opportunity shall occur, by the legates of our trusty Archbishop Lanfranc. Pray for us, and for our kingdom, for we always respected thy predecessors, and we would fain regard thee with sincere affection, and be always thy obedient servant."[1]

Moreover, the Conqueror took occasion to lay down certain "customs" as a summary of the proper relation between the Crown, upon one hand, and the Church, national and œcumenical, upon the other. The clergy were not to acknowledge any one as Pope, until the royal consent had been first obtained; no letters from Rome were to be published, until they had first been approved by the king; the Church of England, in Council assembled under its Primate, might pass no laws or canons but such as were agreeable to the king's pleasure; no bishop might implead or punish any of the king's vassals, even for gravest sin, except by the king's precept; nor might any ecclesiastic leave the country without similar permission.

**The "Customs" of William I.**

On the Conqueror's "customs" was based the ecclesiastical policy of all the strongest and most national of his successors down to Edward III; nor did they need much expansion or adaptation when Henry VIII decided to "break the bonds of Rome". Nevertheless, William's policy did in fact involve contradictory principles, though the contradiction was disguised by the good understanding between a wise archbishop and a statesmanlike king.

His son and successor, William Rufus (1087–1100), was a man of very different type. The Conqueror was an autocrat; Rufus was a tyrant, cruel, vicious and rapacious, a blasphemer of God, an oppressor of men. After Lanfranc's death (1089) Rufus gave full rein to his worst vices. The Church he regarded merely as a source of profit to the Crown: the feudal principle of land tenure, already tentatively applied to Church property by the Conqueror, was carried by Rufus to its extreme logical conclusion. More than that: bishoprics, abbacies and other benefices were deliberately kept vacant for years in order that the Crown might confiscate their revenues. Worst of all, on Lanfranc's death, the vacancy at Canterbury was not filled.

**William Rufus.**

"The king," wrote a contemporary chronicler, Eadmer,

[1] Peter's Pence, nevertheless, continued to be paid until the Reformation.

"seized the church at Canterbury, the mother of all England, Scotland, and Ireland and all the neighbouring isles: all that belonged to it within and without he caused to be inventoried by his officers. . . . So he put up the Church of Christ to sale. . . . The same savage cruelty raged in all her daughter churches in England, which, when bishop or abbot died at that time, fell into widowhood. . . . And thus wherever you looked there was wretchedness before your eyes . . . always increasing, always as time went on growing more cruel and evil."

**Anselm.**

In 1093, however, Rufus fell grievously sick, and, thinking himself at the point of death, determined to make peace with the Church. There chanced to be in England at the moment Anselm, the abbot of Bec. Anselm was the most learned scholar of his day, a man of saintly character, lovable, gentle and retiring, but, as the sequel proved, a man who, in defence of principle, could exhibit dauntless courage and undeviating persistence. Summoning Anselm to his bedside, Rufus forced on him the archbishopric of Canterbury. Anselm insisted on conditions: Rufus must restore all the property of the see; accept Anselm as his spiritual father and ghostly adviser; and recognize Pope Urban II (already recognized by Anselm), as against the anti-Pope. On his recovery Rufus confirmed the appointment of Anselm, who was, "according to the custom of the land, made the king's man, and ordered to be seised of the whole archbishopric as Lanfranc had been". On the two other conditions no agreement was reached. The king soon resumed all his evil ways, and between him and his archbishop there ensued bitter and wellnigh continuous strife. Obedient to a law which he deemed higher than any human laws, Anselm more than once put himself technically in the wrong. Rufus was quick to take advantage of any slip on the part of the archbishop, and at last, in despair, Anselm demanded leave to go to Rome and take counsel with the Pope. He was absent for three years (1097–1100). When he returned Rufus was dead: the world was well rid of a bad man, his kingdom of a cruel king.

Anselm's sojourn in Rome coincided with the meeting of a council which not only renewed the decrees against simony and clerical marriage, but pronounced anathema against those who gave or received lay investiture.

**Investitures.**

Investiture was a symbolic ceremony. The king invested the bishop with crozier and ring; the bishop, placing his hands between those of the king, did homage as his " man ". Against this ceremony Hildebrand stoutly protested, as tending to exalt Cæsar to the detriment of the clergy whose primary allegiance was owed to God. At the Lenten Synod of 1075 Pope Gregory VII forbade lay investiture and summoned the Emperor Henry IV to Rome. The emperor defied the Pope, but his defiance issued in his humiliation at Canossa (1077). To modern minds the point at issue may seem trivial, but the quarrel that ensued perturbed the mediæval world for half a century, until, at long last, a compromise was reached in the Concordat of Worms (1122). Nor was the matter, in truth, trivial. It involved a problem old as time and still unsolved, the conflict between Ethics and Politics, between the things that are Cæsar's and the things that are God's. To yield on the symbolic point meant to a Hildebrand and an Anselm not the surrender of claims put forward by a human institution, but disloyalty to a Heavenly Master. A Hohenstaufen emperor or an English king might, on the contrary, reasonably hold that, in acknowledging the supremacy of a "foreign" potentate, he was surrendering something essential to the conception of feudal kingship.

**Henry I and Anselm.**

Henry I had no sooner succeeded to the throne than he recalled Anselm, who reached England in September, 1100. At his coronation the new king issued a Charter of Liberties, the first words of which ran as follows: " Ye know that by the mercy of God and the Common Counsel of the barons of the whole kingdom of England I have been crowned king of that kingdom: and whereas the kingdom was oppressed by unjust exactions I, in my reverence to God and my love towards you, in the first place make God's Holy Church free, that is I will neither sell nor let to farm, nor will I, on the death of an archbishop, bishop or abbot, take anything of the demesne of the church or its vassals until the successor shall enter into possession."

So the bad customs of William II were to be abrogated, but the "customs" of William I were in their integrity to be maintained. Anselm must, therefore, do homage on the restitution of the properties of his see, and accept investiture at his hands.

Anselm, fresh from the Council at Rome, refused. "If the king will obey the decrees of that Council there will be peace between us", but "I have not returned to England to remain here at the cost of disobedience to my spiritual chief the Roman Pontiff".

Henry, greatly perturbed, proposed, as a compromise, that the new Pope Paschal should be petitioned to grant to England exemption from the decrees. But Paschal proved adamant; Anselm would not disobey the Pope. At length, however (1107), a reasonable compromise was effected which anticipated by twenty years that reached for the Church at large in the famous Concordat of Worms (1122). Bishops and abbots were not henceforth to receive the ring and the pastoral staff at the hands of laymen, but as "barons" were to do homage for their temporalities. Henry proved faithless. After Anselm's death (1109) he kept the see of Canterbury vacant for five years, and appropriated its revenues.

**Stephen.**

Under Stephen the Church was able to demonstrate its power. Henry I, leaving no son, had tried to secure the succession for his daughter Matilda. But owing to support of the Church, led by Stephen's brother Henry, Bishop of Winchester, and Roger, Bishop of Salisbury, the throne was secured by Stephen, a grandson of the Conqueror. Stephen, as faithless as he was weak, made large promises to the Church but did not keep them, and in 1139 completely alienated his best friends by an act of incredible folly. The whole administrative machinery of the kingdom was in the hands of Roger of Salisbury, as Justiciar, and of his son and nephew, who were respectively Chancellor and Treasurer. The nephew Nigel was also Bishop of Ely; and Alexander, another nephew, was Bishop of Lincoln. In view of the prevailing anarchy, and following the example of the lay barons, Roger and his nephews built and fortified a number of strong castles in their dioceses. Treating this as an act of treason, Stephen arrested the bishops, and thus not only alienated the Church but brought the whole administrative machine to a standstill. The fourteen years of civil war and anarchy that followed were terminated only by the Treaty of Wallingford (1153).

A year later Stephen died and Henry of Anjou succeeded to the throne.

Henry's first act was to issue a Charter confirming the concessions made by his grandfather. There followed thereon a decade of peace, prosperity, and happiness guaranteed by the strong and orderly administration of Henry II and his chief minister. The minister was the Chancellor, Thomas Becket, a " notary ", and, though only in deacon's orders, Archdeacon of Canterbury.

**Henry II and Becket.**

In an evil hour, but in the well-grounded belief that he could count upon Becket's continued co-operation in the task of government, Henry forced on his reluctant Chancellor the archbishopric of Canterbury (1162).

Far from slothful in business, Becket was also fervent in spirit, but his fervour was henceforward transferred from the State to the Church. He refused to remain Chancellor, adopted the monastic habit, and surprised and irritated the king by his sudden and violent championship of clerical rights and immunities. In 1163 in a Council at Woodstock the archbishop successfully opposed the king on a question of taxation (memorable as the first recorded case of the kind in England), and in the same year a still more serious quarrel broke out between the old friends on the subject of criminous clerks.

Clerical immunities constituted a grave scandal. More than one hundred serious crimes committed by clerks since the accession of Henry—including two murders by highly placed ecclesiastics—had gone unpunished. The Church claimed that all " clerks "—even those in minor orders—could be tried only by ecclesiastical courts and sentenced only to ecclesiastical punishments. To an orderly administrator like Henry II such a claim was intolerable. Becket vehemently supported it. A committee of barons was then appointed to draft a statement of the " ancient customs of the realm " concerning the relations of Church and State.

**The Constitutions of Clarendon.**

The *Constitutions of Clarendon* (1164) were the outcome of their labours.[1] This famous document purported to be, and in large measure was, a codification of the usages of Henry I, but some of its clauses were evidently fresh developments and applications of customs then in force. Disputes about advowsons and presentations were to be determined in the King's Court. Elections of bishops and abbots were to be in the King's Chapel, with the assent of the king and " by the counsel of the clergy summoned for that purpose ". The person elected was, before consecration, to do homage to the king for his lands and to hold them as a barony subject to all feudal incidents, and was to attend the King's Court. No ecclesiastic was to leave the realm without the king's leave or, without the same, to carry an appeal beyond the court of the archbishop. No tenant-in-chief or royal servant was to be excommunicated, or his lands placed under interdict, without consultation with the king. Sons of villeins were not to be ordained without their lord's leave. On these points there was no great difference of opinion. Far otherwise was it in regard to the trial and punishment of criminous clerks. They were to be tried in the ecclesiastical court, but if found guilty to be handed over to the secular arm for punishment.

The Constitutions of Clarendon are, as Stubbs justly says, " no mere engines of tyranny, or secular spite against a Churchman; they are really a part of a great scheme of administrative reform, by which the debatable ground between the spiritual and temporal powers can be brought within the reach of common justice, and the lawlessness arising from professional jealousies abolished ".[2] Becket at first gave his assent to the Code, though in ambiguous

[1] For text, cf. Stubbs: *Select Charters*, pp. 131–4. [2] *Constitutional History*, I, p. 465.

terms, but subsequently withdrew it, and after a violent quarrel fled the country, and obtained condemnation of the Constitutions from Pope Alexander III. Henry, deeply hurt and angered, confiscated the property of the see, banished Becket's kinsmen, and had the young Henry, his heir, crowned by the Archbishop of York. Becket, in exile, retorted by excommunicating seven of Henry's leading councillors, including two bishops. At last, however, after six years of blasts and counterblasts a truce was patched up (1170). Becket returned to England, still breathing fire, slaughter, and excommunications against his enemies. Henry, holding his Christmas court in Normandy, lost all patience with the "low-born clerk". His hasty words were caught up by the courtiers, and four knights crossed the sea to arrest the archbishop. Becket fled for sanctuary to his own minster at Canterbury, and there on the steps of the altar was foully done to death.

**Murder of Becket.**

The brutal crime created a profound sensation throughout Christendom. Becket was canonized by the Pope. Henry, distraught with grief, cleared himself of all complicity in the crime, but, nevertheless, on his return to England did public penance and founded three monasteries, having already at Avranches (1172) abrogated the Constitutions of Clarendon. But the abrogation was hardly more than formal; many of the Constitutions, being mostly declaratory, were only partially affected by abrogation.

Both Becket and the king had stood for important principles, but in essentials the work done by the king for the State had greater permanent significance than any achieved by the archbishop for the Church. Nevertheless, sympathy was naturally extended to the victim of a detestable crime: Becket was crowned with a halo of martyrdom, earned less by wisdom than by courage.

Except for the point already[1] noted, the reign of Richard I may, in the present connexion, be passed over.

Not so the reign of John, whose intemperate folly produced a crisis in the affairs of the State no less than of the Church.

[1] *Supra*, pp. 62–3.

## CHAPTER VII

# The Great Charter

IN 1591 there was published a Chronicle play, *The Troublesome Reign of King John*. Whether that play, like a later and more famous one, was also from Shakespeare's pen is uncertain. But whoever the author he chose well his epithet. John's reign was "troublesome", but it was also of high significance.

John's succession was not, either in his island kingdom or his continental empire, undisputed: it was secured to him mainly by the efforts of his mother, Queen Eleanor, and the Archbishop Hubert Walter.

The deaths, in rapid succession, of these two supporters gave a fatal shock to John's position. That position had from the first been threatened by a rival claimant to the throne, his nephew Arthur, the thirteen-year-old son of his elder brother Geoffrey and Constance of Brittany. The cause of Arthur was championed by John's overlord, Philip IV of France, but thanks partly to John's own genius for war, partly to the support of his mother, John made good his position alike in England and in Normandy, Anjou, Maine, Poitou and Guienne. Prince Arthur was captured and murdered by John in 1203. In 1204 Queen Eleanor died. Shameless in her varied conjugal relations, Eleanor was a woman of strong character and immense ability, which she devoted to the interests of her sons. On her death John's position collapsed. All his continental possessions were taken by Philip IV, to the manifest advantage, as many hold, of the insular kingdom.

**Death of Queen Eleanor.**

Be that as it may, John was thus left face to face with his English subjects. It soon became clear that the administrative system, initiated by Henry I, perfected by Henry II, and further refined and developed during Richard's absence by a succession of able and devoted ministers, was doubled-edged in operation. John proved that, in the hands of a tyrant, it might easily be perverted into a peculiarly effective instrument of financial extortion, pressing upon all classes of the people, and particularly upon the baronage and the Church, who had most to lose.

The clerical Estate was the first to feel the pressure. Archbishop Hubert Walter died in 1205, and disputes at once arose about the election of a successor. Three parties put forward their claims: the monks of Christ Church, Canterbury; the suffragan bishops of the Province; and the king.

**Death of Archbishop Hubert.**

The formal right of election undoubtedly belonged to the Chapter—the monks of Christ Church—as it belongs to a Chapter to-day; but, then as now, the nomination was virtually in the hands of the king. John meant to nominate John de Gray, Bishop of Norwich, upon whose complaisance he could rely. The bishops would have raised no objection to this choice, and the majority of the monks, while maintaining their own right to elect, were willing on this occasion to accept the nomination. But the younger monks, thinking that the unpopularity and misfortunes of the king gave the Chapter a chance of successfully asserting its claims, met by night, elected their sub-prior Reginald, sent him off, post-haste, to Rome to obtain from the Pope the *Pallium*. Reginald, though sworn to secrecy, could not resist the temptation to reveal himself to friends in Flanders as the archbishop-elect. When the news reached John his anger knew no bounds; the Chapter, in dire alarm, joined with the suffragan bishops in electing John de Gray, and sent delegates to Rome to obtain Papal confirmation (December, 1205). John also appealed to the Pope, but bound the delegates from the Chapter by a secret oath to elect his own nominee.

The Papal chair was at the moment occupied by Innocent III, who has commonly been described as " the greatest of

**Pope Innocent III.**

all the Popes ". If not the greatest Churchman among the successors of St. Peter, he was undeniably the shrewdest lawyer. He outwitted John by treating him as an honest man, by regarding his appeal as genuine, and his delegates as plenipotentiaries. Setting aside both elections, he induced the Chapter-delegates to elect Stephen Langton, a cardinal of English birth and high reputation, and, despite the protest of John's delegates, invested him with the Pallium.

The wisdom of the Pope's choice, the signal services rendered by his nominee to the English people, have obscured the fact that Innocent III was guilty of a piece of chicanery more worthy of a " peddling attorney " than of the successor of St. Peter. John had committed almost every conceivable folly, in particular the folly of misjudging and underrating his astute opponent, but his anger was intelligible and not unjustified.

A greater man would have smothered his anger and acquiesced in an appointment which, if dubious in origin, was in itself wholly admirable. Not so John. He mendaciously declared that he had never heard of Langton, charged the monks with perjury (thereby revealing his own attempt at bribery), sequestrated their property, threatened the Pope with the withdrawal of obedience and of revenue, and absolutely refused to accept Langton as archbishop.

**The Interdict.**

Innocent retorted by placing the whole of England under interdict, a punishment which fell heavily on the clergy and the pious laity, but was accepted with equanimity by a great part of the nation. The king's threat to exile all the clergy was withdrawn almost as soon as uttered, but all Church property was sequestrated, the clergy being allowed barely enough to sustain life. The bishops, with two exceptions, fled the country, but many of the clergy made submission to the king and obtained in return partial restoration of their property. The Interdict, though not lifted until John's submission in 1213, was never very strictly enforced; pious folk were able to obtain most of the religious consolations they needed, and they shared with the impious the material consolation of considerable remissions of taxation, rendered possible by the confiscation of Church property.

John himself was excommunicated in 1209, a sentence which he bore with equanimity. But it was a different matter when in 1212 Innocent took the further step of deposing him, and committed the execution of the sentence to Philip Augustus of France. Excommunication had encouraged John's enemies and had scared his friends more than it scared the king himself. But he was genuinely alarmed by the sentence of deposition, combined as it was with a threat of foreign invasion and accumulating troubles at home. Accordingly in May, 1213, John made an abject but not impolitic surrender; received Archbishop Langton, recalled the exiled bishops and monks, and undertook to restore Church property and make compensation for the injuries the Church had suffered. More than that; he resigned the crowns of England and Ireland into the hands of the Papal legate, and agreed to hold his kingdoms henceforward as a Papal fief at a rental of 1000 marks. Protestant historians, following the lead of Shakespeare, have represented John's action as shameless and ignominious. Contemporaries saw little shame in Papal vassalage, and commended the unjust steward for making friends with a righteous Pontiff. The country was freed from the threat of invasion and the domestic crisis was postponed. John had at least gained time, though he made little use of it. Innocent regarded the vassaldom as no mere formality, but the efforts of his successors to make it a reality reacted disadvantageously upon Papal authority in England, and gave a powerful stimulus to the growing nationalism of the English people.

**Excommunication.**

Meanwhile, the astuteness of the king's sudden surrender was soon manifested. The Pope became his staunch ally, his champion against opponents foreign and domestic.

**Stephen Langton.**

Archbishop Langton, on the contrary, deeply disapproved John's pusillanimous if politic surrender, and stood forth, at this crisis, not merely as a great Churchman, but as an intrepid patriot.

After Langton's return to England (16th July, 1213) things moved rapidly. On 4th August a Council met at St. Albans and was attended not only by barons and bishops, but by the reeve and four loyal men from each township on the royal demesne. The immediate object of the Assembly was to ascertain the amount due as restitution to the bishops plundered by John during the Interdict, but the proceedings took on a wider aspect when the Justiciar promised, on the king's behalf, a restoration of the "good laws" of Henry I. Three weeks later, at another Council called at St. Paul's (25th August), the archbishop produced a copy of the Coronation Charter of Henry I, which was promptly adopted as a basis for the demands to be made upon John.

The king retorted by summoning to Oxford (November) a Council which was to include, besides barons and armed knights, four discreet men from each county to "speak with the king concerning the affairs of the realm".[1] There is, however, no record that this Council ever met. The barons, meanwhile, were quarrelling with the king about their obligation to serve abroad and pay scutage (November, 1214). Philip's victory at Bouvines (1214), shattered John's hopes of a successful confederacy against the French king, and on his return to England, a defeated man, John found all classes of his people, led by the archbishop, united in their determination to put an end to his tyranny, and extort from him a comprehensive charter of liberties.

The barons, having secured the adhesion of London (May, 1215), and backed by the bishops, presented their demands to the king.

John, surrendering at discretion, issued on 15th June the great Charter.

**Magna Carta.**

*Magna Carta* has suffered many vicissitudes of interpretation at the hands of commentators. The latest of them observes, somewhat cryptically, that "the real history of

[1] For the constitutional significance of these Councils see *infra*, p. 87.

the Great Charter . . . belongs to a later age ".[1] It may be so. It may be that Stubbs indulged in unwonted exaggeration when he said: " The whole of the Constitutional History of England is little more than a commentary on it." That great historian-ecclesiastic taught a whole generation of historians that the Great Charter " is the act of the united nation, the Church, the barons and the commons for the first time thoroughly at one. . . . In substance and in historical position it is the first effort of a corporate life that has reached full consciousness, resolved to act for itself, and able to carry out the resolution."[2] A great German historian emphasized the same point—the significance of the Charter as the seal and symbol of national unity. " In other countries also at this epoch," wrote Ranke, " emperors and kings made very comprehensive concessions to the several estates: the distinctive point in the case of England is that they were not made to each estate separately, but to all at the same time. While elsewhere each estate was caring for itself, here a common interest of all grew up which bound them together for ever."

Thus *Magna Carta* was accepted as " the Bible of the Constitution ", the corner-stone of English liberty. Did it not in fact guarantee the " freedom " of the Church, prompt and equal justice to all sorts and conditions of men, the equal rights of all " free men "? Did it not contain the germ of the doctrine of *Habeas Corpus*, the most effective guarantee of personal liberty, the germ of trial by jury—the right of a man to be tried by his peers? Did it not proclaim the " fundamental principles of the Constitution ", notably the principle that there should be no taxation without the consent of the " common counsel of the realm "?

The answers to these questions, of course affirmative, represent the popular and indeed the critical view of the Great Charter that was universally accepted from the seventeenth century to the twentieth. But in the last thirty years the clauses of the Charter have been subjected to closer and more critical analysis, notably by Mr. W. S.

[1] F. M. Powicke: *ap. Cambridge Mediæval History*, VI, p. 245. [2] *C. H.*, I, p. 543.

McKechnie[1] and by M. Petit-Dutaillis.[2] Dr. McIlwain[3] and Dr. Baldwin,[4] two American professors, writing with scholarly caution and profound erudition, have indeed given to the whole history of mediæval England an entirely new emphasis, but in less responsible hands the reaction against the "orthodox" view of the Great Charter has undoubtedly been carried too far.

That the Charter was the invention of the lawyers of the seventeenth century is a view designated by Dr. T. F. Tout as "ridiculous"—and justly. Nor need we pay too much heed to the paradoxical views of Dr. Jenks, who did not scruple to write of *The Myth of Magna Carta*, and to argue that by reason of its reactionary character and its consecration of the past it proved "a stumbling block in the path of progress".[5]

The temperate and scholarly criticism of Mr. McKechnie and M. Petit-Dutaillis cannot, however, be ignored. Briefly, the main point made by them is that *Magna Carta* was primarily and almost exclusively a feudal compact extorted by the baronage, assisted by the Church, and drawn up in the interests of a class which had been severely repressed by King John, and not less effectively by his predecessors. We are now taught that the "freedom" promised to the Church meant merely the privileges of the clerical order, and that the "free men" (*liberi homines*) to whom so many concessions are made are not ordinary citizens, but the limited class of "freeholders"—and much to similar effect. Of the 63 clauses of the Charter, 14 were temporary or executive; two referred to the Church, viz. the famous first clause declaring that the Church should be "free", and a second (§ 22) declaring that "no clerk should be amerced for his lay tenement", save in the manner prescribed [for other classes] and not according to the value of his ecclesiastical benefice; while no fewer than 24 clauses referred specifically and exclusively to baronial privileges. Of these several (notably § 34, which dealt with the writ

[1] *Magna Carta* (1905). [2] *Studies in Constitutional History* (1908).
[3] *The High Court of Parliament and its Supremacy* (1910).
[4] *King's Council in the Middle Ages* (1914). [5] *Independent Review* (Nov., 1904).

*Praecipe*—a process by which suits concerning free tenures were evoked to the King's Court) were evidently intended to restore to the baronial courts the jurisdiction of which, during the preceding century, they had been deprived. Others protected feudal privileges against recent " encroachments " on the part of the Crown, and from the point of view of the legal reformer were indisputably reactionary.[1] On the other hand, there were several clauses which definitely developed the reforming principles of Henry I and II, and extended the jurisdiction of the Crown and its judges. A notable example is the clause (§ 24) forbidding sheriffs, constables, coroners or bailiffs of the king to hold trials of criminal charges (" pleas of the Crown ").

Even the older commentators had to admit that the clauses, greatly extolled, dealing with the Common Council of the Realm and its right to assent to taxation were " reactionary ", since they took no account of the recent tendency to summon knights from the shire-court, still less representative burghers. M. Petit-Dutaillis, on his part, had to admit that the benefit of the clauses dealing with the administration of royal justice " could not be confined to the barons alone ". Nevertheless, he stoutly maintained that the clauses referring to the City of London (§ 13), to the merchants (§§ 20, 35 and 41), and the clause saving from forfeiture the wainage (working tools) of the villein, were " really made in the interests of the barons ". This is surely special pleading, and it will take still more special pleading to dislodge from the popular imagination the general effect of the famous clauses 40 and 60. The former runs: " To none will we sell, to none will we deny or delay, right or justice." On this Chief Justice Coke commented in words which have become part of the fibre of all free-born Britons: "All men, for all kinds of injuries, may have justice and right, freely without sale, fully without denial, and speedily

[1] Most reactionary of all, perhaps, and most misinterpreted in later centuries, was the famous clause *nisi per legale judicium parium suorum*. Interpreted as establishing the right of trial by jury, this clause was simply intended to secure the privilege of a peer to be tried by peers. This claim was finally established, as regards civil treason and felony (but not in civil actions), under Edward III.

without delay." Not less pregnant is the promise of clause 60, by which "all the rights, customs and liberties conceded to the king's men (*erga nostros*) were by all his subjects, cleric and lay, to be extended to their men (*erga suos*).

It may be, as Petit-Dutaillis argues, that *suo* refers only to the subtenants, but "all his subjects" (*omnes de regno suo*) would still remain to be explained away; and assuming the explanation to be satisfactory, does it matter?

Conceding everything that the "higher criticism" claims, the same question may, indeed, be repeated: Does it matter? To the legal specialist it matters much; to the historian it matters little. He may well be satisfied with the common-sense summary of two eminent lawyers—Sir Frederick Pollock and Dr. Maitland. Of the Great Charter they write: "With all its faults this document becomes and rightly becomes a sacred text, the nearest approach to an unrepealable 'fundamental statute' that England has ever had. In age after age a confirmation of it will be demanded and granted as a remedy for those oppressions for which the realm is suffering, and this when some of its clauses, at least in their original meaning, have become hopelessly antiquated. For, in brief, it means this, that the king is and shall be below the law." Precisely: and so said Bracton, a great jurist of the thirteenth century: "The king hath one superior, namely God; and another the law by which he is made king" (1259). So said Hooker, an Elizabethan bishop: "Lex facit regem . . . whatever power the king hath, he hath it by law, the bounds and limits of it are known." So said, with one voice, all the lawyers of the seventeenth century.

*Magna Carta* for the first time, and in a comprehensive way, made those limits known. Legally interpreted, many of its clauses may be "conservative and even reactionary". But the political significance of this great document consisted less in what it said than in what, through the ages, it was popularly supposed to have meant. The Charter would not have been confirmed thirty-eight times had it been regarded as a "myth".

## CHAPTER VIII

# The King and Parliament
## Representative Government

NO two nations have exactly the same conception of Liberty. The Hebrew weeping by the waters of Babylon thought of it in terms of national independence. A modern German finds its highest fulfilment in the privilege of "compulsory" service. An American still thinks of it as the "right to do what he likes with his own". To a Frenchman it is almost synonymous with the possession of a plot, however small, of land. The Englishman associates it with Runnymede and Westminster. Runnymede stands for that personal liberty which the average Englishman, rightly or wrongly, believes to have been guaranteed to him by *Magna Carta*; Westminster is the traditional home of the Parliament which enshrines for him the idea of political liberty —the right to assent to the making of the laws to which he owes obedience.

**Roots of Parliament.**

Yet representation in Parliament was in its origin less a privilege conceded by the king to the people than an obligation imposed upon the people by the king. Bishop Stubbs declared that the idea of constitutional government, summarized in the legal meaning of the word *parliament*, implied four principles: (1) the existence of a central or national assembly, a "*commune concilium regni*"; (2) the representation in that assembly of all classes of the people regularly summoned; (3) the reality of the representation of the whole people secured either by its presence in the council, or by the free election of the persons who are to represent it or any portion of it; and (4) the assembly so summoned and elected must possess definite forms of taxation, legislation and general political deliberation. That is an accurate analysis of Parliament as it ultimately took shape. But for its roots we must look in three directions. All are deep down in the soil. The deepest are the Ecclesiastical Synods, dating back at least to the days of Theodore of Tarsus. A second root is found in the central assemblies of the Saxon Witenagemot and of the Norman Curia Regis; the third is in the local "moots" of the hundred and the shire. Although we are bidden by a modern scholar[1] to abandon the "myth" of the Three Estates, it is undeniable that Parliament in its final form contained at least three elements, and that these corresponded to the roots uncovered above. Westminster is popularly described as the Mother of Parliaments, but representative assemblies were not, in fact, peculiar to England. The Spanish kingdoms were well ahead of England in this respect. It was in Leon that delegates from the communes were first summoned (1188) to take part with the nobles and ecclesiastics in the Cortes. Popular representation in Aragon dates back at least to 1163, in Catalonia to 1218, and in Castile to 1250 or perhaps earlier. The States-General in France—a body representative of nobles, clergy and communes—was convoked by Philip the Fair in 1302, though some authorities date the institution at least from 1241. Premature development is generally inimical to vigorous growth. The States-General seemed destined in the fourteenth and fifteenth centuries to play in the history of France a part hardly less important than Parliaments in England. But the hope was disappointed: between 1614 and 1789 the States-General never met, and not until the definite establishment of the Third Republic (1875), if then, did the Parliaments created under the varied constitutional experiments of the nineteenth century begin effectually to function. The Spanish Cortes was never entirely suspended as was the French States-General, but after the development of the centralized monarchy in the sixteenth century Par-

**Origins.**

**Parliaments in Spain and in France.**

[1] A. F. Pollard: *The Evolution of Parliament* (1920).

liament ceased to exercise any real influence upon the government of Spain. It may be that the decay of parliamentary institutions in France and Spain was due to the fact that they were based on the principle of Estates, that they exaggerated and perpetuated class distinctions, and that consequently they were ill-qualified to offer a solid and united opposition to the encroachments of the Crown. Be this as it may, Englishmen take legitimate pride in the fact that the English Parliament has, with some inevitable vicissitudes of fortune, enjoyed a continuous existence from the day of its birth until the present hour.

**Central Representation.**

About the day of its birth there is, however, no general agreement. Perhaps, like Topsy, the English Constitution "was never born" but "just grew". The idea and habit of representation derived from the remote past; but the presence of representatives, locally chosen, in a central assembly dates only from the thirteenth century. And even then the development was tentative and slow. The first instance is afforded by the Council held at St. Albans on 4th August, 1213. It was attended not only by bishops and barons, but by the reeve and four representative men from each villa on the royal demesne. Later in the same year, the king addressed to the sheriffs a writ summoning to a Council at Oxford "four discreet knights" to speak with him concerning the business of his kingdom.

*Magna Carta* made no provision for representatives in the Common Council of the Realm; that document characteristically required the assent to taxation of an assembly exclusively feudal in composition. The Charter was frequently reissued under Henry III, but with omissions which were evidently designed to enhance the power of the dominant aristocracy. The Charter of 1215 was, then, at the highest, the product of a coalition which did not survive the crisis which called it into being. Strengthened by his recent compact with the Pope, John appealed to his suzerain against his vassals. Innocent III promptly ordered the archbishop to pronounce sentence of excommunication upon the king's enemies, and annulled the Charter. The barons thereupon appealed to Philip Augustus of France and offered the Crown to his son Lewis. In November, 1215, a large body of French troops landed in England and were followed in May, 1216, by Lewis himself. Yet King John had still a powerful section of the baronage on his side, and his position, though serious, was perhaps not quite hopeless when, on 19th October, he died at Newark.

**Henry III.**

Henry III, a child of nine, succeeded to a kingdom in virtual possession of a foreign prince and an army largely composed of foreigners. But the death of the perjured tyrant encouraged the re-formation of the coalition which had extorted the Great Charter. National sentiment reasserted itself. William Marshall, Earl of Pembroke, a man of high character, ripe experience, and genuine patriotism, was appointed Regent of the realm and guardian of the king, and with him were associated, as chief counsellors, the Papal legate and (in Archbishop Langton's absence at Rome) Peter des Roches, Bishop of Winchester. Pembroke waged energetic war against the foreigner, and before the end of 1217 Lewis agreed to evacuate the country, and the general pacification was signalized and completed by a second reissue of the Charter. This contained several new clauses. One, imposing a legal restraint on the alienation of land, anticipated the later statute *Quia Emptores*; a second, forbidding the fraudulent transfer of land to religious houses, similarly contained the germ of the statute of *Mortmain*; a third ordered the destruction of adulterine castles, symptoms of a disorder that recalled the time of Stephen. The Charter was frequently reissued, but in future without amendment: the Charter of 1217 constitutes its final form.

**English Nationalism**

Whether the Charter represented the triumph of nationalism or of feudalism, certain it is that during the thirteenth century the idea of national unity made rapid progress, and that the idea was ultimately enshrined in a Parliament truly representative of the nation.

To the development of nationalism many things obviously contributed—the "sea-frontier", the existence of the common law, &c.—but nothing more directly than the loss of the continental possessions of the Norman Angevin kings. Hardly less responsible was the presence of the " swarms of foreign locusts " (to use a contemporary description) who, thanks to the complaisant uxoriousness of a weak king, infested England and preyed upon her resources.

**Anti-national Policy of the Papacy.**

Nothing, however, did more to develop national feeling in England than the ambition and rapacity of successive Popes. The attempt of Honorius III to rule England, during Henry's minority, as a Papal fief was deeply and increasingly resented. William Marshall, Stephen Langton and Hubert de Burgh—three stout-hearted Englishmen—resisted to the utmost of their power the impudent and extortionate demands of Rome. But Marshall died in 1219, Langton in 1228, and Hubert de Burgh was finally dismissed from all his offices in 1242. The king was then able to give full rein to his partiality for foreigners and to demonstrate his devotion to Holy Church. That devotion was probably sincere. Henry III was certainly susceptible to the externals of religion, and, feeble, fickle and capricious though he was, something may be forgiven to the man whose taste in architecture was impeccable, who enriched and enlarged the castle at Windsor, beautified St. Stephen's Chapel, transformed the palace of Westminster, and bequeathed to us, in all its exquisite beauty, the Abbey Church. " A connoisseur to the finger tips," is Dr. Jacob's happy description. But England looked for qualities in her king other than those of a consummate artist, and in all the endowments that make for greatness in a ruler Henry III was gravely deficient.

**Henry III.**

Yet his weakness was not without its political compensations. His subservience to Rome and his partiality for foreign ecclesiastics had a happy result. There was formed in the English Church a strong national party which found great leaders in men like Thomas and Walter de Cantelupe, Bishops, respectively, of Hereford and Worcester, in Archbishop Edmund Rich, and greatest of all in Robert Grosseteste.

Robert Grosseteste was from 1235 to 1253 Bishop of

**Nationalism in the English Church.**

Lincoln. But for ten years previously he had been the Rector of the Franciscans who in 1224 had established themselves at Oxford. Grosseteste, though not himself a Friar, admirably exemplified, alike in his life and work, the highest ideals of the movement to which he paid a noble tribute. " Your holiness may be assured " (so he wrote to Pope Gregory IX) " that in England inestimable blessings have been produced by the Friars, for they illuminate our whole country with the light of their preaching and learning. . . . If your holiness could see with what devotion and humility the people run to hear the word of life from them . . . and how much improvement the clergy and regulars have obtained by imitating them, you would indeed say that they who dwell in the land of the shadow of death, upon them hath the light shined." Grosseteste invited scholars to settle in Oxford, and he himself superintended the translation of Aristotle's *Ethics*. As a student of scientific theology he anticipated the methods of the leaders of the Oxford Renaissance, of John Colet and Linacre, of Grocyn and Erasmus; in his fearless exposure of abuses in the Church —of the prevalent greed, indolence and ignorance of the clergy; of the scandals connected with the clerical courts, with patronage, pluralities and non-residence, he was the precursor of the Protestant reformers of the sixteenth century. In all things, indeed, he showed himself an ardent patriot and a keen, if conservative, reformer.

**The Constitutional Struggle.**

The patriotic and reforming party in the Church was naturally in close alliance with the political " Opposition ". The last word has a modern ring, and the precocity of the thirteenth century must not beguile us into unjustified anticipation of later developments. The temptation is real, for the political thought of the period was amazingly advanced. The political songs collected by Dr. Wright prove it.[1] The tone of the song of Lewes is almost that of a Whig of the Revolution. Many of the sentiments are expressed in words which verbally anticipate the speeches of the opposition leaders under the early Stuarts. " If a

[1] *Camden Society*.

king be less wise than he ought to be, what advantage will the kingdom gain by his reign? Is he to seek by his own opinion on whom he should depend to have his failing supplied? If he alone choose, he will be easily deceived. Therefore let the community of the kingdom advise. . . . We give the first place to the community; we say also that the law is the light without which he who rules will wander from the right path."

Embryonic Parliaments.

Such an atmosphere was evidently favourable to the rapid, perhaps too rapid, development of political theory and constitutional reform. The National Council comes into prominence, and in 1246 is, for the first time, designated a *Parlamentum.* Modern critics warn us to lay no special stress on a word which was commonly used as synonymous with *colloquium* to describe any meeting for speech or conference. Nor will they draw any distinction between Parlamentum, Curia and Concilium. Before 1246 there had been at least three important meetings of the Council, at which the barons had proposed plans of reform designed to limit the autocracy of the king by the appointment of a body of responsible advisers. Matthew Paris has preserved the record of a highly instructive debate in the Council of 1242. The king requested an aid for the recovery of his foreign possessions. The Council, according to the chronicler, "withstood him to the face", but after long debate gave a conditional promise of assistance. Two years later (1244) the king again demanded money to pay the expenses of his disastrous campaign in Gascony. A small committee of twelve, four prelates, four earls and four barons, was appointed to consider the demand. Of this committee, Grosseteste, Walter Cantelupe, Richard Earl of Cornwall, the king's brother, and his brother-in-law, Simon de Montfort, Earl of Leicester were members. The committee agreed to a grant to be expended under their own supervision, but only on condition that the king would appoint such counsellors and adopt such reforms as the Council could approve. On his refusal, a much more drastic scheme of reform was put forward. A new revised and strengthened Charter was to be issued and its execution committed to four counsellors, chosen by common assent, two of whom were to be in constant attendance on the king, and to hear and remedy all complaints, to guard the treasure and to supervise the expenditure of all money granted to the king. Nothing was done, and the next eight years present a monotonous repetition of Papal exactions, royal demands, baronial refusals, and so on. Most of the money was extorted from the Jews and the City of London.

The Council which met in 1254 is commonly regarded as an important landmark in the development of Parliament, because to it were summoned, in addition to the magnates, two knights elected in full county court in each county, as well as representative clergy from each diocese. The Crown gained nothing, however, by this manœuvre, and matters drifted on to the crisis of 1258.

**Simon de Montfort.**

Further and larger demands for money, mainly to meet the insatiable greed of the Papacy, were made by the king to a Parliament which met in London. It was then that Simon de Montfort came definitely to the front as the leader of the Opposition. For the next seven years interest is centred on the contest between the great earl and the king. There are cross-currents, and the details are confused, but the broad issues are fairly clear. On the one side stood the king, the plunderer of England less in his own interests than in those of his foreign kinsmen and friends, and particularly of the Pope; facile in promises of reform, but faithless and evasive in performance. Opposed to him was his intrepid brother-in-law, Simon de Montfort, supported by the bulk of the clergy, the towns (notably London), and a considerable section of the baronage. But the baronage was divided. Simon could count on most of the lesser barons and the knights, but among the greater barons there was a strong party whose views were oligarchical rather than popular, who were determined to assert the claims of their order, as against the Crown, and thought more of their class privileges than of the liberties of the nation. This oligarchical party played a most important part in the politics of the fourteenth century, notably in relation to the crises of 1310 and 1388. Meanwhile, their attitude impaired the solidarity of the opposition to Henry III.

**The Provisions of Oxford.**

The scheme of reform presented to Henry at Oxford in 1258 was largely their work, and was conceived entirely in the spirit of oligarchy. The list of grievances covered much of the same ground as the Great Charter of 1215, the fiscal exactions of the sheriffs and the king's justices, the evasion of the forest laws, the oppressive insistence of the Crown upon its feudal rights, and the like; but mention was also made of the multiplication of castles, the custody of which was largely committed to aliens. A committee of twenty-four was appointed to deal with these matters, and, by a cumbrous process, a council of fifteen members was nominated to act as the permanent advisers of the Crown. Three times a year this Standing Committee was to meet a body of twelve persons chosen by the barons to discuss on behalf of the community the business of the realm in Parliament. Thus the Great Council was to be superseded by a select body representative only of the great barons.

**King, Barons and Knights.**

The scheme, though reactionary in character, operated continuously until the end of 1259, and then again with interruptions until the outbreak of civil war (1263). But in 1261 the king was absolved by a Papal Bull from his oath to observe the *Provisions*. Both sides then took up arms, though for the moment a battle was avoided. Particularly noteworthy were the endeavours of both parties to strengthen their position by alliance with the knights. The Council of Barons summoned to St. Albans an assembly to which the sheriffs were invited to send three representative knights from each county. The king ordered the knights to meet him at Windsor. The importance of securing the help of this intermediate class was, then, plainly recognized. For the moment, however, conflict was averted by referring to the arbitration of St. Louis the whole question of the validity of the *Provisions*. In January, 1264, the French king decided all the points in favour of Henry (*Mise of Amiens*) and annulled the *Provisions*. Simon de Montfort and the barons refused to abide by the award: war broke out, and at Lewes Simon inflicted a heavy defeat on the king (14th May, 1264). Simon de Montfort was now in power. The king, who had been taken prisoner at Lewes, was released on terms, and a fresh scheme of government was drafted, under which the king could act only on the advice of ministers approved by the baronial party.

**Parliament of 1265.**

Another Parliament met at Westminster on 20th January, 1265. Summoned in the king's name by Simon, its meeting is popularly regarded as a landmark in the development of representative government. In virtue of it Simon has been hailed as " the founder of the House of Commons ". The ascription is extravagant. The Parliament of 1265 did, indeed, for the first time bring together representative knights from the shires and representatives from a certain number of towns. It contained also five earls, eighteen barons and a large number of clergy. The clergy as a body were the stoutest supporters of Simon; the knights were mainly on his side, and of the earls, barons and boroughs only those were summoned which could be counted on to support him. More accurately, then, the " Parliament " of 1265 may be described as a glorified Party Convention.

Nor did it end the war. Prince Edward, joined by the inconstant Earl Gilbert of Gloucester, renewed the struggle, and on 4th August, 1265, inflicted a crushing defeat on Earl Simon at Evesham. In the battle Earl Simon was killed, and his party dissipated.

Simon de Montfort had played a great part in the history of his time; but the character and value of his work have been variously estimated. Consonant with his view that down to this time all the opposition to the Crown was *feudal*—conceived in the interests not of the nation but of a class—McIlwain insists that Simon was contending " for feudal immunity rather than national well-being ".[1] Be that as it may, there is no doubt that he was a great popular hero, that he focussed in himself, and brought to a head, the accumulating discontent of the English nation. Whether

[1] *Op. cit.*, p. 16.

he can be regarded as a great constructive statesman is more doubtful. Of his famous Parliament the most that can be said is that it marked a stage in the development of representative institutions. And even that is disputed. But of his popularity there is no question. It is attested by much contemporary evidence, not least by that derived from the Political Songs of the day. The following is typical of many:

> Salve, Symon Montis-Fortis
> Totius flos militiae,
> Duras poenas passus mortis
> Protector gentis Angliae:
> Sunt de Sanctis inaudita,
> Cunctis passis in hac vita,
> Quemquam passum talia.
> . . . . . . .
> Sis pro nobis intercessor
> Apud Deum qui defensor
> In terra extiteras.[1]

With the remnant of the reign of Henry III this narrative is not concerned. Between 1265 and 1272 several Parliaments were called, but neither their structure nor their procedure demands notice.

**Edward I.**

Henry III died in 1272 and was succeeded by his eldest son Prince Edward, destined to prove the best, perhaps the greatest, of our kings. That he had learnt the art of war was shown conclusively at Evesham. Yet great soldier as he was, conqueror of Wales and Scotland, it is not as a soldier he is held in everlasting remembrance, but as a great lawgiver and reformer—the "English Justinian", as a great administrator, as the man who has more right than anyone else to be called the Father of the English Parliament. No one, indeed, can strictly claim that title. All that Edward I can claim is that a most important stage in the evolution of Parliament was registered at his instance.

The years between 1265 and 1295 were, as regards that evolution, plainly experimental. In 1273 four knights from

[1] Wright: *Political Songs*, p. 124.

**Parliamentary Experiments.**

each county and four persons from each city were summoned, together with the earls, barons, prelates and abbots, to take the oath of allegiance to King Edward, who was still absent in Palestine. After his return and coronation (1274) Edward summoned his first Parliament, to which considerable importance has been justly attached. This Parliament met at Westminster and contained besides archbishops and bishops, abbots and priors, earls and barons, "the commonalty of the land". Among the latter were knights from each county and representatives not only from boroughs and cities, but from *villa* (or *villate*) *mercatorie*. Whether (as some hold) the latter designation applies to "market towns" or, more probably, to "towns of merchants" is disputed. But all these town representatives were summoned, like the knights, by writs addressed to the sheriffs, and like them were summoned *ad tractandum una cum magnatibus*. Further, the knights were to be chosen (another variation from the usual formula) *de discretioribus in lege militibus*. All these things may well indicate an occasion of some special importance—a view confirmed by the output of the Parliament. For it was responsible for the *Statute of Westminster I*, which is, indeed, "almost a code by itself", containing fifty-one clauses, and covering "the whole ground of legislation".[1] But the primary object of this, as of other early parliaments, was not legislation but supply, and the king duly obtained from it a grant of custom on wool, woolfells and leather.[2] This was a new departure in the history of public finance. For the first time trade as well as land was to contribute to the revenue. The king resorted to a curious expedient in 1282–3. The Welsh war was proving expensive; money was imperatively required; but the magnates, many knights and freeholders, indeed the whole military force of the realm, were with the king in Wales. Two *provincial* councils were therefore summoned to meet at York and Northampton respectively, and

**Embryonic Parliaments.**

**Statute of Westminster I (1275).**

[1] Stubbs, ii, 109.

[2] For a valuable article on the Parliament of 1275, cf. C. H. Jenkinson, *ap. E. H. R.*, XXV, pp. 231 f.

writs were thereupon addressed to the sheriffs ordering them to send thither all freeholders, not serving in the army, capable of bearing arms and holding lands of £20 annual value, or more, together with four knights from each county and two men from each city, borough and *villa mercatorie*. The archbishops were at the same time ordered to attend with the bishops, abbots, priors, and proctors of the cathedral clergy. The laymen made a grant; the clergy demurred and delayed. But the granting or withholding of supplies does not constitute the special significance of these "provincial" assemblies. Had the experiment been repeated it might well have emphasized the ecclesiastical provincialism of the Church to the detriment of the incipient nationalism of the State. Happily, that danger was, perhaps undesignedly but not less effectually, averted.

**Assembly at Shrewsbury (1283).**

Later in the same year a Council or Parliament was summoned to Shrewsbury to witness the trial of David, brother and successor of Llewelyn, Prince of Wales. It met primarily as a Court, but to it were summoned besides the earls and barons, two knights from each county, and representatives of London and twenty other towns. But the town representatives were summoned not as in 1275, through the sheriffs, but by special writs addressed to the towns concerned. No clergy were summoned, since the occasion was a trial on a capital charge. David was duly tried, condemned, and executed, but the king took advantage of the "Parliament" to issue the Statute of Merchants—commonly known as the *Statute of Acton Burnell*, the place to which the Commons had adjourned. The *Statute de Mercatoribus*, by providing a simpler and more effective remedy for the recovery of debts, facilitated the giving of credit, and may thus be regarded as the first step towards a commercial code. Towards the close of the reign the *Carta Mercatoria* (1303) encouraged foreign trade and foreign traders. Import and export duties on their transactions were to be at a fixed rate, and a special court was set up in London to give them the guarantee of prompt and even-handed justice. If, then, Edward's financial demands were frequent and heavy, he did not neglect the sources of revenue. His subjects were not required to make bricks without straw.

**Court or Council?**

The "Parliament" of Shrewsbury was, however, primarily a court of justice. Does the same character attach to all the earlier Parliaments? With great emphasis and an imposing display of erudition Dr. Pollard argues that it does.[1] He recalls the fact that week by week we pray for the "High Court of Parliament"; but he ignores the fact that the "Bidding Prayer" exhorts us to pray for the "Great Council of the Realm now assembled in Parliament". Parliament is in truth both "Court" and "Council".[2] It combines the functions of the French *Parlements*—which, though primarily law courts, had in the right of registration a semblance of legislative power—with those of the French *Estates*, which were political not judicial. This truth is, indeed, emphasized by Dr. Pollard himself in reference to the later evolution of Parliament: "The English Estates were the grand jury of the nation because they sat in a parliament which was a court of law. There was no national presentment of offenders in France, because the *parlements* excluded the estates, just as lower French courts extruded the jury" (p. 147). The only point, then, that remains in dispute is whether in its origin the institution which we recognize and acclaim as the English Parliament was primarily judicial, or primarily financial and conciliar. For our present purpose it may suffice to say that it very soon became both. Between justice and finance it is, indeed, difficult to draw a line. *Justitia magnum emolumentum.*

**"Estates".**

Dr. Pollard is, however, right in repudiating the old idea that our early Parliaments represented the "Three Estates". The first official reference to "three estates" is in 1421, and may have been due, as he ingeniously suggests, to the fact that the Treaty of Troyes concluded between Henry V and

[1] *The Evolution of Parliament* (1920).

[2] Against the views of Dr. Pollard and Dr. McIlwain, Dr. Tout gently protests, showing that *Curia* "is not essentially a law court in mediæval phrase, but the king and his entourage". The prayer for the "High Court of Parliament" only came into the Prayer Book in 1662, having been written (and printed) about 1625, perhaps by Laud.

Charles VI in 1420 contained a stipulation that, for additional security and sanctity, the peace between the two monarchs should be "sworn to by the *three estates* of the two realms". Thenceforward the phrase comes "slowly and doubtingly into English official and popular use".[1]

**The "Model" Parliament (1295).**

Nevertheless, no research, however ingenious and meticulous, can dislodge Edward I from his position in relation to the evolution of Parliament. Whether the Parliament of 1295 was more of a "model" than that of 1275 or that of 1298 is, in the present context, immaterial. It is enough that that famous Parliament contained representatives of all classes. Seven earls and forty-one barons were summoned individually by name, as were twenty archbishops and bishops, sixty-seven abbots, and three heads of monastic orders. Nor was the representation of the clergy confined to the princes of the Church. By the *Praemunientes* clause the bishops were bidden to bring with them, the dean or prior of the Cathedral church, the archdeacons, one proctor representing the capitular, and two proctors representing the parochial clergy of each diocese. The rest, the "commons", were summoned by writs addressed to the sheriffs, who were to cause two knights of each shire, two citizens of each city, and two burgesses of each borough to be elected with full powers to carry out what should be ordained by common counsel. The number of counties thus represented was 37, of cities and boroughs 166. The "Third Estate" would then number 406. But the word "Estate" is better avoided if it implies a rigid distinction of classes. No such distinction has ever been recognized in England. There is among us no noble caste. The sons and brothers of nobles are, despite courtesy titles, commoners. As commoners they sit in a House of Commons, while the House of Lords has been regularly recruited from ranks which have no claim to noble blood. But this is to anticipate future developments.

Many years were to elapse before the definition of the English polity. But by the end of the thirteenth century

[1] Pollard, p. 70, and see references there cited.

the foundations had been well and truly laid. We are rightly warned to avoid the temptation to over-precise and premature definition: but with all its legitimate caution, modern scholarship has but slightly diminished the reputation of the greatest of our statesmen-kings, and has not greatly dimmed the glory of a great century. Whatever be the precise interpretation put upon its clauses, *Magna Carta* remains one of the most important documents in our history. However we assess the credit due to Edward I, it is indisputable that by the close of his reign the outlines of the English polity have been drawn. The courts of law are sitting and functioning at Westminster, and to the highest court there have been summoned suitors who come as representatives of their respective shires and towns, who come no longer merely to present their petitions to the king, but empowered, in return for justice, to make grants to meet the expenses of the State, and by their presence, if not by vote and voice, to add weight and authority to the statutes enacted by the king.

## CHAPTER IX

# Monarchy v. Oligarchy
# The Evolution of Parliament

THE three kings of the thirteenth century made, each in his own way, a notable contribution to the development of the English polity: John by his folly, Henry III by his weakness, Edward I by his wisdom and strength.

The work of the fourteenth century differed essentially from that of the thirteenth. The thirteenth century laid the foundations of a parliamentary constitution; the fourteenth added several stories to the structure. But there was a preliminary issue still to be decided. Was the King to continue to govern? Or was government to pass into the hands of a group of great nobles? The principle of Monarchy was opposed to that of Oligarchy. Nor was it as yet clear which of the two claimants to the estate would be more likely to favour the expectations of the residuary legatee—Democracy. But of the position of that residuary legatee contemporaries can have taken little account. What they saw was a conflict between an hereditary monarch and a group of magnates headed by a powerful and ambitious prince of the Royal House.

In this conflict personalities counted for much. A Thomas of Lancaster is opposed to an Edward II; a Henry of Lancaster—" that vile politician Bolingbroke "—triumphs over a redeless Richard of Bordeaux.

**Edward II and Piers Gaveston.**

Edward II was three and twenty when he began to reign. He was not lacking in personal attractions, but of any kingly qualities he was utterly devoid. A keen sportsman, pleasure loving, fond of music and acting, artistic and wildly extravagant, he preferred the company of mimes to that of soldiers or statesmen. But his ruling passion was devotion to an attractive and amusing foreigner, the Gascon-born Piers Gaveston. Edward I, mistrusting the friendship of the two young men, had sent his son's favourite out of the country. Edward II was no sooner king than, in defiance of his sworn promise, he recalled Gaveston and loaded him with wealth and honours. The king conferred on Gaveston the earldom of Cornwall—an appanage of the Crown—and married him to Margaret, his own niece, the daughter of his favourite sister Jean and sister of the young Earl of Gloucester. But Gaveston, like his master, was a trifler, and by his insolence bitterly offended the great nobles.

**Thomas of Lancaster.**

Of the baronial party, Thomas of Lancaster was the acknowledged leader. Thomas was, moreover, the first representative of a new type of magnates destined, until Tudor days, to play a great part in English history. As the feudal baronage of the Conquest had given place to the official baronage created by the Plantagenet kings, so the latter were superseded by a group of great territorial magnates whose deliberate policy evidently was to substitute the rule of a baronial committee for that of the king.

Cousin to the king, uncle to the queen, Thomas of Lancaster possessed in his own right the earldoms of Lancaster, Leicester and Derby, and was married to the heiress of Henry de Lacy, Earl of Salisbury and Lincoln. A victim of Gaveston's wit and insolence, he insisted that the favourite should for the second time be exiled (1308), but the king sent Gaveston as his deputy to Dublin, and, relying, like his grandfather, on a Papal dispensation, within a year's time recalled his favourite.

The wild extravagance of the two young men compelled the king to go to a Parliament for supplies. They were granted only on conditions: there must be a redress of grievances and a reform of the administration. To work out a detailed scheme recourse was had to the precedent set by the Provisions of Oxford. A committee was appointed to " ordain and establish the state of our realm and our household ". Consisting of seven bishops, eight earls and six barons, this committee published (1311) the famous *Ordinances*.

**The Lords Ordainers.**

The *Ordinances* set forth a comprehensive scheme of reform. Some of the articles dealt with the grievances of the hour; others affirmed principles of government designed for permanence. Four articles provided for the perpetual banishment and forfeiture of Gaveston, who had " misguided the king and turned away the heart of his people "; several more dealt with the removal of other bad companions, with the reform of the king's household and the expulsion of the Friscobaldi, the Italian financiers, who had enjoyed the lucrative privilege of farming the taxes; with the recall of grants to favourites and the payment of the king's debts and the limitation of his expenditure, and so on. More permanently important were the ordinances dealing with the powers of the Crown, of Parliament and of the Lords Ordainers; the king was to make no gifts or alienate property without the consent of the Ordainers; Parliaments were to meet at least once a year, and the king was not to leave the realm to declare war without their consent; above all, ministers were to be appointed only with the assent of the baronage in Parliament. To the " commons " there is naturally no reference in a scheme so purely oligarchical.

For the third time Gaveston was banished, but within a few months he rejoined the king, who issued a proclamation quashing the favourite's banishment. But the patience of the magnates was exhausted: Gaveston was captured by them, and on 19th June, 1312, was, without trial, beheaded at Blacklow Hill near Warwick.

Gaveston had become a personal nuisance if not a political danger. Nevertheless, his death was a brutal crime, for which Lancaster had ultimately to make appropriate expiation.

Terrible were the sufferings of the people, and bitter the humiliation of the realm during the years that followed the execution of Piers Gaveston. The king did not mend his

Anarchy and Civil War.

ways; he was, indeed, compelled to accept for a time Lancaster as his chief minister, but he gave his confidence not to him but to Hugh le Despenser, whom he made Earl of Winchester, and to his son, Hugh the Younger. Divisions in England inevitably reacted upon external policy. The northern counties were again and again raided by the Scots, and in 1314 Robert Bruce won his historic victory at Bannockburn. His brother, Edward Bruce, accepted from the rebel chieftains in Ireland the throne of Ireland and was crowned king in 1316. Robert captured Berwick in 1318 and in 1322 ravaged Yorkshire. The country was afflicted by terrible famines in 1315 and 1316: the prices of necessaries rose so high that only the wealthy could procure them, and in the wake of famine pestilence stalked through the land.

A truce was patched up in 1318, and in the same year a "full" Parliament met at York. It sat for the unusual period of seven weeks; the king confirmed the Ordinances, issued charters of pardon to Lancaster and his party, and agreed "in all weighty matters . . . which can or ought to be transacted without the assent of Parliament" to act only on the advice of a small standing committee of bishops and barons.

Progressive improvement in the situation was unfortunately interrupted by personal quarrels among the magnates; the king refused, at the bidding of their rivals, to part with the Despensers, consequently Lancaster and his party came in arms to the Parliament summoned by the king to meet at Westminster in July, 1321. The Parliament was fully representative, being attended not only by barons and higher clergy, but by representatives of the counties, towns, and lower clergy. The main work of this Parliament was to formulate charges against the Despensers and to procure their banishment. They had come between the king and his constitutional advisers, had usurped the royal power, had "estranged the heart of the king from his people, and had engrossed the sole government of the realm".

To the demands of the armed confederates the king was

compelled, for the moment, to assent. The Despensers were banished, and their rivals secured themselves by a statutory indemnity. But the magnates had gone too far; the tide turned in the king's favour, and Edward, acting with unprecedented energy, took the offensive against Lancaster, who was defeated and captured at the battle of Boroughbridge (16th March, 1322). In his own castle of Pontefract the great earl was tried and condemned by his peers, and as a rebel and a traitor suffered death.

That this prince of the blood, vicious and cruel, greedy of wealth and power, yet incapable of using power for any but purely selfish ends, should have been mourned as a martyr and worshipped as a saint is a measure of Edward's unpopularity. The rising tide of national sentiment floated the enemy of a foreign favourite into undeserved favour with the populace. Nor did his posthumous fame suffer by reason of his benefactions to the Church. As the leader of opposition to a worthless king, as the representative of the royal baronage, he has a place in history: to the orderly development of the Constitution he contributed nothing.

**The Statute of York (1322).**

The execution of Lancaster was immediately followed by the meeting of a Parliament at York (May, 1322). To its proceedings great importance has been commonly attached. The Parliament contained besides the council, the lords temporal and spiritual, the ecclesiastical proctors, and representatives of counties and towns. There also attended, for the first time, twenty-four discreet men empowered to act for the *communitas* of each half of the principality of Wales—though it was not until the reign of Henry VIII that this procedure was regularized. The Ordinances were repealed, and it was laid down that for the future " the matters which are to be established for the estate of our lord the king and of his heirs, and for the estate of the realm of the people, shall be treated, accorded and established in parliaments by our lord the king, and by the consent of the prelates, earls and barons, and the commonalty of the realm, according as has been heretofore accustomed ".

**The "Commons".**

Upon the interpretation of this remarkable enactment much learning has been recently expended. It cannot, indeed, be questioned that the Statute of York assisted, if it did not finally establish, the right of the "commonalty", as represented by knights and burgesses, to concur in legislation. On the broad issue, then, Stubbs and his disciples were right. It is on narrower issues that recent critics quarrel with them, and they are divided among themselves.[1] However these narrower issues may ultimately be decided, the fact plainly emerges that the "House of Commons" was rapidly moving towards the assertion of its right to be regarded as an essential element in the constitution of a Parliament. Dr. Pollard—one of the most distinguished of the critics—himself quotes three illustrations of this movement in little more than a decade (1332–43). In 1332 certain measures "ordained" by the earls, barons and other magnates were read before them, the king, the knights of the shires, and the *gentz du commun*, were found pleasing to them all, and were fully agreed to.[2] In 1340, twelve knights of the shire and six borough members were added to a committee of magnates to try and examine certain petitions *et de les mettre en estatut*. This is clear evidence of a notable advance in the position of the "Commons". Further evidence is furnished by the proceedings of 1343, when not only were articles drafted by the magnates submitted for the consent of the Commons, but the latter added provisions on their own initiative, and the resulting statute was "ordained" by *la commune* as well as by the king and the lords.[3]

Meanwhile, the Commons had been summoned to take part in the last act of the tragic drama of the reign. For four years after the Parliament of York the king and the Despensers had things all their own way. The Earl of Hereford had been killed at Boroughbridge; Lancaster had

[1] G. Conwy Davies: *Baronial Opposition to Edward II*, appendix, pp. 582–3; Lapsley: *ap. E. H. R.*, XXVIII, pp. 118–24; and Tout: *Reign of Edward II*, p. 150. On the whole matter, cf. Pollard: *Evolution of Parliament*, pp. 129, 241.

[2] Rot. Parl. II, 65, quoted by Pollard, p. 243.

[3] Pollard: *Parliament*, pp. 242–3.

died on the scaffold; the party they had led was annihilated. But the triumph of the king and the Despensers only exhibited their incapacity to rule, and in 1326 the final catastrophe was reached. It arose from sordid domestic circumstances. Confronted with a conspiracy between his adulterous Queen Isabella and the opposition nobles, King Edward found himself friendless, and fled with Hugh Despenser to Wales. There they fell into the hands of the new Earl of Lancaster. Despenser was hanged, and Edward was imprisoned to await the verdict of a Parliament specially summoned to decide his fate.

The Parliament, constituted on precisely the same basis as the York Parliament of 1322, met at Westminster on the 7th of January, 1327. Six specific charges were made against the king, who was required to renounce the throne in favour of his young son. Resistance was impossible, and after a further period of imprisonment the ex-king died at Berkeley Castle on the 21st of September, 1327. It was publicly notified that he died a natural death; but almost certainly he was murdered. His deposition, though manifestly illegal, set a constitutional precedent of undeniable significance. Before the century closed it was followed in the case of his great-grandson. But between the two cases there was no parallel. In 1327 the issue was personal; in 1399 there was a real conflict of principles. Richard II stood, like Charles I, for a theory of government which Parliament successfully repudiated.

**The Structure and Powers of Parliament.**

The contrast is significant. Between 1327 and 1399 the power of Parliament had notably increased, and its structure had been defined. By 1399 the English Parliament had taken on the shape which was destined in the nineteenth century to afford a model for parliamentary constitutions throughout the world.

Parliament consists to-day of the King and two "Houses", but the bicameral form of the Legislature is the result less of design than of circumstances which were in part fortuitous. The English Parliament might well have been organized, as was the Castilian Cortes, the French States-General and the Scottish Parliament, on the basis of *Estates*. The Aragonese Cortes was organized in four "arms" or "branches": the clergy, the great nobles (*Ricos Hombres*), the caballeros or knights, and the towns. The Swedish Diet included, in addition to the nobles, the clergy and the towns, 250 representatives of the peasantry. The bicameral arrangement in England was, but for the exception of Hungary, unique.

**Two Chambers.**

How and why did the English Parliament assume that form? The *Modus Tenendi Parliamentum* enumerates six "grades" or elements in Parliament—the clergy, higher and lower, earls and barons, the barons of the Cinque Ports, knights, citizens and burgesses. These elements might well have disposed themselves like the Aragonese Cortes in four "Houses", or like the French Estates in three. As a fact they all met originally in one assembly, but by the middle of the fourteenth century we find them sitting as two bodies, which by a convenient anticipation of terms we may describe as "Houses". Not, however, until the sixteenth century were the "Lords" officially described as a "House"; not until 1547 did the "Commons" keep a separate "Journal". Even now there is but one "Clerk of Parliament", whose place is in the Upper Chamber, and on occasions of the highest ceremony or formality, when the king is present personally or "by commission", Parliament still assembles in a single Chamber, in which the peers, temporal and spiritual (and the judges when summoned), are entitled to sit while the Commons humbly stand at the "Bar".

**The Clerical Estate.**

The bicameral arrangement was reached partly by elimination, partly by amalgamation. Attendance at a Parliament was regarded less as an honour than an obligation—in much the same light as service on a jury. Consequently, the same individuals were not, as a rule, called upon to serve more than once. Nor were any persons so anxious to evade the obligation as the representatives of the lower clergy. Their reluctance was due partly, no doubt, to considerations of personal convenience, but not less to professional exclusiveness. They had their own ecclesiastical assemblies, greatly exceeding parliaments in antiquity. Why, then, should they be at pains to attend the Common Council of the Realm, when with more obvious convenience and with greater independence they could vote supplies to the king in their Convocations of Canterbury and York? Anyway, the ecclesiastical proctors soon dropped out of Parliament and made their grants in Convocation. This practice continued until the privilege was surrendered by a verbal agreement between Archbishop Sheldon and Lord Chancellor Clarendon in 1663. But the surrender of an historic right was not followed, as logically it should have been, by the removal of a disability. Clergymen of the Established Church are still ineligible for election to the House of Commons. The position is anomalous. Self-deprived of their position as an Estate, the lower clergy have never obtained the complete right of citizenship.

The higher clergy were naturally associated with the temporal baronage. Like the latter, they held their land *per baroniam*, for their baronies (*temporalities*) they still do homage to the king, and it was by reason of their baronial tenure that they were liable to service in the King's Court, and took their place, when summoned by special writ,[1] in Parliament. Membership of one House of Parliament depended, then, and depends still, on the receipt of a special summons which the peers have successfully maintained cannot be withheld from anyone who can prove himself the heir of a magnate who was ever summoned by special writs to the Parliament, and who actually took his seat therein. Thus was the composition of the Upper Chamber in due course defined.

**The Knights of the Shire.**

Yet the definition seems somewhat arbitrary. It might have been expected that the knights of the shire, united with the barons in economic interests, and belonging to a similar social class, would have politically attached themselves to the baronage. They followed the example of the

[1] *Fide et Dilectione.*

barons in their grants to the Crown, and they may at times have sat with them and apart from the burgesses. But information is scanty. The knights are recorded as deliberating apart from the prelates and barons in 1332, and it is fairly certain that by the middle of the century they had joined the burgesses, who sat in the Chapter House of the Abbey while the barons and prelates sat in the Palace of Westminster.

**Union with the Burgesses.**

The junction of the knights of the shire with the representatives of the towns in a "House of Commons" is the most fateful event in the constitutional history of England: more than any other it differentiates the political development of England from that of its continental neighbours; more than any other it accounts for the virility, the efficiency and the continuity of parliamentary institutions in this country. That the knights did join the burgesses in the High Court of Parliament was due primarily to their association in the local court of the shire, to the fact that both classes were summoned to the Great Council of the Realm in a representative capacity, by writ addressed to the sheriff, and were by him selected to serve on behalf of their respective constituents, with an identical object, *ad tractandum, ordinandum et faciendum*, &c.

Of the two elements in the House of Commons the knights of the shire were, for many years, much the more important. Nor has their importance ever been more eloquently estimated than by the greatest of our constitutional historians: "If we ask who were the men or the classes of men who worked out the political scheme of the thirteenth century, the whole history of the fourteenth century supplies a harmonious answer. It was not men like Thomas of Lancaster. . . . It was not the clerical body generally. . . . It was not the town communities . . . nor the great merchants. . . . The victory of the constitution was won by the knights of the shires. . . . They are very distinctly the depositories of the constitutional tradition; and this fact is one of the most distinctive features of our political history, as compared with most other nations in which representative institutions have been tried with less success."[1]

The knights of the shire might very well have become a separate Estate. So also, but for the junction of the knights with the burgesses, might other classes. The lawyers were in a favourable position for establishing their claim to this distinction, and seemed, at one time, not unlikely to press it. The judges of the High Court have from time immemorial been summoned to attend the king in the Highest Court, and they are still required "to be at the said day and place personally present with Us and with the rest of Our Council to treat and give [your] advice upon the affairs aforesaid". In obedience to this summons the judges still attend the opening of Parliament, though they have never established their right regularly to sit and vote there. In the Parliament of 1381, however, their position appears to have been co-ordinate with that of other Estates. In that year the Commons petitioned the king that "the prelates, peers, judges, and *all the other Estates* might deliberate severally".

**The Lawyers.**

More dangerous to the solidarity of the "Third Estate" than the lawyers were the great merchants, whose claim to separate Estateship was fiscally, if not constitutionally, more substantial. The basis of representation in this country has, from the first, thanks to the virility of our local institutions, been local not vocational. But in the fourteenth century the great merchants were sufficiently important as contributors to the revenue to make independent arrangements with the Crown, and were, indeed, encouraged to do so by the king's officials. That constituted a serious menace to the cohesion and solidarity of the "Third Estate". Moreover, the position was further complicated by the fact that the "customs", being regarded as fees for licence to trade, were naturally the subject of direct bargaining between the grantor and the grantee. None the less, the practice was dangerous—a truth of which the Commons were far from oblivious. Consequently, Parliament enacted

**The Merchants.**

[1] Stubbs: *op. cit.*, II, 513.

in 1362 that henceforward " no subsidy or charge should be set upon wool by the merchants or any other body without consent of Parliament ". That further and similar legislation was passed in 1371 and 1387 affords convincing proof both of the anxiety of the Commons, and of their failure to arrest the dreaded development by legislation. Nor was the confusion entirely cleared up until the seventeenth century. " Impositions " and " Tonnage and Poundage " were a fertile source of dispute between the first two Stuarts and their Parliaments; nor is it certain that the decisions of the courts in such cases as that of ship-money were so entirely due to the " subservience " of the judges as some of the Whig historians supposed. We may take it, however, that by the end of the fourteenth century the broad principle had been laid down and accepted, that there should be no taxation without consent of Parliament. It further resulted that the danger of a multiplication of Estates had been dissipated and that the principle of local representation had been successfully affirmed.[1]

**Appropriation and Audit.**

The broad principle had, moreover, been substantiated by detailed concessions. Among these the most important related to the spending of the grants made to the Crown by Parliament. All supplies still take the form of a grant made in response to a demand on behalf of the Crown. It is still the rule, and there is none more salutary, that only the Crown can propose expenditure. It is for the House of Commons to grant or refuse " supply ". But, in any sound scheme of public finance, the guardian of the public purse has a further duty: to assign expenditure to objects approved in detail by Parliament, and to make sure that the supplies voted by it have been expended on those objects, and on none other. Here we have the principle of " appropriation ", and the practice of audit. Both are secured by the elaborate machinery which has been gradually devised and which now controls financial procedure in Parliament.[2]

[1] Marriott: *Mechanism of the Modern State*, I, Chap. VII, *passim*.

[2] For details of this procedure, cf. Marriott: *Mechanism of the Modern State*, I Chaps. xx and xxi, and for all the relevant documents, Vol II, Appendix D.

The beginnings of appropriation and audit are to be traced to the reign of Edward III. Thus in the "Walton Ordinances" (12th July, 1338) elaborate rules are laid down for financial procedure. A specific warrant under the Privy Seal was required for any payments out of the Exchequer, and in order to see that the money thus issued was properly expended, a committee of audit, consisting of a bishop, a banneret, and a clerk, was appointed. But this was administrative action designed to secure not the control of Parliament over expenditure, but that of the king and his household over the public departments.

The turn of Parliament came in 1341. The French war had compelled the king to make large demands of money. But no section of the people was prepared to meet them unconditionally. Irritated by opposition, the king plunged from one blunder into another, and was finally compelled, in exchange for supplies, to make large and important concessions. In November, 1340, King Edward suddenly returned from France, made a clean sweep of his chief ministers, judges, and officials, and appointed as Chancellor Sir Robert Bouchier, the first layman to hold that office. In particular, Edward's anger fell upon John of Stratford, Archbishop of Canterbury, who with his brother Robert, Bishop of Chichester, had for some years been mainly responsible for the administration of affairs. Ordered to answer for his supposed irregularities in the Court of Exchequer, Archbishop Stratford demanded to be tried by his "peers" in Parliament. The peers supported his demand; the King was obliged to give way, and the peers secured the important privilege that none of their number might be judged on a criminal charge except in full Parliament and before his peers.

**Ministerial Responsibility.**

Further concessions, of wider constitutional significance, followed. Parliament demanded and the king agreed that a committee should be elected in Parliament to audit accounts, and that certain high officials should be appointed, with the advice of the magnates, in Parliament. The statute in which these and other concessions were embodied was repealed in 1343, and in any case it would be premature to find in the crisis of 1341 a definitive assertion of the doctrine of ministerial responsibility. But equally to be deprecated is the tendency to minimize the significance of these proceedings. Stubbs is clearly justified in claiming that they prove the determination of the country, as represented by Parliament, " not to be governed by irresponsible officials or by royal tyranny ".[1]

Another crisis arose in 1371 when Parliament successfully demanded the dismissal of the Chancellor, William of Wykeham, and the other clerical ministers. Wykeham was succeeded by Sir Robert Thorpe, and another layman, Sir Richard le Scrope, became Treasurer. The removal of Wykeham and his clerical colleagues may have been due to the wave of anti-clericalism, and more notably anti-papalism, then sweeping over the country, but there was substance in the complaint of the lay members of Parliament that good administration suffered from the fact that clerics could not be brought to book for their actions. In return for the removal of the ministers, Parliament made a grant of £50,000 to be raised by a contribution of 22*s.* 3*d.* from each parish, and a statute was enacted that without consent of Parliament no impost should be laid upon wool.

A curious blunder had, however, been made. The number of parishes, assumed for the purpose of the subsidy to be 40,000, turned out to be only 8600. To remedy the blunder a Great Council was summoned to meet the king at Winchester, and the assessment per parish was raised to 116*s.*

Wykeham's dismissal brought no improvement in the general situation. After the death of Queen Philippa in 1369 the King sank into premature senility, and allowed his mistress, Alice Perrers, not merely to rule his household, but to pervert justice and interfere constantly and mischievously in affairs of State. In 1371 the Black Prince came home from his Duchy of Acquitaine a sick man. His younger brother, John of Gaunt, virtually ruled the kingdom during

[1] *Constitutional History*, II, p. 390.

the last years of the reign, though the Black Prince recovered sufficiently to support the attack upon the administration in the Parliament of 1376.

**The Good Parliament.**

This "Good Parliament" was remarkable for the unprecedented length of the session—nine weeks—and on other grounds as well. Never before had the Commons played so important a part in Parliament. For the first time they elected a President to speak on their behalf, to be known from 1377 onwards as "the Speaker". By the mouth of Sir Peter de la Mare, the first occupant of this new office, the Commons laid before the Lords their complaints of maladministration and fraud, on the part of the king's favourites and officials. In particular they impeached Lord Latimer, the king's chamberlain, and Richard Lyons, the king's agent with the merchants. They were sentenced to forfeiture and imprisonment. Alice Perrers was sentenced to banishment and forfeiture, and Wykeham, with his clerical and conservative colleagues, was reinstated in office. But in June, 1376, the Black Prince died; John of Gaunt regained power; Wykeham, accused of malversation, was dismissed, deprived of the "temporalities" of his see and banished from court. Sir Peter de la Mare was imprisoned, and the impeached officials and favourites were pardoned.

The work of the Good Parliament might well seem to have gone for nothing. It was not so. Although Gaunt and the Lancastrian party momentarily triumphed, an important stage in the development of parliamentary government had been registered. The House of Commons, as never before, had asserted itself, and in an important political crisis had played the foremost part.

It is, then, clear that in the period 1340–77 Parliament was moving towards the assertion of the principle of ministerial responsibility, and was, if tentatively, claiming that the Legislature should control the Executive. But the employment of such terms indicates the necessity of caution. In an historical constitution, the result of continuous development, the temptation to anticipation demands constant watchfulness. Moreover, it must be remembered that the differentiation between legislative and executive business is a relatively late development. It certainly was very far from complete in the fourteenth century. Nor was legislation exclusively the function of Parliament. Down to the thirteenth century it was exclusively the act of the Crown; from the fourteenth century onwards statutes were enacted by the Crown in Parliament, but the Crown also retained the right to legislate by Ordinance independent of Parliament.

**Statutes and Ordinances.**

The distinction between Statutes and Ordinances is, however, less clear-cut than the last sentence suggests, and much confusion has arisen from the attempt at over-precision. The generally accepted view is that a Statute implies permanence, while an Ordinance is a temporary regulation; that the former is the solemn act of the Legislature, while the latter proceeds from the Executive. The distinction thus drawn may be accepted as sufficiently accurate, but only so long as no attempt is made to differentiate too precisely between legislative and executive acts.

Statutes were originally based on petitions presented by the Commons and enacted by the king with the advice and consent of the lords spiritual and temporal. The right of the Commons to an equal share in the process of legislation was a matter of very gradual growth, and could not be complete until, in the fifteenth century, the process of legislation by bill superseded the earlier process by petition. Until then there could be no guarantee that the essential point of the petition would be met by the resulting legislation. Nor, indeed, was there any security that the petition would not be simply ignored. These defects were increasingly recognized by the Commons in the fourteenth century; various expedients were adopted to provide a remedy, but it was not until the last years of Henry VI that statutes were brought forward in the shape that they were ultimately intended to take. Bills gradually superseded petitions, and the co-ordinate share of the Commons in legislation was thus finally assured.

Edward III.

The reign of Edward III is, in respect of the evolution of Parliament, exceedingly important. But the King himself contributed little to its evolution except in so far as constitutional concessions were wrung from him as the price of financial supplies. The heavy expenditure was necessitated by an ambitious and futile foreign policy, with the details of which this work is not concerned. To contemporaries Edward III stood out in pleasing contrast with his father and with the grandson who succeeded him. And the opinion of contemporaries has been generally accepted in modern textbooks. " Little Arthur " was taught that Edward III was a " wise and good King ", that his name was made " glorious by his victories, and that his people were happy and prosperous ". J. R. Green, despite his protest against " drum and trumpet history ", declared that " a sudden burst of military glory threw its glamour over the age of Cressy and Poitiers ". Even a later generation accepts Edward III as " the ideal king of chivalry ".

A closer and more critical examination reveals him as a pinchbeck hero, whose " glorious " victories resulted in the loss of all the English possessions in France except Calais, Bayonne, Bordeaux and a few towns upon the Dordogne; whose personal contribution to the history of his country was almost entirely negative; and who bequeathed to his grandson problems that were beyond the capacity of that " redeless " ruler to solve.

## CHAPTER X

# Richard of Bordeaux and Henry of Lancaster

## The Lancastrian Revolution

**The Revolution of 1399.**

THE Revolution of 1399 was at once the climax of the fourteenth century and the prelude to the fifteenth. It explains both centuries; it reveals the forces that operated to bring the Lancastrians to the throne, and made it difficult for them to keep it. Like other "revolutions" in English history, it was essentially conservative in character: it stood for social order against the ferment of ideas which found expression in the Peasants' Revolt of 1381; it represented the triumph of orthodox Churchmanship over the "heresies" preached by Wyclif and disseminated by the Lollards; and it set the seal of success upon the movement towards a limitation of monarchical autocracy and the development of parliamentary control. But there was another side to it. If Henry of Lancaster was a Conservative, he was also a usurper.[1] Richard of Bordeaux aimed at the establishment of absolute monarchy, but he was the legitimate sovereign. His successful rival asserted the principle of parliamentary control; but Lancaster's accession also registered the triumph of the oligarchy which had extorted the Great Charter from John, had imposed the Provisions of Oxford on Henry III and the "Ordinances" on Edward II, and had formed the backbone of the opposition to Richard II.

[1] I do not ignore Mr. Lapsley's learned article on the title of Henry IV in *English Historical Review*, xlix (1934). He writes (p. 606): "I suggest that . . . Henry could have had a complete and technically correct Parliamentary title, that his supporters intended that the revolution should be accomplished in that way, and that Henry, by a *coup de main* at the last moment, was able to obtain the Crown on the grounds of conquest, inheritance, and some loose form of acceptance."

The baronage had, indeed, become more oligarchical during the century preceding the Lancastrian Revolution. The average number of lay barons summoned to Great Councils and Parliaments by Edward II was 74; under Edward III it was only 43. Of these a considerable proportion were of the blood royal. The later Plantagenets imagined that by giving great heiresses in marriage to princes of the blood they would strengthen the Crown. The policy proved to be a blunder; it diminished the number of magnates, but increased the number of pretenders. The wise policy of William the Conqueror was reversed. The Normans and the earlier Plantagenets had killed the feudalism that might have threatened the throne in their day. The later Plantagenets created a "bastard feudalism" represented by powerful satraps who ruled in almost complete independence over a great part of English soil, who surrounded themselves with retainers who wore their livery, and supplied them, in effect, with private armies, and whose quarrels they "maintained" even against the representatives of the king's justice. The full effect of this policy was not revealed until the fifteenth century, but the forces which ultimately produced the so-called "Wars of the Roses" were already operating in the fourteenth, and supplied one of the elements in the Revolution with which it closed.

**The Baronial Oligarchy.**

The consistent purpose of the oligarchical baronage was to substitute for the English monarchy a Venetian Doge. But oligarchy is the foe not only of monarchy but of democracy. To speak of democracy in connexion with mediæval England is, of course, a misleading anachronism. Nevertheless, it is possible in the fourteenth century to discern the existence of embryonic forces destined, centuries later, to put England in the forefront of the nations who were to find in "parliamentary democracy" a solution of some of the most baffling problems in the art of politics.

**Embryonic Democracy.**

Among those forces three were especially obtrusive in the period under review: representation in Parliament, a wealthy bourgeoisie, and a free, but landless, peasantry. Reference to these forces must be brief, but they cannot be ignored.

**The Economic and Social Revolution.**

Constitutional development was undoubtedly accentuated by the break up, in the fourteenth century, of the *manorial* economy. For at least four centuries—from the eleventh century to the fourteenth—the soil of rural England was occupied by agricultural communities, known by the Norman name of *manors*, and numbering in Domesday no fewer than 9250. Each manor was vested in a " lord " who held it, though not in absolute ownership, from the king or from some intermediate lord, to whom services, chiefly of a military character, were owed.[1] Of the inhabitants of the manors, surveyed in Domesday, about 4 per cent were freeholders, 9 per cent were slaves, the rest were villeins of various grades who held their cottages and land in virtue of agricultural services rendered to the lord.

**The Manor.**

The lord's own land, the *demesne*, was cultivated mostly by the villeins, but partly by wage-paid labourers, whose wages were paid partly in kind, and partly in money which the lords obtained as " quit rents " from those villeins who commuted their agricultural services for a fixed money payment. The break up of this manorial economy was unquestionably accelerated, if not caused, by a terrible visitation of the bubonic plague. This " Black Death " first reached England in 1348–9, and recurred two or three times during the next half century.

**The Black Death.**

The results of the visitation have become matters of controversy, but that they were immensely important is not open to question. At least one-third of the whole population perished, thus reducing the inhabitants from perhaps rather over 4,000,000 to 2,700,000—or fewer. Not until the reign of Elizabeth did the population regain the former figure. This meant a sudden dearth of labour, a rise in wages, and a rapid fall in the value of money. The money " rents " for which villein services had been, especially since the imposition of *scutage*, increasingly commuted, were no longer adequate to provide wages for the " free " labourers. The labourers naturally took advantage of the new economic conditions

[1] A lord might hold several manors, and apart from this there was infinite variety in the manorial economy.

to demand (and, despite prohibiting legislation, to obtain) higher wages. The lords, as naturally, attempted to keep such of their villeins as were still legally tied to the soil, and, it may be, to reimpose villein services upon those who had escaped them by commutation.[1]

**The Peasants' Revolt.**

That these attempts were in part responsible for the Peasants' Revolt of 1381 is certain. Greatly resented, also, were the attempts made, first by an Ordinance of the Council (1349) and later (1351) by Parliament, to fix wages at the rate of wages current before the Plague. The frequency with which the statute was re-enacted and, with ever stiffening penalties, proves its futility. But if wages were fixed by authority, so were prices. Neither side was to be allowed to take advantage of temporary scarcity. All victuals and other necessaries of life were to be sold at reasonable prices. These regulations were embodied in a statute in 1350, and the statute was re-enacted, at short intervals, no fewer than ten times before the middle of the fifteenth century.

This legislation, though entirely consonant with the spirit of the fourteenth century, was severely condemned by the economists of the nineteenth. It may be more leniently regarded by a generation which has been taught by totalitarian (and other) States to accept if not to welcome Government interference in economic affairs. In the fourteenth century the legislation was almost entirely ineffective. Nevertheless, it stimulated the movement that issued in the Revolt of 1381.

> When Adam delved and Eve span,
> Who was then the gentleman?

The popular rhyme re-echoed the teaching of John Ball, the "mad priest of Kent", who for twenty years had been turning Wyclifite doctrine to the service of communistic propaganda. Wyclif had taught that power, privilege, and property can be justified only by the use made of them:

[1] The whole of this subject is treated in greater detail in Marriott: *The English Land System* (Murray, 1934), Chap. II. See also H. S. Bennett: *Life on the English Manor*, Cambridge, 1937.

but that he was in any way directly responsible for the Rising of 1381 is improbable. That some of his more extreme disciples were, is certain. The prevailing discontent was, however, brought to a head by a new form of taxation, imposed as a graduated poll-tax, in 1379, and reapplied with increasing severity in 1380. But the outstanding feature of the insurrection is that, although the whole thing lasted only a fortnight, it broke out in no fewer than seventeen counties stretching from Kent to Yorkshire and from Yorkshire to Devonshire. Such perfect timing could have been achieved only by the most careful preliminary organization, and there is some ground for attributing it to Wyclif's itinerant missioners. Not many people would in those days have had equal opportunities. The first object of the peasants was to burn the manorial rolls which recorded their services, but many unpopular lords lost not only their records but their lives. The peasants found support among the Londoners, who hated the French war, hated the poll-tax, and hated John of Gaunt, whose palace of the Savoy they burnt. Gaunt himself was in Scotland, but Archbishop Sudbury, who as Chancellor was head of the ministry, was caught and murdered.

Serious, then, the insurrection was, but it was not directed against the young king, by whose courageous intervention it was brought to an abrupt end. The chivalrous spirit of his grandfather and father shone forth in the lad of fourteen who rode forth, with a few attendants, to meet the insurgents at Mile End and, when their leader, Wat Tyler, had fallen mortally wounded, put himself at their head: "What need ye, my masters? I am your captain and your king." Satisfied with the king's solemn promise of redress, the rebels dispersed: the insurrection was at an end. Could Richard II have sustained the part, thus instinctively and dramatically assumed, there would have been no Revolution in 1399. Unfortunately Richard allowed his ministers to repudiate his promises of pardon and redress. The collapse of the insurrection was succeeded by a bloody assize which in its ferocity anticipated that of Judge Jeffreys. But though an attempt was made to reimpose villein services, the economic forces tending in the opposite direction were too strong. The Black Death had given the *coup de grâce* to a system already in process of dissolution. Some of the villeins became labourers, free but landless; some of them became copyholders in the manors where they had served as villeins. But for much land neither tenants nor labourers could be found. Of necessity it was put down to grass and on the grass were grazed the sheep that brought England for the first time to the fore in commerce.

**The Growth of Trade.**

Economics was evidently beginning to play a part, destined steadily to increase, in politics. It supplied a factor unobtrusive but vital in the Revolution of 1399. That Revolution primarily represented the triumph of the oligarchical principle: but not the less clearly was it a victory for the parliamentary principle. Yet in the drama which reached its catastrophe in 1399 Parliament could never have played the part it did had not the House of Commons contained wealthy burgesses as well as knights of the shire.

Their wealth was derived almost entirely from the trade in raw wool. Even before the Black Death, and much more rapidly after it, the soil of England was dedicated to the provision of pasture for sheep. English wool was of a peculiar quality indispensable for the manufacture of the finest cloths. To the manufacturing cities of the Netherlands and even to Italy, English wool was therefore exported in ever-increasing quantity and with ever-increasing profit to English merchants. To the production of raw wool were subsequently if slowly added supplementary trades in fulling, dyeing, bleaching, and even weaving the coarser kinds of cloth.

**Mercantilism.**

Under Richard II the Government interested itself increasingly in trade, and anticipated the policy subsequently known as mercantilism. To obtain the favourable " balance of trade ", exports were encouraged, and imports discouraged. An Act of 1381 forbade the export of gold and silver; in 1382 English merchants were forbidden to import goods except in English ships; in 1392 foreigners were forbidden to sell imported goods by retail in England; and in 1394 the export of corn, forbidden by Edward III, was freely permitted except to enemy countries. The policy which governed English trade until the nineteenth century was, then, already in embryo adopted.

The economic movement was, however, ancillary. The outstanding importance of the reign of Richard II consists in the struggle between two, or it may be three, opposing principles of government.

**Monarchy, Oligarchy and " Democracy ".**

The first struggle lay between the magnates and Parliament. The King, though only ten years of age, was not treated as a minor. On his accession the Great Council appointed a standing council to advise if not to control the ministers of the Crown. But the Commons were not to be thus thrust aside. Having again elected Sir Peter de la Mare as Speaker, they laid three demands before the king and the magnates: that no law ordained in Parliament be repealed except in Parliament; that a council of eight persons should be nominated in Parliament to be in continuous session and to co-operate with the king's ministers; and that during the king's tender years his household attendants should be nominated in Parliament. The last request, curiously anticipating the " bed-chamber question " at issue between Queen Victoria and Sir Robert Peel, was refused by the magnates, and was dropped. On the two other points the Commons had their way. It is far too much to say with Hallam, that " the whole executive government was transferred to the two Houses "; but that we have in 1377 a noteworthy anticipation of much later developments is undeniable. In the same Parliament two London merchants, Walworth and Philpot, were appointed as parliamentary treasurers, to receive and disburse the subsidy voted for the French war.

Neither Parliament nor the magnates earned much credit by their conduct of affairs during this " minority " period: Parliaments met regularly—generally two a year—but with the exceptions already mentioned left no record worth recalling. In 1386 Gaunt left England for Spain to assert, at the expense of the English taxpayer and with the help of English adventurers, his rights to the Crown of Castile. For the next three years England and its king were rid of a troublesome and potentially dangerous personality.

Richard II.

Richard was now approaching twenty and was rapidly developing those doctrines of absolute monarchy which provoked the crisis of 1386, and in the end led to his deposition. With a fervour worthy of a Stuart he embraced the doctrine of Divine Right:

> Not all the water in the rough rude sea
> Can wash the balm from an anointed king;
> The breath of worldly men cannot depose
> The deputy elected by the Lord.

This absolutist doctrine encountered stout opposition. Richard, for his part, if no trifler like Edward II, was a *poseur* with a dramatic, not to say a melodramatic, sense of the pose appropriate for an " anointed king ".

Crisis of 1386.

Thus between King and Parliament there emerged, as in 1640, a real conflict of principle. But the conflict was triangular, complicated by the pretensions of the baronial magnates led by the king's uncle, Thomas of Woodstock, Earl of Gloucester, and Gaunt's eldest son Henry, Earl of Derby and later Duke of Hereford. Gloucester was a far more dangerous leader of opposition than Gaunt: abler, more cruel, and even more selfish. Henry was more dangerous than either. In character he was the exact antithesis of his cousin: cautious, cool, and crafty; temperate in his personal habits; an orthodox Churchman; patient and capable of taking infinite pains in pursuit of a predetermined purpose.

The Parliament of 1386 had many grievances to allege against the king, but it began by demanding the dismissal of the Chancellor and the Treasurer. The Chancellor was Michael de la Pole, Earl of Suffolk, no Gaveston or Despenser, but an official of high competence and complete integrity. To the demand of Parliament Richard haughtily replied that " he would not for them or at their instance remove the meanest scullion from his kitchen ". But being reminded, deferentially if not obscurely, of the fate of Edward II, he gave way. De la Pole was impeached on a number of charges, including, of course, malversation; some of them he successfully rebutted, on others he was condemned to forfeiture and imprisonment; but after the dispersal of Parliament was released. The attack on him was purely political, and he was replaced at the Chancery by Thomas Arundel, afterwards Archbishop of Canterbury, and a leading actor in the drama of 1399. As the price of a subsidy Richard was compelled to consent to the appointment of a commission of fourteen persons who for one year were virtually to take over the government. Before Parliament was dissolved Richard made a formal protest against the legality of their proceedings, and a few months later obtained from the judges a decision, on all points, in his favour. The judges of 1386, like those of 1637, were, of course, declared to be " subservient ": but it may well be that they impartially declared the " law ", which, as in 1637, was in conflict with the " Constitution ". English judges, unlike American, can, indeed, take no account of a Constitution, except in so far as it is embodied in statutes. Armed with this decision, Richard prepared a *coup d'état*, but was forestalled by Gloucester and four other earls, who " appealed ", took up arms, and accused of high treason the king's chief friends and counsellors.

**The Lords Appellant and the " Merciless " Parliament.**

At Radcot Bridge (1387) they defeated the king's favourite de Vere, whom he had created Marquis and then Duke of Ireland, and on the meeting (1388) of a Parliament, well named " merciless ", they impeached the king's friends, six of whom were, with some of the " subservient " judges, sent to the block.

Incidentally, the House of Lords put forward a claim of the highest constitutional significance. The king attempted to protect his friends by a legal opinion that the charges of the Appellants did not comply with the civil law or " the law of the land ". The Lords of Parliament brushed aside this plea and declared that " they only, with the king's assent, were judges in such cases, for that the realm of England had never been and ought not to be governed by the civil law, nor according to the laws of any other court or place, for that such inferior courts were but the executors of the laws of the realm and the ordinances of Parliament ". In this notable declaration a modern commentator discerns an implicit assertion of the ultimate sovereignty of Parliament, and its supremacy alike over the Judiciary and the Executive.[1] Interesting as the suggestion is, it must, for reasons already given, be received with caution.

A Parliament which met later in the year at Cambridge passed some important legislation: it re-enacted and enlarged the Statute of Labourers; re-enacted the statute against Papal " Provisions "; provided for quarterly sessions of Justices of the Peace, and for their payment; and laid the foundations of the English Poor Law, in particular the principle of " settlement ". The break up of the manorial system had flooded the country with vagrants and beggars. The Act of 1388 prohibited vagrancy, provided for severe penalties against " sturdy vagabonds " and " valiant beggars ", and ordered all beggars " impotent to serve " to remain in the place where they were at the time the Act was proclaimed. Failing maintenance there, they were to be sent back to their birthplaces. Such legislation affords interesting testimony to the social conditions of the time. The issues immediately in conflict were not, however, social but political.

**The Personal Government of Richard II.**

Gloucester and the Appellants were, for nearly a year, mainly responsible for the government, though Richard retained many of his household officials. At the close of it Richard quietly asked his uncle how old he was. " Twenty-two," replied Gloucester. " Then," said the king, " I am certainly old enough to manage my own affairs. I thank you, my lords, for your past services; I want them no longer." Gloucester and Arundel were dismissed from the council; Arundel was replaced as Chancellor by William of Wykeham, and Wykeham's friend Brantingham, another

[1] Tout: *Mediæval Administration,* III, p. 432.

old official, became Treasurer. Gaunt, having returned to England, gave valuable support to Richard, who, for the next eight years, "governed England" (in Stubbs's words) "as to all appearance a constitutional and popular king". Parliaments were only half as frequent in the ensuing nine years as they had been from 1380–8; but that was in itself popular: the fewer the Parliaments the less onerous was taxation. Not that there was a lack of useful legislation. Further precautions against the scandal of Papal patronage were taken by the Act of 1390; the Second Statute of Præmunire (1393) restrained appeals to the Roman Curia; and legislation (1390–3) against "livery and maintenance" testified to increasing anxiety about practices which were becoming a political danger as well as a social nuisance.

In 1394 a great blow fell upon Richard: he lost his wife, Anne of Bohemia, to whom he was devotedly attached, and whose influence had been consistently exerted for the good of her husband and his people. Two years later he concluded a twenty-five years' truce with France and sealed it by a marriage with the five-year-old daughter of Charles VI. From that moment a rapid deterioration in Richard's character is discernible. Craftily and cautiously he begins to prepare for a *coup d'état*. He proceeded in strict legal form; his chief agents being Sir William Bushy, the Speaker of the House of Commons, Sir Henry Green, and Sir William Bagot. Three out of the five "Lords Appellant" were, together with Archbishop Arundel, impeached, and suffered death or banishment. Gloucester died by violence at Calais —a fate not undeserved. A Parliament summoned in 1390 to Shrewsbury, annulled all the proceedings of the Merciless Parliament; vindicated the judicial decisions of 1388; declared a general amnesty; granted to the king the customs for life; and finally appointed, according to custom, a committee of eighteen to deal with petitions and in particular with the charge of treason laid by the Duke of Hereford against the Duke of Norfolk. The committee ordered trial by combat: but just as the lists were about to be opened Richard dramatically intervened, sentenced his enemy

Hereford to banishment for ten years, and his friend Norfolk to banishment for life.

On 3rd February, 1399, John of Gaunt died, and in the absence of his heir, Richard, with incredible tactlessness and without legal warrant, confiscated his uncle's vast estates. In July, Henry, the new Duke of Lancaster, returned to England to claim his inheritance. Landing at Ravenspur, he was joined by the Percies, Nevilles and other great nobles, and soon found himself at the head of a force to which Richard's friends could offer no resistance.

**Richard's Deposition and Death.**

Richard himself had in May gone to Ireland to avenge the death of Roger, Earl of March, the man whom, to the exclusion of the Lancasters, he had declared heir to the throne (1385). Henry of Lancaster, meanwhile, carried everything before him. Bushy, Green, William le Scrope, Earl of Wiltshire and other friends of the king—the "caterpillars of the Commonwealth"—were captured at Bristol and executed. Richard returned from Ireland to find himself friendless and deserted, and at Flint Castle made an abject surrender. In his attitude towards his triumphant rival there is a characteristic mingling of regal dignity and acquiescent servility. As ever Richard luxuriates in feeling: he is gluttonous of emotions. He is as abject in defeat as a few short months ago he had been arrogant in success:

> Of comfort no man speak;
> Let's talk of graves, of worms, of epitaphs;
> . . . . . . . . .
> For God's sake let us sit upon the ground
> And tell sad stories of the death of kings.

Taken as a prisoner to London, Richard was compelled to execute a deed of abdication. On the meeting of Parliament a detailed indictment was preferred against him: he was solemnly deposed; Henry of Lancaster claimed the throne by descent, conquest and election; the claim was acknowledged. Henry was enthroned; Richard was sentenced by the peers to life-long imprisonment, and in February, 1400, a corpse, believed to be that of Richard, was exhibited in London at St. Paul's.

From Richard himself it is impossible to withhold sympathy. He was out of tune with the times: his instincts were autocratic at a stage in history when England was moving towards parliamentary government, but personally he was one of the most interesting and not the least attractive of our kings. He was " the sweet lovely rose " that blossomed early and untimely died. But, though there were in his career flashes of manliness and vigour, he lacked virility and consistency of character. If he was never at fault for the apt pose, the dramatic sense too often failed to translate itself into action. Politically, therefore, he was a failure, incapable of coping with a man of coarser mould, of tougher fibre, the " vile politician Bolingbroke ". Yet a question obtrudes itself: may not Richard have sincerely believed that the alternatives for his day were autocracy and anarchy? He attempted—though feebly—to make for himself the position which the Wars of the Roses created for the Tudors.

CHAPTER XI

# Lancastrians and Yorkists

## An "Unquiet Time"

HENRY OF LANCASTER had been scurvily treated by his cousin; his treatment was generally resented by his peers; and his accession to the throne was popular. He claimed it, however, not only by election and conquest, but by right of blood. The descent of the Crown was never, in fact, legally defined until the passing of the Act of Settlement (1701). Nevertheless, there was an uneasy sense that Henry IV was a "usurper":

**Title of the Lancastrians.**

> God knows, my son,
> By what bye-paths and indirect crook'd ways
> I met this crown; and I myself know well
> How troublesome it sat upon my head.

"Troublesome", indeed, was the Crown; "unquiet" was the reign; and the trouble was largely due to the fact that Henry's position was a contradiction in terms. Oligarch and parliamentarian; a usurper and a conservative; at once successful rebel and stern represser of rebellion, Henry's reign was bound to be "unquiet".

To the unquiet, Scotland and Wales both contributed, but Henry's main trouble arose from his relations with his baronial colleagues, especially the Percies. The men who had helped him to the throne naturally expected to share the spoils of victory; the king on his side was naturally suspicious of men who knowing

> the way
> To plant unrightful kings [would] know again
> Being so little urged, another way
> To pluck him headlong from the usurped throne.

Not until the defeat and death of the Earl of Northumberland at Bramham Moor was Henry quit of a danger which had repeatedly threatened both his throne and person.

**Constitutional significance of the Fifteenth Century.**

With regard to the constitutional significance of the fifteenth century widely divergent views have been expressed. Bishop Stubbs says, rather surprisingly, that in a parliamentary sense the period from 1399–1487 is a blank. But his practice is not consistent with his precept. It is true that the fifteenth century differed markedly from the fourteenth. It registered not the acquisition of fundamental powers and privileges, but a detailed definition of rights already acknowledged—a process that Stubbs himself happily describes as " hardening and sharpening ". This process was applied to finance, legislation, and privileges, to the relations between the two Houses, between the legislature as a whole and the executive, as well as to the electorate and the method of election.

**Finance.**

Take finance. The fourteenth century had established the broad principle of parliamentary control. For the fifteenth, broad principles were not enough: it required precise definition. In 1406 the Commons insisted on an effective audit of expenditure, and in 1407 obtained a recognition of their right to originate all money grants, which were to be *made* by the Commons, by the Lords *assented to*, and *reported* to the King by the Speaker of the Commons. With the exception of a money-bill, any bill might originate in either House.

**Legislature and Executive.**

Of even greater importance was the change in the relations between the legislative and executive sides of government. It was in the Cabinet system—the system under which the Crown acts in all political matters on the advice of a small committee of ministers who collectively command the confidence of Parliament—that England ultimately found the solution of the central problem in the art of politics. Parliamentary democracy rests fundamentally on this device. Monarchy is held to be " constitutional " only when the device has been adopted. It has been the essence of the concession whereby " Responsible Government " has been established in the British Dominions. All the more, then, must we resist the temptation to discern in the Lancastrian Council the lineal ancestor of the Hanoverian Cabinet, or to assign to the " experiment " of the fifteenth century a proleptic significance.

Nevertheless, real importance does attach to the formal declaration made on the King's behalf to Parliament by Archbishop Arundel, that King Henry meant to govern by the " common advice, counsel and consent " of " the honourable, wise, and discreet persons of his kingdom ". To the promise thus made Henry and his son were consistently faithful. " Never before," says Bishop Stubbs, " and never again for more than two hundred years were the Commons so strong as they were under Henry IV." It remains to be shown how that strength was manifested, and how in detail the King's promise was fulfilled.

**The Council.**

The King agreed in 1401 not to intervene in matters pending in Parliament, but there was no mutuality in the agreement. On the contrary, an attack was made in Parliament (1404) on the royal household: on a petition from the Commons, four persons were dismissed and the King was requested to appoint his servants in Parliament, and those only who were " honest, virtuous, and well renowned ". The King agreed; and, further, communicated to Parliament the names of the twenty-two persons whom he had appointed to be his continual council. Nevertheless, in 1406 the Commons returned to the attack. In their name the Speaker required of the King " good and abundant government ", and having secured the nomination in Parliament of a council of seventeen persons, some of whom were to be in constant attendance on his person and by whose advice he undertook in all cases to govern, the Commons made a grant " for the great confidence which they had in the lords elected and ordained to be of the continual council ". In these proceedings we cannot but discern some approach (to put it at the lowest) towards " responsible government ".

In the same Parliament was enacted a statute against

the Lollard heretics, and also an Act of Settlement declaring the Crown to be heritable by the King's sons and their male heirs in succession. To the problem of the Executive the Commons recurred in 1410, and, after prolonged discussion, the King agreed to nominate " the most valiant, wise and discreet of the lords, spiritual and temporal, to be of his council, in aid and support of good and substantial government ".

**The First Regency.**

During the reign of Henry V no dispute on this or any other question arose between Crown and Parliament; but on his death the Crown passed to an infant nine months old. For the first time the question of a regency arose. The Privy Council at once took command of the situation, and claimed to act, and did act, as a council of regency. Henry V had entrusted the regency of France to his elder brother John, Duke of Bedford, and that of England to his younger brother Humphrey, Duke of Gloucester. But the council set these dispositions aside, issued writs for the election of a Parliament, appointed Gloucester to open it as High Commissioner, repudiated Gloucester's claim to the regency, and appointed Bedford, or in his absence oversea, Gloucester, to be protector and defender of the kingdom and Church and chief counsellor to the King. Gloucester accepted the position, and Parliament proceeded to nominate a council of seventeen persons with Gloucester as chief, and to confer upon it extensive, but clearly defined powers. A few additional members were added to the council in 1423 and a few more in 1430. In 1437 the young King assumed the right to nominate his council, and its connexion with Parliament ceased. But by that time new forces were operating which will demand analysis later on.

**Parliament.**

Parliament had by now come to consist of two Houses. But both were much smaller bodies than they have since become. The temporal peers never exceeded 50 in the reign of Henry IV; under Henry V they only once numbered as many as 40; by the accession of Henry VI they had diminished to 23, but under Edward IV were sometimes as many as 50. In addition, 20 archbishops and bishops were regularly summoned, but the abbots, who in 1295 numbered 70, were increasingly anxious to evade the tiresome and expensive duty of attendance in Parliament, and in the fifteenth century never exceeded 30. We may put the House of Lords, therefore, at a maximum of 100, not unequally divided between temporal and spiritual peers.

In the House of Commons the county members invariably numbered 74; the number of burgesses varied considerably, partly perhaps at the discretion of the sheriffs, and partly according to the success of boroughs in evading the expensive obligation of sending representatives to Parliament. The burgesses received only 2*s.* a day, as against 4*s.* paid to the knights of the shire, but as they were paid for the days of their journeys to and fro, the wages-bill mounted up, especially for the northern towns, whose reluctance to send up members was intelligible and persistent. On the occasion of the coronation of Edward V the members for York received eight additional days' wages; the borough of Cambridge made a bargain with their members to accept half wages in 1427; but 2*s.* a day was the normal rate.

**The Electorate.**

In regard to the process of election there was room for considerable variety. But in 1406 an important statute was passed to regulate county elections. The election was to be made, freely and independently, by the whole county in the next county court, and the return of the chosen knights was to be made in an indenture containing the names, and sealed with the seals, of all who took part in the election. The return was to be made to Chancery. The injunctions issued to the sheriff as to the choice of fit persons varied considerably from Parliament to Parliament, according to the circumstances of the hour. Wherever possible "belted knights" were to be preferred; but in default esquires, especially if "honest and peaceful, not pleaders or maintainers of quarrels", might serve. In 1372 lawyers and sheriffs were by ordinance excluded from candidature, and the disqualification of sheriffs, but not of lawyers, afterwards became permanent. A statute of 1413 made residence within the county or borough an essential qualification both for electors and elected.

**The County Franchise.**

The county franchise reached its maximum under Henry IV, when it included not only all freeholders but all freemen. But in 1430 the franchise was restricted to residents possessed of a freehold worth 40*s*. a year. Two years later it was ordained that the qualifying freehold must be within the county. The qualification remained unaltered (save by the Constitutions of the Cromwellian Protectorate) until the Reform Act of 1832, but the rapid fall in the value of money had, in the meantime, by diminishing the rigidity of the qualification, enormously extended the electorate, and the 40*s*. freeholder had become the most popular element.

**Borough Representation.**

Not until 1832 was there any real simplification and regularization of the borough franchise. The original problem as regards borough representation was whether the towns should be treated as independent and extra-county units, or merely as more closely and largely populated townships within the county borders. Simon de Montfort treated the towns as independent units and, for obvious reasons, addressed his writs to selected boroughs. In the first Parliament to which he summoned burgesses Edward I followed that precedent. But as Parliament assumed its more permanent form the boroughs fell, so to say, into the shire system. The writs were addressed to the sheriff, the formal election of borough members took place in the county court, and the returns were included in the document which certified the election of the knights of the shire. It was the sheriff's duty on receipt of the writ to transmit a copy of it, together with his precept, to the town magistrates. The method of electing the burgesses varied from town to town, perhaps from Parliament to Parliament; as did the selection of the boroughs themselves. Until borough representation became a privilege, and the exercise of the franchise a legal right, boroughs were only too thankful to be overlooked or deliberately omitted by the sheriffs, and prosperous burgesses had little temptation to seek employment at 2*s*. a day—though as money then went the pay was not despicable—instead of attending to their own business. A few cities which, like York, were counties followed, it would seem, the county rules in regard to the franchise. For the rest there was infinite variety, not to say confusion. But whatever the method adopted in this borough or that, the formal certification was the duty of the sheriff.

**Constitutional Progress.**

Whether regarded in gross or in detail the progress made, during the period between the reign of John and that of Henry VI, towards government by consent was extraordinarily rapid. Fundamental rights had been affirmed and acknowledged; the machinery for giving practical effect to them had been worked out in considerable detail. The progress was too rapid; the development was premature. That is the lesson drawn by Bishop Stubbs from his brilliant review of this period. It may well be that as regards the nature of the Lancastrian "experiment" Stubbs was over-precise and attributed to Henry IV and V a design of which they were innocent. A recent writer has pertinently pointed out that the "later splendours of the Constitution have been reflected back upon the fifteenth century, throwing certain features of it into undue relief, and enveloping the whole structure with an appearance of maturity and completeness which is in fact illusory".[1] That may well be; but Stubbs's analysis was essentially sound, and his conclusion is irrefutable. In the art of politics there is nothing so fatal as premature development. The Fascist dictatorship is the penalty which Italy has to pay (if penalty it is) for the adoption of parliamentary democracy, before the social conditions and political education of Italy justified the experiment, and offered some guarantee of its success. If the strength of the parliamentary system was subjected to a premature test in Italy in the nineteenth century, England suffered the same experience in the fifteenth. In both cases the result was disastrous. "The Constitution had in its growth outrun the capacity of the nation; the nation needed rest and renewal, discipline and reformation before it could enter into the enjoyment of its birthright." So Stubbs wrote of

[1] T. F. T. Plucknett: *ap. Tudor Studies* (1924), p. 161.

fifteenth-century England. Upon the collapse of government under Henry VI there ensued a period of grave social disorder; once again, as in the evil days of Stephen, we can discern all the familiar symptoms of social disorganization and governmental impotence. The least important element in the Wars of the Roses was the dynastic issue. There was not one civil war but as many wars as there were great nobles. There was no hope for the country but from a saviour of society. Premature parliamentary development necessitated a dictatorship. Fortunate was it for England that the dictators were of the Tudor type. But before that dictatorship was established, England suffered deep humiliation in the French wars, and at home was distracted by civil strife, general lawlessness, and impotent administration. No fewer than three kings were murdered in the course of a century and a fourth was killed in a faction fight. Three dukes and other great nobles died similarly violent deaths. The classes responsible for the social anarchy were thus, in the main, its victims: the towns were, relatively, little affected by the baronial wars, and many of the merchants were exceptionally prosperous.

**Social Disorder.**

The root of the trouble lay, as Fortescue acutely discerned, in the predominance of the "over-mighty subject". Sir John Fortescue was Chief Justice of the King's Bench under Henry VI and was a member of the commissions to inquire into the disturbances in Yorkshire and East Anglia (1443). He had, therefore, special opportunities for forming a sound judgment on the causes of the prevailing anarchy. An ardent adherent of the Lancastrian House, he was attainted by Edward IV in 1461, and possibly acted as tutor to the young Prince Edward—the heir of Henry VI. During the Lancastrian exile in France he wrote his famous treatise *De Laudibus Angliae* (1468–70) for the instruction of his pupil. A later work, *The Governance of England*, is "of special interest as being the earliest constitutional treatise written in the English language".[1] Moreover, it contains a particularly penetrating analysis of the social and

**The "Over-mighty Subject".**

[1] Plummer: *Governance*, p. 86.

political conditions of the time. "For certainly," he wrote, "ther mey no grettir perell growe to a prince than to have a subgett equepolent to hymselff." The whole history of the fifteenth century is one extended commentary on that pregnant aphorism. The causes which contributed to this peril are not far to seek.

The vast wealth of the great barons like Percy or Warwick contrasted with the poverty of the Crown; the concentration of landed property in very few hands; the revival of the feudal temper in a spurious or bastard form; the practice of "maintenance" and "livery"; the idea that a great lord must surround himself with bands of semi-military retainers whom he must protect from the penalties of their lawless misdeeds; the new military system which put the barons in command of professional armies; the breakdown of local government; the maladministration of justice; the insolent interference of the barons with the independence of juries and even of judges—of all these things there are abundant illustrations in Fortescue's treatise, and a still more vivid picture in the *Paston Letters*. "The two cankers of the time," says Thorold Rogers, "were the total corruption of the Church and the utter lawlessness of the aristocracy." The full consequences of this were not apparent until the reign of Henry VI; but Henry IV himself was far too shrewd a man not to perceive the danger which threatened his dynasty. Hence his sagacious though somewhat unprincipled advice to Henry of Monmouth:

> Therefore, my Harry,
> Be it thy course to busy giddy minds
> With foreign quarrels; that action, hence borne out,
> May waste the memory of the former days.

In this advice we may perhaps discover one of the reasons for the renewal of the French war under Henry V. But the glories of Harfleur and Agincourt were evanescent, and the nemesis of the Lancastrian crime descended with dramatic rapidity upon the devoted head of Henry VI. No king was ever less responsible for the miseries which accumulated during his reign than this " Royal Saint ". The dissensions in the Lancastrian House; the disastrous quarrel between Cardinal Beaufort and the Duke of Gloucester; the healing of the internecine rivalries in France; the consequent withdrawal of Burgundy from the alliance which was essential to English success abroad; the intervention of Joan of Arc; the foolish and petulant partisanship of Queen Margaret of Anjou; the social anarchy made manifest at home by the rebellion of Jack Cade; the final exasperation of Richard Duke of York owing to the ill-omened birth of a Prince of Wales—all these things contributed to the downfall of the Lancastrian dynasty, to the outbreak or rather the culmination of the social disturbances misleadingly known as the Wars of the Roses.

**The Wars of the Roses.**

The significance of these wars is entirely missed by those who regard them primarily as a dynastic struggle. " The Rising of Cade," says Mr. Plummer, " was but the climax of a process which had long been going on. The Government had gradually been losing all hold upon the country, and in the general paralysis of the central administration local disorder had increased to a frightful extent."[1] It was, in fact, the complete breakdown of the executive, combined with fierce family feuds and perpetual private wars, that furnished the opportunity for the House of York.

The original cause of the mischief is undoubtedly to be discerned in the new military system under which the Crown " indented " with great lords and others for the supply of men at a fixed rate of pay.[2] When the war for which the contract had been made came to an end the commanders returned, not only enriched by the profits of their enterprise, but surrounded " by bands of men accustomed to obey their orders, incapacitated by long warfare for the pursuits of settled and peaceful life, and ready to follow their masters on any turbulent enterprise ".[3] One of Suffolk's men boasted " that his lord was able to keep daily in his house more men than his adversary had hairs on his head ".

[1] Plummer: *Fortescue*, p. 27; [2] Sir C. Oman: *Warwick the Kingmaker* (p. 36), prints a typical indenture of 1449. [3] Plummer: *Ibidem*, p. 15.

In 1406 " the Commons had complained that baronets, knights and esquires gave liveries of cloth to as many as three hundred men or more to uphold their unjust quarrels, and in order to be able to oppress others at their pleasure. And no remedy could be had against them because of their confederacy and maintenance ". " The livery of a great lord," said Stubbs, " was as effective security to a malefactor as was the benefit of clergy to a criminous clerk."

Closely connected with the change in the military system and with the custom of livery was the increasing prevalence of private wars. Noble was at war with noble; the Earl of Northumberland at war with the Earl of Westmoreland; the Earl of Devon at war with Lord Bonneville; the heir male was at war with the heirs general of the House of Berkeley from 1421 to 1475; counties like Shropshire were invaded by the men of Cheshire; Archbishop Kemp's tenants at Ripon were fighting the king's tenants of Knaresborough Forest; the students of Oxford were at war with the county. Worse still, this bastard feudalism infected the administration of justice. The Paston correspondence teems with illustrations of the intimidation of juries, the bribery of sheriffs, and even the corruption of the judges. " Nothing is more curious," says Mr. Plummer, " than the way in which it is assumed that it is idle to indict a criminal who is maintained by a powerful person; that it is useless to institute legal proceedings unless the sheriff and jury can be secured beforehand; nothing can be more naïve than the complaints as to the difficulty of being sure of jurymen, because either they are ' ambidexter ', i.e. take bribes from both sides, or they fear a ' turning world ', i.e. some sudden change in the relations of parties. Very quaint too is the astonishment expressed by John Paston *not* at being attacked in an unprovoked manner at the door of Norwich Cathedral, so much as at being attacked by a dependant of the Duke of Norfolk who was his ' good lord '; for it is evidently regarded as a great scandal to a lord that two of his dependants should be at feud. Bribes are offered and looked for as a matter of course; it is assumed that an officer will use his official position in favour of his friends, and the only hope of redressing evils is considered to lie in the influence of the great."

**The Yorkists.**

Particular illustrations of these malpractices might be multiplied to any extent. More to the purpose is it to investigate the causes rather than describe the symptoms of the prevailing epidemic. Many convergent causes operated, but the *causa causans* was, in Stubbs's pregnant phrase, that " constitutional progress had outrun administrative order ".

That progress was arrested under the last Lancastrian and the Yorkist kings. Parliaments which under the later Plantagenets and the first two Lancastrians had met at least once and frequently twice a year, were under Edward IV exceedingly irregular. No Parliament sat between January, 1465, and June, 1467, or between May, 1468, and October, 1472, and between 1475 and 1483 Parliament sat only once, for six weeks, in order to pass an Act of Attainder against the Duke of Clarence. Only seven times, during the twenty-five years of Yorkist rule, was a new Parliament elected.

It is doubtful whether the suspension of Parliaments was so unpopular as in retrospect we might imagine. Suspension of Parliaments meant the abeyance of regular taxation. Some taxes had, indeed, been voted to Edward IV for life, early in the reign, and these were supplemented by " benevolences ". But these " free-will offerings " were extorted from the relatively rich: the average citizen escaped, and consequently did not greatly lament over the abeyance of Parliaments. Edward IV made money, too, like his subjects, in trade, and amassed great wealth by numerous forfeitures. Benevolences were, naturally, very unpopular with those from whom they were collected, and when in 1483 Richard of Gloucester was invited to assume the Crown, the opportunity was taken to make a strong protest against the practice. " For certainly we be determined rather to aventure and committe us to the perill of owre lyfs and jopardie of deth, than to lyve in such thraldome and bondage as we have lived long time heretofore, oppressed and injured by extortions and new impositions agenst the lawes of God and man, and the libertie, old policie and lawes of this realme, whereyn every Englishman is inherited." So ran the remarkable address presented to Richard when he held a Parliament in January, 1484. Of several statutes it enacted the most important was one abolishing the practice of benevolences. They were, nevertheless, collected, though Richard had obtained from Parliament a grant of tonnage and poundage and the subsidy on wool for life. Parliament also confirmed the king's title to the Crown, basing it upon the right of consanguinity and inheritance, as well as upon lawful election, consecration and coronation. But the perfection of his title did not secure Richard against defeat at the hands of a rival. On 7th August, 1485, Henry Earl of Richmond landed at Milford Haven, and on the 22nd Richard was defeated and killed on Bosworth Field.

**Battle of Bosworth.**

If the Yorkist ascendancy was brief, and in the present connexion unimportant, it was due to the circumstances of the time, not to any lack of ability or energy on the part of the kings themselves. Neither Edward IV nor Richard III lacked brains, but both were entirely selfish and unscrupulous; both had a large share of the callous brutality characteristic of that period. Ruthlessly they swept aside anyone who stood in the path of their ambition or was suspected of disloyalty to themselves. Yet Edward IV was undeniably popular; nor, until the imprisonment of his nephews, was the popularity of Richard III markedly less than that of Edward IV. Neither of them had any organized political opposition to encounter. The magnates had committed suicide in the "Wars of the Roses"; the Church had completely lost the sympathy of the people; its leaders were identified with the interests of Rome; for spiritual sustenance the people looked rather to the cruelly persecuted Lollards than to their orthodox persecutors; the "Third Estate", weakened perhaps by the disfranchising statute of Henry VI, were not yet in a position, single-handed, to control the Crown.

Nor, indeed, is there any evidence that they wished to do so. Edward IV in particular was high in favour with the trading classes whose interests he shared and promoted. Cordial friendship with Burgundy meant far more to the average citizen than any " constitutional " advance registered in Parliament. The stronger the government the better for trade, and only the monarchy could give strength to the government. The mischief was that the Yorkist monarchs, though strong enough to deal drastically with personal rivals, were not sufficiently secure on the throne to give the country the strong executive so urgently needed, if not consciously demanded.

Richmond's victory at Bosworth meant to contemporaries merely one more turn in the wheel of dynastic fortunes. Historians, with the advantages of retrospect, can perceive that it opened a new era in the evolution of the English Constitution, that it registered the passing of another stage in the making of the English nation.

## CHAPTER XII

# The Tudor Monarchy

THE historians of the nineteenth century were apt to look askance at the sixteenth. The straiter sect of constitutionalists would gladly have ignored it altogether. To them the Tudors were not merely usurpers, but intruders breaking in, with their despotic methods, upon the orderly evolution of English government. Henry VII was everything that was unlovely: despotic, pitiless, avaricious. Henry VIII was a " spot of blood and grease upon the page of English history ". Queen Mary was " bloody ". Worst of all was Queen Elizabeth. Her sagacity and success as a sovereign were undeniable, but her personality was detestable. Captious critics insisted that she never knew her own mind, and was habitually in two minds; that her hesitations, procrastinations and prevarications were the result not of profound policy, but of inconstancy of temper and infirmity of will. They declared that she was consumed by vanity and insatiate in her appetite for admiration; that her conduct was indecorous to the verge and beyond the verge of scandal; that she lured men to make love to her only to hold them up to scorn, or punish them for their temerity; that she treated with base ingratitude her most trusted counsellors, and showered favours upon worthless sycophants and audacious admirers; that her natural and commendable frugality hardened into parsimony and at critical moments endangered the safety of the State. In fine she was, in Goldwin Smith's phrase, a " little figure in a great age ".

The fashion has changed. The Tudor period is now more justly appreciated alike on its own merits and by

The Tudor Dictatorship.

reason of a more correct apprehension of the constitutional significance of the preceding century. It may, under the circumstances of the hour (1937), be misleading to describe the Tudor régime as a dictatorship; but dictatorships, like the Greek " Tyrannies ", may be good or bad. The Tudors were called to the throne (unconsciously, of course) for a definite purpose; without a standing army they could occupy it only by popular consent; their rule was limited in duration, and was terminated as soon as the emergency was over. All this is of the essence of a dictatorship as originally devised for the Republican Constitution of Rome. A dictatorship must be judged by its ultimate effect upon its legatees. A good dictatorship should provide for its own supersession. Only if the people are taught to do without it can its passing existence be justified.

To this exacting test the Tudors successfully reacted. They were not tyrants, but in the true sense dictators. If they ruled as well as reigned, they ruled through Parliament. If they erected extraordinary tribunals, with special or local jurisdiction, it was in order that the people might have speedier and cheaper justice. If Henry VIII dealt somewhat summarily with a succession of unattractive wives, it was obviously not for the satisfaction of his own lust, but that he might provide for an undisputed succession and so avert the disaster of a recurrence of civil wars. In their ecclesiastical reforms the Tudors went as far as, but no farther than, the vast majority of the people desired. They reorganized the whole system of local government on lines so sound that it worked with general approval until the reforms of 1888 and 1894. Dictators, then, the Tudors were: not despots.

Henry VII.

Of this dictatorship the foundations were well and truly laid by Henry VII. His reign was, in a sense, preliminary; he cleared the ground for the new dynasty, and laid down the lines of policy which in the main were followed by his successors—most conspicuously by his grand-daughter Elizabeth.

Henry VII was, with the exception of Mary, the least

popular of the Tudor sovereigns; but he was, perhaps, the ablest: clear of brain; strong in will; inflexible in pursuit of the policy which he deemed essential to the good of the realm and the strength of the monarchy. "He was," said Stowe, "a prince of marvellous wisdom, policy, justice, temperance and gravity, and . . . he kept his realm in right good order." "A wise man and an excellent King," was Bacon's estimate.

**His Title.**

His first business was to establish the new dynasty on the throne. Their title must be unquestioned and unquestionable. Henry, accordingly, claimed the throne not only by "the judgment of God in the field" but by hereditary right. The latter claim, if disputable, was not disputed; Parliament, without inquiring too nicely into rights, simply enacted that the inheritance of the Crown should "rest, remain and abide" in Henry and "the heirs of his body lawfully coming". Having thus obtained admission of his independent rights, Henry further strengthened them by marriage with the Lady Elizabeth of York, and by obtaining a Papal Bull which enumerated, but without discrimination, the various titles by which Henry held the throne. In particular, while not ignoring his marriage with the Lady Elizabeth, the Bull provided that the King's children by any future marriage were to have an equally undisputed title to the throne. Later on, when the Warbeck scare was at its worst (1495), the Statute of Treason was passed providing for the immunity of persons adhering to a king *de facto*. That Henry's precautions, if elaborate, were not superfluous was proved by the persistence of the Yorkist insurrections associated with the names of Lambert Simnel and Perkin Warbeck but largely sustained by the Duchess Margaret of Burgundy, the sister of Edward IV. The death of that intrepid old lady in 1503 removed the main source of danger, and in 1506 a lucky accident brought into the King's hands her nephew, Edmund de la Pole, Earl of Suffolk, who was committed to the Tower, only to emerge from it, seven years later, to suffer death at the hands of Henry VIII. Warbeck's final defeat and condemnation

(1499) involved also the death of the young Earl of Warwick, " the winding ivy of a Plantagenet thus killing " in Bacon's phrase, " the true tree itself ".

**Financial Independence.**

Second only in importance to an unquestioned title was the financial independence of the Crown. The poverty of the Lancastrians had been their undoing. Henry Tudor took to heart the wise words of Fortescue: " We must hold it for undoubted that there may no realm prosper or be worshipful, under a poore king " (chap. v.). To avoid this peril Fortescue recommended " a general resumption, by authority of Parliament, of alienated lands, and when the king, by the means aforesaid or otherwise, hath gotten again his livelihood " he should then " amortise the same livelihood to his Crown, so as it may never be alienated therefrom without the assent of his Parliament, which then would be as a new foundation of his Crown " (chap. xix). Henry followed this advice and vast sums were by this and other means accumulated. Parliament confirmed to the King possession of the duchies of Lancaster and Cornwall, the earldoms of Chester and Richmond, and sanctioned the resumption of all the Crown lands which had been alienated since 2nd October, 1455, besides many properties alienated as far back as the reign of Edward III. The Yorkist insurrections also helped, by escheats and forfeitures, to fill the Exchequer. Clemency too was profitable. " The less blood he drew," says Bacon, " the more he took of treasure." Feudal dues were enforced to the last penny; obsolete statutes revived; fines imposed; municipal liberties granted or reconfirmed for money payments. Morton's ingenious " fork " has become proverbial; Empson and Dudley, the later and less scrupulous of Henry's agents, were described by Holinshed as the " two ravening wolves ". The first Parliament granted to the king the duties on tonnage and poundage for life, but during the remainder of the reign only five requests for grants were made to Parliament.

**Parliament under the Tudors.**

Though Parliament plays little part in the reign of Henry VII, no attempt was made to supersede it. Henry VIII made great use of it. In his reign there were nine distinct Parliaments; one sat for seven years, and two others sat for three. During the short reigns of Edward VI and Queen Mary Parliament was practically continuous. The first Parliament of Edward VI held four sessions extending over nearly five years; the second had one. In the five years of Mary's reign there were five Parliaments.

Elizabeth, being more economical than her predecessors, had less need of Parliaments; but she "summoned ten Parliaments, which held in all thirteen sessions. Parliament met, then, on the average about once in every three and a half years."[1] And all the Tudors gave it plenty to do. The additions to the statute book during this period were, as Prothero pointed out, "more copious and not less important than in any previous age".[2] Maitland emphasized the use which Henry VIII made of Parliament. "The part," he wrote, "which the assembled estates of the realm have to play in the Great Acts of Henry VIII may in truth be a subservient and an ignoble part, but the Acts are Great and they are all done by the authority of Parliament."[3]

**The House of Lords.**

The composition of Parliament at this time is, therefore, a matter of importance. The lay baronage was much attenuated in numbers and weakened in prestige. In the first Parliament of Henry VII there were only twenty-nine lay peers; in the first Parliament of Henry VIII there were but thirty-six, and in that of Elizabeth forty-three. Elizabeth nearly doubled the numbers of the lay peerage, so that James I could on his accession summon over eighty. But these new creations needed time before they found their political legs in the Upper House. They were not long in doing so under the Stuarts. The spiritual peers far outnumbered, during the reign of Henry VII and the first part of Henry VIII, their lay brethren, but the dissolution of the abbeys reduced their number from forty-eight (ultimately) to twenty-six, the figure at which they still remain.[4] The mitred abbots had been probably the most independent

[1] Stubbs: *Mediæval and Modern History*, p. 269.

[2] *Statutes and Documents*, p. xxiv. [3] *ap. Social England*, II, p. 477.

[4] Until the abolition of the bishopric of Westminster (Ed. VI) there were twenty-seven; and from the Irish Union to the Disestablishment of the Irish Church, thirty.

element in the House of Lords under the early Tudors. They disappeared, however, in 1536, while the bishops were by the Act of 1534 reduced to still further dependence on the Crown. From a House thus constituted—a House which from this time onwards becomes almost exclusively secular and hereditary in character—the Crown had little opposition to fear in the sixteenth century. Nor is any development in this respect discernible during the period.

**The House of Commons.**

With the House of Commons it was otherwise. The difference of temper displayed by the Commons in the earlier and later years of the century is immensely significant. At neither period is it accurate to describe it as " disgracefully subservient and sycophantic ", and it is doubtful whether it can fairly be described as " packed ". But it must be admitted that if not " servile ", it was usually submissive, and it is true that if not " packed ", its numbers were considerably increased under the Tudors. Thus in 1543 Henry VIII added thirty-two knights and burgesses " by bestowing representation on the towns and counties of Wales, Calais, and Chester ". " Preston also, Lancaster, Thetford, Orford, Berwick, and possibly one or two more towns, gained the privilege of representation." [1] Eighteen new parliamentary boroughs were created under Edward VI. Some of these were, as Dr. Pollard pertinently pointed out, towns like Wigan, Liverpool, Peterborough and Westminster, which " were certainly entitled by their growing population and importance to elect members to Parliament, and their creation, so far from being evidence of a design to pack the House of Commons, really indicates the adoption of a liberal policy which had to wait three centuries for its consummation." [2] Most of the new boroughs were, however, in Cornwall; and though there were many rapidly rising towns in that county—especially the fishing towns on the coast—it is difficult to resist the conclusion that Cornwall was specially favoured as a royal duchy, and as being, on that account, particularly amenable to Crown influence. Queen Mary created fourteen new boroughs, while Queen Elizabeth added

[1] Stubbs's *Lectures*, p. 271. [2] Pollard: *England under Protector Somerset*, p. 70.

to the House of Commons no less than sixty-two new members. Thus during the century the membership of the Lower House was nearly doubled. But with Dr. Prothero we may repudiate the sinister interpretation which by the older generation of historians was placed upon this fact. " The main reason," as he pointed out, " for the large increase . . . is probably to be found in the growing prosperity of the country, and in the reliance which the Tudors placed on the commercial and industrial classes." [1]

Assuming the creation of new boroughs to be satisfactorily and even honourably accounted for, what are we to say of the charge of direct interference with freedom of election? Did the Tudors secure subservient Parliaments by bringing pressure to bear upon returning officers and upon electors? This is a point which is hardly susceptible of conclusive proof one way or the other. It is probable that there was a regular form which, with some variations to suit particular occasions, was issued by the Government to the sheriffs on the dissolution of each Parliament. But it is not easy to decide how far these letters of advice or instruction really carried. In some cases the instructions appear to be quite general, bidding the freeholders elect " men of knowledge and experience ". In others they are much more precise. Thus Northumberland in 1553 actually gave the names of those whom the Crown wished to be returned. Again in 1554 Queen Mary required the sheriffs to admonish the electors to choose " such as being eligible by order of the laws were of a grave, wise and catholic sort ". In 1570 Queen Elizabeth complained that " though the greater number of knights, citizens and burgesses for the most part are duly and orderly chosen, yet in many places such consideration is not usually had herein as reason would, that is to choose persons able to give good information and advice for the places for which they are nominated, and to treat and consult discreetly upon such matters as are to be propounded to them ". The Queen, therefore, appointed Archbishop Parker and Lord Cobham to confer with the returning

[1] *Statutes and Documents*, p. lxvi.

officers in Kent, and take care that the persons returned " be well qualified with knowledge, discretion, and modesty ". Her successor similarly admonished the electors " to avoid the choice of any persons either noted for their superstitious blindness one way or for their turbulent humours other ways ".

How far these admonitions actually served to secure the subservience of the House of Commons is a question not easy to answer; but two things are indisputable: the first is that under the Tudors Crown and Parliament were in close accord with each other; the second is that under the Stuarts, employing though they did the same methods to secure subservience, Crown and Parliament were perpetually at variance. Perhaps, after all, the simplest explanation may be the true one—that in the main the Tudor Parliaments were " subservient " to the Crown because they believed that the several sovereigns of that line did faithfully and honestly seek to promote the well being, and even carry out the will, of the vast majority of the people over whom they ruled.

The Tudors were, moreover, singularly adroit in the management, if not the manipulation, of Parliament. They never raised unnecessarily a point of principle, and they invariably took the line of least resistance. The consequence was that the actual collisions between Crown and Parliament were as rare under the Tudors as they were common under their successors.

**Finance.**

Take the crucial question of finance. The revenue of the Crown was, indeed, only in small part dependent upon regular parliamentary grants. Henry VII and Elizabeth could almost manage to " live of their own ", i.e. on the permanent hereditary revenues of the Crown, rents of Crown lands, monastic property (after 1539), feudal incidents, purveyance, ecclesiastical first-fruits and tenths (after 1534), and fines and other proceeds of justice. Indirect taxation —customs, tonnage and poundage—was at the disposal of Parliament, but to each Tudor sovereign Parliament voted it, at the beginning of every reign, for life. Only over direct taxation did Parliament exercise real control, and the Tudors rarely had recourse to it, and only to meet exceptional expenditure. A poll tax, the yield of which was much short of the estimate, was voted in 1512; a subsidy was voted in 1514, and in 1523 Wolsey demanded a large subsidy for the expenses of the war. The House of Commons demurred to the demand and declined to discuss it in the Cardinal's presence: "The fashion of the Nether House," he was bluntly informed, "was to hear, and not to reason but among themselves." Debate, in fine, was to be free and unimpeded by the presence of the Chancellor. Ultimately, a somewhat smaller subsidy was voted, but in a form wherewith the Cardinal was "sore discontent". In 1534 another subsidy was demanded for national defence, for the expenses of the war with Scotland, and "to bring the wilful, wild, unreasonable and savage people of his said land of Ireland . . . to such conformity, rule, order and obedience as the same for ever hereafter shall be much utile and profitable to the kings of this realm, and a great surety and quietness to the subjects and inhabitants of the same." National defence was the ground alleged for the demand for another subsidy voted in 1548.

**Subsidies and Monopolies.**

During the reign of Elizabeth almost every session of Parliament was marked by the vote of a subsidy, with its invariable accompaniment of two fifteenths and tenths. During the first thirty-five years of her reign these sources yielded an average of £40,000 to £50,000 a year; but during the last ten years the average exceeded £120,000. These grants were made almost as a matter of course. Far otherwise was it in regard to monopolies and patents, from the sale of which the Crown derived a considerable revenue. To grant monopolies in respect of such commodities as coal, salt, leather, oil, iron, lead and yarn was to raise the cost of living to almost every householder, and the practice was, in consequence, bitterly resented. A certain Mr. Bell brought the abuse to the notice of the House of Commons in 1571, but was summoned before the council and returned to the House "with such an amazed countenance" that, according to D'Ewes, " it daunted all the rest ". In 1597, however, the Commons presented a remonstrance to the Queen, who, while claiming the prerogative as " the choicest flower in her garden and the principal and head pearl in her crown and diadem ", graciously promised to give the matter close consideration. But the scandal only increased, and on 20th November, 1601, Mr. Lawrence Hyde introduced a bill " for the explanation of the Common Law in certain cases of Letters Patent ". A long and somewhat tumultuous debate ensued. " Never," said Mr. Secretary Cecil, " did I see the House in so great confusion . . . more fit for a grammar school than a Court of Parliament." Certainly feeling ran high, and when Sir Robert Wroth recited a long list of additional monopolies granted since the last Parliament, " Mr. Hakewill of Lincoln's Inn " up and cried, " Is not bread among them? No! but if order be not taken for these bread will be there before the next Parliament."

The Queen realized the strength of the feeling, and, though not abandoning her cherished prerogative, promised that some monopolies should be immediately withdrawn, some suspended, and " none put in execution but such as should first have a trial according to the law for the good of the people ". To the thanks of the Commons conveyed by the Speaker and a large deputation, the old Queen personally replied with a graciousness and tact that won every heart: " I have more cause to thank you all than you me . . . for had I not received a knowledge from you I might have fallen into the lap of an error only for lack of true information." Never had she done anything but what she believed to be her people's good, for " above all earthly treasure I esteem my people's love . . . and never thought was cherished in my heart that tended not to my people's good ". The appeal went home; with all her defects the old Queen's first thought had ever been her people. Therein lay the secret of her success and her popularity.

One other source of revenue demands brief mention—benevolences and forced loans—taxes in all but name and incidence. Queen Elizabeth almost invariably, Henry VII invariably, repaid the loans. If Henry VIII repudiated them, he did so, characteristically, always by authority of Parliament.

Parliament, then, was the instrument of Tudor policy, and so far from betraying any jealousy of parliamentary privileges the Tudors confirmed and enlarged them.

**Privileges of Parliament.**

The privileges of the peers attach to them individually as peers: those of the House of Commons are both individual and collective. The first duty of the Speaker, after the approval of his election by the Crown, still is to make claim, on behalf of the Commons, " to all their undoubted Rights and Privileges, particularly to freedom of speech in Debate, freedom from arrest, freedom of access to His Majesty whenever occasion may require, and that the most favourable construction should be placed upon all their proceedings ". It is the invariable practice for His Majesty to " confirm them in as ample a manner as they have . . . ever been granted or confirmed by His Majesty, or any of His Majesty's Royal Predecessors ". Among those predecessors not the least conspicuous were the Tudors.

Even before the Tudors there were isolated cases of " Privilege ", as, for example, that of Thomas Haxey, whose sentence of imprisonment (1397) was quashed by Henry IV, and those of Speaker Thorpe (1453) and Thomas Yonge (1455); but in this respect the Tudor precedents were exceptionally important.

**Freedom from Arrest.**

The arrest and imprisonment of Richard Strode, member for the borough of Plympton, for putting forth certain bills to regulate the " tinners " in Devonshire led to the enactment of a statute (4 Henry VIII, c. 8) *Pro Ricardo Strode.* Strode had been fined and imprisoned by a court of special jurisdiction, the court for the Stannaries of Cornwall and Devon, and had been delivered " by a writ of privilege out of the King's Exchequer at Westminster ". The statute declared the proceedings of the Stannary Court void, and further enacted that suits, amercements, punishments, &c., " put or had, or hereafter to be put or had unto or upon the said Richard, and to every other of the person or persons afore specified that now be of this present Parliament or that of any Parliament hereafter shall be, for any bill, speaking, reasoning or declaring of any matters concerning the Parliament to be communed, treated, and be utterly void and of none effect". Unlike the cases previously cited, Strode's did not raise any issue between Crown and Parliament. It merely vindicated the authority of a superior court against an inferior court, but the resulting statute appeared to affirm, and was, in after times, held to have affirmed, a much wider and even more important principle.

Still more important was the action of the Commons in 1542 when for the first time Speaker Moyle, on their behalf, claimed as general privileges the right of freedom of speech, and, in grave matters, of access to the sovereign. The claim was admitted *maxima cum humanitate* by the King, with the stipulation that "access" should be confined to a small deputation.

**Freedom of Speech and Access.**

In the case of George Ferrers (1543) the House of Commons advanced a further claim—the right to effect the release of a member from custody by their own serjeant. The London sheriffs, despite the hasty release of Ferrers, whom they had arrested, were summoned to the Bar and committed to the Tower for contempt. Of these proceedings the King expressed his cordial approval and associated himself to the full with the rights of Parliament: "We are," he declared, "informed by our judges that we at no time stand so highly in our estate royal, as in the time of Parliament; wherein we as head, and you as members, are conjoined and knit together into one body-politick, so as whatsoever offence or injury, during that time, is offered to the meanest member of the House is to be judged as done against our person and the whole Court of Parliament." [1]

This speech, if accurately reported by Holinshed, is, like Elizabeth's speech on monopolies, admirably illustrative of the attitude of the Tudors towards Parliament. "The discussions in the English Parliament are free and un-

[1] Holinshed: *Chronicle*, I, p. 824; May: *Parliamentary Practice*, p. 120.

restricted; the Crown has no power to limit their debates or to control the votes of their members." Henry VIII had his own reasons for addressing this reminder to Pope Clement VII in 1529; but the words were not wholly ironical. The Tudor sovereigns, if in effect dictatorial, invariably exercised their power under the forms of law.

**The Executive and the Legislature.**

In their dealings with Parliament the Tudors enjoyed conspicuous advantages. One was the virtual nomination of the Speaker.

The Speaker's control of the proceedings in the "Nether House" was all but absolute. Until the development of the ministerial system he was the sole channel of communication between the House and the Crown, though it was through the Chancellor that the Crown, as a rule, addressed the Commons.

Hardly less important was the increasingly frequent presence of the members of the Privy Council—the ministers of the Crown—in Parliament. We moderns are apt to miss the significance of this. The books teach us that the presence of ministers in the English Parliament is at once the symbol and the seal of the control of the legislature over the Executive. It was not so regarded by our forefathers, and in the sixteenth century its significance was all the other way. It was, on the contrary, a powerful instrument in the hands of the Executive for influencing the legislature. Is it quite certain that even now the "books" are right? Were the fathers of the American Commonwealth altogether unwise in their generation? Is not the increasing power of the Executive in the sphere of legislation no less than in that of administration the most significant of the constitutional symptoms of to-day? Not the most autocratic of modern ministers ever ventured to re-echo the language of the Lord Keeper of 1593: "Wherefore, Mr. Speaker, Her Majesty's pleasure is, that if you perceive any idle heads, which will not stick to hazard their own estates, which will meddle with reforming the Church and transforming the Commonwealth, and do exhibit any bills to such purpose, that you receive them not until they be viewed and considered by those who it is fitter should consider of such things and can better judge of them." The better judges were, of course, the Crown and its Councillors.

**The Council.**

The position of the Council under the Tudors demands closer examination. "To his Council he did refer much and sat oft in person, knowing it to be the way to assist his power and inform his judgment." So Bacon wrote of Henry VII. The Council, which under the Lancastrians had acted as a check upon the power of the Crown, became under the Tudors the main instrument of regal government. Fortescue had shrewdly attributed the weakness of the Lancastrian Crown to the composition of the Council, which "was wont to be chosen of great princes and of the greatest lords of the land who were more intent on their own affairs than the King's". The suggestions which he made for the reorganization of the Council were, consciously or unconsciously, closely followed by the Tudors.

**Composition of the Council.**

Of whom did the Tudor Council consist? Despite much laborious research, the only safe answer is that the Council consisted of the men whom the King summoned for consultation, precisely as a modern Cabinet consists of the men whom the Prime Minister summons. One of the first acts of Henry VII (September, 1485) was to nominate a Council of only sixteen members. Among them were John Morton, who in 1486 became Archbishop of Canterbury, Chancellor in 1487, and in 1493 a cardinal; Courtenay, who was entrusted with the Privy Seal; five peers (of whom four were new creations), a second bishop, and eight other persons. Many more persons were summoned to the Council in 1486; the numbers steadily increased; and by 1501 no fewer than 41 attended. Privy Councillors took a special oath by which they were sworn, *inter alia*, to secrecy and to defend the royal prerogatives: but not all who from time to time were summoned to the Council were thus sworn.

Henry VIII by an Ordinance issued in 1526 provided, with great precision, for the establishment of a Council of 20 persons, of whom no fewer than 14 were officials. Among

**The Ministers of the Crown.**

these were included the Chancellor (Wolsey), the Lord Treasurer, the Keeper of the Privy Seal, various Household officers, the King's Secretary, and the Chancellor of the Duchy of Lancaster (Sir Thomas More). The President of the Council was not included. Though that new officer came into existence in 1497, it was not until 1539 that the office was regularly filled. In that year an Act of Parliament gave the President precedence after the Chancellor and the Treasurer and before the Privy Seal—a place he still holds. "The King's Secretary", on the other hand, appears in front of the Chancellor of the Duchy. The office of Secretary dates from the reign of Henry III, but not until the Tudors did it become of political importance. An Ordinance of 1526 and the statute of 1539 gave the Secretary a definite precedence in Parliament, which he was to attend whether he was otherwise qualified or not. If a baron or a bishop, he was to take precedence of the others of his order; if not, he was to be placed "at the uppermost part of the sacks in the midst of the said Parliament Chamber". Not until 1601 did "the beloved clerk who stays continually at our side" become Secretary of State, but to recall the names of some of the Secretaries of the sixteenth century is sufficient to prove the increasing importance of the office. Richard Fox and Thomas Ruthall (afterwards Bishop of Durham) served under Henry VII. Thomas Cromwell, the first layman to hold the office, was virtually a Prime Minister; so was Sir William Cecil (1558–73). When in 1573 Cecil was "promoted" to the office of Treasurer he found in Sir Francis Walsingham, who succeeded him as Secretary, a dangerous rival, and after the latter's death (1590) he kept the office vacant until in 1596 he secured it for his son Robert.[1]

Throughout the sixteenth century membership of the Council was mainly confined to great ministers of State and officials of the royal household, and rarely exceeded twenty.

[1] The duties of a Secretary in 1600 are precisely enumerated by (probably) Dr. John Herbert in *State Papers* (Domestic Eliz., cclxxiv, p. 118; *ap.* Prothero: *Documents*, p. 166.

**Functions of the Council.**

But if the members were few, their functions were many. By the issue of *Proclamations*, on a great variety of subjects, they exercised quasi-legislative authority, largely supplementing, and to some extent superseding, the function of Parliament. Outlying portions of the kingdom were specially subjected to the control of the Council: Jersey and Guernsey, for example, and still more notably Ireland. The Statute of Drogheda, popularly known as Poyning's Law (1494), subordinated the Irish Parliament to the English Council. No bill could be passed in Ireland until it had received the assent of the King in Council.

**Local Councils.**

Localized Councils, in subordination to, and on the model of, the Council, were set up in different parts of the country. Of these the most important were the Council of the North, the Council of Wales and the Marches, and the Council of the West. The problem of maintaining order on the Scottish border had long baffled the English Government, and it was accentuated in 1536 by the insurrection evoked by social and ecclesiastical changes, and known as the Pilgrimage of Grace. After the suppression of the rebellion Henry VIII decided to establish a permanent Council at York "for the conservation in quiet and the administration of common justice" in the counties of York, Northumberland, Westmorland and Durham, and the cities of York, Hull and Newcastle. The Council consisted of a Lord President and six other councillors, who were charged to administer justice, promptly, economically and with special consideration for poor suitors. The Council functioned most efficiently, but in 1641 it shared, at the hands of the Long Parliament,[1] the fate of the Star Chamber and other Prerogative Courts.

The Council of the Marches in Wales had existed from the time of Edward IV, if not earlier, but was reorganized by an Act of 1534. Its jurisdiction extended not only to Wales and the Marches lordships, but to the adjacent counties of Salop, Hereford, Gloucester and Worcester.[2]

[1] Cf. R. R. Reid: *The King's Council in the North* (1921).
[2] C. A. J. Skeel: *The Council in the Marches of Wales* (1904).

Like the Council of the North, and the Council of the West which was established at the same time, it made the King's government respected in districts which had too long been the scene of aristocratic turbulence and tyranny.

The work of these local Councils, like that of the Privy Council itself, was administrative as well as judicial. Popular tradition has not, however, been wholly at fault in magnifying the latter at the expense of the former function. Tudor policy was, indeed, largely designed to bring the administration of the law under the control of the Council. This was to be effected partly by setting up new courts, such as the Court of Requests—a sort of poor man's Court of Chancery; the Court of Augmentations—set up to deal with the spoils of the monasteries; various Financial Courts, and the famous Court of High Commission. More important, however, than these ancillary and special courts was the extension of the judicial functions of the Council itself, exercised in the *Star Chamber*.

**The Court of the Star Chamber.**

Had historians paid more heed to the warning of William Lambarde, a famous antiquary of the sixteenth century, whose *Archeion*, written in 1591, was published in 1635, much controversy would have been avoided. Referring to the statute of 1487 and its relation to the Court of Star Chamber, he wrote, "the which some men (but much deceived) do take to have laid the first stone of this far more ancient and stately erection (i.e. the Star Chamber Court)". "This Statute, as some have thought," he adds, "was made for the restraint of that absolute authority which beforetime was exercised by the King's Council, so as after the making thereof they were to take knowledge of these few causes only, and of none others. But I do rather expound it by way of enlargement of their judicial authority. . . ."

Lambarde was right. The Act of 1487, like many previous Acts passed under the Lancastrians, was almost certainly intended to give statutory sanction to certain common-law powers exercised by the Privy Council, and at the same time to hand over the exercise of those powers to a special committee composed only in part of Privy Councillors. But, leaving technical details aside, the important point is to realize the place of the Star Chamber Court in the dictatorial scheme of the Tudor sovereigns. Composed of three royal officials, the Chancellor, the Treasurer, and the Keeper of the Privy Seal, of one bishop, one temporal peer, and two judges, the Court was intended to supplement the obvious deficiencies of the ordinary courts, to assist in the restoration of social order, and above all to bring to justice those powerful and highly placed offenders who had long defied the King's ordinary courts. It was extraordinarily successful in attaining these objects, and won golden opinions from men of the most opposite opinions. "Si vetustatem spectemus est antiquissima," wrote Camden; "si dignitatem honoratissima." Lambarde writes almost ecstatically "of this most noble and praiseworthy Court, the beams of whose bright justice, equal in beauty with Hesperus and Lucifer, do blaze and spread themselves as far as the realm is long and wide, and by the influence of whose super-eminent authority all other Courts of law and justice that we have are both the more surely supported and the more evenly kept and managed". Sir Thomas Smith commends it as able "to bridle such stout noblemen or gentlemen which would offer wrong by force to any meaner men". "This Court," wrote Bacon, "is one of the sagest and noblest institutions of this kingdom." His eulogy you would expect; but far more remarkable is that of his great opponent, Chief Justice Coke. "It is the most honourable Court (our Parliament excepted) that is in the Christian world, both in respect of the judges of the Court, and of their honourable proceeding according to their just jurisdiction and the ancient and just orders of the Court. . . . This Court, the right institution and ancient orders thereof being observed, doth keep all England in quiet." Nor is there any reason to doubt that it was as popular with the people, particularly the poorer sort, as it was with the jurists. "The Star Chamber," writes a modern historian, "found its main difficulty in the number of suitors which flocked to a Court where the King was Judge, the laws' delays minimized, counsel's fees moderate, and justice rarely denied merely because it might happen to be illegal."[1] "Its situation," writes the most recent authority, "made it fearless: it could assert its jurisdiction over anyone: it could be set in motion by anyone: its procedure was admirably adapted for extracting the facts of a case: its special function was to do what good government required even when the law as previously expounded had not authorized it. . . . Never was there a judicial organ better suited to facilitate administration."[2]

Thus the Court of the Star Chamber and the Prerogative Courts fitted in to the general frame of the Tudor dictatorship. They were extraordinary expedients designed to meet temporary needs; and they were popular. No doubt they lopped off the heads of the exceptionally tall poppies; but those who were not poppies and did not grow too tall, had little to complain of in Tudor justice.

**Local Government.**

Closely connected with the work of the Councils was that assigned by the Tudors to local administrators. The whole system of local government was in fact reorganized during this period. Reform was urgently required. Nowhere had the Lancastrian breakdown been more conspicuous and complete than in the sphere of local government. The feudal organization, administrative and judicial, had fallen into decay in the fourteenth century, though in some parts the Courts Baron and Courts Leet still survived in the sixteenth century. Much older than the feudal Courts were the communal Courts of the shire and the hundred, remnants of which still survived in a mangled form. The sheriff, though stripped of many of his functions, still remained to preside over parliamentary elections, and with him and for the same reason the ancient Court of the shire. Thanks to the persistence of the parish priest in his contest with the feudal baron, the parish meeting also survived, although its ecclesiastical connexion had given it the name of Vestry.

[1] A. F. Pollard: *Henry VIII*, p. 26.

[2] Pickthorn: *Early Tudors*, I, 49. On the Star Chamber generally, cf. *Select Cases* (Selden Society), ed. I. S. Leadam; Tanner: *Tudor Documents*, p. 249 f.; Prothero: *Documents*, p. cii f.

But neither shire-court nor vestry had any genuine vitality. Power was passing into new hands. Of these the highest in dignity was a new official appointed to act as the chief military officer of the Crown in every county. Henry VIII issued special commissions to Lieutenants to act on particular occasions in this or that locality. Under Edward VI they were appointed in most counties in view of possible Catholic insurrections in 1550 and 1551. Under Mary (4 and 5 Phil. and Mary, c.s 2 and 3) they were authorized for every county by statute and thenceforward superseded the sheriff for all military purposes. Their duty was to levy, array and arm all the subjects of the Crown " meet and apt for the wars " in every county, to lead them against all foreign invaders and domestic rebels; to execute martial law; to appoint " deputies ", and to superintend the work of the Justices of the Peace in the " conservation of [the sovereign's] person and peace ". The Lord Lieutenant was also, as a rule, Keeper of the Records of the Peace (*Custos Rotulorum*), and in this capacity appointed the Clerk of the Peace.

**The Lord Lieutenant.**

Most of the work of local government was, however, committed by the Tudors to the Justice of the Peace. His office, as a statutory institution, dates from 1360, though *Conservatores Pacis* were appointed by proclamation as early as 1195. The Justices were and are appointed by the Chancellor. A property qualification of £20 a year was imposed under Henry VI, but might be waived in the case of " discreet persons learned in the law ".[1] Upon these officials the Tudors based their reorganization of local government. With their sure instinct for the vitalities they took the *parish* as their administrative unit, and they made the Justice of the Peace their man of all work. They thus laid the foundation of the system under which rural England was governed, and in the main admirably governed, until the last decade of the nineteenth century. Lambarde, in his *Eirenarcha*, published in 1581, with a tract (1583) on the duties of constables, gives a detailed account of the position

**Justice of the Peace.**

[1] Tanner, *op. cit.*, p. 453, who also prints the pertinent documents. Prothero (*op. cit.*, p. 154 f.) prints a Commission of Lieutenancy, of 27 Eliz.

and functions of the Justice of the Peace. Bitterly he complains that he and his brother magistrates were burdened with " stacks of statutes ". There was some justification for his groans. Henry VII passed twelve, Henry VIII no less than fifty, Edward VI nineteen, Queen Mary nineteen, and Queen Elizabeth fifty-four statutes (down to 1579 only) affecting in one way or another the functions of this overburdened official. Well might Sir Thomas Smith, also writing under Queen Elizabeth, declare that " the Justices of the Peace be those . . . in whom the Prince putteth his special trust ".

The Justice of the Peace was at once judge, policeman, and administrative man-of-all-work; he was responsible for the trial of criminals, for the maintenance of order, and for carrying into effect that huge mass of social and economic legislation which the Tudors were not slow to enact. In his own parish he sat alone and tried petty cases without a jury; four times a year he met his brother magistrates of the whole county in Quarter Sessions; later on (in 1605), an intermediate division was created in which he sat with two or more brethren in Petty Sessions. But his special significance in relation to the Tudor dictatorship consists in the multitude of administrative duties which he was expected to perform. He had to fix the rate of wages for servants and labourers; to bind apprentices and cancel indentures; to fix the prices of commodities; to appoint and dismiss constables; to see to the maintenance of gaols and bridges and highways; to supervise the payment of pensions to maimed soldiers and sailors; to determine all questions of settlement and affiliation; to search out recusants and enforce the law against them, and to see that Sunday was properly observed. He was the sole sanitary authority, the sole licensing authority (for all trades except monopolies), and the chief poor law and vagrancy authority. Such were some of the many duties under which Lambarde groaned. And no shirking was possible; for at every assize the Clerk of the Peace had to hand in a certificate giving the names of all justices absent from Quarter Sessions since the last assize, and the judge had to examine into the cause of absence, and report thereon to the Lord Chancellor.

There can, however, be no question that on the whole the work was admirably done, and that social order was gradually evolved out of the welter and chaos to which the Tudors had succeeded. The work of the Justices of the Peace was good for the country, and it was good for the Justices. Nothing could be more striking than the contrast between the turbulent neo-feudal barons of the fifteenth century—the Nevilles, the Percies, and the rest—and the legally-minded squires of the seventeenth century—the Pyms, Eliots, and Hampdens. The explanation of that contrast must be sought, and will be found, in the discipline and training of the Tudor J.P. " Nothing," writes Dr. Prothero, " could so well have prepared the country gentry and the burgesses of the great towns for the share they were to take in the Parliaments of the coming age."

The education was not, however, confined to squires and burgesses; it extended to all classes. The people at large were taught, as a great lawyer of our own day has pointed out, " to govern themselves, from the humbler classes who were obliged to serve as constables, surveyors, overseers or churchwardens, to the higher classes who were obliged to serve as lord lieutenants, sheriffs or justices ".[1]

**Results of Tudor Dictatorship.**

Self-government, then, was the ultimate result, if not the immediate purpose, of the Tudor dictatorship. The process was disciplinary; and the nation emerged from the discipline braced, stimulated and invigorated, ready to embark upon the contest with the luckless sovereigns who inherited the Tudor throne, but not the prerogatives of the Tudor monarchs.

Of those prerogatives not the least important were those which belonged to the Crown as " supreme governor of this realm . . . as well in all spiritual or ecclesiastical things or causes as temporal ".

With the royal supremacy and all things pertaining to it the next chapter will deal.

[1] Sir W. S. Holdsworth: *A History of English Law*, iv, 165.

## CHAPTER XIII

# The Crown and the Reformation

THE Established Church is, in Anson's phrase, " built into the fabric of the State ": the King is " for all constitutional purposes the head of a National Church ".[1]

Ever since England was converted to Christianity the Church has been a national institution; " national in its comprehensiveness as well as in its exclusiveness ". Its national character was emphasized by the legislation of the sixteenth century, but that legislation was in large measure declaratory and conservative, not revolutionary. Thus the *Act in Restraint of Appeals* (1533) declared " that this realm of England is an empire, and so hath been accepted in the world governed by one Supreme Head and King . . . without the intermeddling of any exterior person or persons ". The *Act of Appeals*, then, asserted the historic independence of the realm as against any external authority, that of Popes no less than that of Emperors. The Act also provided that no appeals were to be carried beyond the Archbishops of Canterbury and York. The *Act of Supremacy* (1534) was similarly declaratory and corroborative. It declared that " the King our Sovereign Lord, his heirs and successors, shall be taken, accepted and reported the only Supreme Head in earth of the Church of England, called *Ecclesia Anglicana* ", and that he had " authority to reform and redress all errors, heresies and abuses in the same ".

**The Reformation Parliament (1529–36).**

These were the crucial Acts of the Reformation as effected under Henry VIII. But hardly less important was the *Act in Restraint of the Payment of Annates* (1534),

[1] *Law and Custom of the Constitution*: The Crown, Vol. II, p. 254.

ECCLESIASTICAL ENGLAND BEFORE HENRY VIII

which not only forbade the payment of annates, first-fruits, &c., to Rome, but provided for the appointment of bishops and other high dignitaries of the Church by the Crown. Under the *Congé d'élire* the right of electing bishops was and is nominally vested in the Chapter, but the Chapter is obliged, under the mysterious " dangers, pains and penalties " of the statutes of *Provisors* (1351) and *Praemunire* (1393), to elect the Crown's nominee. By the *Act for the Submission of the Clergy* (1534) Convocation was completely subordinated to the Crown. Only by the authority of the Crown could the Convocations meet or enact canons, nor could any canons made therein bind the laity without the royal assent in Parliament. Moreover, appeals from the archbishops' courts were to go to the Crown in Chancery. So the law remained until in 1832 ecclesiastical appeals were transferred from the Crown in Chancery to the Crown in Council. A year later the Judicial Committee of the Privy Council was set up for this and other purposes.

**Dissolution of the Monastaries.**

The *Acts for the Dissolution of the Monasteries* (1536 and 1539), apart from social and economic results of the highest importance, reacted in two ways upon the Constitution. The House of Lords now became an almost exclusively hereditary body and predominantly and increasingly a secular body. Six new bishoprics were indeed founded and endowed out of monastic properties, but of these one (the bishopric of Westminster), was abolished by Edward VI. Henceforward, the spiritual peers in the House of Lords numbered only 26, save during the period from 1800 to 1869, when they were reinforced by four bishops representing the Established Church in Ireland.

The new bishoprics absorbed only a very small proportion of the confiscated land of the abbeys; far the largest portion went to the endowment of a new nobility and squirearchy. The " new men " gave staunch support to the Crown under the Tudors. Under the early Stuarts, however, they asserted their political independence, and supplied some of the most conspicuous leaders to the parliamentary opposition.

The general effect of Henry VIII's policy was to subordinate the Church completely to the Crown. In matters of doctrine, however, there was little change. The Bible was, indeed, translated into English, and in 1538 a copy of the authorized version was ordered to be kept in every parish church. The " Ten Articles " published in 1536 showed a marked movement towards Protestant doctrine, but Henry was quick to perceive that the movement commanded little popular support. To repudiate allegiance to the Papacy, to stop the drain of English treasure to Rome, was one thing: it was quite another to tamper with the Catholic ritual, to which for centuries English folk had been accustomed, and with the doctrine of the Catholic Church. In the Ten Articles Cranmer had evidently gone too far, and the *Act of Six Articles* (1539) practically reaffirmed in their entirety the old doctrines of the Catholic faith. Moreover, there was to be no " diversity in opinions ", and though the penalties for heresy were mitigated, heresy became " a secular offence ".

**Catholicism without the Pope.**

So matters stood when Henry VIII died: England was to be " Catholic without the Pope ". The reigns of Edward VI and Mary proved the difficulty of maintaining that position. Under Edward VI things began to move, gradually under Protector Somerset, precipitately under Northumberland, in a Protestant direction. The rights of the Crown as " Head " of the Church were exercised by both Protectors even more drastically than by Henry VIII. Under the authority of a statute (1 Edw. VI, c. 2) bishops were appointed directly by the Crown by letters patent without any pretence of capitular election. The bishops were required by order of the Council to take out new licences for the exercise of their ecclesiastical jurisdiction, and the writs of the ecclesiastical Court were henceforth to run in the King's name. A book of homilies, composed by Cranmer, was authorized, and injunctions were sent out (1547). The injunctions ordered the clergy to " take away, utterly extinct and destroy ", all images and to discontinue pilgrimages and other customs tending to superstition. They

**Violent Oscillations.**

also enjoined further use of the vulgar tongue in Church services. The marriage of the clergy was legalized; the property of the chantries was vested in the Crown, and a new communion office was authorized. The First Act of Uniformity (1549) ordered the use of a new Prayer Book, which, though simplifying the Liturgy and enjoining the use of English throughout all services, did not, doctrinally, register a complete breach with Catholic tradition. The Second Prayer Book ordered by the Second Act of Uniformity (1552) was, on the contrary, frankly Protestant, not to say Calvinistic, in doctrine, though the episcopal government of the Church was retained. A year later the Forty-Two Articles were issued on the authority of the Council.

Thus was the Church, a Protestant Church, completely subordinated in its government and ordinances to the State. How little the Protestant policy was liked by the nation was shown by the insurrections under Edward VI, and still more by the unanimity of the welcome accorded on his death to the daughter of Catherine of Aragon. But Queen Mary was not merely, like her subjects, a fervent Catholic, but, unlike them, a fanatical Papist. The whole of the Edwardian legislation was repealed by Parliament before the end of 1553. Cardinal Pole arrived in 1554 as a special legate from the Pope, and the English people received absolution at his hands. In 1554–5 all the anti-papal legislation passed since 1529 was repealed, and the laws against heresy were revived. Parliament, however, insisted that the restoration of Roman obedience should be accompanied by a confirmation of the titles of the existing proprietors to the monastic lands.

After the death of Bishop Gardiner in November, 1555, the Queen gave full rein to her lust for the blood of heretics. The victims numbered, in fact, less than 300, but the persecutions sufficed to give a considerable impulse to Protestantism. The Queen's Spanish marriage, and the continental complications in which the country was thereby involved, gave an impulse even more decided to the growing sense of nationalism.

**The Elizabethan Settlement**

Queen Elizabeth represented both sentiments. Personally she was a *politique* rather than a Protestant; but the Pope had pronounced her illegitimate; he was presently to declare her excommunicate and to release her subjects from their allegiance to a heretic queen. Moreover, the situation on the Continent and in Scotland forced upon Elizabeth the championship of Protestantism. But she went no further in that direction than she was obliged to. The "Elizabethan Settlement", as embodied in the Acts of Supremacy (1559) and Uniformity (1559), in the revised Prayer Book, and the Thirty-Nine Articles drafted by Convocation in 1562 and approved by Parliament in 1571, was admittedly a compromise. Under the *Act of Supremacy* the title of "Supreme Head of the Church" was, out of deference to the Catholics, dropped, and for it was substituted "Supreme Governor of this Realm . . . as well in all spiritual or ecclesiastical things or causes as temporal". All ecclesiastical jurisdiction was annexed to the Crown, which was to have the right of visiting and reforming the Church; no foreign potentate was to exercise authority in this realm, and all office-holders, on pain of loss of office, were to take the oath of supremacy. The *Act of Uniformity* enjoined the exclusive use of the new Prayer Book, which, when subsequently issued, proved to be a compromise between, or rather a combination of, the "Catholic" and the "Protestant" Prayer Books of Edward VI. The emphasis on, and interpretation of, the more controversial parts was left to the individual worshipper; as much as possible of the old Liturgy was retained; but the services were to be in English. As for doctrine, the people could take their choice between Trent and Geneva; so long as they went regularly to Church they could believe what they chose. The Church was to be ruled by bishops, but the bishops were to be subject to the Crown.

Such was the Elizabethan compromise. It did not satisfy either the zealous Catholic or the convinced Calvinist. But the great mass of the nation were for the moment reasonably content. Not, however, permanently. No one who looked at all below the surface could doubt that the deeper issues would have to be faced and fought out.

Those issues were at once ecclesiastical and constitutional. Protestantism expressed itself not less clearly in the reviving independence of Parliament than in a demand for changes in the ritual, the doctrine, and the government of the Church. Under Henry VIII, as under his father, Parliament had done little more than register the King's will. Under the last three Tudors it was otherwise. The action taken by the Crown to secure the election of members well disposed towards the policy of the Government was in itself evidence that Parliament had a will of its own.

**Crown and Parliament**

The first Parliament of Edward VI showed its independence by abolishing all the new treasons and felonies created under Henry VIII and repealing the statute which had given to Royal Proclamations the force of law. It is true that in 1552, after the fall of Somerset, there was a reversion to the treason laws of Henry VIII, but Parliament rejected the more drastic proposals of the Government and inserted in the new statute a provision of the highest importance to the liberty of the subject. Henceforward, no person was to be convicted of treason except on the testimony of two lawful witnesses, who were to be confronted with the accused in open court. Under Mary, Parliament, though acquiescing in the restoration of Roman Catholic obedience, doctrine and ritual, refused to restore ecclesiastical property. Under Elizabeth it accepted the compromise embodied in the statutes enumerated above. The Marian and Elizabethan Parliaments were, we may surmise, equally representative of the prevailing temper of the country.

As Elizabeth's reign went on, Parliament showed, notably after 1570, steadily increasing independence. That an actual breach with the Crown was avoided was due partly to the wisdom of the Queen, partly to a recognition by Parliament of the extreme gravity of the situation, domestic and international.

Elizabeth was by nature at least as autocratic as any other member of her family. But she had remarkable tact; she had learnt self-control in a hard school, and she was a true patriot. Her heart was given to Lord Robert Dudley, but not her hand; and her head taught her that to marry him would be the act of a political adulteress: she had pledged her troth to England. No other husband would she take. It may well be that her self-renunciation preserved the integrity and independence of her country.

In order to estimate the debt the nation owed to the Virgin Queen it needs only to compare the situation on her accession with that towards the close of the reign. In 1558 it was unspeakably grave. The Queen's accession was in itself a defiance of Papal authority, at a moment when the Papacy had regained much of its prestige and power, and the Counter-Reformation was at full tide. The Pope had declared the Princess Elizabeth illegitimate, and was presently to pronounce her excommunicate, and to release her subjects from their allegiance. Parliament retorted (1571) by enacting severe laws against Roman Catholics, by declaring the introduction of Papal Bulls high treason, and by proposing an attainder (estopped by the queen) against Mary, Queen of Scots.

**Mary, Queen of Scots.**

For nearly thirty years Mary Stuart was a thorn, periodically threatening a septic wound, in Elizabeth's side. Mary Stuart's position was dynastically very strong. Queen of Scotland, she was also Dauphiness, and for a short time (1559–60) Queen, of France. In the eyes of many Englishmen she was also, by right of birth, Queen of England, and by all was regarded as heiress-presumptive to the throne. Consequently, until Mary's death, the danger to the life and throne of Elizabeth was always real if latent and was periodically acute. Yet in one sense Mary was a shield to Elizabeth. So long as she lived Philip of Spain, despite all the provocations offered to him by the Elizabethan sea-dogs and by the apparent vacillations of Elizabeth's continental policy, would not strike his blow at England. Never would he have dethroned Elizabeth to crown in her stead Mary Stuart, and so give to France the hegemony of Europe. After Mary's death he could strike without the apprehension that his success would redound to the advan-

**England and Spain.**

tage of his rivals. In 1588 he struck: the great Armada came; but English seamen knew their job; the fire-ships struck terror into the heart of the Spaniards; the winds of Heaven blew; the Armada was scattered.

The defeat of the Armada closed an epoch; the great dangers that had threatened England were dispersed; the need for the Tudor dictatorship had ceased.

But the sequel will make it clear that, in order to avoid the risk of a real conflict with the Crown, Parliament deliberately deferred the assertion of its rights. Towards such a conflict matters had, nevertheless, been tending ever since the beginning of the reign.

**The Succession.**

Hardly was Elizabeth seated on the throne when Parliament raised the question of the succession. To a petition that she would marry, the Queen had replied (1559) that she wanted nothing but her people's love and had already given herself in marriage to them. The matter seemed more pressing when in the autumn of 1562 the Queen fell ill of the smallpox and lay for some days at the point of death. Accordingly, in 1563 both Houses petitioned the Queen to marry or at least to name her successor. But again she evaded the question. The birth of an heir to Mary Stuart rendered the matter still more urgent, and in the Parliament of 1566 a hot debate arose. The Queen, deeply offended, ordered that "they should no further proceed in their suit, but to satisfy themselves with her promise to marry". Paul Wentworth, thereupon, raised the question of privilege, desiring to be informed whether "the Queen's commandment was not against the liberties". The Queen, however, peremptorily commanded that "there should not be further talk of that matter". The Commons insisted, and before the session ended the Queen, to the joy and gratitude of Parliament, "did revoke her two former commandments". But though liberty of speech was vindicated, the question of the succession was still undetermined, and in 1571 the Commons were warned that "they should do well to meddle with no matters of State but such as should be propounded unto them, and to occupy themselves with other matters concerning the Commonwealth ".

**Puritanism in Parliament.**

With other matters they did occupy themselves, and in particular with a new factor which after 1570 entered into the problem. The country was beginning to move definitely in a Protestant direction; a Puritan party, discontented with the compromise of 1559, and bent upon a religious, as opposed to a political Reformation, appeared in Parliament. In 1571 Mr. Strickland, " a grave and ancient man of great ziel ", introduced a bill for the revision of the Prayer Book. Summoned before the Council, he was ordered not to appear again in his place in Parliament. The Commons resented the order as a breach of their privileges: Strickland resumed his place; but Parliament was rebuked by the Queen for its " audacious, arrogant and presumptuous folly . . . in meddling with matters neither pertaining to them nor within the capacity of their understanding ". In 1572 the Speaker reported the Queen's pleasure that " henceforth no bills concerning religion shall be received into the House unless the same be first considered and liked by the clergy ".

**The Court of High Commission.**

The Queen had become seriously alarmed by the growth of Puritanism; the " favourers thereof " she was determined to " root out ". Accordingly, Archbishop Parker had been instructed in 1565 to issue a series of directions for the ordering of public worship. A large number of clergy resigned in protest against *Parker's Advertisements*; laymen began to assemble for common worship in " conventicles "; and Grindal, who in 1576 succeeded Parker as archbishop, was shortly afterwards sequestered from his see for refusing to suppress the Puritan " prophesyings ". There was an instrument ready to his hand had he chosen to use it. By the *Act of Supremacy* the Queen was empowered to nominate commissions, and give them authority to " correct and amend all errors, abuses and offences " which by any manner of spiritual or ecclesiastical power may lawfully be amended or corrected ".

Between 1559 and 1601 a series of commissions were issued, the result of which was to set up a group of courts which collectively formed the famous Court of High Commission. The commissioners had wide powers: they could compel attendance on mere suspicion; examine the suspect and witnesses on oath; punish by fine or imprisonment all who offended against the Acts of Supremacy and Uniformity; and, in particular, administer to all ecclesiastics (and afterwards to laymen) the oath of supremacy.

The High Commission Court became increasingly unpopular, and in 1584 Lord Burghley was moved to protest to Whitgift (who in 1583 had become archbishop) against his proceedings "so vehement and so general against ministers and preachers. The inquisitors of Spain," added Burghley, "use not so many questions to comprehend and trap their preys."

**The Parliamentary Opposition.**

Burghley undoubtedly represented the prevailing temper of Parliament, where the questions of Puritanism and parliamentary privilege were becoming inextricably interwoven. The conjunction of religious and political independence gradually led to the formation of an "Opposition" which from 1570 became increasingly articulate. Thus in 1576 Peter Wentworth, brother of Paul and member for Tregony, made a vehement attack upon the Queen for her attempts to limit liberty of speech—particularly on religious questions—in Parliament. Alarmed by his outspokenness, the House committed Wentworth to the Tower, whence he was released, a month later, at the instance of the Queen herself. Wentworth, wholly undismayed, returned to the charge, and in 1577 asserted the right of the House "freely and without controlment of any person, or danger of laws . . . to utter any of the griefs of this Commonwealth whatsoever, touching the service of God, the safety of the prince, and this noble realm".

**The Ecclesiastical Position.**

On the question of privilege the Wentworths enjoyed much support, but in the sphere of religion things were moving towards Puritanism faster than Parliament approved. To the severities of the "Anglican Inquisition" Parliament was as strongly opposed as Burghley, and in 1584 the Commons went so far towards Presbyterianism as to petition that in the rite of ordination a certain number of inferior clergy should be associated with the bishops. But alarmed by the " Marprelate " libels (1588) and other manifestations of hostility to episcopacy, Parliament passed an Act (1593) against " seditious sectaires and disloyal persons " and authorizing the penalty of imprisonment, banishment, and even death, against frequenters of conventicles and other persistent assailants of ecclesiastical supremacy.

This legislation, combined with Whitgift's firm administration, had considerable effect: the last years of Elizabeth's reign were less disturbed by religious differences. But the ecclesiastical problem, like the constitutional problem, was merely postponed, to reappear in a more acute form under the Stuarts.

**Tudors and Stuarts.**

On the part of responsible persons the postponement was plainly intentional. In the *Apology* of 1604 James I was bluntly informed to that effect: " In regard to her [Queen Elizabeth's] sex and age which we had great cause to tender . . . *those actions were then passed over* which we hoped in succeeding time of freer access to Your Highness . . . to restore, redress and rectify." Precisely. Queen Elizabeth was an old lady: by sleepless vigilance, with consummate tact, with superb self-control and self-abnegation, she had brought her country safely through great perils. She deserved consideration; and Parliament was determined that, so far as possible, she should receive it. No body of men could fail to be touched by the grace with which the autocratic old lady withdrew, as in the matter of monopolies, from an untenable position, and conceded claims she could no longer resist.

But the postponement of curative treatment only rendered the subsequent operation more severe. The Stuarts were the victims of Tudor popularity; the success of the Tudor dictatorship made its prolongation unnecessary; exceptional powers readily conceded to sovereigns who, whatever their faults and failings, were ardent nationalists, were inevitably denied to Kings who came to the throne as foreigners.

## CHAPTER XIV

# The Stuart Monarchy
# Crown v. Parliament

IN the history of the English monarchy the seventeenth century was, in the strict sense, critical. The Tudor sovereigns, like their predecessors, were the rulers of England: the monarchy to which James I succeeded was a Personal monarchy. All the successors of Queen Anne have, on the contrary, been "constitutional" sovereigns. They have reigned but not ruled. The issue between the two types of monarchy was fought out between 1603 and 1714. It was decided by the death on the scaffold of Charles I and by the "abdication" of James II. The decision was clenched by the success of the Whig *coup d'état* in 1714 and by the failure of the Tories in the '15 and the '45. Time was naturally needed to work out all the implications of "Responsible Government"; but from the days of George I and Sir Robert Walpole the principle was established. Although English sovereigns have never become mere cyphers, the seat of power, ever since a Prime Minister began to emerge, has been transferred from the palace, which still and properly remains the scene of all the splendid ritual of State, to the unpretentious tenements in Downing Street.

**King and Premier.**

From the day when the Stuarts came to England their position was difficult. Nor did their personal qualities make it easier. Their high pretensions combined with unsuccessful practice to produce disaster. The Tudors, in true English fashion, had been content with the substance of power and avoided definition. The Stuarts, obstinate in adherence to theory, were compelled to sacrifice the substance. The Tudor dictatorship was accepted as a fact. James I, with all the obstinacy of a Scot and with all the national aptitude for metaphysics, not only maintained the philosophy of absolutism, but claimed that his southern subjects should acknowledge its validity. The rejection of that claim meant revolution.

**Crown and Parliament (1603–29).**

The conflict has often been represented as one between the Crown and Parliament. But Parliament had no desire to abolish the monarchy; even the Stuart kings had no designs against the existence of Parliament. Like Oliver Cromwell himself, however, they wished to keep Parliament in its " proper place ".

What was its " proper place "? That Parliament should, with the assent of the King, make laws; that its consent was necessary to taxation; that it should keep the Crown informed on the state of public feeling—all this was acknowledged by both parties. But who was to control the executive government? That was the core of the contest. Hitherto executive power had been indisputably vested in the Crown. The monarch ruled. He had his counsellors; but they were responsible to him alone. With him lay the real and final decision. Preceding chapters have shown that periodically the magnates had attempted to control the Crown by means of a Council appointed by themselves, and occasionally Parliament had attacked and even displaced the King's confidential advisers. But ministers were the servants of the King, not of Parliament.

**The Economic Revolution.**

From the moment that the Stuarts came to the throne they were confronted by demands on the part of Parliament that were new, if not revolutionary. It was not only the specific demands that were new; the whole temper of Parliament was different from anything that England had known before. The difference was due partly to Tudor discipline and to political causes already noted, but Parliament would never have won its battle against the Crown but for the economic revolution of the sixteenth century. At the accession of Henry VII the House of Lords contained 77 members. Of these 48 were spiritual peers, and of the spiritual peers only 21 were bishops. By 1603 the total membership had increased to 107, of whom only 26 were spiritual peers—and these were all prelates. But the dissolution of the monastic foundations had done more than diminish the spiritual peerage and almost double the number of lay peers: it contributed not a little to that spirit of independence which, under the Stuarts, manifested itself in the House of Commons. As of old the Lower House was composed of squires, merchants and lawyers. But these classes occupied a new place in the body politic, and were emboldened by a great access of wealth to speak with a new voice in Parliament. Squires and merchants had alike grown rich on wool. Sheep-breeding necessitated enclosures; arable fields, open and unfenced, were laid down to grass; capitalist farming superseded subsistence farming; men were displaced to make room for sheep. This agrarian revolution was already in progress before the assault upon the abbeys, but the substitution of keen business men for monks as landlords gave to the revolution a powerful impulse. Many contemporaries, especially those who could make their voices heard from pulpits, bewailed the change. "O what a lamentable thing it is to consider that there are not at this day ten plows whereas were wont to be forty or fifty." Such was the text of Bishop Scory's sermon addressed to Edward VI. "Where there were once a great many householders and inhabitants," complained Bishop Latimer, "there is now but a shepherd and his dog."

We must not look to the pulpit for far-sighted views on Economics: but it affords evidence on the state of popular feeling. The gain to English commerce ultimately balanced the loss inflicted upon the peasants. But the present sufferings of individual contemporaries are imperfectly compensated by the future prosperity accruing to the community. As to the political significance of the economic change, there is, however, no ambiguity. The new temper of the House of Commons was unmistakable, and was manifested in the remarkable *Apology* drafted by the House in June, 1604.

The *Apology*.

The *Apology* expressed their " grief and anguish of mind " at realizing that the King had been " greatly wronged by misinformation " about the " estate " of his English subjects and the privileges of the House of Commons to the " extreme prejudice " of both. They bluntly reminded James that they had postponed an assertion of their rights in the latter days of the late Queen mainly in order " to avoid all trouble which by wicked practice might have been drawn to impeach the fact of Your Majesty's right in the succession ". Having delivered this shrewd thrust, the Commons proceeded to set forth certain facts on which the King had been misinformed. The privileges of the Commons were not of " grace " but of " right "; the members were not " Puritans or Brownists ", though they were anxious to " reform certain abuses crept into the ecclesiastical state even as into the temporal ". Mr. Gardiner insists that " to understand this Apology is to understand the success of the English Revolution ". Quite justly. But it is difficult to concede his claim that the address was " conservative and monarchical to the core ".

Upon the institution of monarchy there was, indeed, no attack; but it is idle to suggest that Parliament did not seize the opportunity of the accession of a new dynasty to register a further stage in the process by which sovereignty was to be gradually transferred from a Personal ruler to the King-in-Parliament.

The Theory of Absolutism.

Had the moment arrived for that transference? According as that question is answered must we condemn or approve the " Puritan Revolution ". The point at issue was the location of sovereignty. James I was bent not only on exercising absolute power, but on obtaining assent to the Theory of Absolutism. In 1598 he had published anonymously his *True Law of Free Monarchies*, claiming that " although a good King will frame all his actions to be according to the law, yet is he not bound thereto but of his good will, and for good example—giving to his subjects ". This theory he insisted on expounding in 1616 to the English Privy Council:

" As for the absolute prerogative of the Crown, that is no

subject for the tongue of a lawyer, nor is it lawful to be disputed. It is atheism and blasphemy to dispute what God can do; good Christians content themselves with His will revealed in His Word, so it is presumptious and high contempt in a subject to dispute what a King can do, or say that a King cannot do this or that, but rest in that which is the King's will revealed in his law."

Such doctrines sounded strangely in the ears of statesmen and lawyers trained in the traditions of Bracton, Fortescue and Hooker. But had James been content with the composition of philosophical treatises and the delivery of philosophical homilies, all might have been well. Unfortunately, he was determined to translate philosophy into politics; and that determination was at the root of all the disputes between Crown and Parliament.

These disputes covered the whole field: finance, legislation, ecclesiastical policy, foreign policy—all these questions raised the same fundamental issue.

**Finance**

Finance came first. The right of Parliament to control taxation was unquestioned. But custom duties? Did it not lie within the function of the Executive to regulate external commerce? What were custom duties but licences to trade? The legal point was raised in the case of a certain Levant merchant, Bates, who refused to pay the new custom duties on currants. The Court of Exchequer decided in favour of the Crown, and even Sir Edward Coke admitted that in law the decision was right. Similar in principle was the much later and still more famous case of ship-money. Was not the Executive responsible for the defence of the realm? The charge of providing ships was an ancient obligation—at least upon certain counties. Were not all counties equally concerned in national defence? John Hampden refused to pay the small sum in which he was assessed. Again the judges decided, though with characteristic caution, in favour of the Crown. Must the judges, therefore, be condemned as "subservient"? Notoriously, Charles I levied ship-money in order to avoid the necessity of summoning Parliament and getting from it the needed supplies. But that does not prove that in law the judges were wrong.

The truth is that law and politics were in conflict. Evidently between the prerogative of the Crown and the rights of Parliament there lay a large tract of debatable ground. Tactful kings would, under the circumstances of the hour, have kept clear of it. The early Stuarts, as anxious to establish a theory as to obtain a revenue, rushed on to it, only, in the end, to provoke the Long Parliament to erect statutory barriers against their intrusion.

**Currency Depreciation.**

But there was more to these disputes on finance than political theory. In many respects the Stuarts had cruel luck, and in none more conspicuously than in this matter of finance. Behind financial disputes there lay an economic fact, too little emphasized by historians, but of immense significance. Much less would have been heard about impositions and ship-money, but for the recent exploitation of the mines of Central and Southern America. Europe was flooded with silver, and inflation was the inevitable result. Even if James I had been as thrifty as Henry VII, he could not have kept up the government on the revenue that sufficed for that monarch. To the trouble of depreciation Henry VIII added the evil device of debasement. Elizabeth restored the purity of the coinage, though she minted one pound of silver into sixty instead of twenty shillings. And even that careful Queen, with all her parsimony, had been compelled by the rise of prices incident to inflation to sell Crown lands to the value of £327,000 and also to incur a debt of £400,000. James's necessity was Parliament's opportunity. No economy on the part of the Crown—and James was, in fact, hopelessly extravagant—could have avoided recourse to Parliament, and Parliament would vote money only on terms.

**Legislation.**

As in finance, so in ordinary legislation there was an area of debatable ground. Legislation proper belonged to the King-in-Parliament; but the Crown had never abandoned the right to supplement parliamentary Statutes by Ordinances or Proclamations. The Tudors issued Proclamations freely, but within constitutional limits. James I ignored the limits, and in 1610 the House of Commons demanded "justice and due redress" in this matter. The dispute was referred to the judges, who gave an opinion that "the King hath no prerogative but that which the law of the land allows him. But the King may by Proclamation admonish his subjects that they keep the laws." In practice, however, the abuse was not stopped until the Long Parliament abolished the extraordinary tribunals by which Royal Proclamations were enforced.

**Religion.**

Crown and Parliament were at loggerheads also on ecclesiastical matters. James I, though brought up as a Presbyterian, was quick to perceive that Episcopacy accorded much better than Calvinism with his political theory. "Presbyterianism agreeth as well with monarchy as God and the devil. Let that government be once up we shall all of us have work enough, both our hands full." So James declared at the Hampton Court Conference (1604). "No bishop, no king" was his final word to the Conference. The alliance was struck. The fortunes of the Stuart dynasty and the Anglican Church were henceforward inextricably intermingled.

In Parliament, on the other hand, Puritanism was predominant. Not that, at this stage, Parliament desired to see Presbyterianism established. It was James's fatal, if very natural, blunder to confound Presbyterianism with Puritanism. All Presbyterians were indeed Puritans, but not all Puritans were Presbyterians. Some favoured "moderate" Episcopacy; some were opposed equally to Canterbury and Geneva. "New Presbyter is but old Priest writ large." Milton crystallized into an epigram the objection of the Independents to any unified system of Church government.

The compromise embodied in the Elizabethan settlement was probably acceptable to, and was certainly accepted by, the great mass of the English people, but it could not satisfy religious zealots on either side, Roman Catholics, or non-episcopalian Puritans. But none of the religious parties ever entertained the idea of toleration. *Cujus regio ejus religio*. The religion of the sovereign must determine the religion of his subjects. Each party, then, was aiming at ascendancy and exclusiveness. So long as it was a minority and in opposition it demanded toleration: but the history of New England is a standing illustration of the difference between Puritans in opposition and Puritans in power. The Roger Williamses and Mrs. Hutchinsons got short shrift from the Puritans in New England. Under Puritan rule in old England there was to be toleration for all Christians—except Papists and Prelatists—an exception which probably represented the majority of Englishmen.

But this is to anticipate. The first two Stuarts remained steadfast in their alliance with Anglicanism, or Arminianism as it was then called.

**Foreign Policy.**

Divergent views on foreign policy reflected and accentuated religious differences. On foreign affairs Parliament was less well informed than the King. James knew that since the time of the Armada a great change had taken place in the European situation. Spain was no longer likely to dominate Europe; Henry IV, king of both Catholics and Protestants in France, was all in favour of equilibrium; the Northern Netherlands were on the way to the establishment of their own independence, but were soon to realize that they could not conquer the Southern Netherlands, known to us as Belgium. In 1609 they concluded a truce with Spain. James I had anticipated their action. With Cecil's help he negotiated in 1604 a peace with Spain, which secured to England everything she could have hoped to obtain by war. England reserved her right to trade with Spanish America, to carry Dutch goods in her neutral bottoms, and even to permit her nationals to volunteer for service on behalf of the Netherlands against Spain. Thenceforward, alliance with Spain was the keynote of James's foreign policy. *Beati Pacifici* was his text, and he sincerely believed that the peace of Europe would be most effectually guaranteed by an alliance between Catholic Spain and Protestant England.

***Beati Pacifici.***

To the achievement of that laudable purpose Sir Walter

Raleigh was cruelly sacrificed. After thirteen years' imprisonment that great Elizabethan was suddenly released, and sent out, under a promise to avoid fighting, to explore Spanish Guiana for gold. The Spaniards barred his way and inflicted heavy losses on his men. Raleigh got no gold; he lost his son; and returned home to pay the penalty of failure. Gondomar, the Spanish ambassador, demanded his head, and James did not refuse it. The friendship of Spain was worth more than a brave Englishman's life. For the next six years (1618–24) James was intent on obtaining the hand of the Spanish Infanta for his heir, Prince Charles.

**The Spanish Marriage Project.**

To the vast majority of Englishmen the idea of the Spanish marriage was odious on political and still more on religious grounds. The outbreak in 1618 of the Thirty Years' War accentuated their feelings. The occasion, though not the cause, of that war was the acceptance of the Crown of Bohemia by James's son-in-law, Frederick the Elector Palatine. The Elector's folly brought the Austrian Hapsburgs down upon Bohemia, and the Spanish Hapsburgs into the Palatinate. James very properly refused to support the Elector's claims in Bohemia, out of which he was driven by Tilly (1620). The Palatinate was a different matter. James had no wish to see his daughter's throne lost to her, but his hope of saving it by his alliance with Spain was inevitably destined to disappointment.

**Impeachment of Bacon (1621).**

His subjects, on the other hand, were eager for war on behalf of the Protestant cause—more particularly for a naval war against Spain. Apart from his genuine desire for peace, the King had neither ships nor money wherewith to wage war. Accordingly in 1621 he summoned his third Parliament. Seven years had elapsed since the dissolution of the "Addled Parliament" (1614), and the Parliament of 1621 was in no amiable mood. Having voted two subsidies to the King, it turned impatiently to the redress of accumulating grievances. Two of the most prominent monopolists, Sir Giles Mompesson and Sir Francis Mitchell, were successfully impeached and punished, and other impeachments, mainly for judicial corruption, followed. Among those accused of this high crime was Lord Chancellor Bacon. Bacon admitted that he was " frail and partook of the abuses of the time ", but he was the victim not the inventor of a bad system: never had he taken " rewards to pervert justice ". But, conducted with consummate ability by Bacon's old enemy and rival Coke, the prosecution prevailed: Bacon was disgraced and sentenced. The fallen Chancellor acknowledged " the sentence just and for reformation fit: nevertheless, he had been the justest Chancellor since his father's death ". The sentence, though severe, was not vindictively executed. The fine of £40,000 was made over by the King to trustees to be administered for Bacon's benefit: his imprisonment lasted only a few days; but his disgrace was final, and five years later he was released from ignominy by death.

Meanwhile, the Commons, further irritated by a prosecution launched against Coke, proceeded, on Coke's motion, to petition the King against the growth of Popery and the Spanish match. They prayed the King to marry his heir to a Protestant princess and make war against Spain. James angrily bade the House not to " meddle with mysteries of State ". The Commons asserted their claim to freedom of speech, " the same being our undoubted right and an inheritance received from our ancestors ". The King retorted with a lecture on the incompetence of Parliament to handle high matters of State; *ne sutor supra crepidam*; so long as they " contained themselves within the limits of their duty " he would be as careful of their liberties as of his own prerogative, but let them remember that their liberties were not as of right but were " derived from the grace and permission of our ancestors and us ". In hot anger the Commons refused to admit the King's contention, and vehemently reaffirmed the position taken up in the *Apology*. The King sent for the *Journal* and himself tore out the page on which the obnoxious claim was inscribed.[1]

Parliament was at once dissolved, and Coke, with other

[1] The torn page was recovered, restored to its place, and can still be seen in the Library of the House of Commons.

leaders of the Opposition, was imprisoned. Three years later Parliament met again. The scene was completely changed. The Spanish marriage project had miscarried: Buckingham and Prince Charles, dispatched to Madrid to conclude it, had returned not only without the Infanta, but deeply incensed against Spain. On hearing the joyful news the Commons voted supplies for the prosecution of a war against Spain, for the recovery of the Palatinate. James agreed that the money thus voted (about £300,000) should be entrusted to treasurers appointed by the Parliament and accountable to it for the manner in which the subsidies were expended. This novel procedure may be taken as a tentative assertion of the principle of appropriation. The Parliament of 1624 was also memorable for passing an Act against monopolies, and for the successful impeachment, on a charge of bribery, of the Lord Treasurer, Lionel Cranfield, Earl of Middlesex. As regards the promised war against Spain, all that James did was to get together a force—a mere rabble—of 12,000 men, put them under the command of Count Mansfeld, a German adventurer, and send them off, untrained and ill-equipped, for service on the Rhine. They got no farther than the mouth of the Scheldt, where most of them perished in the swamps of the Isle of Walcheren.

**Parliament of 1624.**

James I died in 1625. Charles I was a better man than his father, but a worse king. A strong Churchman, a good husband, a warm friend, he would as a private citizen have been wholly estimable. Called to high place in difficult days, he showed himself a double-minded man and therefore in all his ways unstable.

**Charles I and Parliament.**

For the first three years of the new reign the country was ruled by a worthless and incompetent favourite, the worst of several bad legacies bequeathed to his son by James I—George Villiers, Duke of Buckingham. By frustrating the Spanish marriage Buckingham earned a transient popularity, but it could not survive the revelation of his trickery in diplomacy and his ineptitude in war. The trickery was revealed in connexion with his master's marriage. The Spanish Infanta was replaced by a French princess. Louis XIII, in consenting to the marriage of his sister Henrietta Maria with a Protestant King of England, stipulated that the English Catholics should not suffer persecution. Parliament was assured that they should not be tolerated. Charles's first Parliament (1625) wanted to fight Spain, but only at sea. It showed its mistrust of the King by voting tonnage and poundage for one year only, instead, as was customary, for life, and limited its grant of subsidies to £140,000, a sum wholly inadequate to the prosecution of war at sea or on land. More money, however, Parliament would not grant, except on condition that its expenditure was entrusted to ministers in whom it had confidence.

Charles refused to allow Parliament to interfere with his choice of servants. The Executive was to remain independent of the Legislature. To maintain ministerial independence the first Parliament of the reign was dissolved. But England was at war; money was essential; another Parliament was, therefore, summoned for February, 1626.

**Second Parliament (Feb.–June, 1626).**

Before the second Parliament met a fresh disaster had occurred to English arms. In the hope of emulating Drake's achievements, an expedition was sent to intercept Spanish treasure ships and singe the King of Spain's beard again at Cadiz. It was a hopeless fiasco, and Buckingham, as Lord Admiral, was held responsible. Before the new Parliament met, some of the leading members of the Opposition, including Coke and Sir Thomas Wentworth, were picked as sheriffs, to prevent their election to Westminster. Charles warned the Commons against an attack on his servants who took their orders from him. The Commons resolved to vote supplies, but with the proviso that grievances must first be redressed, and promptly impeached Buckingham. In order to obstruct the prosecution Charles sent the two leading managers of the impeachment—Sir John Eliot and Sir Dudley Digges—to the Tower. The Commons refused to proceed with business until they were released. The Lords also had their grievance. The Earl of Arundel had, on a trumped-up charge but really as an enemy to Buckingham, been sent to the Tower. The Earl of Bristol, who as Ambassador at Madrid could tell tales of the favourite, received no summons to this Parliament. The Lords were as insistent as the Commons on their privileges. In order to save Buckingham from his deserved fate there was nothing for it but to dissolve Parliament (June, 1626).

**The Forced Loan.**

In desperate straits for money, Charles had recourse to a forced loan which brought in a large sum (£236,000) but involved the King in a conflict with the law. For pronouncing against the legality of the loan, Chief Justice Crew was dismissed. Many people were imprisoned for refusing to lend, and five intrepid knights, including Sir Thomas Darnel and John Hampden's cousin, Sir Edmund, sued out a writ of *Habeas Corpus*. The Court of King's Bench, however, held that the knights, having been committed *per speciale mandatum regis*, could be detained in custody without further cause shown.

This decision raised big issues. But before Charles's third Parliament met to explore them, Buckingham gave further demonstrations of his egregious folly and complete incompetence. Having (1625) lent English ships to Louis XIII to overpower the resistance of the great Huguenot stronghold La Rochelle, he led Charles into war with France in 1626, and in 1627 he organized and commanded a great expedition to La Rochelle for the relief of the besieged Huguenots. Out of some 7000 Englishmen dispatched on that disastrous expedition less than 3000 men, sick and starving, returned. As Gardiner tersely put it: "mismanagement completed the ruin which an evil policy began".

**The Petition of Right.**

Under the shadow of this blow to England's honour Charles's third Parliament met (1628). In the new House Coke and Eliot, Pym and Hampden were included, but it was Sir Thomas Wentworth who led it. Wentworth was no Puritan and no democrat. He believed in monarchy and worshipped efficiency. Buckingham's outrageous inefficiency was damaging the repute, if not threatening the existence, of the monarchical office. For the King to part with Buckingham was, however, to accept a new principle governing the relations between the Executive and the Legislature, between Crown and Parliament. We are again on the bedrock of conflicting theories of government. Buckingham must evidently go, but his dismissal at the bidding of Parliament would signalize a momentous shifting in the centre of political gravity.

Recent events had, moreover, compelled Parliament to discharge a more elementary duty. Of nothing are Englishmen at all times more jealous than an infringement of personal liberty. The system of *lettres de cachet*, the methods of the *Cheka*, are abhorrent to them. If the judges were right in ordering the detention, without cause shown or charge preferred, of Darnel and his companions; if the King could compel his subjects to pay taxes, under the guise of forced loans; if Buckingham could billet his undisciplined soldiers upon private families, and rule the country by martial law, there was an end to the boasted liberty of the individual citizen.

These were the points raised in the brief, business-like document known as the *Petition of Right.* Here was no flatulent declaration of the abstract " rights of man ". Here was a simple enumeration of actual and recent grievances and an appeal (whether historically justified or not matters little) to *Magna Carta.*

King Charles struggled hard to escape from the toils: but he needed money and hoped to save Buckingham. He was compelled to promise that henceforward there should be no billeting, no martial law in time of peace, no arbitrary taxation, no arbitrary imprisonment.

On 7th June, 1628, the King gave his assent to the *Petition of Right.* Satisfactory as far as it went, it was necessarily ambiguous on points of detail and left undecided the two fundamental issues of the century, the relations between the Executive and the Justiciary, the Crown and the Judges, and the relations between the Executive and the Legislature.

In less than a week the latter issue was again raised. On 11th June the Commons demanded the dismissal of Buckingham. The King, thereupon, prorogued Parliament,

**Murder of Buckingham.**

and Buckingham prepared to renew the attempt to relieve Rochelle. At Portsmouth, when making ready to embark, he was suddenly assassinated (23rd August). The expedition sailed under another commander, but there was no fight in the men, no capacity in the commanders. Rochelle fell, and Richelieu imposed terms, not ungenerous, on the Huguenots.

Charles, bereaved of his favourite, had to face Parliament in the session of 1629 without him. Before the prorogation a fresh dispute had arisen about finance. The Commons insisted that the *Petition* covered not only direct *taxation*, but custom duties. It was the old quarrel about "impositions"—tonnage and poundage. The King protested, and with reason, that the Commons were taking up fresh ground. They were—justifiably perhaps, but disingenuously.

There was, however, a larger issue. The Commons were greatly alarmed by the spread of "Popery", and the favour shown by the Crown to High Churchmen. A committee, under Pym's chairmanship, drafted a series of Resolutions on Religion. The breach between Crown and Parliament was further widened by a quarrel on a point of privilege involving a claim—on the part of Parliament—declared by the highest modern authorities to be "outrageous". Charles, not unreasonably angered, resolved to prorogue Parliament (2nd March) and on 10th March dissolved it. But before the prorogation, and while a protesting Speaker (Finch) was violently held down in his chair, the Commons adopted these resolutions: all persons who favoured Popery or Arminianism, or levied or paid tonnage and poundage (except as voted by Parliament), were declared "betrayers of the liberties of England". The King issued an elaborate justification of his policy, and nine members of Parliament were committed to custody. Eliot, refusing to make submission, died in the Tower in 1632. Holles and Valentine remained in prison until the Short Parliament met in 1640. The rest were presently released.

It was eleven years before Parliament met again.

CHAPTER XV

# The Rule of Thorough
# The Great Rebellion

KING CHARLES had, at last, an opportunity of showing what guns he carried. They proved to be too light for the campaign on which he had embarked. He might, indeed, have made a better fight had he taken as his chief counsellor Wentworth instead of Laud. William Laud, translated in 1633 from the see of London to the Primacy, was a great Churchman. He had proved his vigour and foresight as an administrator at Oxford, and Mr. Gladstone's fine tribute [1] to his work for the English Church is now generally endorsed by all competent commentators. Even his enemies acknowledged his personal integrity and saintliness of life. But this Arminian zealot was no fit adviser for Charles, at a moment when England was moving steadily towards Puritanism. Wentworth urged patience and caution on his friend, and might himself have supplied the deficiencies both of that friend and of his master had he not, during the years from 1629 to 1639, been immersed in the problems of local administration, first at York as President of the Council of the North, and from 1633 onwards as the King's Deputy in Ireland. Not until Charles and Laud had become hopelessly entangled in English and Scottish politics was Wentworth called into the inner councils of the King. It was too late.

**Personal Government.**

Meanwhile, the account against a King bent on emulating the example of his brother-in-law of France steadily mounted up. Between 1614 and 1789 the States-General never met

[1] *An Academic Sketch* (1892), pp. 38-9; and Marriott: *Crisis of English Liberty* (1930), Chap. V.

in France. To contemporaries it might well have seemed that in 1629 England also had said good-bye to Parliaments. Charles had not only dissolved three Parliaments in four years, but after the dismissal of the third had by proclamation inhibited all men to speak of another Parliament. By the generality of men the suspension of the Legislature was, however, less resented than the heavy hand of the Executive.

**The Crown and the Judges.**

That was felt chiefly in two ways: in the administration of justice and in demands for money. Nor were the two grievances unconnected. The subserviency of the Judiciary under the Stuarts may have been exaggerated, but the facts remain that until the Act of Settlement (1701) the judges held office at the good pleasure of the Crown, and that on important issues the Courts usually supported the Executive. They had good reason. Sir Edward Coke was dismissed by James I in 1616 for refusing to assent to the King's wishes in the case of *Commendams*, Chief Justice Crew was dismissed by Charles I for refusing to admit the legality of forced loans (1626), and Chief Justice Heath for his opposition to ship-money in 1634.

**Prerogative Courts.**

Moreover, during the ten years' "Tyranny", the Prerogative Courts greatly extended their jurisdiction: the Court of the Marches, set up in the border shires of England and Wales; the Council of the North at York; the Stannary Courts in the far south-west; the Court of High Commission, which as the *Grand Remonstrance* afterwards complained "grew to such an excess of sharpness and severity as was not much less than the Roman Inquisition"; above all, the famous Court of the Star Chamber. In the sixteenth century the Star Chamber had been far from unpopular; it had put fear into the hearts of powerful offenders, but for the common sort it had meant cheap and speedy justice. Conditions had, however, altered: a Court which had been accepted as an appropriate appendage of a popular dictatorship had degenerated into the oppressive instrument of an unpopular despotism. "The Court of Star Chamber hath abounded in extravagant censure whereby His Majesty's subjects have been oppressed by grievous fines, imprisonments, stigmatizings, mutilations, whippings, pillories, gags, &c." Thus the *Grand Remonstrance*. Clarendon is not less emphatic in his condemnation of a Court that held "for honourable that which pleased and for just that which profited. . . . Those foundations of right by which men valued their security were to the apprehension and understanding of wise men never more in danger to be destroyed."

**Financial Expedients.**

If personal liberty was menaced, so also was security of property. Money had to be raised somehow. Direct taxation was barred by the *Petition of Right*. Indirect taxation in the form of Impositions the King still continued to collect; but though the duties were raised to the highest possible point, the resulting revenue was inadequate to the King's needs. The sale of some articles of daily use such as soap, salt and wine was, contrary to Statute, handed over to monopolists; obsolete feudal obligations such as "distraint of knighthood", whereby country squires were compelled to pay for titles they did not want, or in the alternative to pay for not taking them, were revived; the claims of the Crown to royal forests were asserted in the most extravagant manner; villagers who had settled on "forest" lands were constrained to ransom their property and to come under the jurisdiction of the old forest law; profits were made by the sale of great offices of State, and a petty fraud was practised upon the counties by the exaction of "coat and conduct money"—provision for the militia regiments which were not in fact called up. In these and other ways, some paltry, all irritating, the necessities of the King were partially supplied.

Of all the devices, however, to which a hard-pressed Treasury resorted none aroused so much popular clamour or evoked such conspicuous and influential resistance as the collection of ship-money.

**Ship-money.**

The writs for the collection of ship-money were, in the first instance (1634), directed only to London and other seaports, but in the following year the device was extended with more questionable legality to the inland counties. Lord Saye and Sale in Oxfordshire, John Hampden in Bucks, and other influential individuals refused to pay their assessments, but the judges were decisively in favour of the legality of the impost. Their law may have been good, but they were foolish enough to base their decision on politics, on the absolute power of the Crown. "It was," even Clarendon admits, "a logic that left no man anything that he might call his own".

More potent, however, as an irritant even than taxation, was the ecclesiastical policy carried out by Archbishop Laud and cordially supported by the King. "Believe it, Sir," said Rudyard, speaking in the Long Parliament (7th November, 1640), "religion hath been for a long time and still is the great design upon this kingdom." Rudyard spoke the thoughts of Puritan England. Only the Brownists and the Quakers (relatively small parties) dreamt of impugning the idea of a National Church established in connexion with the State. Most Englishmen also agreed that the Church was best governed by bishops. But Charles and Laud were much more than Episcopalians of the Falkland type. To them the bishops represented not merely a convenient and orderly system of Church government; they were *jure divino*, in direct and unbroken succession from the Apostles. Doctrinally the Church was to be purged of any Calvinistic taint: it was to maintain the "Catholic" faith, and to follow the ritual familiar to all worshippers before the Reformation, save that all services were to be in the vulgar tongue. English Catholics were, moreover, to be entirely independent of the Bishop of Rome.

**The Bellum Episcopale**

To impose Anglo-Catholicism upon Puritan England was difficult; to impose it upon Presbyterian Scotland was impossible. But Charles and Laud were resolved to bring the two National Churches into conformity. The attempt to do so proved in both countries the ruin of the monarchy.

The introduction of a new Prayer Book into Scotland, more "Catholic" even than the English Liturgy, led to brawls inside and riots outside the churches (1637). With slight exceptions the whole Scottish nation "bristled", as has been strikingly said, "into resistance". In February,

1638, a national Covenant was drafted. It pledged the subscribers to restore the " purity and liberty of the Gospel, as it was established and professed before the innovations ", and was signed by almost the whole adult manhood of the Scottish nation. A General Assembly, meeting at Glasgow on the summons of the King (November, 1638), abolished Episcopacy and re-established in its entirety the Presbyterian ritual, discipline and government.

Charles, however, would not hear of surrender. He was determined to impose his will upon the Scots by force. Accordingly, in January, 1639, he summoned the English nobles to appear in person with their due quota of followers for the defence of the borders. The Scots raised an army of 20,000 men, mostly veterans who had seen service in Germany, well armed and well disciplined. The King's army was slightly superior to that of the Scots in numbers, but in all else hopelessly inferior—most of all in conviction. " Never were the people of England so averse from any war, as neither hating the enemy against whom, nor approving the cause for which they were engaged." So wrote Thomas May, the Puritan clerk and historian of the Long Parliament. The two armies faced each other: the Scots near North Berwick; the English on the Tweed. But battle was not joined. A peace patched up at Berwick (18th June, 1639) proved, however, to be no more than a hollow truce. " Nobody," as Clarendon pithily observed, " meant what others believed he did."

**The Short Parliament (13th April to 5th May, 1640).**

In September, 1639, Charles took his first, almost his only, wise step. He sent for Wentworth from Ireland, and created him Earl of Strafford.[1] For some nine months Strafford was virtually Prime Minister. On his advice Charles summoned Parliament.

Parliament met on 13th April. Charles bluntly told them that they were called not to offer counsel still less " to interpose in any " office of mediation, but " to give His Majesty such a supply as he might provide for the vindication of his honour ". The Commons were more

[1] 12th January, 1640.

concerned to vindicate their own liberties. From the first, John Pym, West Country squire, Oxford graduate, trained lawyer and stern Puritan, took the lead. In a "set discourse of about two hours", respectful to the King but "very plain", he arraigned the Government. Many specific grievances awaited redress, but at the root of all grievances lay the "intermission of Parliaments". "The powers of Parliament," he declared, "are to the body politic as the rational faculties of the soul to a man." Sir Harry Vane, then Secretary of State, retorted with a demand for twelve subsidies. Convocation, at Laud's bidding, voted six, but the Commons insisted that redress of grievances must precede supply. From that position nothing would move them—not even (perhaps least of all) the news that the Scots were threatening to invade England.

On 5th May the Short Parliament was dissolved. Every expedient to raise money was tried—mostly in vain. An army was got together by the aid of the press-gang, but it was a mere rabble, more ready to murder their officers than fight the Scots. On 20th August the Scots crossed the Tweed, 25,000 strong. On the 28th they crossed the Tyne, driving before them the English rabble, panic-stricken and in headlong flight, and were soon in possession of the northern counties. In October they came to terms with the King, in the Treaty of Ripon. A two-months' truce was concluded, and the Scots were to be paid £850 a day until a definitive treaty could be agreed upon.

**The Long Parliament.**

The King had, meanwhile, summoned another Parliament. It met on 3rd November. "So long as the lads about Newcastle sat still" (the phrase is Baillie's), the Puritan leaders in Parliament felt secure; and the Scots, drawing £850 a day for their expenses, were in no hurry to go.

The Commons, again led by Pym, showed a temper very different from that exhibited in May. The new Parliament was barely a week old when Pym suddenly moved the impeachment of Strafford, and he was immediately committed to the Tower. Pym's action looked precipitate and was certainly vindictive, but it may be that he only anticipated an attack on the Puritan leaders by Strafford. Anyway, the lion was caged.

**Strafford.**

Strafford's trial was not opened until 22nd March, 1641. The impeachment broke down; high treason—however widely the doctrine was stretched—could not be proved against him. But the victim must not escape. A Bill of Attainder was substituted and by 8th May had passed both Houses. Strafford's fate now rested with the King, who had pledged himself that his faithful servant should not suffer "in life, honour or fortune". But on 10th May the King, distraught by anxiety for his Queen, gave his assent to the Bill of Attainder. Two days later Strafford was executed. He grudged not his life for the master who had betrayed him. "Stone-dead hath no fellow" was the grim excuse made by the Earl of Essex for the condemnation of Strafford. None other is valid. Pursued to the death by his enemies, Strafford was, until lately, shamelessly maligned by historians. He was no "apostate". He changed sides but he never deserted his principles. His ideal was good administration. To secure it he looked to a strong monarchy in harmony with Parliament, but, like Cromwell, he favoured Parliaments only so long as they kept their hands off the Executive Government.

A month after Strafford's arrest Laud was committed to custody, and there he remained until he was brought to trial in 1645. In his case, as in Strafford's, the impeachment broke down, but an *Ordinance* of Attainder sufficed to bring the old archbishop to the block. The King had no part in the crime. In his absence no Act of Parliament could legally be passed. The murder of Laud acquired no sanction from an "Ordinance" beyond the competence of Parliament. Secretary Windebank and Lord Keeper Finch escaped the fate of Strafford and Laud only by flight to the Continent (December, 1640).

**The Machinery of Thorough.**

The chief agents of "Thorough" having been secured or dispersed, Pym and his colleagues proceeded to break up the machinery. The regular meeting of Parliament—a preliminary essential to all other reforms—was guaranteed by a

*Triennial Act*; an Act was also passed against the dissolution of the present Parliament without its own consent—unconstitutional but, in view of recent experience, not unjustifiable; the Courts of Star Chamber and High Commission were, with the rest of the Prerogative Courts, abolished, and their victims were released and generously compensated; Acts were passed declaring ship-money illegal, prohibiting the exaction of knighthood fines, limiting forest boundaries, and making tonnage and poundage payable only under Act of Parliament. The judgment against Hampden was declared illegal, and the King consented that henceforth judges should hold office during good behaviour and no longer at the pleasure of the Crown. That was a crucial concession. That the judges should be (in Bacon's words) "lions under the throne" was an essential element in the Stuart theory of government. As affecting the liberty of the subject, the relations between the Executive and the Judiciary, between the Crown and the Judges, are at least as important as the relations between Legislature and Executive. The concession now made was a triumph for the view which Coke had persistently maintained against Bacon: that there must be one law for all—officials and private citizens alike; that in the administration of justice in England there must be no intrusion of the principle of *droit administratif*, so largely adopted elsewhere, to the strengthening of the Executive, if not to the protection of the subject.[1]

Early in August, 1641, the King left London for Edinburgh. A treaty was signed with the Scots and their army recrossed the Tweed (August). At the end of the same month Parliament itself adjourned. After nine months of hectic work the constitutional fabric had been restored, and, provided the King was sincere in accepting the restrictions imposed upon the Prerogative by Parliament, it seemed possible that things might settle down. But the ecclesiastical problem had not been solved. A large party in Parliament wished to curtail the power of the bishops; many would

[1] For a full discussion of this subject cf. Marriott: *Crisis of English Liberty* (especially civ).

have excluded them from the House of Lords and the Privy Council; some would have abolished them altogether. But no decision had been reached, and the violence of the abolitionists, the supporters of the " Root and Branch " Bill, was partly responsible for the reaction in the King's favour which was clearly manifest in the late summer of 1641.

**Royalist Reaction.**

There were other reasons for the reaction, notably the heavy taxation imposed by Parliament, and the feeling that the King had made every concession that could be reasonably demanded from him. The reaction alarmed the parliamentary leaders, and when Parliament reassembled (20th October) it was clear that they meant to provoke an open rupture with the King.

Their suspicions of the King's motives in going to Scotland were deepened by the disclosure of a plot for the assassination of the Covenanter leaders Argyle and Hamilton. There was no evidence that the King was concerned in this " incident ", but the news alarmed the extreme Puritans at Westminster. Still more were they alarmed by the news (1st November) that a rebellion had broken out in Ireland, ostensibly in the King's interest, and that a large number of Protestants had been massacred by the dispossessed Catholic peasants in Ulster. Rumour exaggerated the extent of the massacre, but it was bad enough, and for it the King was, unjustly, held responsible. That he had been negotiating with certain Irish lords was true: rebellion and massacre were the last things he wanted.

**The Grand Remonstrance.**

The rumours were a godsend to Pym. On 8th November he presented to the House the famous document known as the *Grand Remonstrance*. Not, however, until after long and heated debate did the House adopt it (22nd November), and then only by 159 votes against 148—a minority unprecedented in that Parliament.

The *Grand Remonstrance* was presented to the King on 1st December. It was at once a powerful indictment preferred against the King, and an effective manifesto to the people, setting out the case for Parliament. It preluded the Civil War which, from the moment it was carried, became inevitable. Had it been rejected, Cromwell would, he declared, "never have seen England more, and many other honest men were of the same resolution". "So near," adds Clarendon, who tells the story, "was this poor kingdom at that time to its deliverance."

Of the 204 clauses of this momentous document the first 103 consisted mainly of an historical recital of the "distempers and disorders" which had marked the reign of King Charles. Then followed a summary justification of the work accomplished by the Long Parliament (§§ 104–68). Finally, after a reference to various "army plots" and the intrigues of "venomous counsellors, bishops, and Popish lords", the Remonstrance enumerated a number of substantive proposals. These included the calling of an ecclesiastical synod for a reformation of religion, a universities' commission, and the appointment of ministers responsible to Parliament.

**Responsibility of Ministers.**

The last proposal crystallized the whole issue between Parliament and the Crown. Who was to control the Executive? The King, Pym insisted, must henceforward "employ such counsellors, ambassadors and other ministers, in managing his business at home and abroad, as Parliament may have cause to confide in".[1] There was the kernel of the whole matter. Pym, a great Parliamentarian, had lighted on the solution that was to give its peculiar significance to English democracy, to supply the English Constitution with its mainspring. The King's reply to the Remonstrance dealt mainly with the religious question. In reference thereto he did not refuse the calling of a synod, but reaffirmed his determination to maintain the Church as established by law and to defend it "not only against all intrusions of Popery, but also from the irreverence of those many schismatics and separatists wherewith of late this kingdom and this city abound, to the great dishonour and hazard both of Church and State". As to the demand for parliamentary ministers, he promised to make careful choice of fit persons, but refused to part with the "undoubted right of the Crown of England to select its own ministers".

[1] § 197. For the text of the *Remonstrance*, Gardiner: *Documents*, pp. 127–54.

Thus was the issue fairly joined. The King's practical retort to the Remonstrance was the attempt to arrest the five members. The attempt was the extreme of folly; failure was the prelude to the Civil War. The actual breach came on the question of the control of the army. Ireland was in rebellion; both parties agreed that an army must be sent to suppress it; but Parliament would not raise an army or put the control of it in the King's hands: the King very naturally would not hand it over to Parliament.

**Attempted Arrest of the Five Members.**

The King had, much against the grain, assented to a bill for the exclusion of the bishops from Parliament: on the Militia Ordinance there could be no compromise.

**The First Civil War.**

Acts of war quickly followed. Hull, the most important arsenal, perhaps the most important seaport in the kingdom, was promptly secured for the Parliament by the Hothams, who refused the King's demand for admission (23rd April). Hull played a vitally important part in the war that followed, for Parliament had the command of the fleet. "The loss of the whole Navy was," as Clarendon said, "of unspeakable ill-consequence to the King's affairs." Clarendon's statement is in no wise exaggerated; but its significance has not, as a rule, been sufficiently emphasized. The holding by Parliament of Plymouth and Gloucester was inferior in this connexion only to the possession of Hull.

There was great hesitation about the choice of sides among common folk, and on both sides great reluctance to draw the sword. "The great God who is the searcher of my heart knows with what reluctance I go upon this service and with what perfect hatred I look upon a war without an enemy." So Sir William Waller, a Parliamentary general, wrote to a friend. "I do not like the quarrel," said Sir Edmund Verney, the King's standard-bearer, to Hyde. So was it with a vast number of people, whose primary anxiety was to keep the armies on both sides out of their own localities. But war came, with much misery in its train, and the sword drawn from the scabbard in 1642 was not finally sheathed until Charles II was restored to his dead father's throne, nearly twenty years later.

The details of the war are outside the scope of this narrative. The King, making Oxford his headquarters, worked out a remarkably able plan for the campaign of 1643. The plan, though proof of his skill as a strategist, was foiled by Parliament's command of the sea. The objective was, of course, London. Newcastle's men were to have made a descent on London by the Great North Road: with Hull untaken they would not come south of Yorkshire. Gloucester barred the way to the Welshmen, who were to cross the Severn and advance by the Thames valley. The men of Cornwall and Devon, who were to reach London by the route now followed by the South-Western Railway, would not leave Plymouth untaken in their rear.

**Sea-power.**

Nevertheless, by the autumn of 1643 things were looking bad for Parliament, and in desperation they turned to the Scots, whose price was the acceptance of the *Solemn League and Covenant*—the establishment of Presbyterianism in England. That price Parliament reluctantly agreed to pay (September, 1643), and on 2nd July, 1644, David Leslie helped Cromwell to turn a Parliamentary defeat into a victory at Marston Moor. That battle ruined the King's cause in the north; but elsewhere Parliament was faring so ill that in April, 1645, Cromwell was able to persuade Parliament to supersede their half-hearted and incompetent generals and allow him to reorganize the army on the lines of his own " New Model ".

**The Solemn League and Covenant.**

The worth of the New Model was amply proved in 1645, notably at Naseby (19th June). The surrender of Oxford in June, 1646, brought the first Civil War to an end.

The victory was due primarily to Cromwell and the Independents. But in July, 1646, Parliament and the Presbyterians offered terms to the King, who, after the fall of Oxford, had surrendered his person to the Scots. Politically the King would have been wise to accept these " Newcastle Propositions ". But it was an essential condition that he should take the Covenant. His Anglican conscience forbade.

The acceptance of the Newcastle terms would have meant a defeat for Cromwell and his army. The refusal

**Army and Parliament.**

led Cromwell to hope that he might make terms with the King and save the monarchy. Army and Parliament were now openly at loggerheads, and the King, to his undoing, conceived the hope that he could hold the balance between them, and so "be really King again". The Army, having taken the precaution to secure the King's person (June, 1647), offered terms to him at Hampton Court in August. The terms were at once more democratic and less anti-monarchical than any yet offered to Charles. He would have been wise to accept them; but buoyed up by a belief in his own indispensability to both parties he refused them, fled from Hampton Court and took refuge at Carisbrooke.

From Carisbrooke, where he was virtually a prisoner in the hands of the Army, the King entered into secret negotiations both with Parliament and with the Scots. The Army, learning of this dubious diplomacy, lost patience, and for the first time demanded the life of the King.

**The Second Civil War (1648).**

In 1648 there were sporadic risings in the King's favour, but the only serious effort on his behalf was made by the Scots, who invaded England in force (July) only to suffer a crushing defeat at Cromwell's hands in a running fight at Preston, Wigan, and Warrington (17th–19th August). Cromwell's victory ended the second Civil War and sealed the fate of the King—and of Parliament.

**Trial and Execution of Charles.**

Colonel Pride, on behalf of the Army, carried out a thorough "purge" of Parliament (8th December, 1648). The Independent Rump, some fifty or sixty strong, set up a special court to try the King. It was a mere masquerade of justice. Charles refused to plead, and on 30th January, 1649, went to his death on the scaffold at Whitehall, with a dignity that compelled the respect of his enemies:

> He nothing common did or mean
> Upon that memorable scene
> . . . . . . .
> But bowed his comely head
> Down, as upon a bed.

Charles believed that he died a martyr in the cause of

"liberty". Many people have shared that belief, and it is certain that his death brought no immediate gain to that cause. Equally certain is it that the King could, by the sacrifice of his convictions, have saved his life. In that sense he was undeniably a martyr. But his martyrdom was due to a canker of personal character. He protested that a king "could not be bound": his enemies forcefully retorted that Charles Stuart could not be trusted. In his case, as in that of the great servant he deserted, "stone-dead had no fellow". If Charles would not be bound he must die.

## CHAPTER XVI

# Interregnum
# Military Dictatorship

SUCH remnant of legal authority as survived the execution of the king was vested in the pitiful remnant—less than one hundred members—of the Long Parliament, popularly known as the " Rump ".

**The Commonwealth.**

During the ensuing years (1649–60) a series of constitutional experiments were tried. Without exception they failed, but they are nevertheless of pre-eminent and permanent interest to all students of Political Institutions, in particular to those who are familiar with the working of Presidential Democracy in the United States of America. Of the many points which were raised by the experiments tried during the Interregnum three stand out conspicuously. The first referred to the structure of Parliament: should it be bicameral or unicameral? Secondly, as to its powers: should Parliament be omnipotent, entrusted with power not only to legislate within the limits of the Constitution, but to amend the Constitution itself? A third question raised the position of the Executive: ought it, as Pym and his friends had contended, to be controlled by and responsible to Parliament; or, as the American Constitution subsequently decreed, to be vested in a single person, outside the Legislature and not answerable to it?

**The Council of State.**

The first experiment was a Republic, dominated by a unicameral Parliament with an Executive Council subordinate thereto. On 13th February, 1649, the Rump set up a Council of State, consisting of forty-one members, mostly squires possessed of some parliamentary experience, together with a few soldiers, lawyers and merchants,—a highly competent body. Of the forty-one members, thirty-one were members of Parliament, which remained in continuous session. Whether the other ten were entitled to sit, speak, or vote, in Parliament is not known.

The Rump then proceeded to abolish "the office of king" (17th March), and having found "by too long experience that the House of Lords is useless and dangerous to the people of England to be continued", abolished it also (19th March). On 19th May an Act was passed declaring "England and all the dominions and territories thereto belonging to be a Commonwealth and Free State". But the authority of the new Government was promptly challenged not only by Ireland, Scotland, the Isle of Man, Jersey, Guernsey, and several Colonies, but in the heart of England itself.

**Ireland.**

In Ireland, Lord Ormonde, the Lord Lieutenant, had temporarily united the Anglo-Irish Catholics, the Presbyterians, and the Episcopalians in support of Charles II, while Parliament maintained a precarious hold upon the island by its continued occupation of Dublin. The Irish situation was, then, a real menace to the infant Commonwealth. To Ireland, accordingly, Cromwell set off (August, 1649), and striking terror into the country by the sack of Drogheda (September) and of Wexford (October), re-established the authority of Parliament over a great part of the country. Cromwell himself was recalled to other tasks in May, 1650; but within two years Ireton had completed his work. Ireland was for the first time really conquered, and the drastic settlement known as Cromwell's was imposed upon it. Had that settlement been carried out in its entirety, such Irish Celts as had not fled or been shipped off to Barbados would have been cooped up in Connaught. The other three provinces would have been colonized by English and Scottish Protestants, who would have been represented in the united Parliament at Westminster.

**Scotland.**

On the death of Charles I, Scotland, like Ireland, promptly acknowledged Charles II, who in June, 1649, arrived in Scotland, took the Covenant, and was proclaimed King.

Not even under the first two Stuarts had Scotland been organically united with England. But Cromwell, a staunch Unionist, was determined on a legislative union. To Scotland, accordingly, he went in July, 1650; he routed the Scots at Dunbar (3rd September) and occupied Edinburgh. The Scots were not (for the most part) Papists to be exterminated like the Irish, but Puritan brethren to be won over by gentler methods. The kirk, however, was no longer to be allowed to dominate the State, which was presently united with England. Meanwhile, Charles II, having been crowned at Scone (1st January, 1651), but cut off from the Highlands by Cromwell's rapid advance, slipped past him into England and on 22nd August raised his standard at Worcester. His reception, even in northern England, was tepid; Cromwell was in hot pursuit, and on 3rd September inflicted a crushing defeat upon the Royalists at Worcester. It was his last battle —" the crowning mercy ". The young King, after forty-four days of wandering and hiding, during which he was the recipient of innumerable tokens of selfless devotion, escaped to Normandy (16th October).

**Democrats and Communists.**

Meanwhile, the Commonwealth had to deal with the opposition of democrats, of Levellers like John Lilburne and social visionaries like Gerard Winstanley. The authority of the Commonwealth rested, indeed, on a very narrow basis, and between the Royalists on the one side and these left-wing opponents on the other, it had great difficulty in maintaining itself. The only chance of stability was to obtain a verdict from the electorate, but a self-appointed Government dare not appeal to it. On the contrary, the Rump pressed on a bill to secure that, in a future Parliament, the existing members should retain their seats. Cromwell's patience was exhausted. The rule of the Rump seemed to him the " horridest arbitrariness " that ever existed. The nation, he told them, " loathes your sitting. We have had an end of this: I will put an end to your prating." He did. The musketeers were called in. " Take away that bauble," he cried in passion. The mace was removed; Speaker Lenthall was " assisted " out of the Chair; the House was cleared and the door locked (20th April, 1653). " I have sought the Lord night and day that He would rather slay me than put upon me the doing of this work." But it had to be done. That deed done, Cromwell held himself to be the sole residuary of quasi-legal authority.

**The " Barebones " Parliament.**

Nevertheless, Cromwell had no desire to assume a dictatorship, and one constitutional experiment followed another. A small (140) Convention of Puritan notables was summoned in June, 1653, but after the manner of well-meaning doctrinaires, tried to crowd the work of years into a few weeks. Cromwell was now " more troubled with the fool than with the knave ", and on 12th December, 1653, the Convention, stimulated by the timely appearance of a military guard, resigned its power into the hands of the Lord General. Four days later Cromwell was installed as Protector under a new Constitution drafted by a committee of officers and civilians, and known as *The Instrument of Government.*

**The Instrument of Government.**

The *Instrument* provided for an Executive consisting of an elective Protector and a Council, and a single-chamber Legislature of 460 members, 30 of whom were to represent Scotland and 30 Ireland, to be elected triennially by a reformed electorate. But Parliament was to have no power to " alter the Government as it is hereby settled ". The *Instrument* was to prove a rigid as well as a written Constitution. Nevertheless, the new Parliament no sooner met (3rd September, 1634) than it claimed constituent powers. Cromwell insisted that their functions were merely legislative; their business was to make laws, but only within the limits of the " fundamentals " laid down by the *Instrument of Government.* Above all, they must not meddle with the Executive.

Parliament was not willing to accept the subordinate position thus assigned to it, and after five (lunar) months, wasted in wranglings, was dissolved by Cromwell, at the earliest possible moment permitted by the *Instrument* (22nd January, 1655).[1]

[1] For further details of these experiments see Marriott: *The Crisis of English Liberty*, Chaps. XI and XIII.

Thereafter, for nearly two years, England was under a naked military despotism, which recalled the worst features of "Thorough". The main difference between the two periods was that Cromwell had a large and disciplined army at his command, Charles had none. In 1655 the whole country was divided into eleven districts, and each was placed under a Major General in command of a local militia consisting of well-disciplined cavalry, selected for loyalty to the Protector.

**The Major Generals (1655–6).**

But Cromwell, great soldier though he was, had no liking for military rule. Besides, like the Stuart kings, he needed money, more particularly to carry on the war on which in 1655 he had embarked against Spain. Accordingly, in September, 1656, he summoned another Parliament. Great efforts were made to secure the election of "well-affected persons", but even so it was found necessary to exclude no fewer than one hundred irreconcilables.

**Second Protectorate Parliament.**

This "sifting and winnowing" failed to solve the problem. Between Parliament, permeated by the constitutional principles of Pym, and Cromwell, resolved, like Charles I, to retain in his own hands the Executive, no reconciliation was possible. Nevertheless, all parties being anxious for a "settlement", another effort to devise one was embodied in the *Humble Petition and Advice* (May, 1657). Cromwell was to take the title of King, and a new Second Chamber was to be constituted. In deference to the republican prejudices of his army, though much against his own better judgment, Cromwell refused the Crown, but was installed, with great ceremony, as Lord Protector and authorized to name his successor. The "other House" was to consist of not more than 70 and not less than 40 members, nominated for life by "his Highness" and approved by "this" House. The case for a Second Chamber was never put with more conclusive effect than by Cromwell,[1] and the proposal for setting it up was carried with an unexpected degree of unanimity. Of the 63 members of the Second Chamber nominated by Cromwell only 42

[1] Marriott: *Second Chambers* (2nd Ed., 1927), pp. 27–31.

answered his summons; of the seven English peers so nominated only two.

The reconstructed Parliament proved as obstructive and dilatory as its predecessors. A week of "foolery" exhausted the Protector's patience, and on 4th February, 1658, he angrily dissolved it. "Let God be judge between you and me." "Amen," responded some of the irreconcilables.

Death of Cromwell.

Seven months later (3rd September, 1658) the great Protector died. "Great" Cromwell undeniably was: a great Imperialist, a great Unionist, and conspicuously great in opposition; but as a constructive builder of the Constitution a failure. He failed because, under the circumstances of his day, he could not succeed. No more than the Stuart kings was Cromwell prepared to concede to Parliament the control of the Executive. As compared with Pym he was constitutionally a reactionary. Towards a solution of the problem of sovereignty he made no advance. During the Interregnum sovereignty was vested neither in Parliament nor in the people. Cromwell's power rested on the army, and anxious as he was to restore a parliamentary monarchy, there was no disguising that awkward truth. "I don't love him, but he was a mighty big fellow." So said Mr. Gladstone, and Mr. Gladstone had a knack of speaking at times the mind of his countrymen.

Richard Cromwell.

Still less could it be disguised under his son Richard, who showed himself quite unequal to the difficult task of reconciling the army chiefs and the civil power. The sword was the arbiter of the stituation. The only question was whether the sword should be wielded by General Lambert, a violent Republican, or by General Monk with his doubtful opinions and unrevealed intentions. In December, 1658, Royalist agents were instructed to open negotiations with Monk, who secured the strong places in Scotland and cashiered his more fanatical officers.[1] In London all was confusion. The Rump of the Long Parliament was recalled by Protector Richard in May, 1659. It was Richard's last authoritative act. In July "Tumbledown Dick" was virtually deposed;

[1] Bryant: *Charles II*, pp. 64–9.

he left Whitehall, and until his death half a century later (1712) he lived in suburban obscurity as "Mr. Clarke". The Rump was expelled a second time in October by Lambert, only to march back to Westminster with Speaker Lenthall at their head on Boxing Day of that year. The cry was now all for a "free Parliament", and there was little doubt what a free Parliament would do.

**General Monk.**

Monk and his army crossed the Tweed in December, and amid the acclamations of the populace reached London on 3rd February. The General kept his lips sealed, but having been nominated Lieutenant General of the Commonwealth, joined the City in their demand for a "full and free Parliament".

On 23rd February the members excluded by Pride[1] were, under pressure from Monk, restored to their seats, and at once gave the Presbyterians a majority. The Long Parliament, thereupon, summoned a new Parliament, to be freely elected and to meet on 25th April. This done, the Long Parliament at last dissolved itself (16th March), after a broken and not untroubled existence of nearly twenty years.

**Declaration of Breda.**

The exiles at Brussels were on the tiptoe of expectation, and on 30th March, Sir John Greenvil arrived with instructions, unwritten but carefully learnt by heart. Charles was required to move from Catholic Brussels into Puritan Holland, to promise to confirm the sales of Crown lands, and to proclaim an amnesty with complete liberty of conscience. These promises were embodied in a Declaration issued on 4th April from Breda.

A Parliament known as a "Convention", since it lacked a royal summons, met on 25th April. On 1st May it resolved that "according to the ancient and fundamental laws of this kingdom the Government is, and ought to be by King, Lords and Commons". An invitation was forthwith dispatched to Breda; on the 25th of May the King landed at Dover and, escorted by General Monk, made a triumphant progress to London, which he entered, amid

[1] Some had been restored soon after the King's death.

scenes of tumultuous enthusiasm, on the 29th. There was point in Dryden's satire:

> Crowds err not, though to both extremes they run;
> To kill the father, and recall the son.

Nevertheless, there can be no question that the enthusiasm displayed for the restoration of the monarchy was genuine as well as general. Oliver Cromwell was undeniably one of the greatest uncrowned kings that ever ruled a proud and independent people. But the English people have never loved a military dictatorship, and Cromwell's dictatorship rested, not like that of the Tudors on consent, but on naked force. "The Teuton," according to a brilliant but dangerous generalization, "loves laws and Parliaments, the Celt loves a king." The English people are not predominantly Celts, but, with characteristic love of compromise, they believe both in the principle of hereditary monarchy and in that of parliamentary democracy. The Stuarts accepted a parliamentary legislature only so long as it did not encroach upon the Executive government, vested in "a single person". Cromwell held the same convictions. But his Parliaments, like those of the Stuarts, wanted something more than the "single person" was prepared to concede. They strained after an acknowledgment of the principle now accepted as the corner-stone of "responsible government". It may well be that few members of Cromwell's Parliaments were as clear-sighted as John Pym in discerning the solution of the problem. But they were feeling after it. Cromwell would not, perhaps could not, help them to find it. He was a great soldier and a great ruler; he was not a great parliamentarian. He was impatient of that "chatter of the monkey-house" which is inseparable from Parliamentary Democracy. The architects of the American Constitution built their democratic structure not on Pym's model but on Cromwell's. Federalism may be inconsistent with Cabinet government, and the Cabinet system with Federalism. Our experience of the attempts made to combine the two principles has been too limited to warrant any dogmatic

**Crown and Parliament.**

conclusions. The experience gained during the Interregnum does, on the contrary, suffice to establish two propositions: (1) that Parliamentary Democracy is incompatible with any form of dictatorship, and (2) that an Hereditary Monarchy, if not an indispensable adjunct to Parliamentary Democracy, contributes a most valuable element to its successful operation —an element with which Englishmen will never lightly dispense. A seventeenth-century Parliament would not work without a king. Of this truth Cromwell became convinced. But monarchy calls for sanctions other than those derived either from military force or political expediency. An English king is not only *Rex et Imperator* but *Sacerdos*: he is consecrated as well as crowned. The jurist may reject the theory of indefeasible hereditary right; but popular instinct rightly discerns something more than utility in the hereditary principle. Moreover, it seemed, in 1660, to the vast majority of Englishmen only reasonable that the principle, if valid, should operate in favour of the descendant of kings rather than of the son of a Protector. If a " single person ", why not Charles II? was a question frequently asked between the death of Oliver and the restoration of Charles. It was answered by the Convention Parliament on 1st May, 1660, and before the end of the month by the returning King.

# CHAPTER XVII

## The Restoration
## The Later Stuart Monarchy

CHARLES II was welcomed back to his throne with amazing unanimity and vociferous enthusiasm. The nation was delighted to have a King again, even if he was a Stuart. But the problems raised by the Restoration were neither few nor simple. Something more than enthusiasm was needed to solve them.

**Charles II.**

Charles II possessed many of the qualifications essential to the man who, after a period of profound upheaval, was called to preside over a settlement which necessarily impinged upon the rights of individuals, offended many old friends, and completely satisfied none. Personally, Charles II is one of the most interesting in our long line of sovereigns, but also, despite much laborious research, one of the most inscrutable. His vices were, like Falstaff's lies, gross and palpable. The grandson of Henry of Navarre, he inherited many of his characteristics: his tolerance, his ready wit, and his love of women. If Henry IV thought Paris worth a Mass, Charles II thought London not too dearly bought by outward conformity to Anglicanism. He was wholly lacking in the religious devotion of his father and brother, and though, in the agony of his last hours, he received extreme unction from a Catholic priest, he probably oscillated, throughout his life (as was wittily said), " in contented suspense between Roman Catholicism and Atheism ". But he was not more crooked than his father or more obstinate than his brother. He loved and was beloved by one, if not both his sisters, and, despite the irregularities of his married life, retained to the end the affection of his wife. His sense of humour, though far from delicate, was keen, but he never indulged it to the sacrifice of his dignity. In daily intercourse he was genial, gentle, and invariably courteous; he was adroit in the management of men, but tenacious in adherence to his principles. His indolence was, perhaps, like Lord Melbourne's, a calculated pose, for he had a real capacity for business and dispatched it with concentration and rapidity. He did his best, if with indifferent success, to restrain the vindictiveness and intolerance of the more violent Royalists, but gave full rein to his own passions. Intellectually he was more highly endowed than any other sovereign of his House: he was the first patron of the Royal Society (1662), a keen musician, a discriminating collector, and genuinely interested in art. He made science fashionable; architecturally England owed much to the close supervision he exercised over the rebuilding of the City after the Great Fire, and no one was more cordial than the King in admiration for the genius of Sir Christopher Wren.

**Commerce and Colonization.**

The reign of Charles II was a time of great prosperity: overseas trade noticeably expanded; the East India Company not only paid large dividends, but was able to purchase Bombay—part of the Queen's dowry—from the King. Another portion of Catherine's dowry proved a liability instead of an asset. A large garrison and heavy expenditure were required to hold Tangier against the Moors; Charles spent nearly £2,000,000 upon it, but Parliament refused its help, and in 1683 the garrison was withdrawn and the town and fortifications were destroyed.[1] Twenty years later England secured a more defensible base in the Mediterranean, but while Tangier was a symbol of Portuguese amity, Gibraltar perpetuated the hostility of Spain.

**Shipping.**

Not the Mediterranean, however, but the Atlantic was the appropriate sphere of English maritime activity in the seventeenth century. That activity was in every way encouraged by the king. " 'Tis certain," wrote Buckingham, " no Prince was ever more fitted by nature for his country's interest than he was in all his maritime inclinations."

[1] E. M. G. Routh: *Tangier*.

Himself a keen yachtsman, he was constantly on the water, frequently visited the dockyards, and took the greatest personal interest in all the details of shipbuilding and naval administration. The mercantile marine was doubled in size during his reign, but the history of the navy is more chequered. Between 1660 and 1673 there was an increase in naval tonnage of 60,000 tons, in personnel of 20,000 men and 4000 guns, and 147 vessels were added to the 156 inherited from the Commonwealth. In 1675 Pepys boasted that more ships had been built since 1670 than in any other quinquennium in English history.[1] But activity was spasmodic and naval administration, owing chiefly to recurrent fits of parsimony on the part of Parliament, was irregular and on the whole inefficient.

Navigation Acts.

Parliament did, however, consistently support the policy embodied in the *Navigation Acts*. The Act or Ordinance passed by the Long Parliament in 1651 was aimed against the Dutch, who in the words of Thomas More "undermine, hurt and eclipse us daily in our Navigation and Trade". Amendments passed in 1660 and 1662 greatly extended the scope of the original Act. They prohibited the importation into England, or the exportation from any plantation in Africa, Asia, or America, of any goods, except in English-built and English-manned ships. Certain "enumerated" commodities could be exported from the colonies only to England or to other English Plantations. The purpose of the Acts was partly political and partly economic; the method was frankly protectionist. The Acts were in complete harmony with the accepted mercantilist theories of that day, but were bitterly assailed a century later by Adam Smith and his disciples of the Manchester School. Yet they were undeniably effective in transferring commercial and naval supremacy from Holland to England, and without inflicting any hardship on the colonies. It has, indeed, been plausibly argued that they were as much to the advantage of New England as of old England—at any rate until 1760.[2]

[1] Ogg: *Charles II*, I, p. 280, and references there quoted.
[2] Cf. Sir W. Ashley: *Surveys Historic and Economic*, pp. 309 f.

Imperial interests were, indeed, a matter of constant solicitude to Charles II, whose name is perpetuated in the Carolinas. In 1663 the King granted the region between Florida and Virginia, with its vast hinterland to the Pacific, to a body of eight proprietors, among whom were Clarendon, Monk (by now Duke of Albemarle), Sir George Carteret, and Ashley, afterwards Earl of Shaftesbury. No colony had yet been established under such influential auspices, and it was wisely governed. The grantees insisted on a policy of religious toleration, and Charles himself was responsible for reinforcing the English settlers by a body of Huguenots. Jamaica, conquered from Spain during Cromwell's Protectorate (1655), owed to Charles its first civil governor and embryonic Constitution, but North America owed him a still heavier debt. Between New England and the southern group of colonies there was until 1664 an ugly gap, but in that year Charles picked up the threads of one of Cromwell's projects, dropped in 1654. He dispatched a small fleet under the command of Colonel Nicholls to the Hudson River, with orders to seize the New Netherlands. The Dutch settlers made no resistance, and the New Netherlands, together with New Sweden, passed into the hands of England, who then held the whole Atlantic seaboard from the Kennebrek to the Savannah. Charles handed over the new acquisitions to the Duke of York, after whom the colony and its capital were renamed. New Sweden was, after a time, formed into a separate colony as Delaware. In 1664 the Duke of York transferred the territory between the Hudson River and the Delaware to Lord Berkeley and Sir George Carteret. In compliment to Carteret, who had held Jersey for the King during the Civil War, the territory was named New Jersey.

**The Carolinas.**

**New York and New Jersey.**

Of all the North American colonies none, however, started under happier auspices than Pennsylvania. The name perpetuates the memory of a remarkable man, William Penn, lawgiver and philanthropist. The son of Admiral Penn, the conqueror of Jamaica, William Penn was the friend of the Duke of York, who in 1682, in liquidation of a

**Pennsylvania.**

debt of £16,000 owed by the Crown to the father, assigned to the son a vast territory on the west bank of the Delaware. Primarily established as a refuge for Penn's persecuted co-religionists, the Quakers, the new colony welcomed other immigrants in large numbers alike from England and from Germany, Holland, and Scandinavia.

**Committee of Trade and Plantations.**

The interest of Charles II in colonial and commercial matters was further proved by an important reform in the administrative machine. In 1662 a Standing Committee on Trade and Plantations was set up to assist the work of the great trading companies and in particular their trade with the Plantations. This Committee—the ancestor of the Board of Trade—was to consist of forty " understanding able persons ", some of whom were to be merchants representing the East India and other trading companies, others were to represent the " unincorporated trades for Spain, France, Portugal, Italy, and the West India Plantations ", while the Board was to be " dignified also with the presence and assistance of some of His Majesty's Privy Council ". The Board was to take a special care for the strict application of the Navigation Act, to encourage and control emigration to the Plantations, to keep themselves informed of the state of the Plantations, of their government and their trade, and to inquire into any grievances of which they might complain.

Of this Committee Shaftesbury was president, and John Locke was for a short time (1673–4) secretary. After the fall of Shaftesbury, however, the Joint Committee was abolished, and its functions were transferred to a Committee of the Privy Council consisting of the Lord Treasurer, the Privy Seal, and seventeen other members. This Committee continued to control colonial affairs until after the Revolution, when a new Board of Trade was set up (1696).

**Foreign Policy.**

Charles's foreign policy has not received the unanimous approval accorded to his administration of colonial and commercial affairs. Between the almost indiscriminate eulogy of Mr. Bryant and the stern condemnation of Dr. Keith Feiling no reconciliation is possible. To the former

Charles II was the " patriot king " whose efforts to promote national interests were frustrated by the parsimony of Parliament and the treasonable conduct of the Whigs. " There are abominations about him and his rule," wrote Dr. Feiling, " which cannot be whitewashed . . . he threw away the passionate affection of England by an unprincipled vacillation . . . he was false to his friends, false to all the Churches, false to himself. And yet," he adds, " the earth lies soft on his royal ashes." These incisive and sharply opposed judgments are typical of many. It is outside the scope of this work to argue the question in detail, but certain facts emerge on which there can be no controversy.

The foreign policy of Charles II was (superficially at any rate) a continuation of Cromwell's. The Dutch wars were a direct legacy from the Protectorate: so also was friendship with France and hostility to Spain. The marriage of Charles II with Catherine of Portugal (1662) was an event of the first political importance. Menacing to Spain, it strengthened the connexion of Charles II with France, to whom, instead of to its owner, Spain, Clarendon sold Dunkirk. The first Dutch War (1665–7), a stern fight between two well-matched combatants, was a legacy from the Protectorate, though France was, this time, on the side of the Dutch. The first-fruit of the peace concluded with Holland (July, 1667) was, however, the adhesion of England to a Triple Alliance with Holland and Sweden to arrest the progress of Louis XIV in the Netherlands (1668). Louis, though compelled to surrender his immediate object, was determined to teach the insolent merchants of Amsterdam what it was to thwart the ambition of a King of France. But to make their punishment certain he purchased the support of his cousin of England by the secret Treaty of Dover (1670).

**Clarendon.**

In August, 1667, Clarendon had with singular ingratitude been dismissed by the King, impeached (abortively) by Parliament, and had fled the country never to return. Clarendon had alienated all parties. As a royal minister of the Elizabethan type he was unacceptable to a

Parliament grotesquely misdescribed by Macaulay as "more zealous for royalty than the King". At the same time he was too loyal to Parliament (understood again in the Elizabethan sense) to be acceptable to the King. His antique respectability was a reproach to a profligate court; his strict fulfilment of the Indemnity Act was an offence to the cavaliers. The sale of Dunkirk, the Plague, the Great Fire, the wound to national pride inflicted by the appearance of the Dutch fleet in the Medway—for all these things Clarendon was held responsible, and in 1670 he was replaced by the "Cabal".

Clarendon's enforced retirement from politics was not without compensations. It enabled him to complete, at leisure, his *History of the Great Rebellion* and to write his *Autobiography*, thus permanently enriching English literature as well as the University of Oxford.[1]

**Parliament and Foreign Affairs.**

In 1672 Charles earned his French pension by issuing the Declaration of Indulgence, repealing by prerogative action all *Acts* against Catholics and Nonconformists, and by declaring war, in conjunction with his patron, upon the Dutch Republic. But Charles had gone too far. Parliament compelled him to withdraw the Declaration, and in place of it passed the *Test Act*, linking all public service with a profession of Anglicanism. This necessitated the immediate retirement from office of the Duke of York and the fiery Clifford. The Cabal was broken up (1673), and a resolution against a standing army was passed (1674). A threatened refusal of supplies compelled the King to make peace with Holland in February of the same year. So much did the independent temper of the English Parliament alarm Louis XIV and impoverish Charles, that the former agreed to pay, and the latter to accept, a subsidy of £100,000 a year, in return for a dissolution or a prorogation of Parliament. Charles, fearing that a dissolution would mean an even less complaisant House of Commons, adopted the second alternative. Parliament was accordingly prorogued in November, 1675,

[1] To the University he bequeathed his *History of the Great Rebellion*, and out of the profits derived therefrom the "Clarendon Building"—the first home of the Clarendon (University) Press—was built.

and did not meet again until February, 1677. In order to reduce the political temperature the coffee-houses were also closed.

**England and France.**

A secret treaty with Louis was signed by Charles in February, 1676; it consolidated their previous engagements and included a mutual undertaking not to negotiate, except conjointly, with Holland. Charles was, nevertheless, anxious to relieve himself of domestic embarrassments by inducing Louis to make peace on reasonable terms with the Dutch. But Louis, with Charles in his pocket, was inexorable in his demands upon the Dutch Republic. Meanwhile, on the eve of the reassembly of Parliament (14th February, 1677), an Anglo-French maritime treaty was signed which made very valuable concessions to English ships in the matter of trade with belligerents. This treaty, though little noticed by most historians, is said truly by a careful commentator to have been "of more value to our carrying trade than the winning of several naval battles".[1] It also provides further proof of the King's solicitude about English commerce.

When, at long last, Parliament reassembled (15th February) it was induced to vote £600,000 for ship-building, though stipulating that the subsidy should be paid into the hands of receivers appointed by itself. Charles had, indeed, no intention of allowing the forces of the Crown to be employed on behalf of the Dutch, though in November, 1677, he consented to the marriage of the Princess Mary, daughter of Anne Hyde and the Duke of York, with William of Orange.

**Danby.**

This momentous marriage was primarily, no doubt, the work of George Osborne, Earl of Danby, who on the fall of the Cabal had succeeded Clifford as Lord High Treasurer and become virtually the first minister of the Crown. Danby, a shrewd Yorkshireman, a skilled financier, and a stout Protestant, was, like Clarendon, at once a genuine believer in Parliament and a loyal servant of a King who wished to rule as absolutely as his cousin in France. The Dutch marriage was Danby's master-stroke of policy.

[1] Ogg: *Charles II*, II, p. 539.

Why Charles consented to it is almost unintelligible, unless it were to annoy and embarrass the brother he hated, or to raise his own value (and price) against the cousin he admired. Danby's influence was also manifested in the conclusion (31st December, 1677) of a treaty with Holland designed to force reasonable terms of peace on France.

Parliament met in February, 1678, and voted supplies for an increase in the fighting services to be employed against France. Louis, in alarm, lavished bribes on the Opposition, but nevertheless concluded (with Danby's reluctant connivance) another secret treaty with Charles, in return for a promise to withhold support from the Dutch and to dissolve Parliament.

**The Popish Plot.**

Parliament was saved by the panic created by the revelations of one Titus Oates, who deposed to the existence of a plot to murder Charles, replace him by the Duke of York, and bring England back into the Roman Communion. Oates was an unmitigated scamp, but the mystery of the plot which he pretended to reveal has never been completely solved.

> Some truth there was, but dashed and brewed with lies
> To please the fools and puzzle all the wise.

Such was Dryden's conclusion, and research has not got much beyond it. The result was the savage and almost indiscriminate prosecution of Papists, an Act of Parliament for disabling Papists from sitting in either House of Parliament, and the impeachment of Danby and five Roman Catholic peers. The attack on Danby was, indeed, due to Louis XIV, who, having made peace with the Dutch at Nimwegen (1678), revenged himself upon Charles and his anti-French minister by revealing the terms of the secret treaty of 1678. Danby pleaded a pardon under the Great Seal, and Charles, to save the minister, at long last dissolved the Parliament elected in 1661.

**The Succession.**

The new Parliament, elected amid great excitement, renewed the attack on Danby, but contented itself by sending him to the Tower, whence he emerged in 1684, to resume his place in the House of Lords and his political career. The exultant Whigs, having rid themselves, if only temporarily, of Danby, introduced a bill to exclude from the succession the Duke of York.

The Whigs overreached themselves. For nearly twenty years the King had played the game of the Opposition. The Restoration had been due predominantly to four sentiments: attachment to the principle of hereditary monarchy; fear of a standing army and a dictatorship resting thereon; resentment against Puritan restrictions combined with underlying loyalty to the Established Church; and not least a growing belief in parliamentary institutions. Charles's subservience to France, his leanings towards Roman Catholicism, and his evident dislike to parliamentary government, had gone far to dissipate the loyalty of his people. But the sentiment was by no means extinguished. The Exclusion Bill revived it. An attempt to revivify the Privy Council by confining it to thirty members, and giving it an important place in the machinery of government, was accepted as a constitutional gesture on the part of the Crown, but was not successful. The movement towards an "unconstitutional" Cabinet was too strong to be arrested. The Short Parliament of 1679 is, however, memorable for the enactment of the *Habeas Corpus Act*. The right to personal liberty was an ancient one: it had been reaffirmed in the *Petition of Right* and fortified by the Act of 1640 for the abolition of the Prerogative Courts. The principle that a subject could be deprived of his personal liberty only by regular process of law was, then, established; but the machinery for asserting it was defective. The *Habeas Corpus Act*, though not quite watertight, went far towards providing the machinery, and putting an end to evasions and delays. It was the expiring effort of the Parliament of 1679.

**Whigs and Tories.**

A new Parliament was elected in October of that year, but Louis XIV promised Charles a large pension only on condition that it was not permitted to meet. For twelve months Charles was able to fulfil the condition, though at the cost of an unprecedented political agitation in the country.

Petitions poured in praying that Parliament might meet, only to be countered by petitions expressing abhorrence of the attempt to exclude from the succession the legitimate heir. To that agitation it is customary to assign the genesis of the modern parties, Whigs and Tories. In fact it was only those nicknames that we owe to the agitation of 1680. The parties themselves can be traced back to the debates of the Long Parliament, if not to the divisions which manifested themselves after the passing of the Act of Uniformity (1559). The basis of Toryism was attachment to the Monarchy and the Church; the Whigs mostly held the Puritan creed, and thought less of the Crown than of Parliament.

**The Exclusion Bill.**

The Exclusion Bill tested the strength of these opposing principles and parties. It passed the Commons in November, 1680, but was rejected in the Lords, and the King formally declared that he would never assent to it. The Commons refused supplies, and in January, 1681, Parliament was dissolved. The new Parliament met in March, but at loyal Oxford. The Commons, however, returned to the attack and refused a compromise adroitly offered by the King. The Duke of York was to be banished, and the Prince of Orange was to rule as Regent in his father-in-law's name. The Whigs, however, insisted on the full measure of exclusion. Parliament was thereupon dissolved, only to meet again under James II.

Charles had won. He had defeated the Whigs partly by his superiority in tactics, and still more by his tenacious adherence to a principle to which his people were, like himself, devoted. Charles had no love for his brother, but he had a passionate belief in the monarchical principle, and not even to gratify personal hatred would he betray it. Shaftesbury, the leader of the Opposition and the chief champion of Exclusion, was for the second time sent to the Tower, and arraigned on a charge of treason, but a London grand jury ignored the bill. Released from the Tower, he attempted to raise an armed insurrection. He failed, and fled to Holland, where in 1683 he died.

**Shaftesbury.**

Next to the King himself, Shaftesbury is the most interesting personality of the reign. Revered by Whigs as the real founder of their party, he was bitterly satirized by Dryden as " Achitophel ":

> For close designs and crooked counsels fit,
> Sagacious, bold, and turbulent of wit,
> Restless, unfixed in principles and place,
> In power unpleased, impatient of disgrace;
>
> . . . . . . . .
>
> Achitophel, grown weary to possess
> A lawful fame and lazy happiness,
> Disdained the golden fruit to gather free
> And lent the crowd his arm to shake the tree.
> Now, manifest of crimes contrived long since,
> He stood at bold defiance with his Prince,
> Held up the buckles of the people's cause
> Against the Crown, and skulked behind the laws.

The satire, if severe, was not unjust. Shaftesbury's failure was the measure, and the explanation, of Charles's success. A plot to murder both Charles and his heir presumptive—the " Rye-house Plot "—was fortunately discovered in time (1683). Convicted of participation in the plot, William, Lord Russell, and Algernon Sidney paid the penalty of their criminal folly on the scaffold. The Earl of Essex frustrated the King's intention to save his life by cutting his own throat in the Tower.

The immediate reaction to the Rye-house Plot was to evoke from the University of Oxford—more loyal than discreet—a decree condemning the doctrine that resistance to a king can under any circumstance be lawful (July, 1683)—a decree conveniently ignored, four years later, when James II dissipated its loyalty by his attempt to Catholicize the University.

The folly of his opponents combined with Charles's own tenacity to secure the undisputed succession of a Catholic Sovereign in the person of James II.

Charles II has been very variously judged, but it must be remembered that he was by blood and breeding more

Charles II

French than English. His French grandfather and French cousin were his models of kingship, and never was the French monarchy more brilliantly successful than in their hands. Charles, like Henry IV and Louis XIV, believed in personal monarchy, and he had the example of Cromwell before him. It is easy for the philosophical historian to see in retrospect that with the passing of Queen Elizabeth the day of personal monarchy was over. If the Stuarts lacked the prophetic sagacity to perceive this truth, can they be blamed? Cromwell, exalted to a foremost place in democracy's Pantheon, imperfectly apprehended it: William III, hero of the Whigs, was a personal ruler. Only after the accession of the Hanoverians, and then partly by accident, was "constitutional monarchy" gradually evolved. Charles II was not vindictive nor did his reign witness any set-back in constitutional progress. The Act of Indemnity and Oblivion (1660) alienated many Royalists but implemented the promise given at Breda, only the regicides and five others being excepted from the general pardon. No attempt was made to undo the work legally accomplished by the Long Parliament: the Prerogative Courts were not revived; Parliament was not intermitted until the last days of the reign; feudal tenures, and other feudal rights, were abolished (1660), and the King, but for the help of his cousin, would have been financially dependent on the grants of a suspicious and parsimonious Parliament.

The crucial question is, whether the French subsidies deflected Charles II from the path of patriotism as an English King? Again in retrospect, we can see that English interests were inextricably bound up with the independence of the Low Countries. Spanish rule in Belgium was, in fact, less menacing to England than was French predominance. But in the seventeenth century Englishmen might well have thought of the Dutch rather as trade rivals than as the warders of England's continental frontier. A Protestant Parliament may have been more clear-sighted in this matter than a Catholic King. But perhaps it was England's traditional hatred of France rather than newly conceived love for Holland that compelled Charles to make peace with the Dutch Republic in 1674.

James II and Monmouth.

James II, though treated more generously than his brother by Parliament, was similarly subsidized by Louis XIV. But his first business was to quell the insurrection of Monmouth. Whether Monmouth was the bastard son of Charles II and Lucy Walters, or the nephew of Algernon Sidney, matters not. Charles II loved him as a son, but would not countenance him as an heir. Monmouth's ingratitude, vanity, and ambition, led to his participation in the Rye-house Plot in 1683, and his suicidal attempt to assert his "legitimate" and legal right to the Crown against James II. He landed at Lyme Regis on 11th June, 1685, was proclaimed King at Taunton (20th June), but was disastrously defeated at Sedgemoor (6th July) and was executed in the Tower on the 15th.

Judge Jeffreys.

Terrible was the vengeance wreaked upon the deluded peasants of Dorset and Somerset who had fought under Monmouth's standard at Sedgemoor. Those who escaped military execution, at the hands of Colonel Kirke, on the morrow of the battle, were either hanged or transported to Barbados by Chief Justice Jeffreys, in whom James II found a facile instrument for the execution of his brutal policy.

The Army.

Nor did the King rely only on the robe. He raised the regular army from 6000 to 30,000, and in 1686 formed a camp of 13,000 troops at Hounslow to keep Protestant London in awe. None of his predecessors had ever done the like. Had Charles I taken Strafford into his inner counsels sooner, London might have had a similar experience in 1640, and Pym might have been in Strafford's place in the Tower. But by 1660 popular feeling against a standing army had become irresistibly strong. Clarendon was wise enough to pay the Cromwellian army off to the last penny of their arrears, and Charles was content to retain in his service only Monk's Coldstreamers and a regiment of Horse Guards—the Blues—raised from the garrisons of Dunkirk and Tangiers. James II was less mindful of his subjects' prejudices, but his augmented army served him little.

Declaration of Indulgence.

With perverse ingenuity he contrived simultaneously to offend every party and every creed in the country. Despite the Test Act, he gave a commission in the army to a Roman Catholic, Sir Edward Hales, and, having obtained from the judges an opinion in favour of his dispensing power, proceeded to give more commissions to his co-religionists, and even to appoint them to high positions in the Church. In July, 1686, he set up a new Court of Ecclesiastical Commission, which promptly suspended Dr. Compton, Bishop of London. Massey, a Roman Catholic, was appointed to the deanery of Christ Church, and Mass was publicly celebrated in the Chapel Royal at Whitehall. In April, 1687, James published a *Declaration of Indulgence*, suspending at one stroke all the penal laws against Catholics and Protestant dissenters. Jesuits and other Roman Catholic orders were encouraged to open schools in London, a Papal Nuncio was received, and Catholic peers were admitted to the Privy Council. An attempt was then made to open the universities to Roman Catholics, and also to impose Catholics upon the governing bodies of colleges. But the expulsion of the Protestant Fellows of Magdalen College, Oxford, was resented as an attack not only upon the Established Church, but upon vested rights and the whole principle of property. Protestant landowners throughout the country took alarm.

The first Parliament of the reign having been dissolved in July, 1687, the Lord Lieutenants were bidden to furnish lists of non-Anglicans suitable for election to the new Parliament. Many of the Lieutenants preferred resignation to compliance. Many bishops also refused to order their clergy to read the Proclamation of Indulgence reissued on 4th May, 1688, and ordered to be read on Sundays 20th and 27th May. Six bishops were, together with Archbishop Sancroft, brought to trial for seditious libel, but were acquitted amid scenes of enthusiasm that sounded the doom of the Stuart monarchy.

Thus had James violated every sentiment dear to his people and hopelessly alienated every interest and every class. Things were brought to a crisis by the unexpected birth of a son to Mary of Modena, James's second wife (10th June, 1688). The birth of this child, known to history as the Old Pretender, gave promise of the establishment of a Catholic dynasty and dashed the hopes of the Protestants who might have endured the rule of James, in view of the fact that the princesses, hitherto next in succession, were daughters of James's Protestant wife, and were both married to Protestant husbands. Moreover, James had neglected to summon the officials required to be present at the birth of a prince, and the rumour spread that the Jesuits had foisted a suppositious child upon the country. The "warming pan" tale was without foundation, but it sufficed; and on 30th June an invitation was sent to William, Prince of Orange, to come to England with an army at his back and secure the liberties of the English people. The invitation was signed not only by typical Whigs like Admiral Edward Russell, Henry Sidney and William Cavendish, fourth Earl and first Duke of Devonshire, but by Danby and Bishop Compton.

**William of Orange.**

William of Orange, if not deeply interested in the "liberties" of the English people, was strongly convinced that the adhesion of England was essential to the success of the League (of Augsburg) which he had lately (1686) formed to assert the liberties of Europe against Louis XIV. Accordingly, he accepted the invitation, issued a manifesto (30th September) enumerating the misdeeds of James II, and announcing that he was coming to England with an army and would abide the decision of a freely elected Parliament. He landed at Torbay on 2nd November and advanced on London. James had made a last-hour effort to revoke his blunders: he restored the town charters, which he had confiscated in order to secure the return of Catholic members for borough constituencies; he abolished the Ecclesiastical Commission; restored dispossessed dons, and removed Catholic counsellors. It was too late. The defection of General Lord Churchill sealed his fate. After a frustrated attempt at flight he was wisely permitted to quit the kingdom. William arrived in London, and in consultation with peers and ex-M.P.s summoned a Convention which, after debating several alternative schemes, agreed to settle the throne on William and Mary, and drafted a Declaration of Rights which William and Mary accepted.

They were crowned on 11th April, 1689, not by Archbishop Sancroft, who, as a non-juror, refused to act, but by Bishop Compton of London. They were "recognized" not as "rightful inheritors" but as "King and Queen of this realm", and, unlike James II, were sworn to "maintain . . . the Protestant Religion established by law".

Bloodlessly, without violence, and as far as might be by due process of law, the English Revolution was accomplished.

## CHAPTER XVIII

# The Revolution (1689-1714)
# The End of Personal Monarchy

THE Revolution formally accomplished by the accession of William and Mary in 1689 was confirmed in 1714 by the accession of George I.

The intervening period marked the transition from Personal to Constitutional Monarchy. The " abdication " of James II ended personal monarchy; yet William III was a personal monarch; so was Queen Anne. Both presided at the meetings of the Cabinet; neither had a Prime Minister. George I was the first parliamentary monarch; he soon ceased to attend the meetings of the Cabinet, his place in the chair being taken by a minister who was presently distinguished from his colleagues as the Premier. When that happened the English Sovereign became " constitutional ".

**William III.**

William III might well have prayed, in his lifetime, to be saved from his friends; as an historical figure he still needs to be saved from them. In life the Whigs would like to have made him the figure-head of an oligarchical republic—a Venetian Doge. Whig historians have represented him as a champion of parliamentary institutions, and as the begetter of the Cabinet system. The perspective is false. William III had as little love for Parliament as Cromwell or any Stuart; he met it annually because he could not otherwise get supplies for his armies; but he regarded it as a necessary nuisance. As for the Cabinet, he was persuaded by the Earl of Sunderland to confide the chief offices of State exclusively to Whigs (1693), and he has, in consequence, been regarded as the founder of

Party government. But the significance of the *Junto* as a constitutional landmark has been exaggerated.[1] That William III should be included among great *English* statesmen is verging on the ridiculous. He was a great *Dutch* statesman, and even more emphatically a great *European* statesman, to whom England was a pawn in the game of European diplomacy. With some exaggeration, it may be, but with essential accuracy, Sir Henry Maine described him as " merely a foreign politician and general who submitted to the eccentricities of his subjects for the sake of using their wealth and arms in foreign wars ".

**The Revolution: its Character.**

Nevertheless, in the history of the English monarchy the reign of William and Mary is of outstanding importance. Burke extolled the Revolution of 1688 for its cautious and conservative character. Macaulay held its chief merit to be that, by putting a " usurper " on the throne, it cut away all the remnants of the mischievous doctrines of Divine Right and Passive Obedience. Undeniably, the Revolution did register an important development in Representative, if not in Responsible, Government. For a century, indeed, it was pre-eminently the aristocratic oligarchy that reaped the political advantages of the Revolution, but since the great families used Parliament as their instrument of government, the Revolution was essentially a triumph for Parliament.

**Bill of Rights.**

By its famous resolutions (28th and 29th January, 1689) Parliament affirmed the contractual character of the monarchy, and accepted William and Mary, on the basis of a *Declaration* (subsequently embodied in the Bill) *of Rights.* This Act reaffirmed the theory that James had " abdicated ", and prescribed new forms for the Coronation Oath and the Oaths of Supremacy and Allegiance. It catalogued the chief offences of James II, declared illegal the pretended power of suspending and (" as of late exercised ") of dispensing with laws, of levying money " by Pretence of Prerogative ", and maintaining a standing army without consent of Parliament; it insisted that elections should be free, that Parliament should be held frequently, and its

[1] See *infra*, p. 262.

privileges respected. The annual meeting of Parliament had already been virtually secured by the *Mutiny Act* enacted for twelve months only and still annually re-enacted as the "Army Annual". Later on (1674) a Triennial Act was passed providing not only (somewhat superfluously) that Parliament should meet at least once in every three years, but also that no Parliament should sit for more than three years. It was, however, only the exigencies of foreign affairs that induced William to assent to a bill which he disliked and resented. A year later (1695) Parliament, by refusing to renew the Licensing Act (1662), which had given the Crown a strict censorship over the Press, gave to the written word a freedom limited only by the law of libel.

Toleration.

The *Toleration Act* (1689) did not admit to the rights of citizenship Roman Catholics or Protestant Nonconformists, but it relieved the latter from most of the restrictions imposed by the "Clarendon Code" upon freedom of worship. The *Uniformity Act* of 1662 still defined the position of the Established Church; the *Test Act* of 1673 remained in force until the nineteenth century, but there was an end of the Ecclesiastical Commissions and other like courts, and persecution ceased. Moreover, by the devious path of "Occasional Conformity", many Nonconformists obtained official situations.

The Judiciary.

Of all guarantees of liberty secured by the Revolution perhaps the most important was the emancipation of the judges from the control of the Executive. The *Act of Settlement* (1701) provided that judges should no longer be "lions under the throne", but should hold office during good behaviour, should draw regular salaries, and be removable only on address by both Houses of Parliament. Their complete independence both of the Executive and (virtually) of the Legislature has never since been questioned.

Finance.

An important change was also made in the financial relations of Crown and Parliament. Hitherto the King had borne the whole charge of government, applying thereto his own hereditary revenues, together with any taxes voted by Parliament, and the product of customs and other similar sources of revenue. Between the royal revenue and the national revenue there was no distinction. The principle of "appropriation" was, indeed, established under Charles II, but the practice imperfectly corresponded with the principle, and it was only after the Revolution that the effective control of the House of Commons over national expenditure really began.

**The Civil List.**

William III surrendered the hereditary revenues (excluding the revenue from the Royal Duchies of Lancaster and Cornwall), which were then derived mainly from Crown lands, feudal rights (commuted in 1660 for the hereditary excise duties), the profits of the Post Office, wine licences, &c. In return Parliament voted to him an annual revenue of £1,200,000 a year, divided into two equal portions. Out of one half the King had to meet the cost of the royal household, palaces, &c., the salaries of foreign ministers, of the judges, the civil service at home, and pensions granted in his reign or those of his immediate predecessors. The other half was to provide for other expenses of government and contingent expenditure. The former half—the Civil List (as it came soon to be called)—was in later reigns reduced in amount but relieved of charges for national, as opposed to royal, purposes.

**Bank of England and National Debt.**

In these arrangements nothing was allowed for the maintenance of the fighting services in peace time, still less in war. War expenditure was met until 1694, out of loans raised in a most haphazard manner and at ruinous rates of interest, rising as high as 14 per cent. But in that year some wealthy supporters of the Government were incorporated under the style of the Governor and Company of the Bank of England. The Bank of St. George at Genoa had been established for three centuries, and early in the seventeenth century the Dutch established a national bank at Amsterdam. England was late in this, as in other commercial developments and financial expedients. Down to the Revolution the idea of funding loans was quite unknown, but the Bank of England initiated a new departure. Government was to borrow £1,200,000 at the low rate of 8 per cent, and the Bank was inhibited, under heavy penalties, from lending money to the Crown without the express authority of Parliament. The new Corporation was endowed with no exclusive privileges, but was permitted to trade in bullion and bills of exchange, and like other banks to issue notes. The Tories opposed the new departure on political grounds, and the landlords were jealous of the rising importance of the new "moneyed" interest. But nothing did more than the new system of finance to give stability to the Revolution settlement, and to guarantee the new dynasty against possible "Pretenders".

**The Act of Settlement (1701).**

Further guarantees were provided, and the constitutional edifice of the Revolution was completed, by the Act of Settlement (1701). That Act is one of the most important in the recent history of the English monarchy and of the English people. On 30th July, 1700, the Princess Anne, heiress presumptive to the throne, lost her only child, the Duke of Gloucester, a promising lad of eleven. His death brought the question of the succession again to the front. The Act of Settlement accordingly provided that after William and the Princess Anne, and in default of issue to the latter, the Crown should pass to the children of William, and in default to the Electress Sophia of Hanover, daughter of the much-loved English Princess Elizabeth, late Queen of Bohemia, and to the heirs of Sophia, being Protestants. No Sovereign becoming a Papist or marrying a Papist was to occupy the throne, and no Sovereign was to leave the country without the consent of Parliament, nor was England, without its consent, to be obliged to engage in war for the defence of any foreign dominion belonging to a sovereign of foreign birth. No foreigner was to receive grants from, or hold any office under, the Crown, or to sit in Parliament or the Privy Council. All matters properly cognizable in the Privy Council were to be transacted there, and no person holding an office or place of profit under, or receiving a pension from, the Crown was to be capable of sitting in the House of Commons.

Had the last two provisions not been promptly amended

under Queen Anne, the evolution of the Cabinet would have been frustrated. The whole Act, indeed, betrays equal mistrust of foreigners, of placemen, and of Papists.

**Foreign Policy.**

Towards many of the sentiments of his English subjects William was far from sympathetic; but he assented to much distasteful legislation—notably the Acts against Roman Catholics—in order to obtain the means for carrying out his foreign policy. To avert a French hegemony in Europe was the supreme object of his life. All else was to him of secondary interest.

But strongly as the English people were opposed to the gallophil policy of the later Stuarts, they could not share their King's acute apprehensions about the advance of Louis XIV on the Rhine, and towards the Pyrenees. On the other hand, they deeply resented the interference of a French king in their domestic concerns; and they derived immense satisfaction from the Orange conquest of Ireland (1689–9), partly because it seemed to assure Protestant ascendancy in a Dependency which had been slow to appreciate the blessings of the Anglican Establishment, partly because the victory of a Catholic Stuart would have made Louis XIV master of the island. But the Continent was relatively remote, and what Louis XIV might achieve on the Continent did not directly concern them. Nevertheless, it was a cause of great satisfaction that by the Treaty of Ryswick (1697) Louis XIV was compelled to renounce the cause of the Stuarts, to acknowledge William III as King, and the Princess Anne as his successor.

To William the Treaty of Ryswick was merely a truce; the real struggle lay ahead. Parliament, hoping that it meant the definite end of the war, at once cut down the army to 7000 men—no more than sufficient for police purposes—and sent back to Holland William's Dutch Guards.

William, deeply chagrined, contemplated retirement to the Hague, but refrained from that drastic step in the hope of persuading the English Parliament to recognize that the liberties of England could not be secure so long as Louis XIV threatened to dominate the Continent.

**The Spanish Succession Question.**

From the time of his marriage with the Spanish Infanta, Maria Theresa (1660), Louis XIV had conceived the ambition of securing for a French prince the Spanish Empire—should the male line of the Spanish Habsburgs, as seemed likely, become extinct. So vast, however, was the Spanish inheritance that Louis consented by treaties concluded with England and Holland in 1698 and 1700 to its partition. The Partition Treaties aroused great indignation in England, partly because they appeared to threaten English trade in the Mediterranean, partly because William had presumed to commit England to the treaties on his sole responsibility. Charles II of Spain died on 1st November, 1700, having secretly made a will leaving the whole of his possessions to Philip Count of Anjou, the younger grandson of Louis XIV.

To the astonishment and indignation of William III the English people preferred the will to the Partition Treaties. The presence of a French prince on the Spanish throne seemed to them less menacing to English interests than the direct aggrandizement of France in the Mediterranean. William, therefore, was compelled to recognize Philip Count of Anjou as King of Spain.

William's popularity in England was now (1701) at the nadir. Parliament, resenting his grants of Irish land to his mistress and his Dutch friends, passed an Act of Resumption, and impeached William's intimate friend Lord Portland (Bentinck), Somers, Oxford and Halifax (Charles Montague), though the impeachment was presently discharged.

**Louis XIV and the Stuarts.**

The whole position was, indeed, suddenly transformed in William's favour by two colossal blunders committed by his adversary. Louis advertised the real significance of the will of Charles II by sending French troops to occupy the strong places in the Netherlands. Worse still, when James II died at St. Germains (16th September, 1701) he recognized the Prince of Wales as *de jure* King of England.

The anger aroused by these acts in England was instantaneous and profound. William promptly dissolved Parliament: the constituencies gave him the Whig majority he wanted; the Tory ministers were dismissed; one Bill was immediately passed to attaint the "Pretender", and was followed by another to maintain the Protestant succession and to impose an oath to that effect upon all office-holders in Church or State. And then, amid a blaze of unaccustomed popularity, William III died.

He died happy in the knowledge that his object was achieved. England was brought whole-heartedly into a war with France, destined only to end, more than a century later, with Wellington's victory at Waterloo.

Queen Anne.

"I know my own heart to be entirely English." So said Queen Anne in her first Speech from the Throne. Her self-knowledge was not at fault. "Entirely English" she was, alike in her virtues and her limitations. She was not clever but she was good. Her resignation under bereavements beyond the common lot, and her unaffected piety, endeared her to her people. Her devotion to the English Church was worthy of Clarendon's grand-daughter, and her Toryism was of an even deeper hue than his. She shared her people's dislike for her predecessor, though she gave her entire confidence to the great general whose victories achieved the end for which William had striven, but which his indifferent skill as a soldier might have denied to him. Marlborough's great victories added glamour to a reign memorable on many grounds. Queen Anne had the honour of conferring a knighthood upon Isaac Newton, who from 1703 until his death (1727) was President of the Royal Society. In the annals of literature her reign was rendered illustrious by Addison and Steele, Pope and Defoe, by Dean Swift and Henry St. John (Lord Bolingbroke). Politically, also, it was important. In the history of the English Parliament, as in that of the Scottish Estates, there has been no single act of statesmanship more completely successful than the Legislative Union between England and Scotland. That the Good Queen made any important contribution to the greatness of her reign it were fulsome to pretend: but she did nothing to diminish it, or to obstruct those who rendered it one of the most illustrious in our annals. The epithet attached to the Queen's title was well

The "Augustan Age".

earned; she was "Good", and among her subjects her memory was fragrant.

The War.

On the Queen's accession a Tory Parliament found itself pledged to the conduct of a Whig war. But Bolingbroke recorded his "deliberate conviction after more than twenty years of recollection, re-examination and reflexion, that before this change of policy [in 1707] the war was wise and just, because necessary to maintain that equality among the Powers of Europe on which the public peace and common prosperity depend".[1] He maintained, however, that by 1706 all the essential objects of the war had been obtained. Marlborough had won his great victories at Blenheim (1704) and Ramillies (1706) and had cleared the whole of Flanders (except four great fortresses) of the French. Admiral Rooke had captured Gibraltar; Peterborough had fought a brilliant campaign in Spain. Louis XIV was beaten, and offered terms of peace more favourable to the allies than those they accepted after seven more years of war.

English Parties and the War.

Party interests were, however, becoming involved in the war. Anne's first ministry, headed by Marlborough, Nottingham and Godolphin, was composed both of Whigs and Tories. But the Tory element was, under the exigencies of the war, gradually eliminated. Rochester, a "right wing" Tory, was dismissed in 1702, Nottingham in 1704, and in that year Harley and St. John, Tories of a less robust type, joined the ministry. In 1708 they in turn made way for Whigs. Among the latter was one Robert Walpole, a Norfolk squire who had been returned to Parliament in 1701 and owed his rapid rise partly to his own character and brains, partly to the influence of Sarah, Duchess of Marlborough. The Whigs had secured a small majority at the election of 1705, and having increased it in 1708 they secured the complete control of the Executive government. The Queen would still have preferred a composite ministry, but from 1708 to 1710 the war and the Whigs were too strong for her, and England was ruled by a Party

[1] *Letters on the Study of History*, Letter viii. (*Works*, Vol. II, p. 449.)

government, supported by a Party majority in Parliament.

To the Whigs and in particular to Lord Somers must be ascribed the credit for negotiating the terms—a task none too easy—of the Legislative Union between England and Scotland.

**The Union.**

> The Queen has lately lost a part
> Of her " entirely English " heart,
> For want of which by way of botch,
> She pieced it up again with Scotch,
> Blest Revolution! which creates
> Divided hearts, united States!

Swift might scoff: but the Union, though at first popular in neither of the united countries, was a very great achievement. It guaranteed to the Scots their Presbyterian Establishment, their own laws and forms of judicial procedure, and complete commercial and fiscal equality with England; it wiped out their national debt, and gave them generous compensation for the loss of a separate coinage. England secured the services of some fine regiments, and recruited her public services and commercial life with the best brains of the Scottish manses. For at least four centuries Scotland, in constant alliance with France, had been a serious menace to England. Great Britain, under one monarch and one Parliament, was to play a far greater part in world affairs than that played by either kingdom in its separate existence.

**Parliament and the War.**

For the moment, however, the Union was overshadowed by the war. In 1707 the Whigs passed a Resolution declaring that no peace could be " safe or honourable " if " Spain and the Spanish West Indies " were " suffered to continue in the power of the House of Bourbon ". That Resolution was, both from the party and the national point of view, a grievous blunder. The nation cared little who sat on the throne of Spain, and began to suspect that aristocratic Whigs and their friends in the City were deliberately prolonging the war for the sake of their party and their pockets. Marlborough continued to win great victories, notably at Oudenarde (1708) and at Malplaquet (1709), but the latter was very costly and, coming soon after a second rejection of the peace offers of Louis, evoked no enthusiasm.

**Bolingbroke, Harley and Swift.**

Moreover, the Whigs and their general were losing popular favour. To the Tory reaction several things contributed. The Whigs made the blunder of giving the halo of advertisement, if not of martyrdom, to an obscure Oxford don, Dr. Henry Sacheverell. In pamphlets, and in sermons not only preached but printed, Sacheverell had attacked "revolution doctrines", and condemned toleration and occasional conformity. For this he was impeached. His trial aroused the greatest enthusiasm for the victim of Whig persecution, and the light sentence passed upon him measured his popularity. The Whigs were replaced in office by a ministry homogeneously Tory in texture, and headed by Robert Harley, the "solemn trifler", and Henry St. John, the "brilliant knave". The Queen, tiring of the insolent domination of the Duchess of Marlborough, dismissed her from court; the Duke was accused of peculation and cashiered; Walpole, on the same ground, was sent to the Tower.

The action of the Queen and her Tory ministers was endorsed by the constituencies. The general election of 1710 gave the Tories a large majority, and encouraged them to end the war. They owed much of their success to the pen of the most brilliant pamphleteer of an age remarkable for its political essayists. In *The Examiner* (November, 1710, to June, 1711) Dean Swift attacked the policy of the Whigs, and in *The Conduct of the Allies* (1711) provided the Tories with a conclusive argument in favour of an immediate peace with France.

**The Treaty of Utrecht (1713).**

An argument even more conclusive was the death (April, 1711) of the Emperor Joseph and the succession of the Archduke Charles to the Empire and to the Habsburg dominions in Central Europe. To fight on in order to give him possession of Spain as well as the Indies was demonstrable folly. Philip of Anjou must, perforce, be allowed to retain them. Peace, then, was inevitable. In order to carry it through, the Queen had to create a batch of twelve

Tory peers (December, 1711). In 1712 the English troops were withdrawn from the war, and in 1713 St. John (raised to the peerage in 1712 as Viscount Bolingbroke) induced or compelled the Dutch and the minor members of the Alliance to join with England in concluding the Peace of Utrecht. The Emperor Charles VI concluded peace at Rastadt in 1714. "In this Peace," said Voltaire, "France accepted terms from England and dictated them to the Empire." Bolingbroke, on the contrary, was inclined to apologize for the terms of a Peace which he nevertheless deemed inevitable. "I shall not be surprised," he wrote, "if you think the Peace of Utrecht was not answerable to the success of the war, nor to the efforts made in it. I think so myself, and have always owned, even when it was making and made, that I thought so."

What Peace has ever really been answerable to the efforts made in the preceding war? Yet no one now questions that it was right to make peace in 1713, or denies that it represented a great triumph for England. France was constrained to acknowledge the Protestant succession in England; the acquisition of Gibraltar and Minorca gave us the command of the Mediterranean; England for the first time began to make headway against the French in North America, and obtained valuable, if shameful, rights of trade with Spanish South America. Sir John Seeley had no misgivings about a treaty which "left England the first State in the world".

Did the Tories hurry on the Peace in order to clear the way for a Stuart restoration? The accusation was made at the time, and has been frequently repeated. Bolingbroke vehemently denied that there existed any design to set aside the succession of the House of Hanover. But, before the Queen's death, there were admittedly many men, on both sides, who were in correspondence simultaneously with St. Germains and Hanover.

**The Succession.**

Any hope of a Stuart restoration was frustrated, on the one hand, by the firm refusal of James Edward to abjure his religion, and on the other by the greatly superior cohesion and organization of the Whigs. The Tories were divided on the crucial question of policy, and their leaders were quarrelling on personal issues. Harley (now Lord Oxford), doubtfully honest, was undoubtedly irresolute and procrastinating. Bolingbroke, putting himself at the head of the High Tories, pushed through the Schism Act (1714) in the hope of crushing the Dissenters, and putting his own friends in all posts, civil and military, "down to the meanest". On 27th July, Bolingbroke induced the Queen to dismiss Oxford: but, as she lay dying, the Whigs effected a *coup d'état*, got Shrewsbury put into Oxford's place as Lord Treasurer, and summoned the Electoral Prince from Hanover. Bolingbroke was outplayed. Queen Anne died on 1st August. "The Earl of Oxford was removed on Tuesday," wrote Bolingbroke to Swift, "the Queen died on Sunday. What a world is this! And how doth fortune banter us!" Fortune did, indeed, banter Bolingbroke. He knew himself beaten, and joined with the Whig leaders in proclaiming the Electoral Prince George as King.

The Whig Triumph.

King George arrived in England in September, 1714, entrusted all the chief offices of State to Whigs, who in the new Parliament (March, 1715) found themselves in a large majority. For nearly half a century the Whig supremacy was practically unbroken.

Bolingbroke fled to France in order to avoid prosecution —a colossal blunder from the effects of which he never recovered. Oxford was impeached and committed to the Tower, but after two years' imprisonment was brought to trial and acquitted. Bolingbroke was pardoned in 1723 and returned to England, where for twelve years he made violent but vain efforts to regain his position in English politics. He recovered his property, but his enemies were too shrewd and too suspicious to allow him to re-enter the House of Lords. Foiled in his political ambitions, he retired in 1735 to France, and devoted his remaining years to literary composition. His voluminous works were intended primarily as an *apologia* for a political career which, despite brilliant gifts, was ruined by ineradicable defects of character.

They remain, however, as examples of eloquent and stately English prose; as party pamphlets they inspired George III and Disraeli; as contributing to the scientific study of political philosophy they are of little value.

**Queen Anne's Death.**

"Good" Queen Anne was not a great Queen, and yet until her death the Crown was the centre of political gravity. Much influenced as she was by favourites, she was the last "personal monarch" in England. But the principle was rapidly weakening. Though the ministers were "Her Majesty's servants" in a sense less purely technical than they have ever since been, they relied less and less upon royal favour and increasingly upon the support of a party majority in Parliament. The Queen's title to the throne, if not divine, was predominantly hereditary. That of her successor was predominantly parliamentary. The death of Queen Anne marks, then, the close of an epoch, the passing of yet another stage in the evolution both of the monarchy and of parliamentary democracy.

## CHAPTER XIX

# Constitutional Monarchy

## The Early Hanoverians and the Cabinet

THE accession of the Hanoverians has been described as "the greatest miracle in English history". But the "miracle" was no inexplicable phenomenon. There was, in fact, no visible opposition, even in the Catholic parts of Ireland or Scotland, to the recognition of the Elector George. On the death of Queen Anne he was immediately proclaimed King, and some six weeks later arrived in England. Behind the "miracle" substantial forces were operating. In one sense the peaceful succession of King George was a party triumph, being unanimously and fervently supported by the Whigs. The Tories, distracted by internal quarrels, lost the game because they could not make up their minds what stakes they were playing for. The nation, though as a whole apathetic, was on one issue determined. As in 1688, so again in 1714 there was a conflict of loyalties; but again loyalty to the Church proved stronger than loyalty to the hereditary monarchy. Had James Edward been willing, like his uncle, to purchase the Crown by repudiation of his creed, he would almost certainly have been recalled to the throne. On the purely political issue the Jacobites were in a large majority. But the people were Protestants first and Jacobites afterwards. On the other hand, the Whigs, if outnumbered in the country districts, dominated the towns, especially those towns which increasingly relied upon commerce for their prosperity. Moreover, if the squires were mainly Tory in sympathies, many of the greatest landowners were Whigs, as were all the Nonconformists and the moneyed men. A party which is compact, coherent,

**The "Miracle".**

well organized, and clear as to its goal, is bound to win in a contest against a party which, even if in a majority, lacks cohesion and unity of purpose.

**George I.** The Whig nominee for the throne was not a man to evoke enthusiasm. As the personal ruler of a German principality he was popular and successful: and he left his heart in Hanover. He also left there his wife, who had long been, and until her death (1727) continued to be, imprisoned for alleged infidelity. Born in 1660, the King was in advanced middle age when he responded, reluctantly, to the invitation of the Whigs. Unlike his mother, he lacked all the Stuart graces, and in manners and person, in outlook and sympathies, was purely German: but he was punctual, methodical, and, though no miser like George II, was far from extravagant. As a soldier he had proved himself possessed of courage and skill. He was more interested in foreign than in domestic politics, but continental affairs, though complicated, were not during his reign of primary consequence to England. The Whigs, though foolish enough to impeach the Tory chiefs for " betraying the interests and honour of England " in concluding the Treaty of Utrecht, fixed upon the maintenance of the settlement it provided as the mainspring of their own foreign policy. After the death of Louis XIV (1715), it was to the manifest advantage both of England and of the Regency Government in France that the terms of the treaty should be scrupulously observed. Twice during the reign of George I was the Utrecht settlement endangered by the ambition of Spain, but the Triple Alliance of England, France and Holland (1717) sufficed to localize such fighting as took place.

**The Whig Ministry.** George I naturally selected his ministers exclusively from the Whig party. In October, 1714, the Duke of Shrewsbury resigned the white staff, and his office of Lord High Treasurer was not filled up. Since then the Treasury has always been in commission. The Chancellor of the Exchequer, though not invariably included in the Cabinet until the days of the younger Pitt, gradually assumed the position of Finance Minister, especially when, as was frequently the case, the office was combined with the First Lordship of the Treasury. Robert Walpole combined the two offices from 1721 to 1742, and since his day the First Lord of the Treasury has generally, but not invariably, been accepted as the Head of the Ministry.[1] From 1714 to 1717 Viscount Townshend, one of the two Secretaries of State, was the leading minister; from 1717 to 1721 General Stanhope took that position, but neither claimed or was accorded the title of Prime Minister.

**Jacobite Rising (1715).**

It was Stanhope who was mainly responsible for the suppression of the Rising of 1715. Bolingbroke ascribes the outbreak of the Rebellion to the vindictiveness with which the Whigs had pursued their Tory opponents. The folly of the Whigs may have furnished some excuse; it may have encouraged Bolingbroke to join a desperate enterprise; but the actual outbreak was due partly to the hopes held out to the Pretender by Catholic zealots in Scotland, Ireland and in less degree in England, and still more to the European situation. The advancement of the Hanoverian Elector was keenly resented not only by Louis XIV, but by the Emperor Charles VI, by Charles XII of Sweden, and by Cardinal Alberoni, who in the name of Philip V was ruling Spain. The European situation, then, was highly favourable to the enterprise. But three conditions were essential to success: perfect timing between the movements in England, Scotland and Ireland; competent leadership; and above all effective help from Louis XIV. None of the conditions was fulfilled. Louis XIV died on 1st September, five days before the Stuart standard was raised and James VIII was proclaimed in Scotland. Not until 22nd December did James VIII himself land in Scotland; exactly two months later (22nd February) he left his disillusioned kingdom, a disillusioned man. James Edward was not the man to inspire enthusiasm in the followers of a cause predestined to failure. The Whigs, amply forewarned, were well prepared; they struck hard;

[1] Under the *Ministers of the Crown Act* (1937), the Prime Minister henceforth will always hold the office of First Lord of the Treasury, and for the dual office will receive a salary of £10,000 a year.

and the Jacobites were in no condition to resist their well-directed blows. Of the insurgents who were taken prisoners, Lord Derwentwater and Lord Kenmure were executed, with a few of their followers; many more were deported to the Plantations, the great majority were either released or lightly punished.

General Stanhope and his Government had shown themselves efficient, strong, and not merciless; their King sat secure on a throne greatly strengthened by the fiasco. Nevertheless, the Whigs were not disposed to put their fortunes to the hazard of a general election.

The Septennial Act (1716).

Under the terms of the Triennial Act (1694), the existing Parliament was due to expire in December, 1716. Could the country, so recently perturbed by the Jacobite Rising, be trusted to give a sober verdict—a verdict in favour of the Whigs? The Whigs decided to take no risks, and passed a Bill to extend the possible duration of Parliaments, including the sitting Parliament, from three years to seven. Though intended as a temporary expedient to meet an emergency, the Act remained in force until the Parliament Act of 1911 reduced the period to five years.

Bitterly opposed by the Tories, the Bill was defended by Stanhope mainly on the ground that unless it were passed no foreign power would ally itself with a country which might repudiate the contract when the next Parliament met; but he held out the hope that the Bill would be repealed as soon as " the evil spirit was cast out ". Speaker Onslow declared that this Act " formed the era of the emancipation of the British House of Commons from its former dependence on the Crown and the House of Lords ". It may be so; but that famous Speaker omitted to notice a more important point: that the Act might well have emancipated Parliament from the control also of the electorate.

Archdeacon Coxe, the biographer of Walpole, frankly admitted that the Septennial Act was " one of the most daring uses—or, according to the representations of its opponents, abuses—of parliamentary power since the Revolution ". Nevertheless, he insisted that " many of the most inestimable blessings of our Constitution are to be attributed to this measure which originally appeared to invade its first principles ".[1]

Clearly defensible, if not imperatively demanded by contemporary circumstances, the *Septennial Act* has been acclaimed by the jurists of our own day as the standing illustration and proof that " in a legal point of view Parliament is neither the agent of the electors nor in any sense a trustee of its constituents ".[2] Constitutional purists like Joseph Priestley were aghast at this violation of the " rights " of the people. Hallam derided Priestley's " ignorant assumption ". But Priestley was right. There is no legal obstacle to the indefinite prolongation of the life of a Parliament. The Long Parliament elected in 1640 might, except for Cromwell's Ironsides, still be sitting. Nor are more recent illustrations lacking. The Parliament elected in 1910 should, under the *Parliament Act* of 1911, have expired at latest in 1915. By successive enactments its existence was prolonged until December, 1918, and by the same legal process it might have been prolonged until 1928.

**The Peerage Bill (1719).**

More disputable than the policy of the *Septennial Act* was that involved in the attempt of Stanhope and Sunderland to render impossible for the future the swamping of the House of Lords. The immediate justification for the Peerage Bill of 1719 was the simultaneous creation, at Lord Oxford's instance, of twelve peers, in order to give the Tories a majority in the Upper House (1712). The author of the Bill was Charles, 3rd Earl of Sunderland (1674–1722). He is now best remembered as the collector of the Althorp Library, but in his own day he was regarded as a volatile and incalculable politician who owed his official employment chiefly to his marriage with Anne Churchill. Sunderland represented the quintessence of aristocratic Whiggism: equally suspicious of the Crown and the people, mistrusting the principles alike of monarchy and of democracy.

Sunderland's bill proposed to limit strictly and for all time the membership of the House of Lords. The Crown

[1] *Walpole*, p. 75 f. [2] Dicey: *Law of the Constitution*, p. 44.

was to have the right of creating six new peers, and in addition one new peer for every peerage that became extinct. Scotland was to be represented by twenty-five hereditary in place of sixteen elected peers. The general effect of the Bill would, therefore, have been to make the House of Lords a close body of some 200 temporal and 26 spiritual peers. Its sponsors argued that it was desirable to deprive successive factions of the power to swamp the House of Lords, and that the House of Commons could never be truly independent so long as its leading members were constantly looking to the Crown for promotion to the Upper House.

The Bill, though carried in the House of Lords, was strongly resisted by Walpole, and by 269 votes to 177 the House of Commons rejected it. It is now common ground that the House of Lords would more effectively function as a Second Chamber were its numbers reduced by at least 50 per cent. But Sunderland's proposal was none the less mischievous. Had it been carried, the Second Chamber would have become the close preserve of an oligarchy; it would not have drawn recruits, as in one way or another it should, from all sections of society, nor would it include, as it now does, the best brains in the ranks of industry, commerce and the professions, as well as experienced diplomatists and pro-consuls. The weakness of the House of Lords is that besides these it includes a majority of members who owe their place in it solely to hereditary descent. Most of the work of the House is, in fact, done not by hereditary legislators, but by men who have attained to membership by personal merit and service to the community, and in large measure by men who have served an apprenticeship in the House of Commons. Had Sunderland's Bill become law, there would have been, as Walpole bluntly put it, " no arriving at honour but through the winding sheet of a decrepit lord, or the grave of an extinct noble family ". But in retrospect we can perceive that the conclusive argument against the Bill was that it would have closed the " safety-valve of the Constitution ". Between two legislative chambers, which until 1911 were co-ordinate in authority, conflicts must have periodically occurred. Such conflicts could and can be overcome, in the last resort, only by the Crown's prerogative of creating an unlimited number of new peerages. Written Constitutions may, and do, provide other devices for terminating a deadlock, but Sunderland's Bill would have abolished the only device known to an elastic, and for the most part unwritten, Constitution. That the device has never actually been used, even in 1832 or in 1911, is due to the fact that it was known to be in reserve.

**Walpole.**

It was fortunate for the country that owing to the disruption of the ministry (1717) Sunderland's Bill found Walpole in opposition, and fortunate for Walpole that he was thus free, as a private individual, to speculate successfully in the South Sea Company, and as a private member to oppose the participation of the Government in that discreditable gamble. The details of the South Sea scheme do not concern us; nor does the fact that the Government saw in it an easy way of ridding the Exchequer of the burden of the National Debt. It may suffice to say that the bursting of the "Bubble" killed Stanhope (February, 1721), and left the field open to one of the greatest statesmen of the eighteenth century.

Sir Robert Walpole (1676–1745) was by birth a Norfolk squire, and by education an Etonian and a scholar of King's College.[1] At the age of twenty-five this promising young man was returned to the House of Commons, and, except for a brief interval when he was expelled from the House on suspicion of maladministration of public funds (1712–3), he remained there until the close of his official career and his elevation to the peerage in 1742. After the accession of George I, he rejoined the ministry as Paymaster of the Forces (1714), a subordinate office which a year later he exchanged for the Chancellorship of the Exchequer. Driven out of office by Stanhope and Sunderland in 1717,

[1] Like a more recent Prime Minister, who in temperament is not unlike him, Walpole delighted in Horace.

he resumed it in 1719, again as Paymaster, and in April, 1721, again succeeded, on Aislabie's disgrace, to the Chancellorship of the Exchequer, combining with this office the First Lordship of the Treasury. When, twenty years later, Walpole resigned, it was clear that a change of profound significance in English politics had been consummated. Henceforward England was to be ruled by the Cabinet.

The time, then, has come to trace the evolution of this most characteristic and most differentiating of English political institutions.

**Essentials of the Cabinet System.**

It may help to elucidate a confused, intricate, and prolonged process to set out, as precisely as the subject permits, the implications of the Cabinet system as it exists to-day. (i) All Cabinet ministers are individually "the King's servants", and are solemnly sworn to secrecy as members of his Privy Council. (ii) The Cabinet is (but only since 1937) a legally defined body of Privy Councillors, whose appointment to, or cessation of service in, the Cabinet is officially announced in the *London Gazette*. (iii) Collectively the Cabinet is, in effect, an Executive Committee of the Imperial Parliament, and as such is the Governing Committee of the British Empire, except for the Dominions, each of which has a Cabinet of its own modelled on that of the United Kingdom. (iv) Individually and collectively Cabinet ministers are responsible to the House of Commons, and (v) acknowledge the headship of a "Prime Minister". (vi) Cabinet ministers are, for the most part, heads of administrative departments, and are responsible, individually, for the conduct of their several departments, such as the Home Office, the Foreign Office, &c., but (vii) the Cabinet as a whole is collectively responsible both for the general policy of the Government and also for all the more important acts of individual ministers, so long as the individuals retain their respective offices. Consequently (viii) the Cabinet must represent the Party majority in the House of Commons, by which it is sustained in power, and to which (or to the House of Lords) its members must, by convention, belong.

Although these principles have only been gradually established, it is possible in retrospect to perceive that ever since the seventeenth century things had been moving towards their recognition as essential to the Cabinet system.

The term "Cabinet" began to be used, but without any precise signification, in the seventeenth century. Bacon in his essay *On Council*, after complaining of the inconvenience of large councils, says: "The doctrine of Italy and the custom of France in some kings' times hath introduced Cabinet Councils, a remedy worse than the disease." More specific is the famous passage in Clarendon's *History of the Great Rebellion* (Book II, Vol. I, p. 244). It refers to the period between the dissolution of the Short and the meeting of the Long Parliament (1640) and runs: "The bulk and burden of the State affairs, whereby the envy attended them likewise, lay principally upon the shoulders of" Laud, Strafford, and Cottington, "some others being joined to them," including the Lord High Treasurer and the two Secretaries. "These persons made up the Committee of State (which was reproachfully after called *the juncto*, and enviously then in court, *the Cabinet Council*). . . . The weight and envy of all great matters rested upon the three first." This *juncto* met irregularly and whenever occasion required; "whereas the body of the [Privy] Council observed set days and hours for their meeting, and came not else together except specially summoned." The *juncto* had clearly no connexion with Parliament, nor, apart from the name attached to it by those who were suspicious of the development, did it possess any other attributes of a modern Cabinet.

**Evolution of the Cabinet.**

Pym came much nearer to the cardinal principle of the Cabinet when in the *Grand Remonstrance* (November, 1641) he demanded that the King should "employ such counsellors, ambassadors, and other ministers . . . *as the Parliament* may have cause to confide in, without which we cannot give His Majesty such supplies . . . as is desired." (§ 197.) In the next clause Pym put his finger upon the weak point of impeachment as a device for enforcing ministerial respon-

**The Grand Remonstrance.**

sibility. "It may often fall out that the Commons may have just cause to take exception to some men for being councillors, and yet not charge them with crimes, for there be grounds of diffidence which lie not in proof. . . . . We may be earnest with His Majesty not to put his great affairs into such hands, though we may be unwilling to proceed against them in any legal way of charge or impeachment." (§§ 198–201.)

The King's reply was uncompromising. He reminded the remonstrants that he had not withheld from "the justice of the law" any man however "near to [him] in place or affection" (Strafford, of course, was in his mind), but he insisted that it was "the undoubted right of the Crown . . . to call such persons to our secret counsels, to public employment and our particular service as we shall think fit". He promised that they should be men of unexceptionable ability and integrity, but the choice of them must be left to him.

Thus was the issue clearly joined. The conflict of the seventeenth century centred, as we have seen, in the struggle for the control of the Executive. But for religious differences there might, indeed, have been no clash of arms; those who made the Revolution were Puritans first, and only in a secondary degree Parliamentarians. None the less, they sought to attain their ends by transferring executive authority to ministers who possessed the confidence and therewith the support of Parliament.

**Under Charles II.**

The Civil War did not solve the problem. Still less did Cromwell. But the Restoration of 1660 was as much a triumph for Parliament as for the monarchy. Throughout the reign of Charles II we are clearly moving, though with hesitating steps and by devious paths, towards the Cabinet solution. Clarendon, true to the Elizabethan idea of the Constitution, made a gallant fight on behalf of the Privy Council. To the Council belonged the constitutional right to advise the Crown, to discourage royal favourites, and, while jealous in maintaining the rights of Parliament, to restrain its encroachments upon spheres not its own. "By

**Clarendon and the Privy Council.**

the Constitution of the kingdom," wrote Clarendon, " as the Privy Council and every member of it is of the King's sole choice and election of him to that trust (for the greatest office in the State, though conferred likewise by the King himself, doth not qualify the officers to be of the Privy Council, or to be present in it before by a new assignation that honour is bestowed on him, and that he is sworn of the Council), so the body of it is the most sacred, and hath the greatest authority in the Government next the person of the King himself to whom all other powers are equally subject; and no King of England can so well secure his own just prerogative or preserve it from violation as by a strict defending and supporting the dignity of his Privy Council."[1] Conformably with these ideas Clarendon had resented the ascendancy of Buckingham and of Strafford as keenly as he afterwards resented the intrusion of Parliament upon the functions of the Executive. The Executive belonged to the King-in-Council, as the making of laws belonged to the King-in-Parliament.

Of this old-fashioned theory Charles II was as impatient as his Parliament. But Clarendon, consistently with his general view of the Constitution, refused to listen to the suggestion that he should himself become a " first " or " sole " minister of the type of a Sully or a Richelieu. " England," he declared, " would not bear a favourite nor any one man, who should out of his ambition engross to himself the disposal of the public affairs." " First minister " was a " title so newly translated out of French into English, that it was not enough understood to be liked, and every man would detest it for the burden it was attended with."[2] There spake the genuine Conservative; but the tide was flowing past him. While Clarendon would have made the Council supreme over all the departments (though " departments " in the modern sense were conspicuous by their absence), the King wished to rule by isolating them, and placed each under a commission answerable only to himself. Several such commissions were,

[1] *Autobiography*, § 912. [2] *Ibid*, §§ 85–6.

in fact, set up—one, for instance, for the navy, with the Duke of York as Lord High Admiral. On the death of Lord Southampton, Lord High Treasurer (May, 1667), the Treasury also was put in commission. Downing was appointed secretary to the commissioners, and in his skilful hands the Treasury became the first of the well-organized departments of State. (To him one of the least pretentious and most important streets in Europe owes its name.) The same year (1667) saw also the appointment of regular committees of the Privy Council for (1) Foreign Affairs, (2) the Admiralty, (3) Trade and Plantations, and (4) Petitions of Complaint and Grievances.

Theoretically distinct from these committees (though in personnel identical at times with one or more of them), there was a small group of confidential advisers concerned not with departmental affairs but with general policy. In this group or committee we have the germ of the modern Cabinet.

**Temple's Scheme.**

This new development was in all quarters regarded with resentment and suspicion, but the old Privy Council, with its numbers swollen to more than fifty, was evidently too cumbrous for executive duties. Accordingly, on the advice of Sir William Temple, a new experiment was tried. In dissolving the old Privy Council the King used significant words: " His Majesty gives you all thanks for . . . all the good advices you have given him, which might have been more frequent if the great number of this Council had not made it unfit for the secrecy and dispatch that are necessary in many great affairs. This forced him to use a smaller number of you in a foreign committee and sometimes the advices of some few among them. . . . He is sorry for the ill success he has found in this course. . . . He hath resolved to lay aside the use he may have hitherto made of any single ministry or private advices, or foreign committees for the general direction of His affairs ", and to constitute a new and smaller Privy Council, representing all parties in the State, and " by the constant advice of such a Council, His Majesty is resolved hereafter to govern his kingdoms, together with the frequent use of his Great Council of Parliament which he takes to be the true ancient Constitution of this State and Government." The King then proceeded to outline the scheme devised by Sir William Temple. The Privy Council was to consist of thirty members: fifteen great officers of State, together with ten noblemen and five commoners, men of wealth and influence, and selected for their ability and public repute. The Archbishop of Canterbury and the Bishop of London were to represent the Church; the Lord Chancellor and one of the Lord Chief Justices the law; the Admiral and the Master of the Ordnance the fighting forces; the Chancellor of the Exchequer and the Treasurer (or First Commissioner) finance; the Lord Privy Seal, the Master of the Horse, the Lord Steward, the Lord Chamberlain, the Groom of the Stole, and the two Secretaries of State—these were to constitute the official fifteen, and were all to be sworn of the Privy Council. The rest were to be summoned at the King's discretion: but the number was never to exceed thirty.

This scheme, happily described by Anson as "that transient and embarrassed phantom in our constitutional history", did not work. A Council of thirty is too large for the determination of executive policy, and within a few months the King was again taking counsel only with small groups of statesmen. Shaftesbury's restless ambition helped to wreck the experiment, but the trend towards a Cabinet was, in truth, too strong to be withstood. During the remainder of Charles's reign the Privy Council was not, however, allowed to exceed thirty; under William and Mary it exceeded sixty, and under Anne eighty. But, as in modern practice, only a moiety of the nominal members were, as a rule, summoned to attend. Whether Privy Councillors not so summoned had a right to attend is a disputed point. To the historic Privy Council of 30th July, 1714, the Dukes of Somerset and Argyle were not summoned, but they attended, and their presence proved decisive.

Meanwhile, the evolution of the Cabinet proceeded apace. By the end of the reign of Charles II it consisted of a small body of eight or ten persons meeting every Sunday under the presidency of the King. According to Roger North it was a recognized and formal body which "had the direction of most of the transactions of the Government, foreign and domestic", and consisted (1682–4) of the Lord President (Radnor), the Lord Chancellor (Guilford), the Privy Seal (Halifax), Conway and Jenkins (Secretaries of State), Rochester (Treasurer), Ormonde (Lord Lieutenant of Ireland) and Sidney Godolphin, a Commissioner of the Treasury.[1] It is noticeable that it contained no Household officers, but did include most of the leading ministers, though no representative of the "Services". Clearly, also, its members, though in touch with Parliament, were primarily the King's servants, chosen personally by him, and presided over by him. It lacked, therefore, most of the distinctive marks of a modern Cabinet.

William and Mary.

From 1689 to 1702 William III ruled England; he was his own Prime Minister and his own Foreign Minister. Yet the Cabinet gained in cohesion, and the resignations of Halifax in 1689 and of Shrewsbury in 1690 may, perhaps, indicate a deepening sense, though still ill-defined, of the responsibility of Cabinet ministers to Parliament.[2] Of some sixty Cabinet meetings in the years 1694, 1695 and 1696, we still have the minutes kept by Shrewsbury, showing the composition of the Cabinet to have been much on the lines indicated by North, with the addition of Tenison (who entered the Cabinet as Archbishop of Canterbury in 1694), and the irregular attendance of the Master of the Ordnance and certain Household officers.[3] William preferred to select his ministers indifferently from the two parties, then gaining in definiteness, but in 1697 Sunderland persuaded him to employ only Whigs, as commanding a majority in Parliament. Exaggerated importance has, perhaps, attached to

[1] *Lives of the Norths*, II, 53. [2] See Blanvelt: *Cabinet Government*, pp. 73–4.
[3] *Montagu House Papers* (Hist. MSS. Com.), Vol. II, Part I, quoted *ap*. Anson: *Crown* I, 97.

**The Whig "Junto".**

the formation of this Whig "*Junto*", but the Cabinet for the first time was politically homogeneous, and for the first time was avowedly constructed so as to bring the Executive into political harmony with the Legislature.

**Parliament and Cabinet.**

Yet the hostility of Parliament to a *Cabinet* remained undiminished, and in 1701, by the *Act of Settlement* (§ iii), an attempt was made to exclude all office-holders from the House of Commons and to revive the decadent power of the Privy Council. Moreover, by that same section all resolutions taken by the Privy Council were to be signed by the Councillors assenting thereto, who were thus to accept individual responsibility. None of these provisions ever became operative. The first was modified so as to allow ministers to seek re-election after the acceptance of office. The second was repealed by statute.

**Queen Anne.**

Queen Anne, like her predecessor, personally presided at the weekly meetings of the Cabinet, but there is evidence that the real control of affairs was passing from the formal Cabinet into a *conciliabulum* or Inner Cabinet, which doubtless referred its decisions on major points of policy to the whole Cabinet. Thus in 1703 Godolphin, who was more nearly a Prime Minister than any other statesman of the reign, wrote to Harley: "It is necessary above all that the Duke of Marlborough and you and I should meet regularly at least twice a week if not oftener to advise upon everything that shall occur."[1] Harley was at this time Speaker, and Dr. Trevelyan suggests that it is for that reason a misnomer to call this triumvirate an "Inner Cabinet".[2] Technically he may be right; but in a state of things so inchoate, technicalities are hardly relevant. Harley, though Speaker, was the leader of the moderate Tories, and in 1704 he combined with the Speakership a Secretaryship of State. Towards the end of the reign (1713) Bolingbroke wrote to Harley, then his colleague: "Let the forms of business be regularly carried on in the Cabinet, and the secret of it in your own closet".[3]

[1] *Portland Papers* (Hist. MSS. Com.), IV 75.
[2] *England Under Queen Anne*, I, 289. [3] *Portland Papers*, V, 311.

Meanwhile, though Queen Anne was the ruler of her kingdoms, and appointed and dismissed her ministers, she paid ever increasing heed to the state of parties in Parliament, and in a secondary degree, therefore, to public opinion as reflected thereby.

**Walpole.**

In the history of the English monarchy, and of English constitutional development, the reigns of the first two Hanoverian Kings were decisively important. In the classic phrase of M. Thiers they reigned, but they did not rule. Political control passed from the Sovereign and his court to Parliament and to ministers responsible to the majority therein. Constitutional changes in England are not, indeed, cataclysmic but evolutionary. Preceding paragraphs have disclosed some of the stages in the evolution of the Cabinet system: but the critical stage was reached during the twenty years of Walpole's administration (1721–42). "At whatever date," wrote John Morley, "we choose first to see all the decisive marks of that remarkable system which combines unity, steadfastness and initiative in the Executive with the possession of supreme authority alike over men and measures by the House of Commons, it is certain that it was under Walpole that its principles were first fixed in parliamentary government, and that the Cabinet system received the impression that it bears in our own time."[1] These words are broadly true; but a great jurist wisely cautions us "not to look for precision of outline and regular sequence of development in an institution so dependent on the conditions of the time and the temperament of individuals. . . . The history of the Cabinet is a shifting scene in which events move forward with uncertain step but continuous tendency."[2]

The steps taken during Walpole's ministry were eminently uncertain. The ministers were Whigs and the parliamentary majority was Whig, but so numerous were the factions in the Whig party that, if it had not been for Walpole's skilful manipulation of Parliament, it would have been impossible to say that the Cabinet reflected

[1] *Walpole*, p. 142. [2] Anson: *E. H. R.*, XXIX, p. 57.

or rested upon a parliamentary majority. Party loyalty was not a sentiment which animated Parliament until the last years of the eighteenth century, and until that sentiment developed the Cabinet necessarily lacked the main support on which it now rests. For parallel reasons there was no real collective responsibility in the Cabinet. The Secretaries of State were still, in a special sense, the King's servants, taking their orders direct from him and reporting regularly rather to him than to their chief colleague in the Cabinet. This independent position was accentuated by the fact that Carteret (Secretary, 1721–4) was the only member of the Cabinet who could converse with George I in his native tongue, and by the growing estrangement between Walpole and his honest but hot-tempered brother-in-law, "Turnip" Townshend. But Carteret was relegated to the Viceroyalty of Ireland in 1724, and Townshend was compelled to resign in 1730. Walpole would brook no rival near the throne. From the resignation of Townshend until the death of Queen Caroline (November, 1737) Walpole's ascendancy was unchallenged.

Vehemently as he repudiated the title, Walpole was in effect the first of a long line of Prime Ministers. Two centuries were, however, to elapse before that office received statutory recognition, and before the holder of it—despite the fact that so many Prime Ministers have come from north of the border—received a salary. Before proceeding to trace the evolution of the Prime Minister, it may be convenient to notice another development of the Cabinet system peculiar to the eighteenth century.

**The Inner Cabinet.**

Much evidence has recently been unearthed to prove the existence during a great part of that century of an Outer and an Inner Cabinet, of two sorts of Cabinet ministers, "honorary" and "efficient". In one sense there has generally been an "Inner Cabinet". A Prime Minister is naturally apt, more especially as Cabinets become larger, to consult habitually with two or three colleagues who are in closest personal relations with himself. But in the middle years of the eighteenth century this

"Inner" or "Efficient" Cabinet was formally recognized as consisting of the four ministers to whom confidential papers were regularly circulated and who had the key of the Cabinet boxes. Policy was in fact decided by "those [four or five persons] whom His Majesty usually consults upon matters of importance".[1] More than one Cabinet minister in the middle years of the eighteenth century repudiated responsibility for executive action on the ground that he had ceased to "act as an *efficient* Cabinet minister". That was the excuse given by Lord Mansfield in a debate in 1775, when he declared that from the close of Grenville's ministry (1765) he had only been a member of the "nominal Cabinet". This "nominal Cabinet" was, in fact, tending towards the position of the old Privy Council, though unlike the Privy Council it had no legal status. It met rarely, and only, it would seem, to ratify decisions already reached by the "efficient" Cabinet. After 1782 the larger Cabinet disappeared, or the two Cabinets were fused. Rockingham's Cabinet of that year consisted of eleven members; Pitt's first Cabinet (1783) of ten, and his second (1804) of twelve. The numbers gradually increased until in the last ministry of the nineteenth century (Lord Salisbury's third ministry, 1895) they reached twenty. But the differentiation between an "outer" and an "inner" Cabinet has never been formally recognized since, at latest, the earliest years of the nineteenth century.[2] After Addington succeeded Pitt as Prime Minister (1801), Lord Loughborough, the ex-Lord Chancellor, continued to attend Cabinet meetings, and retained his key of the Cabinet boxes. But this appears to be an isolated instance, and Addington was compelled to inform Lord Loughborough that his attendance at the Cabinet "naturally ceased upon the resignation of the Seals", adding his opinion that "the number of Cabinet ministers should not exceed that of the persons whose

[1] On this Inner Cabinet much light is thrown by the *Newcastle Correspondence*, the *Grenville Papers*, *Rockingham Memoirs*, *Hervey Memoirs*, *Grafton Memoirs*, *Life of Lord Hardwicke*, and among modern writers by Sir R. Lodge, *Studies in Eighteenth Century Diplomacy*, p. 272 f., and Anson, *Crown II*, I, Chap. III.

[2] For the experiments tried in 1916–9 see *infra*, p. 368.

responsible situations in office require their being members of it ".[1]

All this goes, however, to show how indefinite the Cabinet system continued to be until recent times, and how gradual was the process of its evolution. Not less gradual was the evolution of the " office " of Prime Minister.

[1] Campbell: *Lives of the Chancellors*, VI, 326–7; *ap.* Anson, I, 116, who quotes from Colchester *Memoirs*, II, 26, a description of a meeting of a " Grand Cabinet or Honorary Cabinet " to hear, on the eve of the meeting of Parliament, a draft of the King's Speech.

# CHAPTER XX

## Premier, Parties, and Parliament

THE Cabinet, though it has come to have an organic and inseparable connexion with the Legislature, owed its origin to the Executive branch of government. Its members were the confidential councillors of the King, and over its meetings the Sovereign naturally presided. The critical stage in its evolution arrived when the Sovereign ceased to do so. George I appears to have attended twice, but he quickly tired of presiding over deliberations conducted in a language he did not understand. The withdrawal of the Sovereign from the Cabinet was final.[1] Somebody had to occupy the vacant chair, and the occupant became gradually recognized as Prime Minister. The term had already come into occasional use. Swift frequently spoke of Harley as Prime Minister, and in the preface to his *Last Four Years of Queen Anne* he refers to " those who are commonly called Prime Ministers among us ". But the new title, perhaps by reason of its Gallic origin, made slow way towards general acceptance. A *Protest* of dissentient peers, outvoted on the motion to remove Walpole in 1741, declared that " a sole, or even a first minister, is an officer unknown to the law of Britain, inconsistent with the Constitution of this country, and destructive of liberty in any government whatever ". Sandys declared in the House of Commons: " We can have no sole and Prime Minister. We ought always to have several Prime Ministers and officers of State." The attack on Walpole was, for the moment, defeated, but in the views expressed about the Premiership there was general concurrence. Walpole himself cordially concurred in them. So far from justifying the

**The Premier.**

[1] George III possibly attended once; but the authority for his presence is doubtful.

new departure, he hotly repudiated both the title and the encroachment it appeared to suggest. "I unequivocally deny that I am sole and Prime Minister, and that to my influence and direction all the affairs of government must be attributed." He went further and specifically conceded the independence claimed by his "insubordinate" Secretaries of State. "I do not pretend to be a great master of foreign affairs. *In that part it is not my business to meddle*, and as one of His Majesty's Council I have but one voice." Such language, and in particular the words italicized, would sound strange in the mouth of a modern Prime Minister. Whether or not he retains in his own hands (as did Lord Salisbury and Mr. Macdonald) the Foreign Office, the Prime Minister exercises over that department an exceptionally close and continuous supervision.

Walpole's language is, indeed, appropriate not to the Cabinet system, but to the departmentalism preferred by the United States. It is illuminating to contrast it with the emphatic assertion to the contrary made by the younger Pitt in 1803. In March of that year Addington, then Prime Minister, had the effrontery to suggest to Pitt that a new ministry should be formed under a nominal chief with himself and Pitt as Secretaries of State. To Dundas (who conveyed the suggestion) Pitt declared that it was "an absolute necessity in the conduct of the affairs of this country that there should be an avowed and real minister possessing the chief weight in the Council and the principal place in the confidence of the King. That power must rest in the person generally called First Minister." From Pitt's time onwards that constitutional doctrine has never been questioned.

**Walpole's Place in History.**

Notwithstanding Walpole's repudiation of the title, his long tenure of the Premiership marks the decisive stage in the evolution of the office he disclaimed. He was the first minister to resign office as a direct result of an adverse vote in Parliament; to Parliament he owed primarily his prolonged ascendancy in English politics. Pre-eminently a great parliamentarian, Walpole exercised over the House of Commons an influence such as no statesman had ever exercised before, and few have exercised since. That he maintained his influence by cynical corruption is true. How else was a minister, without any control over the boroughs by which 432 out of 558 members were returned, to maintain it? Walpole had a strong hold upon the middle classes, but during the eighteenth century they had little direct representation in Parliament. The 204 English boroughs had an aggregate electorate of about 85,000, and of these only 22 had more than 1000 electors. It was alleged in 1793 by the "Society of the Friends of the People" that 90 members were returned by boroughs with less than 50 votes apiece, and 70 by towns with practically no electors. Almost at any moment between the accession of George I and that of George III, Newcastle, a politician of third-rate abilities but restless and self-seeking character, could have turned out any minister however eminent and imperious. Even Pitt, the elder, was compelled, despite his exceptional popularity, to "borrow Newcastle's majority to carry on the government".

Walpole, then, was constrained to use the only weapon ready to his hand. With all the fervour of a single-minded patriot, he believed that his first and imperative duty was to establish the Hanoverian dynasty on the English throne. He achieved his purpose not merely or mainly by cynical acceptance of the dogma that "every man had his price", but much more because he had the shrewdness to perceive that what England most needed, after a full century of turmoil, was repose—a period of recuperation moral and material. *Quieta non movere.* He believed in letting sleeping dogs lie. Accordingly he avoided, as far as possible, all questions which provoked strife and controversy. Let the country forget politics for a while, and grow fat and prosperous. Walpole's financial policy was designed to that end. He announced its main principle in the King's Speech of 1721:

Walpole's Methods.

"We should be wanting to ourselves if we neglected to improve the favourable opportunity given us of extending our commerce, upon which the riches and grandeur of this nation chiefly depend. . . . Nothing would more conduce to the obtaining so public a good, than to make the exportation of our own manufactures and the importation of the commodities used in the manufacturing of them as practicable and easy as may be."

Within six months Walpole had removed the duties hitherto payable on the export of one hundred and six articles of British manufacture, and the import duties on thirty-eight articles of raw material. Later on, he removed various restrictions on colonial produce, and in 1733 he carried his free-trade principles a stage further in the famous Excise Bill. Walpole's idea was to exchange the customs duty on tobacco imported from the southern colonies for an excise on its consumption. Smuggling would have been discounted, the shipping trade encouraged, and the public revenue benefited. The yield from the excise duties would have enabled Walpole to win over the country gentlemen to the Hanoverian cause by a substantial reduction in the land tax. But the word excise had hateful associations, and a tumultuous agitation, partly spontaneous, partly manufactured, rapidly gained ground. Walpole, preferring peace even to prosperity, was compelled to abandon one of the wisest of his financial proposals. Among the most vociferous of its opponents was Walpole's own brilliant colleague, Lord Chesterfield, who was very properly dismissed from the Lord Stewardship for his disloyalty. This is one of the cases on which Walpole's critics rely to support the charge that he preferred to surround himself with colleagues of inferior ability and to get rid of men who showed special capacity or independence. This accusation, like others preferred against Walpole, though grossly exaggerated, contains a spice of truth. There is no doubt that one of the explanations for his long tenure of office is to be found in the ruthless manner in which he discarded colleagues who were not disposed to support unconditionally the policy he dictated. But, on the other hand, the practice may be attributed less to the arrogance of the Prime Minister than to the growing-pains of the Cabinet system, the cardinal principles of which were only partially accepted, and perhaps imperfectly apprehended.

Be this as it may, Walpole's place in history is assured. To his moderating influence, his wise policy of appeasement, and not least his skill in finance, England mainly owed the remarkable development of national prosperity so conspicuous in the reign of George II. The consequent improvement in national credit enabled Henry Pelham, despite eight years of war (1740–8), to carry through a successful conversion of the National Debt (1750). If, then, Walpole ranks with Pitt, Peel and Gladstone, Henry Pelham may claim a place alongside Lord Goschen and Mr. Neville Chamberlain. Walpole and Pelham had never been accounted eminent Imperialists, but the brilliant victories of British arms in the Seven Years' War could hardly have been won had not those pacific statesmen so carefully husbanded the national resources. Nor can it be doubted that the fiasco which attended the attempt of Prince Charlie in the '45 was largely due to the apathy engendered by prosperity, and to the reluctance of the nation to stake their solid gains on the hazard of domestic rebellion.

**Queen Caroline.**

In 1737 Walpole had suffered an irreparable loss. Without the consistent support of Queen Caroline he could hardly have withstood for so long the persistent attacks of an opposition which was gradually swollen to formidable proportions by his own autocratic methods. The Queen was as shrewd and clear-sighted as the minister, and her support was due less to personal partiality than to her undeviating conviction that Walpole's policy was the surest way towards the establishment of the new dynasty.

After her death the opposition to Walpole increased both in volume and intensity. That he was right to keep England as free as possible from continental entanglements is not open to question. The disputed succession to the throne of Poland was no concern of ours, and Walpole was wholly justified in keeping England out of the war (1733–8) that arose out of that remote imbroglio. But he failed to realize its reactions. His devotion to peace hid from his eyes the operation of forces that rendered a world conflict between Great Britain and the Bourbon Powers almost inevitable. The commercial classes were, moreover, increasingly interested in the trade with the Spanish Indies stimulated by the *Assiento* (1713), and were provoked beyond endurance by the outrages of Spanish authorities upon British traders in the South Atlantic. The faults were not all on one side, but the cry for war became irresistible, and in 1739 Walpole reluctantly yielded to it.

**War (1739–48).**

The war with Spain soon merged in the wider struggle which presently involved all the great European Powers. Hardly had the War of the Polish Succession ended before the death of the Emperor Charles VI again unloosed the dogs of war. The War of the Austrian Succession raised issues far wider than the claim of Maria Theresa to the Hapsburg dominions. It initiated the struggle between Austria and Prussia for hegemony in Germany, and the struggle between England and France for supremacy in India and North America. The latter issue was decided by 1763; the former only in 1866 by the Prussian victory at Sadowa.

The outbreak of war meant the close of Walpole's long reign, though not until 1742 did his defeat on the Chippenham election petition impel him to resign. He went to the House of Lords as Earl of Orford, and power passed to Carteret under the nominal leadership of Sir Spencer Compton, recently raised to the peerage as Lord Wilmington.

**Carteret.**

Carteret had at last got his chance. In sheer ability he was head and shoulders above all his colleagues in the Cabinet, and what was almost equally important, he enjoyed the complete confidence of the King. But he attained a great position only to prove his incapacity to fill it. He had no real conception of the larger opportunities opening out to British policy; his policy was as narrowly continental as that of the King, whom he appropriately accompanied on the successful campaign which culminated in the victory of Dettingen (1743). A few weeks after that famous battle Lord Wilmington died, but it was Henry Pelham, not Carteret, who succeeded to the " Premiership ". For the next ten years and more the ascendancy of the Pelhams was unquestioned. Pitt enjoyed a personal pre-eminence for four years (1757–61), but even he, at the zenith of his popularity, required the solid backing of the Pelhams to keep him in power. Meanwhile, Carteret had been compelled to resign in 1744. His Hanoverian policy was as unpopular in the Cabinet as in the country, nor could the King's support avail against the influence of Walpole exerted—unofficially —in favour of the Pelhams. Walpole died in March, 1745. In July Prince Charles Edward landed in Scotland. Walpole's policy was doubly vindicated: by the outbreak of the rebellion, and by its failure. Nevertheless, the Pelhams thought it prudent to strengthen the Administration by the admission of Pitt. George II remained stubborn in his refusal. The ministry resigned. The King sent for Carteret, whose ministry lasted " forty-eight hours, seven minutes and eleven seconds ". If Carteret (as a contemporary wit put it) " had studied Parliament more and Demosthenes less ", he would not, by attempting to form a government, have brought ridicule upon himself and humiliation upon his master. The Pelhams came back; Pitt was admitted to minor office; and in 1751 Carteret was fain to accept office under his successful rivals as Lord President of the Council. That office he retained until the fall of the Pelhams in 1762, but it was office only, not power. He died in 1763. Disraeli ascribes Carteret's championship of the Crown to the influence of Bolingbroke, who " painted in immortal hues his picture of a patriot King ". That picture, proceeds Disraeli, " touched the heart of Carteret, born a Whig, yet sceptical of the advantages of that patrician constitution which made the Duke of Newcastle, the most incompetent of men but the chosen leader of the Venetian party, virtually sovereign of England. Lord Carteret had many brilliant qualities . . . and though he failed in his premature effort

**The Pelhams.**

**The '45.**

to terminate the dogeship of George the Second, he succeeded in maintaining a considerable though secondary position in public life." [1] Disraeli's views on the English Constitution first set forth in the youthful *Vindication* (1835), and reproduced ten years later in *Sybil*, will be taken at their face value. But if the hues of Bolingbroke's picture are immortal, the drawing is hopelessly out of perspective.

**Bolingbroke's *Patriot King*.**

The *Patriot King*, regarded as a serious contribution to political philosophy, is worthless; as a party pamphlet it was a masterpiece. Written in adulation of the reprobate Prince Frederick Lewis, it had an immense influence upon his more worthy son. It became, indeed, the political bible of George III, and provided with a philosophical manual the "King's Friends". It was not, however, until 1770 that George III got the opportunity of putting into practice the principles he had learnt from Bolingbroke.

**The "Venetian Oligarchy."**

Meanwhile, the power of the "Venetian oligarchy" was hardly broken even by the personal pre-eminence of Pitt. Henry Pelham remained chief minister until his death in 1754. Consequently it fell to him to conclude the Peace of Aix-la-Chapelle (1748), but as regards the conflict between Great Britain and the Bourbon Powers the Peace proved no more than a truce. Both in India and in North America the decisive struggle was still to come. Of that truth, however, Pelham showed no apprehension. Hardly was the ink dry on the treaty before he cut down the army and the navy so ruthlessly as to provoke some unrest among the discharged men. To appease it a scheme of assisted emigration to Nova Scotia was devised, and in 1749 some three or four thousand families took advantage of its generous terms and laid the foundations of the delectable town of Halifax. Apart from the debt conversion already recorded, Halifax stands out as the chief memorial of an Administration otherwise far from memorable.

Henry Pelham's death made no breach in the reign of his dynasty. Newcastle succeeded him as chief minister, but found it difficult to combat his mutinous colleagues,

[1] *Sybil*, Chap. III.

Henry Fox and William Pitt. In 1755 mutiny was temporarily quelled by promoting Fox to be Secretary of State, and dismissing Pitt and his ally George Grenville. Next year, however, war broke out between England and France. The war, waged in three continents, opened disastrously for England. Minorca was surrendered to the French; Braddock was defeated and killed at Fort Duquesne; Calcutta was captured by Surajah-Dowlah. Newcastle, unable to face the indignation of the populace, turned for help to Pitt, but Pitt rightly refused to cover his retreat. Newcastle, therefore, was constrained to resign, and Pitt became Secretary of State under the Duke of Devonshire as nominal Prime Minister. But no ministry could long survive without the parliamentary support of the Pelham battalions and in face of the King's opposition. Pitt was, indeed, the idol of the country; "it rained gold boxes", but he none the less found it difficult to find a seat, and on 9th April, 1756, was dismissed by the King. Newcastle was recalled, but failed to form a ministry, and from 9th April to 29th June the country, in one of the gravest crises in its history, was without a responsible government. Pitt was clearly indispensable, and after three months of humiliation and vacillation, Newcastle was at last compelled to take him on his own terms.

**The Seven Years' War.**

"I am sure that I can save this country and that nobody else can." Such was Pitt's proud but not over-confident assertion. Newcastle might have all the patronage and place-giving, but Pitt was to have power. For four years (1757–61), perhaps the most splendid in our annals, Pitt ruled England. "I want," he said, "to call England out of that enervate state in which twenty-thousand men from France can shake her." He called: and from John o' Groat's house to the Land's End Great Britain responded to his call. The tide turned at once. In the Far East and in the Far West England renewed her strength. Plassey, Wandewash and Pondicherry; Pittsburg, Ticonderoga, Crown Point, Quebec; Minden and Quiberon Bay—the names attest the brilliance and completeness of England's victory. Clive and Coote; Amherst and Wolfe; Boscawen, Rodney, and

**Pitt in Power.**

**The Year of Victories (1759).**

Hawke—great soldiers and sailors played their memorable parts, but the inspiration of the national endeavour came from Pitt. "The ardour of Pitt's soul had indeed set the whole kingdom on fire. It inflamed every soldier who dragged the cannon up the heights of Quebec and every sailor who boarded the French ships among the rocks of Brittany." That is finely said, as only Macaulay could say it.

By 1761 the great issues were decided. England, not France, was to be dominant in India; North America was to be English not French. But in 1760 George III had succeeded his grandfather as King; his favourite, Lord Bute, became Secretary of State, and Pitt, having failed to persuade his colleagues to declare war on Spain, resigned office (1761). In 1762 Newcastle, excluded from power by the favourite, also resigned. Bute concluded peace in 1763. Though its terms were bitterly criticized, the Treaty of Paris was, perhaps, the most splendid Great Britain ever concluded. France restored Minorca and ceded Senegal; she gave up Canada, Nova Scotia,[1] Cape Breton Island and several West India islands, though other West India islands she recovered, as well as her fishing rights off the coast of Newfoundland and the islands of St. Pierre and Miquelon. Spain, though she recovered Cuba and the Philippines, ceded Florida to Great Britain. In India supremacy passed from France to England. The broad result was that Great Britain recovered her position in the Mediterranean and drove France out of India and North America. Splendid as was the Peace, the King could not maintain his favourite in office, and directly it was signed George Grenville became Prime Minister.

George III.

George III was, however, resolved not merely to reign but to rule. For ten years he waged unrelenting war against the Whig oligarchy. In that contest he had many things in his favour. He was born and bred an Englishman, and

[1] Nova Scotia (Acadia) had been ceded to England in 1713, but the great fortress built by the French at Louisburg and retained by them neutralized the cession until the British Settlement at Halifax and the deportation of the French inhabitants, redressed the balance.

if his intellect was as narrow as Queen Anne's, his heart was as " entirely English " as the Good Queen's. His character, too, was as good as hers, and his will not less strong. His Whig opponents were, indeed, strongly entrenched in Parliament, but the House of Commons was becoming less and less representative of the country. " It could no longer be concealed that by virtue of a plausible phrase power had been transferred from the Crown to a Parliament the members of which were appointed by an extremely limited and exclusive class who owed no responsibility to the country, who debated and voted in secret and who were regularly paid by the small knot of great families that by this machinery had secured the permanent possession of the King's treasury. Whiggism was putrescent in the nostrils of the nation." Disraeli wrote with characteristic hyperbole, but his diagnosis was sufficiently accurate to account for the temporary success of the King, which, after ten years of severe economy, had enabled him to copy, if not to improve upon, Whig methods. But if George III borrowed the Whig weapons, he had also taken to heart the lesson taught by Pitt. " You have taught me," said George II to the reluctantly accepted minister, " to look for the voice of my people in other places than within the House of Commons." George III was at pains to secure, by the lavish distribution of honours, pensions and places, by the purchase of boroughs and the bribery of members, a subservient Parliament. The ramifications of this corrupt system were almost incredible. Even the turnspit of the King's kitchen was a member of Parliament. " The royal household," as John Morley says, " was a gigantic nest of costly jobbery and purposeless profusion." No fewer than 70 elections were controlled by the votes of revenue officers, and 192 members of the House of Commons held places under the Government. Parts of the apparatus of corruption were broken by Burke's *Economical Reform Act* of 1782, but much of it survived.

This, however, is only one side of the shield. George III, like Pitt, looked to the classes as yet unrepresented at

Westminster, and no small part of his success was due to convictions, or prejudices, which the King shared with his people. In his unyielding opposition to the demands of the American colonies, in his staunch Protestantism, and his refusal to concede the claims of the Irish (or English) Catholics, in his detestation of French Jacobins and English radicals, George III was completely in accord with a great number, perhaps a clear majority, of his subjects. His virtues, moreover, were such as to appeal to their best feelings—the simplicity and purity of his family life, his unaffected piety, his unflinching courage, his assiduity in business, his devotion to duty and his unquestioned patriotism. Then, as always, the English people prized character above intellect, particularly in those set in authority over them. Thus with all his limitations George III could count on many advantages in his contest with an aristocracy which had already degenerated into an oligarchy.

**The King and the Whigs.**

Moreover, the great Whig majority was rapidly disintegrating. That is the inevitable nemesis of great majorities. Powerful oppositions are, as Mr. Gladstone insisted, not less essential to parliamentary efficiency than strong governments. Until the Tories shed the last remnants of Jacobitism the Whigs had little to fear from them, and could indulge in the luxury of domestic quarrels. By 1760 the Whig party was broken up into family groups, and in its disintegration the young King saw his opportunity. But it was ten years before he could make full use of it.

**Party Confusion.**

In the meantime ministry followed ministry. Bute was frightened out of office in 1763, making way for George Grenville, a statesman of whom Burke drew an imperishable portrait. "I do believe," he wrote, "that [Grenville] had a very real desire to benefit the public. But with no small study of detail he did not seem to have his view at least equally carried to the total circuit of our affairs. He generally considered his objects in lights that were rather too detached." That penetrating criticism would apply to many other statesmen besides Grenville. The capacity to carry their view to the total circuit of our affairs is to all but the greatest denied. The King would gladly have seen Grenville reinforced by the adhesion of Pitt, but Pitt's terms were too high, and Grenville had to content himself with the Bedford group, who towards the end of 1763 came in on the death of Lord Grenville (Carteret).

Wilkes.

Meanwhile, the country had been agitated, to a degree explicable only by the oligarchical character of Parliament, by the proceedings taken against John Wilkes, a notorious but disreputable actor on the political stage. In April, 1763, Wilkes, then member for Aylesbury, made a venomous attack upon the King's Speech in No. 45 of his paper *The North Briton.* His description of the Speech as a "most abandoned instance of ministerial effrontery" was peculiarly offensive to a King who wished the speech to be regarded as emanating from himself. Lord Halifax, as Secretary of State, issued a "general warrant" for the arrest of unspecified persons and a search warrant for the seizure of papers. Forty-nine persons were arrested, but Wilkes acknowledged the authorship of the article and was committed to the Tower. In the Courts, however, Wilkes won all along the line. The judges of the Common Pleas at once released him from custody, on the ground of privilege as a member of Parliament. Lord Mansfield himself ruled that general warrants were illegal. Wilkes ultimately recovered £4000 in damages against Lord Halifax for illegal arrest, on the ground that a Secretary of State is not competent to issue warrants at all, and £1000 against Under-Secretary Wood, who had personally superintended the seizure of his papers and the execution of the general warrant. But Parliament showed less tenderness than the Courts, and retrospectively declared that privilege does not extend to writing and publishing seditious libels, ordered No. 45 be burned by the common hangman, and expelled Wilkes, who (for other reasons) had absconded to Paris. In 1768 Wilkes, still an outlaw, was triumphantly elected member for Middlesex, but was tried and sentenced, on the original charge of libel, to a fine of £1000 and twenty-two months' imprisonment. In the eyes of the House that did not suffice to purge the original offence. Wilkes was accordingly expelled, re-elected, again expelled and again re-elected. To put an end to proceedings which were becoming farcical, the House then declared Colonel Luttrell, Wilkes's defeated opponent, to be the duly elected member for Middlesex, and Luttrell took his seat. At the election of 1774, however, Wilkes was again returned, and without question took his seat, and in 1782 the resolution of 1769 was by 115 votes to 47 ordered to be expunged from the Journals of the House " as being subversive of the rights of the whole Body of Electors of this kingdom ".

The matter was thus, at long last, put upon the right basis. For Wilkes personally no sympathy need be felt. He got more money and fame than he deserved, but the whole episode is, nevertheless, illuminating. It illustrates the autocratic temper of an unrepresentative House of Commons, and, not less strikingly, the incipient revolt of popular opinion against the abuses of an indefensible system.

The American Colonies.

More serious than the affair of Wilkes was the opening act of the American drama. When the terms of the peace of 1763 were under discussion, acute observers, both French and English, had expressed doubts about the wisdom of annexing French Canada to Great Britain. " The English colonies, relieved of all menace to their frontiers, will stand no longer in need of the assistance of the Mother-country. Should the latter attempt to shift on to the colonies any part of the cost of Imperial defence the colonies will retort by declaring their independence." Such was the remarkable prediction of Vergennes. It was fulfilled to the letter.

George Grenville.

Grenville, precise and pedantic, was outraged by the growth of smuggling in America. It was not only a breach of the Trade laws, but meant loss of revenue to the Treasury. He accordingly decided to enforce the Trade laws, to station a small force in America, and by means of a Stamp duty to collect from the colonists one-third of the cost of this military precaution. It was the restraint of smuggling to which the colonists objected, but they could hardly in decency oppose it. The principle of the Stamp Act was new and therefore questioned, and so stout was the resistance that it was immediately repealed (1766).

The repeal was effected by Grenville's successor in office, Lord Rockingham. Grenville had forfeited the King's favour by mishandling a Regency Bill (1765); Pitt refused to come back except in company with his brother-in-law, Lord Temple; Temple was pledged to Grenville; there was, then, nothing for it but to recall the Newcastle group under the leadership of Lord Rockingham, a staunch Whig. He pleased Pitt and Burke by repealing the Stamp Act, but failed to expel from the colonial body-politic the virus of discontent.[1] Nor did Rockingham improve matters by passing a *Declaratory Act* affirming the right of the Imperial Parliament both to tax and to legislate for the colonies. The right was unquestionable; its affirmation was a piece of ill-timed pedantry. Rockingham's ministry survived for barely twelve months, and in July, 1766, Pitt was, at long last, persuaded to form a Government. He formed it under the nominal leadership of the Duke of Grafton: but he was a broken man, tortured by gout, and by accepting an earldom he forfeited much of the popularity justly earned by, and so abundantly vouchsafed to, the " Great Commoner ". The policy of the Government was mainly controlled by Charles Townshend, the Chancellor of the Exchequer: but Townshend died in 1767, having lived only long enough to embitter relations with the American colonies by imposing customs duties on a few articles such as glass and tea. The duties were few and light, and their imposition conformed to the distinction between external duties and internal taxation laid down by the colonists and accepted by Rockingham. But American views had advanced, and Townshend's duties were bitterly resented. Chatham himself finally withdrew from the Government in 1768, and Grafton became indisputably Prime Minister.

**Lord Rockingham.**

**Pitt's Ministry.**

To the constitutional historian it is still a matter of dispute whether Grafton had or had not occupied that position ever since the formation of the " Chatham ministry "

[1] For Burke's contrary view see his *Speech on American Taxation*.

in 1766. That he had been First Lord of the Treasury is quite inconclusive. Not until 1937 did the tenure of that office confer an irrefutable claim to the leadership. Pitt had been entrusted, by Grafton's own admission,[1] with the formation of the ministry in 1766, and with the distribution of offices therein. Lord Rosebery held that Pitt was thereby acknowledged as Prime Minister,[2] and the weight of critical opinion is on his side. But the pertinent point is the fact of ambiguity, not the solution of it, and ambiguous the position of Prime Minister remained down to the time of the younger Pitt.

**Lord North.**

Popular agitation on the Wilkes question compelled Grafton to resign in January, 1770. Once more the King turned to Chatham, despite the fact that he had encouraged the American agitation. But the Bedford group refused to join Chatham. They were, however, less unfriendly to Lord North, who in 1767 had succeeded Townshend as Chancellor of the Exchequer. To North, who combined the office of First Lord of the Treasury with that of Chancellor of the Exchequer, the King, accordingly, entrusted the formation of the new ministry. Grafton rejoined the ministry as Lord Privy Seal in 1771, but only on condition that he should not be summoned to meetings of the "Inner" Cabinet.[3] Grafton was, perhaps, the ablest of the men then in the forefront of politics, but he was lazy, and preferred the company of his horses and his mistresses to that of his Cabinet colleagues. North was a competent financier, and in general ability was superior to his posthumous reputation, which has suffered from the fact that for twelve years he acted as the instrument of the King's will.

**Farmer George as Ruler.**

During North's ministry George III not only reigned but governed. Of the parliamentary groups his was the strongest and most compact. "Everybody," as Horace Walpole reports, "ran to Court and voted as the Court

[1] *Autobiography of the Third Duke of Grafton* (ed. Anson), pp. 88–134. Cf. also *Chatham Correspondence*, III, pp. 22–33, and *Grenville Correspondence*, III, 308.

[2] Lord Rosebery's opinion I state on the authority of private correspondence, arising out of an article of mine in *The Sunday Times* for 28th September, 1924.

[3] See *supra*, p. 265.

desired." The result was politically disastrous. England was reduced to the nadir of humiliation. France was able to take ample revenge for her defeat in the Seven Years' War.

War of American Independence.

It was, indeed, to France, aided by Spain and Holland, and encouraged by the hostility to England of the northern neutrals, that the American colonies owed their independence. North's decision (1770) to remove all the customs duties except that on tea caused a temporary lull in the American agitation, but it revived in 1773, largely owing to the mischievous conduct of Benjamin Franklin, then agent in London for several of the American colonies. Boston harbour witnessed the first act of overt rebellion, and in 1774 twelve out of thirteen colonies sent delegates to a Congress at Philadelphia. This Congress, while affirming the loyalty of the colonies to the Crown, repudiated the sovereignty of the King-in-Parliament. One hundred and fifty-two years later the Self-governing Dominions (as they had come to be called) followed the lead of the Philadelphia Congress. But in 1931 the Imperial Government cordially conceded, if it had not actually initiated, the demand. George III lacked the prudence of George V; there is no question, however, that he was at one with his people in insisting that the rebellious colonists must be reduced to obedience.

To tell again the pitiful story of the bungling inefficiency —military, naval and political—that lost us our first empire is, in the present connexion, happily unnecessary. Yet even the blunders of the Imperial Government would not have given victory to the colonists but for the help rendered to them by France, especially—humiliating to relate—at sea. Burke and Chatham raised their powerful voices in favour of conciliation, though Chatham, with his last breath, opposed the demand for independence. But on 5th May, 1788, Chatham died, and in 1782 Lord North, increasingly restless under royal domination, at last induced the King to accept his resignation. Lord Rockingham succeeded him, but his death, after less than six months of office, opened the way for the accession to power of William Petty, second Earl of Shelburne and first Marquis of Lansdowne.

"The Jesuit of Berkeley Square" was one of the cleverest and least trusted statesmen of the eighteenth century, and he retained office only long enough to concede independence to the American colonies and to make the humiliating Peace of Versailles (1783) with France and Spain. That Peace would have been far more humiliating but for General Eliott's heroic defence of Gibraltar (1779–83), the brilliant exploits of Admiral Rodney in the last phase of the war at sea, and not least, the superb courage and skill with which Warren Hastings beat off the assaults of the powerful confederacy that threatened the extinction of British power in India.

**Ireland.**

To the brief and tragic record contained in the preceding paragraphs a footnote remains to be added. The success of the American colonists stimulated to imitation the British colony in Ireland. Their position was in many respects, economic and political, similar if inferior to that of the colonists in America. Poynings' Law (1494) had reduced the Irish Parliament to complete dependence on the English Council; the Declaratory Act of 6 George I had affirmed the right of the British Parliament to legislate for Ireland; the commercial exclusiveness of England accentuated political domination. A volunteer force, formed in Ireland in 1780, promptly demanded commercial equality and legislative independence. The British Government was not in a position to resist these demands; they were conceded (1780–2), and for eighteen years the Irish Protestants enjoyed, under the "Grattan Constitution", the luxury of legislative independence. But the Irish Executive still took their orders from Whitehall; the outbreak of the French Revolution made a difficult experiment doubly difficult; Ireland lapsed into rebellion, and Pitt decided that for the manifold ills of Ireland a Union of the Parliaments was the only remedy. Only a united Parliament would, he believed, be strong enough to give Ireland what she most needed, complete commercial equality with Great Britain, and escape from the domination of an alien and Protestant Church. That Pitt's wise policy was frustrated was due to the obstinacy of a King rapidly relapsing into insanity.

**The Coalition of 1783.**

The experiment of personal government had demonstrably failed. It had brought disaster and humiliation upon the country. Lord North, who had abetted it, practically acknowledged the failure when, on the resignation of Shelburne (1783), he coalesced with Fox under the nominal leadership of the Duke of Portland. Whether the Whig factions and their venal constituents would have governed the country any better than the King is doubtful. The corrupt and inefficient administration of the Admiralty by Wilkes's friend, Lord Sandwich (the "Jemmy Twitcher" of *The Beggar's Opera*), is only one of many examples to suggest the contrary. Fox's attempt to secure by his *India Bill* (1783) the valuable patronage of the East India Company for his Whig friends is another instance of the corruption which, alike under the oligarchy and under the monarchy, pervaded every branch of the administration. When the King, infuriated by North's coalition with Fox, intervened to defeat Fox's bill, and on its defeat ignominiously dismissed its sponsor and his colleagues, "not a dog barked". The nation loved the Coalition as little as did the King.

**Pitt.**

To dismiss the Coalition was easy; to find a successor to it was difficult. The King, having exhausted all the alternatives offered by the "Revolution Families", at last turned in desperation to Chatham's young son. Pitt accepted the invitation to form a government; but when, on the 19th of December, 1783, a writ was moved for the borough of Appleby, "in the room of the Rt. Hon. W. Pitt who has accepted the office of First Lord of the Treasury and Chancellor of the Exchequer", the motion was received with shouts of derision:

> A sight to make surrounding nations stare,
> A kingdom trusted to a schoolboys care.

The schoolboy soon proved his mettle. Without a single Cabinet colleague to support him in the House of Commons, he fought valiantly against the formidable though rapidly disintegrating host opposed to him. He found only 54 members to support him on 12th January against what was virtually a vote of censure; but defying all the various combinations formed against him, and disregarding defeats in the Lobby, this stripling of four and twenty held on with a grim tenacity which gradually wore down opposition. On 1st March Fox carried a motion for an address praying the King to remove his ministers, but only by 201 to 189; a similar motion was carried a week later only by a majority of one; the Mutiny Bill was passed without a division on 10th March. George III and Pitt had won. On 25th March Parliament was dissolved.

Burke's Economical Reform Act (1782) had cut the King's claws, but he still had large resources at his command, and he used them (as was said) "with all the zeal of an election agent" on Pitt's behalf. The result was a triumphant victory for the King and his nominee. "Fox's martyrs", as they were nicknamed, numbered no fewer than 160. Corruption undoubtedly played its part—a great part—in the election, but none the less it was a great tidal wave of national enthusiasm that carried Pitt and his Sovereign into power.

CHAPTER XXI

# George III and his Ministers (1784-1815)
## The Regency Question
## The French Revolution and English Politics

PITT'S advent to power opened a new chapter in English history. Neither George III nor his successor was a cypher, but Pitt was, in the modern sense, a real Prime Minister. Moreover, he was the first statesman of the century to perceive that new forces, social and economic, were in operation and were destined to bring about a momentous shifting in the centre of political no less than social gravity. Before the effect of those forces was exhausted, the Government of England had passed from the few to the many: Oligarchy had given place to Democracy.

**William Pitt: Prime Minister.**

Pitt did not live to witness the transition, but it is certain that, had not his energies been diverted by the French Revolution to less congenial work, he would have come down to history as the first and one of the greatest of domestic reformers.

**His Reforms (1783–93).**

The anomalous position of the East India Company made the first call upon his attention. Fox's bill, full of faults, had been rejected on its merits, though only by the interposition, perhaps "unconstitutional" in form, if undeniably salutary in effect, of the King. The matter could not, however, rest there, and in 1784 Pitt passed into law a scheme under which British India was governed and, on the whole with eminent success, until the Mutiny. It was a dual system: it virtually transferred political control to a Ministerial Board of Control under a Cabinet minister as

**India Bills.**

President, while leaving patronage and commercial administration in the hands of "John Company".[1]

Irish Policy.

If India could not wait, still less could Ireland. Legislative independence, but without control over the Executive, had been conferred upon Ireland in 1782–3. Yet Pitt believed that the roots of Irish discontent were less political than economic and ecclesiastical. Accordingly, he drafted a scheme (1785) designed to give to Ireland all the advantages of unshackled commercial intercourse with England. Despite great opposition from Lancashire, he carried his proposals, with some modification, through the English Parliament. Fox then stirred up the suspicions of Grattan and his friends in Ireland, and a bill which would certainly have conferred great benefits upon Ireland was defeated in the Irish Parliament.

Pitt's hopes for the complete emancipation of the Irish Catholics were similarly disappointed, but in this case it was the King, not Fox, who was responsible for frustrating Pitt's benevolent intentions. Pitt's determination to effect the Legislative Union (1800) was largely inspired by his conviction that only from a united Parliament could Ireland hope to obtain commercial and religious equality. Such support as the Irish Catholics gave to the Union was mainly secured by the expectation of Catholic Emancipation. George III was obdurate in his refusal to assent to it. Pitt, in protest, resigned. George IV was, on this question, as obdurate as his father; only in the last year of his reign was he compelled, by the insistence of Wellington and Peel, to make the concession wrung from his reluctant ministers by the brilliant tactics of O'Connell.[2]

Finance.

The Parliament at Westminster into which, by the Union, Irish members were introduced was an unreformed Parliament. That was not entirely Pitt's fault. He was the first minister of the Crown to tackle the question of Parliamentary Reform. He proposed (1785) to disfranchise thirty-six rotten boroughs and to transfer their seventy-two

[1] For details cf. Marriott: *The English in India* (1932), p. 74.
[2] For Pitt's Irish policy see Marriott: *Castlereagh* (1936), Chaps, IV, V, VI.

members to London and the counties. It was not an heroic measure; it accepted the principle that boroughs were private property and that their owners, if deprived of it, were entitled to compensation, and Pitt proposed to buy them out at the rate of £7000 per seat. His proposals were decisively rejected, and nearly half a century elapsed before the question was again seriously attacked. It is, however, for his financial reforms that Pitt is best entitled to remembrance in the prae-revolution period of his career. The details lie outside the scope of this narrative. It must suffice to say that Pitt proved himself the loyal disciple of Walpole and Adam Smith, and by a series of bold and wisely conceived reforms restored order to the finances, which had been thrown into confusion by the American war. By reducing the tea duty from 119 to 12½ per cent he checked smuggling, enriched the East India Company, and benefited the English consumer. He devised new and equitable taxes to fill the gap left by the reduction of the tea duty, and by his sinking fund he hoped to reduce the burden of the National Debt. If, in the event, he immensely increased it, the fault cannot be imputed to him.

**Canada Act (1791).**

Pitt was in cordial sympathy with his friend Wilberforce's crusade against slavery: he passed a bill for the control of slave ships in 1788, and in 1791 supported Wilberforce's motion, unhappily defeated, for the abolition of the slave trade. In the latter year he took the first step towards colonial self-government. The *Constitutional Act* conferred representative legislatures upon Upper and Lower Canada, though, like the Grattan Constitution in Ireland, it withheld a responsible executive. Responsible government was to come; but not yet; Pitt took the first step towards retrieving the blunders that lost us the first British Empire; for the second, Lord Durham was, half a century later, responsible.

**Regency Legislation in England.**

Meanwhile, Pitt had been involved in a bitter controversy, provoked by excited partisanship, on the question of a regency.

It is a curious fact that, previous to 1937, no general provisions had ever been made for the government of the realm during the minority, absence, or incapacity, of the Sovereign. Each case was treated, as it arose, with reference to the particular circumstances of the hour. Various provisions were made for dealing with the minority of Henry III, Edward III, Richard II and Edward V. But the first Regency Act, and the only one until 1811 that ever took effect, was that passed under Henry VIII (28 H. VIII, c. 7). After the King's marriage (1530) with Jane Seymour, Parliament gave him the power of nominating, by letters patent or by will, a Council of Regency. The Council was to act in the case of a male successor until he was eighteen years of age, and of a female until sixteen. Henry left the Crown by will to his infant son Edward, and nominated a council of "executors" to act during his minority. Edward VI died in his seventeenth year, and the Council did, in fact, function, though the actual government was successively confided to Somerset and Northumberland.

**Henry VIII.**

During the frequent absences of the Norman and Plantagenet Kings, the usual custom had been to appoint the Justiciar to act for the King; after the death of Queen Mary in 1694, Lord Justices were appointed under the Great Seal to act under similar contingencies. After the death of Frederick Prince of Wales in 1751, an Act was passed appointing the Princess as Regent in the event of the demise of George II before his successor attained the age of eighteen. A Council of Regency was also named in the Act, and power was given to the Sovereign to add four other names by instruments under his sign-manual, to be opened only after his death. The Act never became operative.

**George III.**

The health of George III was, throughout his long reign, precarious. In 1765 he was believed to be dying of consumption, and he was already (though the fact was concealed) giving signs of incipient insanity. The King himself spontaneously suggested that he should be authorized to nominate a Regent. After acrimonious debate, an Act (5 George III, c. 27) was passed providing for the nomination by the King of the Queen, the Princess of Wales (the King's mother), or a member of the royal family descended from George II to be Regent and guardian of his successor, until he should attain the age of eighteen. There was also to be a Council of Regency consisting of his uncle, the Duke of Cumberland, his brothers and various officers of State and Church, whose powers were carefully defined. The name of the Princess of Wales was inserted by the Commons, though the King had been assured by his ministers that if inserted in the draft, the Commons would delete it. Grenville's mishandling of the Bill naturally incensed the King, and was a prime cause of that minister's dismissal.

**Crisis of 1788.**

The King recovered; the Act never became operative; but in 1788 the King had another, much more serious and more prolonged, attack of his distressing malady. A curiously contradictory situation arose. Provision for a regency was imperatively demanded, but while there was general agreement that the Prince of Wales should be Regent and be invested with all necessary authority, Pitt maintained that it was for Parliament to nominate the Regent. Fox insisted that the Prince had as clear a right to the regency as to the Crown itself. Fox was unquestionably led to take this High Tory view of the prerogative by the conviction that the Prince of Wales would install his Whig friends in office. The Prince himself disclaimed any inherent right to the regency, but was none the less offended with Pitt for questioning it. Ultimately, resolutions were proposed affirming the right of the two Houses to arrange for the exercise of the royal authority during the incapacity of the Sovereign, confiding the care of the King's person and household to the Queen, and providing for the appointment of a Regent under limitations based on the assumption that the King's incapacity was temporary. Before the bill based on these resolutions could be passed, the King recovered and further proceedings were dropped.

**The Crisis of 1810–11.**

The King had further attacks in 1801 and 1804, but it was not until the autumn of 1810 that he became hopelessly and finally insane. Spencer Perceval followed the precedents set by Pitt in 1788 and proposed resolutions precisely similar in effect. They met with even more acrimonious opposition from the Whigs; but Perceval extorted the admiration even of his enemies by the courage and tenacity with which he carried them, with some amendments, and placed his Bill on the statute book. A curious hitch arose from the hesitation of Grenville, as the Auditor of the Exchequer, to permit payments out of the Treasury without the usual authority under the Privy Seal and the sign-manual. But this difficulty also was overcome by Perceval's firmness and by the resolution adopted at his instance by the House of Commons. The resolution "required" the Treasury "to issue their warrants to the auditor for the payment of such sums as the exigency may render necessary", and the auditor was "authorized and commanded" to obey such warrants.

The circumstances of 1788 and 1810 have not recurred, but in 1830, during the last illness of George IV, in order to relieve the King from the painful duty of signing numerous documents with his crippled hand, Parliament passed a Bill empowering the King to authorize the use, with stringent precautions against abuse, of a stamp to be affixed, in his presence, and only by a responsible minister, to documents requiring his signature.

**William IV.**

On the accession of William IV, a man of sixty-four, without legitimate issue, an Act was passed appointing the Duchess of Kent as Regent until the heiress presumptive, the Princess Victoria, should reach the age of eighteen. In the improbable event of a posthumous child being born to William IV, the regency was immediately to pass to Queen Adelaide on behalf of her own child. Provision was also made, after the accession of Queen Victoria, for the government of the realm by lords justices, should her successor (as was presumed) be abroad, and on her marriage in 1840 an Act on the lines of that of 1830 was passed. On the accession of King George V, a similar Act was passed, naming the Queen as Regent, in the event of her husband's death before his heir should attain the age of eighteen. During his severe illness in 1928 and again on his death-bed in 1936, King George appointed Counsellors of State to perform

**Act of 1910.**

certain indispensable functions of the Crown. Not, however, until 1937 did Parliament provide permanent machinery to be used in the event of the minority, the incapacity, or the absence of the Sovereign. In case of a minority or total incapacity, the regency will vest in the next adult heir, and in case of illness, not involving total incapacity, and of intended absence abroad, the Sovereign is authorized to delegate certain of the royal functions to Counsellors of State. The Act is, however, in deference to the *Statute of Westminster*, to operate only in the United Kingdom and the Colonies, not in the Dominions. The functions of the Regent are divorced from the guardianship of an infant Sovereign which is by the Act reserved to his or her mother, if she be living.[1]

**Counsellors of State.**

**Regency Act (1937).**

After a prolonged parenthesis we return to the situation in 1788.

Hardly had the King recovered from the illness which attacked him in that year before Great Britain, like the rest of Europe, was startled by the outbreak of the Revolution in France.

**The French Revolution.**

In no country (England not excepted) had social conditions appeared more stable, or the principle of absolute monarchy more sacrosanct, than in France. Yet in a few short months, in the summer of 1789, the old order, social, economic and ecclesiastical, had been swept away, Paris was in the hands of the mob, and a Constituent Assembly was hammering out a new Constitution, designed to set up parliamentary, if not republican, government in France.

English opinion in regard to the French Revolution passed rapidly through several phases. The first phase was one of sympathy and approbation; but approbation quickly dwindled into indifference; and after the September massacres and the murder of the King, indifference gave place to abhorrence. Yet it was not abhorrence of those crimes that brought England into the war.

**Opinion in England.**

During the first stages of the Revolution many English-

[1] Edw. VIII and 1 George VI, c.

men were inclined to share Lord Chesterfield's cynical view that if France were kept well occupied at home " the rest of Europe would be quiet ". Others were flattered by proceedings which appeared, if only superficially, to indicate a desire to imitate English institutions. The more reflective traced in the French Revolution the influence of English philosophers, notably of Locke. When the Bastille was captured by the mob, Charles James Fox exclaimed: " How much the greatest event that has happened in the world, and how much the best." A few ardent spirits shared Fox's delirious enthusiasm.

Moreover, the first effect of the French Revolution was, beyond question, to give an impulse to the reform movement in England, and to encourage the political clubs which had sprung up during the American war. Among these associations was the " Revolution Society ", which advertised itself —after the manner of unimportant busybodies—by sending (November, 1789) an address of congratulation to the National Assembly in Paris. To this Society was addressed the sermon which Edmund Burke took as his text for the *Reflections upon the French Revolution.* To this fact the preacher, one Dr. Price, owes a spurious immortality.

**Burke and the Revolution.**

Burke's *Reflections* were published in November, 1790, and made an immediate and profound impression upon public opinion. 30,000 copies were quickly sold in England, and a large number in France. Burke's analysis of the causes of the Revolution was superficial, and much of his rhetoric was purely sentimental. As Tom Paine truly said: " He pitied the plumage but forgot the dying bird." Nevertheless, Paine's counterblast, *The Rights of Man,* evoked profound anger in England. In Birmingham riots broke out, in the course of which Dissenting chapels were burnt, and Priestley's [1] house with its valuable papers and scientific instruments was burnt. The Government decided to prosecute Paine, who fled to France to evade punishment.

Burke himself was far less concerned with France than

[1] Joseph Priestley (1733–1804), originally a Dissenting minister of unorthodox views and advanced opinions, was a distinguished chemist and discovered oxygen.

with England. The primary purpose of his pamphlet was to vindicate the excellence of the English Constitution and to show that the Whig Revolution of 1688 had nothing in common with the Jacobin Revolution in France. This object he completely attained.

Burke also made a passionate appeal for armed intervention to extirpate " this strange, nameless wild enthusiastic thing " now established " in the heart of Europe ". Austria and Prussia were ready to respond to that appeal. Pitt was not. On the contrary, he struggled hard to keep England out of the war; but France, intoxicated by her success against the German Powers in 1792, rendered Pitt's efforts vain. A Decree issued by the National Convention in December, 1792, challenged the whole existing Order in Europe, and declared war on every monarchy, absolute or limited. In January, 1793, King Louis XVI was executed, a crime which sent a thrill of horror throughout Europe. But the unpardonable offence of the French Republic, in English eyes, was the opening of the Scheldt and the French attack upon the Low Countries. The independence of that region has ever been a matter of profound concern to England; she had specifically guaranteed the closing of the Scheldt, and not until Napoleon was compelled to loosen his grip upon Antwerp did Great Britain ultimately sheathe the sword reluctantly drawn in 1793.

**The Revolutionary Wars.**

With the course of the Revolutionary and Napoleonic wars, save in so far as they reacted upon politics and parties in England, this narrative is not concerned. But the reaction cannot be ignored. The general effect was to hold up, for a quarter of a century, the domestic reforms on the promotion of which Pitt's heart was set. As a statesman, Pitt belonged to the school not of his father Chatham, but of Walpole, Peel, and Gladstone. Forced into war he proved an incapable war minister, though in two important ways he contributed to the victory ultimately achieved by Great Britain. On the one hand he sustained, like his father, the spirit of the nation in days that were dark and difficult; on the other, he enabled this country, by his skilful finance, to

**Effect on England.**

act as the paymaster of the continental coalitions by whose assistance Napoleon was finally overthrown.

**Trade and Finance.**

Neither Pitt nor any other financier could, indeed, have performed that remarkable feat, but for the coincidence of the industrial and agrarian revolutions, and the consequent expansion in production and trade. In 1792 the total imports into this country amounted to less than £20,000,000; in the last year of the war they were valued at £33,000,000. The exports rose, in the same period, from £18,336,851 to £58,624,000. But Great Britain not only enjoyed, at this time, a virtual monopoly in manufactures: thanks to her supremacy at sea she also became the carrier of the world. She also became during the war the entrepôt of international trade to an extent which is measured by re-exports, which rose from 6½ millions (1792) to over 19 millions in 1814.

**Taxation and Loans.**

This expansion of trade, accompanied as it was by an increase of 35 per cent in population, naturally facilitated the task of the Treasury. Pitt's financial methods have, however, been severely criticized—most severely by those who imperfectly realize the political and social conditions which in war-time limit the discretion of a minister responsible for national finance. It is said that Pitt raised too little by taxation and too much by loans, and that by issuing his loans at a low rate of interest but at a heavy discount, he laid an intolerable burden upon posterity without corresponding benefit to contemporaries. The facts are that the tax revenue in 1792 was under £20,000,000, that in 1815 the same taxes, owing to natural expansion, yielded no less than £45,000,000, and that, by doubling the stamp duties, trebling the assessed taxes, and imposing succession duties and an income tax, the total tax revenue was, during the same period, increased to £72,210,512—the largest sum ever raised by taxation in Great Britain until the Crimean War. The debt charge for interest increased from less than 9½ to over 31 millions, and the capital sum from £239,663,421 to £831,171,132. So severely was the strain felt in the first years of the war that in 1797 the Bank of England was compelled to suspend cash payments, and until 1819 did not resume them. Until the closing years of the war, however, paper money maintained its value better than could have been anticipated, but from 1810–3 the premium on gold rose steeply, and in the latter year the £5 note was worth only £3, 10*s*.

**Repressive Legislation.**

Severely as Pitt's finance has been criticized, a more persistent allegation against him is that, having plunged this country into a war for the suppression of Jacobinism in France, he was responsible for the policy of "coercion" designed to extirpate non-existent Jacobinism at home.

The first charge, though maintained by Macaulay and Goldwin Smith, is demonstrably false. The latter is, for obvious reasons, more difficult to disprove. That personal liberty must be curtailed, when the nation is at war, is axiomatic. Whether Pitt's precautions went beyond the necessities of the situation can be decided only by precise knowledge of the facts. More than once, in order to fortify the position of the Executive, Pitt procured the appointment of a Committee of Secrecy, selected by ballot. The Committee of 1794 declared themselves convinced, by irrefutable evidence, that there did exist "a traitorous conspiracy". Lord Salisbury, after a careful review of the evidence, gave it as his opinion that "strenuous efforts were being made to bring about a bloody revolution such as that which was raging in France".[1] If that were so, Pitt deserves the highest credit for frustrating them. The encouragement given to the English Jacobins by alien emissaries was curtailed by an *Aliens Act* passed in January, 1793; a *Traitorous Correspondence Act* (1793) was designed to prevent English subjects from affording assistance to France; a number of prosecutions were initiated both in England and Scotland against persons who made seditious speeches, and upon those who were convicted severe sentences were in some cases passed. The *Habeas Corpus Act* was suspended in 1794; a bill to prevent seditious meetings, and a *Treasonable Practices Bill*, were passed, in the face of violent opposition from Fox, Sheridan and other Whigs, in 1795. Various

**The Habeas Corpus Act.**

[1] *Essays* (Biographical), p. 168.

Corresponding Societies were, under further statutes, suppressed in 1799. Mutinies which in 1797 had broken out in the fleet at Spithead and at the Nore were said to have been instigated by the traitors against whom Pitt's legislation was aimed, and if more serious and more frequent outbreaks were avoided, Pitt's precautions must not be regarded as superfluous. "It is," as Lord Rosebery shrewdly observed, "a grave error to reason or to act as though the existence of a conspiracy that has not succeeded were necessarily susceptible of public proof."

**A National Government.**

Throughout these years Pitt was acting as the leader not of a party but of the nation. In 1794 he had reconstructed his ministry on a national basis. The Duke of Portland, Earl Spencer, Lord Fitzwilliam and other leading Whigs had taken office under him, and the Opposition, led by Fox, Erskine, Sheridan and Grey, was reduced to negligible proportions. It numbered barely fifty in the House of Commons, and fewer in the House of Lords.

**The Irish Union.**

In 1801, however, the National Government was broken up. The Acts for a Legislative Union between England and Ireland had in 1800 passed the Parliaments at Westminster and in Dublin. Ireland was to be represented in the united Parliament by twenty-eight temporal peers elected for life by their fellow Irish peers, by four spiritual peers chosen in rotation from the bishops of the Established Church in Ireland, and by one hundred commoners. The Established Church was to be maintained in Ireland, and the two countries were to enjoy commercial equality. But Pitt never intended that this measure should stand alone. His intention was that it should be supplemented by the complete abolition of Catholic disabilities and the abolition of tithes. The King, however, as we have seen, frustrated Pitt's beneficent intentions. Pitt resigned, and was succeeded by Henry Addington, who as Speaker had been acceptable to the House of Commons and as minister was even more acceptable to the King.

Though not endowed with the brains of a Pitt or a Castlereagh, Addington was a man of high character and of more ability than the defamatory lampoons of Canning suggest. His ministry was equal to the task of making peace with France at Amiens (May, 1802), but was not equal to the conduct of the war when, after little more than a year, it was resumed (May, 1803). In war-time Pitt was evidently indispensable, but the King was not less averse than Addington to his resumption of the Premiership. Efforts were accordingly made to induce him to take office under Addington. He naturally refused so monstrous a proposal, and the King, therefore, reluctantly accepted the resignation of Addington, and, not less reluctantly, took Pitt back again as First Minister.

**Politicians and Parties.**

Pitt urged the King to allow him to form a Coalition with the Whigs. The King agreed, provided Fox was excluded. But Grenville and his friends refused to come in without Fox. Pitt, therefore, was compelled to form a ministry of Pittite and Addingtonian Tories, with Lord Castlereagh as his principal lieutenant in the House of Commons.

Pitt's health was failing; he was greatly distressed by the impeachment of his friend Lord Melville (Henry Dundas), and though he succeeded in bringing Austria, Russia, and Sweden into the Third Coalition against France, he failed to arrest the progress of French arms on the Continent. Napoleon was, indeed, compelled, by the failure of his naval strategy, to abandon his projected invasion of England in 1805; Nelson's great victory at Trafalgar (21st October, 1805) convinced him that England was irresistible at sea, but Napoleon found compensation in inflicting a crushing defeat upon Austria and Russia at Austerlitz (2nd December). In 1806 he annihilated the Prussian army at Jena and Austerstadt, and in 1807 concluded with Russia the famous Treaty of Tilsit. Prussia was to be dismembered, England to be brought to her knees by the ruin of her trade, and the world to be divided between the Emperor of the French and the Czar of Russia.

Austerlitz was said to have killed Pitt. In less than two months after that crushing disaster the great minister passed

**Death of Pitt.**

away (23rd January, 1806). England remained supreme at sea; the Continent was at Napoleon's feet. At this critical juncture the King consented to the inclusion of Fox, as Foreign Secretary, in a ministry " of all the Talents " under the leadership of Lord Grenville. Fox signalized his accession to power by carrying resolutions for the abolition of the slave trade (1806), and in 1807 the resolutions were embodied in a Statute. Before the Bill became an Act Fox was dead (September, 1806), and six months later the King, angered by the refusal of Grenville and his colleagues to pledge themselves against further concessions to the Catholics, dismissed the ministry and commissioned the Duke of Portland to form a government.

**" All the Talents."**

The duke was seventy years of age and in bad health, but his ministry was a strong one. It included, besides Lord Eldon and Lord Castlereagh, three future Prime Ministers —Perceval, Canning and Lord Liverpool. Castlereagh and Canning quarrelled, however, about the conduct of the war. The quarrel led to the resignation of both ministers, who proceeded to settle their differences by a duel. Their secession broke up the ministry; Portland himself resigned, but died before his successor could take office.

**Castlereagh and Canning.**

Efforts were then made to bring in Grenville and Grey, but they refused to join the rump of Portland's administration, and after much unsavoury intrigue a Tory ministry was at last formed under Spencer Perceval.

**Spencer Perceval.**

Perceval has been unfairly depreciated. Though not a statesman of the highest order, he was an effective debater, a sound financier and a politician of unflinching courage and transparent honesty. To him it fell, as we have seen, to deal with the critical situation incidental to the King's final relapse into insanity in 1810. After that relapse George III lingered for five more years, and the Prince of Wales virtually reigned as Regent.

**The Regent and the Ministers.**

The general expectation was that the Regent would use his new powers to dismiss the Tory ministers and put his Whig friends in office. But on the day before the Regency Bill became law the Prince wrote to Perceval in reference to "the persons to be employed by him in the administration of the Executive Government of the country", and intimated his decision to retain Perceval in office. Nevertheless, the idea persisted that as soon as the twelve months for which the restrictions imposed upon him by the Bill had elapsed the Whigs would be called to office. Lord Holland, who was both shrewd and well-informed, was less confident. In August, 1811, he wrote to Lord Grey: "H.R.H. has a strong disinclination to bringing in Grenville and you."[1] And there was another factor in the problem. "The partisans of Lord Wellesley are sanguine . . . that the Prince will place him at the head of affairs." So wrote Lord Buckingham in September, 1811, and on 5th January, 1812, McMahon (the Prince's secretary) was reported to have said: "You may be as sure of it as of your own existence that Lord Wellesley will be at the head of the Government as soon as the Prince is his own master."

Lord Wellesley.

It was not Lord Wellesley's fault that he was not. For months past he had been intriguing against his chief and doing everything in his power to ingratiate himself with the Regent. When Parliament met on 7th January, 1812, it was ascertained that George III had become permanently insane; it was clear, therefore, that the restrictions due to expire on 18th January could not be renewed and that more appropriate provision must be made for the Regent and for the household of the Queen. Wellesley was dissatisfied with the provision proposed in Cabinet, and took the unusual but characteristic course of insisting that his dissent must be recorded and communicated to the Prince. He was on other grounds annoyed with his colleagues and on 16th January resigned the Foreign Secretaryship. The Prince once more endeavoured to persuade Lord Grenville and Lord Grey to join Perceval's Cabinet, but encountered a point-blank refusal.[2] The Foreign Office was then offered to Lord Castlereagh, and accepted with great reluctance

[1] Ilchester: *Home of the Hollands*, p. 249.

[2] See letter of Grenville and Grey to the Duke of York, *ap.* Buckingham: *Regency*, I, 232–5.

on his part, but to the indisputable advantage of this country and of Europe.

A few months later Spencer Perceval was assassinated (11th May), and the Regent thereupon commissioned Wellesley to form a "national" government. Twice he attempted the task, and twice ignominiously failed. His late Tory colleagues naturally refused to serve under him; Grenville and Grey were even more disdainful in their refusal. The King then turned to Lord Liverpool, who formed an exclusively Tory administration with Lord Eldon as Lord Chancellor, Lord Sidmouth (Addington) as Home Secretary, and Lord Castlereagh as Foreign Secretary and leader of the House of Commons.

**Lord Liverpool.**

In all the tangled negotiations that preceded Liverpool's appointment, the outstanding fact was the paramount influence of the Crown. It was for the Sovereign to "employ" ministers, for Parliament to support his nominees. Against this notion haughty Whig noblemen like the Greys and Grenvilles might chafe; but it was to the court that all parties looked for "employment" in the offices of State.

For fifteen years, however, the country was untroubled by further ministerial crises. During the whole of that long period Lord Liverpool retained the Premiership. During the first ten years Liverpool's principal lieutenant was Lord Castlereagh; during the last five George Canning. On coming into power Liverpool had offered the Foreign Office to Canning, who would gladly have accepted it, but insisted that he must also have the leadership of the House. Castlereagh was willing to surrender the Foreign Office but not the leadership. Canning's obduracy cost him dear. During some of the most critical years in our history he was out of office, and not until his rival's death in 1822 did he attain the position he coveted.

**Lord Castlereagh.**

Castlereagh was accordingly responsible for the conduct of foreign affairs during the last four years of the war; he represented his country during the peace negotiations in Paris and Vienna, and was largely responsible for the settlement of 1815. These matters lie outside the scope of this narrative.[1] Not so the domestic situation which supervened on the termination of the war. With that situation the next chapter will deal.

[1] They are dealt with fully in my *History of Europe*, 1815–1936 (Chap. II), and in my *Castlereagh* (Chaps. XV and XVI).

## CHAPTER XXII

# The Aftermath of War

## Social Unrest and Parliamentary Reform

PEACE was concluded; but peace failed to bring plenty or prosperity to the Power which had mainly contributed to victory. That a great war is apt to be followed by a period of economic recoil, of industrial dislocation, of political and social unrest, has now become a commonplace of historical generalization.

**Economic Distress.**

The recoil after 1815 was severe and prolonged in proportion to the severity and length of the struggle from which England had triumphantly emerged. Many of the phenomena, familiarized to the present generation by its own experience of post-War years, were anticipated in the years after Waterloo. During the war England had become literally the workshop of the world; industry, commerce and agriculture were stimulated to unprecedented activity. With the conclusion of peace demand slackened; deep depression ensued both in industry and in agriculture; thousands of demobilized soldiers and sailors were flung into a labour market already surfeited; of the 700 banks which had sprung into existence between 1797 and 1814, more than one-third stopped payment in the critical years 1814–5; credit collapsed; mortgagees could not realize; substantial farmers were becoming parish paupers; manufacturers and shopkeepers were in no better plight; all classes were, indeed, involved in a common ruin. "Trade is gone," wrote Wellesley-Pole, the Master of the Mint, "contracts are gone, paper credit is gone, and there is nothing but stoppage, retrenchments and bankruptcy."

An epidemic of disorder accentuated universal distress.

Starving mobs do not stop to reason. Because bread was at famine prices, ricks and barns were burnt to the ground. Because work was scarce, machinery was smashed and factories were destroyed. Loud and general was the cry for higher wages, more employment, cheaper food.[1]

**Political Agitation.**

Nor was the agitation exclusively economic. With the cries for more work and cheaper food there began to mingle demands for universal suffrage and annual Parliaments. Demagogues like "Orator" Hunt and brilliant pamphleteers like William Cobbett added fuel to the flames. The "Hampden Clubs", founded by Major Cartwright in 1815, began to formulate the demands subsequently embodied in the "Charter". The "Spencerian Clubs" preached communistic doctrines to hungry mobs.

In the background we can discern the more sinister figures of political conspirators and even assassins—men of the type of the Thistlewoods and Watsons. In November, 1816, there were meetings in Spa Fields, Bermondsey, followed by rioting and lootings in the City itself. The Corporation petitioned the Regent to urge upon Parliament measures for the reduction of public expenditure and the reform of Parliament. His curt response did not add to his popularity, and as he drove back from the opening of Parliament (28th January, 1817) the Regent was pelted and the windows of his coach were smashed.

**Peterloo.**

The investigations of the secret committees appointed by Parliament left no room for doubt that mingling with real grievances and legitimate discontent there was on foot a revolutionary movement. Consequently the Habeas Corpus Act was suspended, seditious meetings were prohibited, and measures were passed to provide for the security of the Regent's person, and to prevent the seduction of the armed forces of the Crown. But the agitation continued. Wage-earners from the north organized marches on London; riots took place in industrial towns, and in 1819 a vast

[1] This paragraph and those that immediately follow are to a large extent summaries of Chapters II, III and IV of my *England Since Waterloo* (10th Edition, Methuen), to which for further detail reference may be made.

meeting in St. Peter's Fields in Manchester was dispersed by a force of Hussars and Yeomanry called in by the magistrates to support the overpowered police. One policeman, one Yeoman, and eleven persons in the densely packed crowd were killed and many were injured; but to describe "Peterloo" as a "massacre" is a gross exaggeration. Nevertheless, it aroused great indignation at the time, and has had loud reverberations in history. Hardly less exaggerated is the criticism on the "Six Acts", designed to maintain public order and passed by large majorities with the cordial assent of Canning and the Grenville Whigs. Some of the Six Acts were drastic in their provisions, but they did not seriously curtail political or personal liberty, so long as these rights were exercised within constitutional limits and without detriment to public order.[1] The lawlessness of the post-war period culminated in 1820 in the Cato Street Conspiracy. Arthur Thistlewood and his fanatical associates designed to get rid of the whole of the detested Tory Cabinet by one murderous stroke. The plan was betrayed and miscarried. The Cabinet, being warned, did not dine, as had been arranged, with Lord Harrowby, but elsewhere, and so escaped assassination. Thistlewood and four of his accomplices were executed, the other six were transported for life. How widely the Thistlewood conspiracy extended it is impossible to say, but the story (reported by Greville) went that the murder of the ministry was to be the prelude to an attack on the Bank, the seizure of the Tower, and a general rising in the capital. No sympathy with the would-be assassins was felt, but the plot itself was evidence of the detestation with which in some quarters the Government policy was regarded.

**The Six Acts.**

**The Cato Street Conspiracy.**

Great as was the unpopularity of the ministry, that of the Crown was greater. In 1820 the poor old King died, and was genuinely mourned by his people. George III was not a great ruler, but his private virtues, his honesty, simplicity, and piety had endeared him to his subjects.

[1] For detailed description and discussion of the policy for which Castlereagh was held mainly responsible, see Marriott: *Castlereagh* (Methuen, 1936), pp. 285 f.

George IV, though politically shrewd and not wholly lacking in dignity, had none of his father's virtues, and had many vices conspicuously his own. A shameless voluptuary, a reckless spendthrift, a hard drinker and a confirmed gambler, his conduct was a constant embarrassment to his ministers and a terrible example to his subjects. Nor was the repute of the royal family effectually redeemed by the King's immediate relations. The death in 1817 of the Princess Charlotte, his only legitimate child, brought into prominence the question of the succession. Of the thirteen sons and daughters of George III, not one had a legitimate child; few of them had legitimate spouses. The death of Princess Charlotte and the Regent's separation from his wife imposed an immediate duty upon the royal dukes. In 1818 three royal dukes and the Princess Elizabeth hurried to the altar, and in 1819 a daughter was born to the Duke of Kent, the fourth son of George III. His elder brothers all died without legitimate children. The niggardly provision made by Parliament for the dilatory dukes on their several marriages testified to the low esteem in which the royal family were then held. As the Duke of Wellington characteristically put it: "They [the princes] are the damnedest millstone about the necks of any Government that can be imagined. They have insulted, *personally* insulted, two-thirds of the gentlemen of England, and how can it be wondered at that they take their revenge upon them in the House of Commons." [1]

**The Royal Family.**

Of the whole family the most disreputable, and perhaps the least popular, was the King. Nothing else could explain the amazing, if transient, popularity of his Queen, Caroline of Brunswick. The extent of that popularity, and the extraordinary concentration of political interest upon the "Queen's Business", can be realized only by those who immerse themselves in contemporary sources, official and popular. The Queen was courageous, pertinacious, not lacking in ability herself, and brilliantly, if not wisely, served by her advocates. But she was a frivolous and tiresome

**The Queen's Business.**

[1] *Creevey*, I, 277.

woman, and guilty, if not of infidelity, of imprudence almost amounting to immorality. Her marital connexion with the Prince had ceased even before the birth of their daughter, and in 1806 the Whig ministry humoured their patron by appointing a secret committee to make a "delicate investigation". Nothing came of it; the princess presently withdrew to Italy, only to return in 1820 to claim her rights as Queen.

The Whigs took advantage of her return to annoy the King and embarrass his ministers. They had the support of the London mob, and the fidelity of the London garrison was so doubtful that the Duke ordered one of the regiments of Foot Guards off to Portsmouth.[1] The Government introduced a Bill of Pains and Penalties to deprive the Queen of her title and dissolve her marriage, but so menacingly narrow was the majority by which the bill was carried in the Lords that Lord Liverpool withdrew it, and it never reached the Commons. In 1821 the House of Commons voted the Queen an annuity of £50,000, but happily she did not live to enjoy it. The Privy Council decided against her right to be crowned (10th July), and when (19th July) she attempted to force her way into the Abbey she was ignominiously excluded.

**Coronation of George IV.**

The inconstant mob had already transferred its interest to a King whose coronation was celebrated with unprecedented magnificence; society was bored by the Queen's importunity. A once-famous epigram expressed the general sentiment:

> Gracious Queen, we thee implore
> Go away and sin no more.
> Should that effort be too great,
> Go away—at any rate.

Queen Caroline died, unregretted even by her not disinterested friends, a few weeks after her husband's coronation (7th August).

In the same month the King paid a visit to Ireland,

[1] Pellew: *Sidmouth*, III, 330.

where his condescension and affability evoked wild enthusiasm. He was attended by Lord Castlereagh, who was as much delighted as surprised by the welcome he received. "I am grown, it seems, very popular," he wrote in answer to a friend's congratulations, "but with quite as little merit, I am afraid, as when I was most unpopular."

**Death of Castlereagh.**

Castlereagh never saw Ireland again; he died by his own hand in 1822. Lord Liverpool's ministry was already in process of reconstruction: the Grenville party at last agreed to support the Government: some of them took office; Lord Wellesley's tiresome claims were ill-satisfied by his appointment as Viceroy of Ireland, but it was Canning, Peel and Huskisson who dictated the policy of the reconstructed ministry. Castlereagh's death opened the Foreign Office and the leadership in the Commons to Canning; Peel succeeded Sidmouth at the Home Office; Huskisson went (1823) to the Board of Trade. Lord Liverpool remained Premier until his fatal illness (1827), but a new spirit began to pervade the whole administration of affairs. The year 1822 rather than the accession of the Whigs to power in 1830 marks the end of the Old Toryism.

**Canning and Peel.**

**Parliamentary Reform.**

The high lights of history play around Thrones and Chanceries. Naturally so; but the forces behind the legislative achievements of Grey, Russell and Durham were supplied by the inventors like Kay, Hargreaves, Cartwright, Arkwright, Watt and Stephenson—the creators of the new England—and by the agitators like Francis Place and William Cobbett, who made its demands articulate. The importance of the work done by the politicians must not, however, be underrated. Peel's Currency Act of 1819 made London the financial capital of the world; the movement towards free trade was initiated by the Acts of 1823 and 1824, but it was Francis Place, the literary tailor at Charing Cross, whose persistent and almost unaided efforts got the laws controlling the combinations of both masters and workmen repealed in 1824, as well as the laws fixing weavers' wages and those which impeded the mobility of labour (1823). Place, too, it was who in 1832 produced the placard "Go for gold

**Place and Cobbett.**

and stop the Duke", and in 1838 drafted the People's Charter. It was William Cobbett, peasant born and brilliant pamphleteer, who by his *Political Register* (1802–35) and other periodical publications, prepared the ground from which Grey in 1832, and Disraeli in 1867, reaped their harvests. Parliamentary reform was effected partly no doubt in deference to Benthamite doctrine and to consideration for the abstract Rights of Man; but the compelling cause was the recognition that a new social structure had been erected, and the face of England had been transfigured, by the Industrial and Agrarian Revolutions.

Down to and beyond the middle of the eighteenth century England had been a land of farms, with a thin and scattered population living in villages and small market towns; the landscape consisting of woods and commons and great open fields; the means of transport almost primitive: without railways, with few navigable waterways, and with roads which, according to Arthur Young, were atrociously bad. Manufacturing work or handicrafts were carried on for the most part in farms and cottages, almost all of which had their spinning-wheels, and many also their hand-looms. There were no great "industrial" towns; smelting was done near the forests of Sussex and Gloucester; there was no deep mining; shipbuilding yards were relatively insignificant; foreign trade was exiguous; London was not yet the financial capital of the world; Liverpool was far less important than Bristol; Bradford-on-Avon had not yet yielded pride of place to Bradford-on-Aire; Manchester was less important than Norwich or perhaps even than Stroud.

**The Industrial and Agrarian Revolutions.**

Between 1715 and 1815 a new England came into being. Agriculture was revolutionized by a few great landlords and by the enclosure of open fields and commons. What "Turnip" Townshend and Coke of Norfolk, Ellmann and Bakewell, Tull and Arthur Young did for agriculture was accomplished for the textile industry by Kay and Hargreaves, Arkwright and Crompton, Cartwright and Watt. The cottage gave place to the factory as the unit of manufacturing industry.

The Duke of Bridgwater and Brindley, Telford and Macadam gave to labour a new mobility and immensely facilitated the exchange of commodities. George Stephenson was busy, and locomotives and railroads were soon to make him immortal.

**Parliamentary Representation.**

Parliament reflected—not unfaithfully—the old England. In relation to the new England the state of representation was grotesque. Previous to 1832 there had been, in the whole of the United Kingdom, only 160,000 electors out of a population of 16,000,000. It was said in 1780 that a clear majority of the House of Commons was returned by 6000 persons, and Lord Grey in 1793 declared that 357 members (out of 558) were returned by 154 patrons of whom 40 were peers. More than half the boroughs were in the maritime counties between the Wash and the Severn and the county of Wilts. Bramber, Bossiney and Beer Alston (to name only a few "rotten" boroughs) had two members apiece; Manchester, Birmingham and Sheffield had none. The uniform 40*s*. franchise (dating from the fifteenth century) had made the counties relatively independent, but in the boroughs the franchise was infinitely varied. In some boroughs the franchise went with certain houses—"ancient tenements"; in others all the ratepayers might vote; in others only the hereditary freemen; in others only the "potwallopers", and so on. The result was that the Act of 1832 was in some cases, Preston for example, a disfranchising measure.

Englishmen are not, however, greatly moved by theoretical anomalies: but the social and economic changes were too palpable to be ignored; they could not continue to coexist with an electoral system virtually dating from the sixteenth century. Reform was overdue.

**Ministerial Changes (1827–30).**

Lord Liverpool's long tenure of office came to an end in 1827. Canning was Prime Minister for less than six months; Lord Goderich (F. J. Robinson) was in office from August, 1827, to January, 1828, but never met Parliament as Prime Minister, being succeeded by the Duke of Wellington with

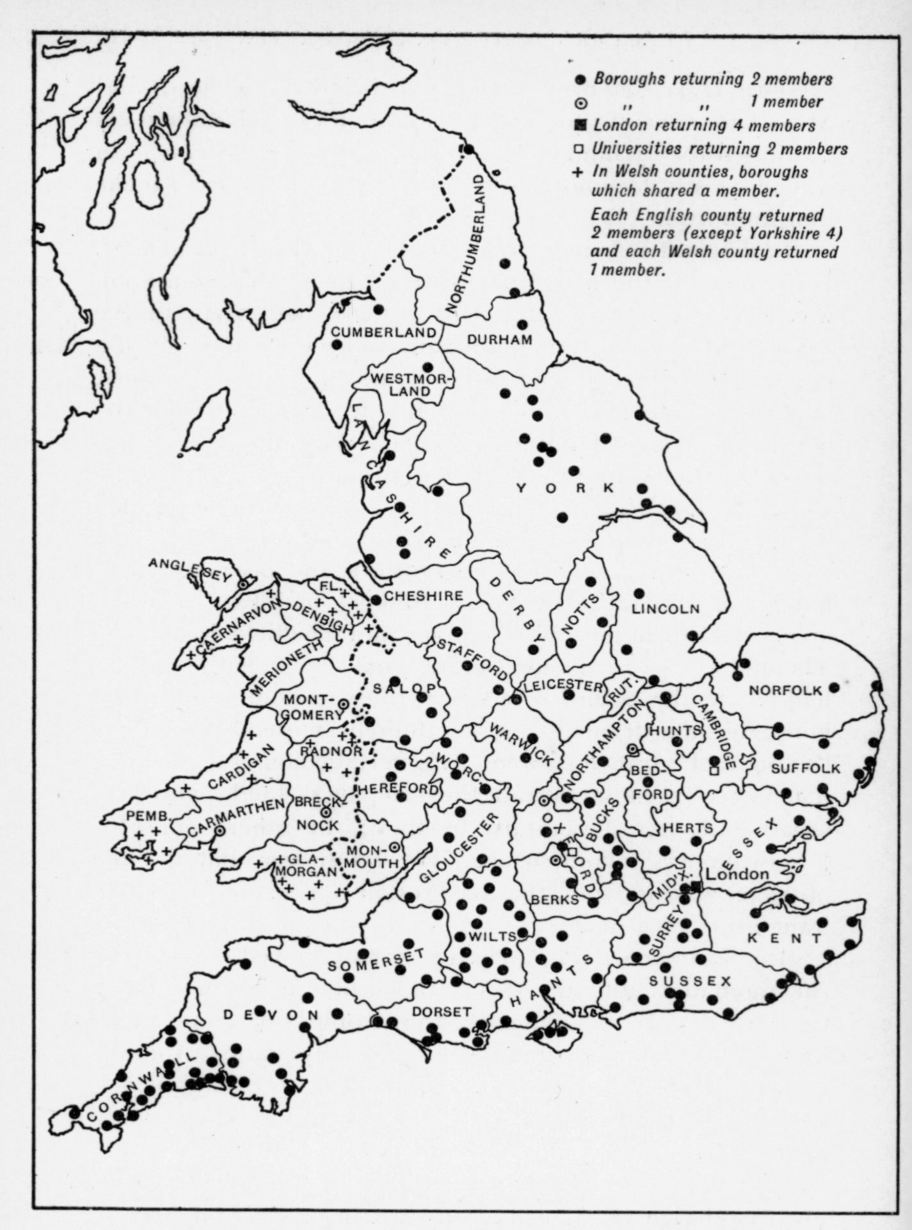


PARLIAMENTARY REPRESENTATION BEFORE 1832

Peel as leader of the Lower House. It was, however, Lord John Russell who in 1828 carried the repeal of the Test and Corporation Acts, though it was Wellington and Peel who overcame the King's resistance to Catholic Emancipation. But if the Duke beat the King, it was O'Connell and the electors of County Clare who beat the Duke. Parliament had long resisted abstract motions for Catholic relief; but O'Connell was eminently concrete. His demand to be admitted to the House of Commons as the duly elected member for an Irish constituency was irresistible.

**William IV.**

On the question of parliamentary reform, however, Wellington was adamant. The new Sovereign was not. George IV had died, wholly unregretted, on 26th June, 1830, and his brother, the Duke of Clarence, had ascended the throne as William IV. The change was greatly for the better. William IV, if inferior in intellect to his predecessor, was by much his superior in character. A bluff, genial, kind-hearted, somewhat eccentric sailor, William IV was commended to his people alike by his profession and his personality. His ministers found in him a man considerate and disinterested, firm but not obstinate, tenacious of the rights of the Crown (not least of the "private rights" of the Duke of Lancaster), and especially concerned to maintain what he termed "the equilibrium of the Three Estates". The King's correspondence with Lord Grey proves that his intelligence has been underrated, that his judgments were shrewd, and his powers of clear expression far from negligible.

**Parliament of 1830.**

The Parliament was dissolved within a month of King George's death, and the new Parliament was elected amid signs of unusual excitement. Even in the old constituencies a new spirit was evidently stirring. The Government lost no fewer than fifty seats, two of Peel's brothers being among the victims.

The King opened the new Parliament on 2nd November, and the attack on the ministry was immediately opened in both Houses. The King's Speech promised prompt and stern repression of public disorder, but there was not a word about reform. Wellington's speech accentuated the significance of the lacuna. He expressed his conviction that all was for the best in the best of all possible Constitutions; he refused to touch the question of reform, and declared with emphasis that " as long as he had any station in the Government of the country, he should always feel it his duty to resist such measures when proposed by others ".

That speech sealed the fate of the Tory party. For the next forty years the Whigs ruled England, and when they were at long last (1874) displaced, it was by a Conservative returned to power by the working men whom he had enfranchised.

**The Grey Ministry.**

On 16th November the Wellington ministry, having already suffered defeat on the Civil List, resigned; and Earl Grey, the veteran champion of reform, formed a ministry which included five Canningites and one other member (Graham) who is best known to history as a leading Peelite.

The new Government at once got to work on a Reform Bill. It was introduced into the House of Commons on 1st March, 1831, by Lord John Russell, who, though not yet a Cabinet minister, had for more than a decade been untiring in his efforts to induce Parliament to tackle what the King and Lord Grey agreed to term " the perilous problem of reform ".

**The Reform Bill.**

Grey insisted that the scheme should be framed on lines so bold and comprehensive as to settle the question once for all. Nor were his colleagues slow to fulfil his injunctions. The scheme when presented proved to be drastic beyond the wildest expectations of the reformers, and caused corresponding dismay among the Tories and borough-mongers. The second reading was carried (21st March), but only by a majority of one. On the motion for committal an instruction, moved by General Gascoyne, stipulating that there should be no diminution in the total number of representatives of England and Wales, was carried against the Government by a majority of eight.

Lord Grey insisted on an immediate appeal to the

country; the King, somewhat reluctantly, assented, and in hot haste dissolved Parliament.

General Election of 1831.

Excitement in the country rose to fever pitch, and the reformers came back with a majority of over one hundred. The Bill, reintroduced with merely minor changes, was carried on the second reading (7th July) by 367 to 231, and after a long and arduous fight in committee was, before the end of September, sent up to the Lords. The only important amendment was carried at the instance of Lord Chandos, and extended the Bill by conferring the county franchise on £50 tenants-at-will. After nearly a week's debate the Lords rejected the Bill (8th October) by 199 to 158.

Second Bill.

The rejection of the Bill revealed a dangerous situation. A mass of social and economic discontent had gradually accumulated during the previous half-century, and, since the close of the war, had periodically become obtrusively manifest. The Lords' action brought the country to the verge of revolution. Serious riots broke out in several large towns, notably in Nottingham, where the castle was burnt down, and in Bristol.[1] The position was, indeed, somewhat paradoxical, since the rioting was evidently the work not of the middle classes who were to be enfranchised under the Bill, but of the workmen who were not. But unlike Grey and Russell, and with sounder instinct, the working men regarded the Bill merely as an instalment. Their time, they were assured, would come, though it might be indefinitely postponed if reform was strangled at the birth.

Third Bill.

Strangled it was not, though the birth pangs were severe. Parliament reassembled in December; a third Reform Bill, considerably amended, was introduced, passed rapidly through all its stages in the Commons and sent up before the end of the month to the Lords, who gave the Bill a second reading by a majority of nine.

Then the real struggle began. Lord Lyndhurst carried by 151 to 116 a motion to postpone the clauses and schedules dealing with disfranchisement until the rest of the Bill had

[1] The Bristol riots are vividly described in Stanley Weyman's *Chippinge*.

been approved. The Cabinet then advised the King to create as many Peers "as might ensure the success of the Bill in all its essential principles".

**King and Peers.**

The King's behaviour throughout the crisis that ensued was by general consent admirable. His study of the whole problem was almost as thorough as Russell's; to the general principles of the Bill he gave cordial assent, though he had made it clear from the first that under no circumstances would he ever accept annual Parliaments, universal suffrage, or vote by ballot. His objections to the first two principles were shared by the Cabinet, and ballot they had expunged, at the King's request, from the first draft. To the coercion of the Peers King William was, however, strongly opposed, and when Grey insisted, reluctantly accepted the resignation of the minister. But neither Lord Lyndhurst nor Manners-Sutton (the Speaker), to whom the King applied, could form a ministry; Wellington, in order to "save the Sovereign from the indignity of having so gross a violation of the Constitution forced upon him", chivalrously attempted the task. On Peel's refusal to join him he failed. Grey was recalled. The King gave way, and promised, if necessary, to create a sufficient number of Peers to carry the Bill, though wisely insisting that as far as possible the new Peers should be eldest sons or collaterals of existing Peers.[1] The battle was won. The opposing Peers seceded, and on 7th June the Bill became law. Bills framed on similar though not identical lines for Scotland and Ireland followed. To the King's "noble conduct" Grey bore generous testimony. "It is indeed," he wrote, "a just theme for praise, and entitles him to all our gratitude and all our zeal in his service." The extreme Radicals did not share Grey's opinion. William IV, they declared, had made more republicans in a week

[1] Not until 1924 was the mystery in regard to the King's famous letter to Lord Grey finally dispelled by the discovery of the original letter, which came into the possession of *The Times* and was described in an important article on 22nd February, 1924. The spurious letter was first printed by I. A. Roebuck, who was in close touch with Lord Brougham, and continued to deceive historians (including the present writer) for more than half a century. Two specialists on this period—Mr. Butler (1914) and Mr. Trevelyan (1920)—have thus been justified in their refusal to accept the letter as authentic.

than all Paine's writings in twenty-five years. But history has endorsed the judgment of Grey.

With the Acts of 1867, 1884 and 1885, 1918 and 1928 in mind, critics are apt to regard the Act of 1832 as almost insignificant. But it is *le premier pas que coûte*; contemporaries were right in discerning in the Act of 1832 the opening of the flood-gates of democracy. Fifty-six boroughs with fewer than 2000 inhabitants apiece were totally disfranchised; thirty with fewer than 4000 apiece lost one of their two members; Weymouth and Melcombe Regis lost two out of four. The 143 seats thus surrendered were redistributed as follows: 65 to counties, 44 to twenty-two English boroughs; 21 to single-member boroughs; 8 to Scotland and 5 to Ireland. The aggregate membership of the House remained, consequently, unchanged at 658. In the boroughs a uniform £10 household franchise was established, with the reservation of the rights of resident freemen in corporate towns. In the counties the old 40*s*. freeholders, who since the fifteenth century had monopolized the county franchise, were reinforced by copyholders and long-leaseholders, and by tenants-at-will rented at £50 a year. In Scotland the county franchise was extended to all owners of property of £10 a year, and to certain leaseholders; in Ireland to owners as in England, and to £20 occupiers. The final result was the addition of 455,000 electors to the roll—thus more than tripling the electorate. In towns, political power was vested mainly in the merchants, manufacturers and shopkeepers; in the counties, in the landowners and the farmers. The Act of 1832 also provided for a proper register of voters, for the division of constituencies into convenient polling districts, and for the restriction of the polling to two successive days.

**Act of 1832.**

The Act did not impair the position of the monarchy, but it did dethrone the aristocracy. For a generation ministerial office was, indeed, monopolized, with few exceptions, by the aristocracy, but legislation reflected the increasing influence of the middle classes, whom the Act established in power.

To the artisans, on the contrary, the Act was a bitter disappointment. They had supplied the driving force behind the bill, but they got nothing out of it. The People's Charter of 1837 was the measure of their disappointment and their ambition. Their refusal to co-operate with the Anti-Corn-Law leaguers was symptomatic of their desire to be revenged. "Don't be deceived by the middle classes again. You helped them to get their votes, but where are the fine promises they made to you? . . . And now they want to get the Corn Laws repealed, not for your benefit but for their own. Cheap bread they cry, but they mean low wages." Such was the advice given by Thomas Cooper to his fellow Chartists. The Chartists demanded annual Parliaments, manhood suffrage, vote by ballot, equal electoral districts, payment of members and abolition of the property qualification for members. Most of those demands have by now (1937) been conceded, but Lord John Russell's famous and fatuous declaration in 1837 that the Act of 1832 was "final" earned him his soubriquet "finality Jack" and was bitterly resented by the working men.

**The Chartists and the Whigs.**

Nevertheless, though far from final, the Act of 1832 was immeasurably important. Modest though it looks on paper, it marks the Great Divide. Down to 1702, perhaps until 1714, England was ruled by a monarch. From 1714 to 1832 the monarch shared the throne with an aristocracy which, as the years went on, became more and more of an oligarchy. The Act of 1832 marks the initiation of the effective rule of Parliament—of King, Lords and Commons.

**Executive and Legislature.**

Never was the "equilibrium", mistakenly described by William IV as that of the "Three Estates", so perfect as it was between 1832 and 1867. Mr. Lecky and Mr. Gladstone concurred in the opinion that in those years parliamentary government was seen at its best. Aristotle, could he have conceived the idea of representative democracy, would have agreed with them: the middle classes ruled. They left the actual executive government in the hands of members of ruling families. Peel and Gladstone, it is true, belonged to the new commercial, not to the old territorial, aristocracy, but at Harrow, Eton and Christ Church they had shared the life and imbibed the traditions of a class to which their sons belonged from birth. Until 1867 Cabinets were composed largely of Peers and almost exclusively of men closely connected with the peerage. Between 1832 and 1866 sixty-four per cent of Cabinet ministers were actually sons of Peers or baronets. Between 1801 and 1831 the same class had contributed seventy-three per cent, and it was not until after 1906 that commoners began to outnumber aristocrats.[1] But if Cabinets were predominantly aristocratic, they were sustained in power by Parliaments increasingly democratic in composition and outlook.

**The Reformed Parliament.**

The first House of Commons elected under the new Act contained an overwhelming preponderance of Whigs, henceforward more commonly described (according to the latest Parisian mode) as Liberals. A new spirit in legislation manifested itself at once. Before William IV died, slavery was abolished, the Poor Law was amended, the municipal corporations were reformed, and, thanks to Lord Shaftesbury, a beginning was made with legislation for the protection of women and children in factories.

**Ministerial Changes.**

Such legislation was the work less of ministers than of Parliament. Ministers succeeded each other rapidly. Lord Grey gave place in 1834 to Lord Melbourne, but the latter had been in office less than four months when he was dismissed by the King, who, on the Duke's advice, entrusted the government to Peel. Peel appealed to the country on the strength of the Tamworth Manifesto, which laid the foundations of the new Conservatism. The old Toryism was decently interred: the new Conservatism promised reform without either revolution or reaction. The Conservatives gained many victories, but not enough to give Peel the requisite majority in Parliament, and in April, 1835, the King was obliged to recall Lord Melbourne. Two years later the old King died, and the Crown descended to a girl of eighteen, the only child of William's younger brother, the Duke of Kent.

[1] Laski: *The British Cabinet* (1928).

CHAPTER XXIII

# The Victorian Era
## The Queen and her Ministers

"THE Elizabethan and the Victorian Ages will appear to the historian of the future as the twin peaks in which English civilization culminated." Dean Inge's opinion will command wide if not universal assent. Twin peaks those periods indubitably are, and it is not without significance that only Queens have, thus far, given their names to the "eras" or "epochs" of our history. The historian must needs be more cautious than the moralist in forecasting the future, though he can be at least as confident about the past. In all its aspects, political, industrial and scientific, the Victorian era was one of the greatest in English history, and in politics, with which alone this work is concerned, the characteristic note of the period was the fruitful partnership of Crown and Parliament. The harmony of the partners was enhanced by the fact that the new Queen was herself in cordial sympathy with the outlook of the middle classes. She shared their outstanding characteristics: their impeccable respectability, their common sense and moderation in all things, their mistrust of enthusiasm and avoidance of extremes, their public philanthropy and their domestic virtues. Nor did she escape some of their limitations and the prejudices to which they obstinately adhered.

**The Middle-Class Monarchy.**

The Princess Victoria ascended a throne which, if not actually tottering, was undeniably unstable. Monarchy was at a discount. Legitimacy had received a fatal blow in France by the collapse of the restored Bourbon monarchy in

**The Monarchy in 1837.**

1830. Of Queen Victoria's immediate predecessors in England one was loved and pitied, but, if respected, was respected rather for his private virtues than his conduct as King; the second was condemned as a notorious profligate, a bad father and an unfaithful husband; the third was the object of good-natured ridicule. The young Queen, though born upon English soil, was brought up by Germans; very quickly, however, she won wide approval by her remarkable combination of simplicity and dignity, of unmistakable shrewdness and uncommon common sense. In the first hours of her reign she made it clear that she was no longer under domestic tutelage, but would look for political guidance only to her constitutional advisers.

**Lord Melbourne.**

Queen Victoria was extraordinarily fortunate in her first Prime Minister. Lord Melbourne had his faults as a man and a politician, but he devoted himself with complete disinterestedness and charming chivalry to the service of his young mistress. He served her not only as First Minister, but as private secretary, and proved himself both a faithful servant and the kindliest, wisest of mentors. The Queen, though quick to detect and reprimand anything amiss in his conduct, soon came to trust him entirely as an adviser and personally to regard him with the affection of a daughter. To his country Lord Melbourne rendered the inestimable service of teaching the young Queen how to preside as a constitutional Sovereign over a parliamentary democracy.

**Tuition of the Queen.**

The soundness of his teaching was first tested when in 1839 the Melbourne ministry, beset by difficulties both at Westminster and in Ireland, resigned. The Queen was distraught with grief and anxiety, but Melbourne, admitting that the situation was "very painful", exhorted her to be "prudent and firm", and in particular not to give any ground for the suspicion of "unfair dealing".

She obeyed; and, albeit reluctantly, sent for Peel, to whom she ingenuously confessed her confidence in Lord Melbourne, "who had been to her quite a parent". Moreover, she told the new ministers "that they might know there was no unfair dealing that I meant" (so she wrote to Melbourne) " to see you often as I owed so much to you ".

After this, Peel might well have seemed to her " awkward and shy ", but the dreaded separation from Melbourne was temporarily averted by the emergence of the " Bedchamber Question ". Peel, with perfect constitutional propriety, insisted that the highest court officials, female as well as male, must change with the Government. The Queen flatly refused to part with her Whig ladies; Peel stood firm; so Melbourne had to be recalled. The young lady was wildly delighted " at having got out of the hands of people who would have sacrificed every personal feeling and instinct of the Queen's to their bad party purposes ". The accusation was palpably absurd, and sixty years later the Queen confessed as much to Lord Stamfordham. Peel's stiff attitude on the matter was perhaps accentuated by the distressing incident arising from the illness of Lady Flora Hastings, lady-in-waiting to the Duchess of Kent. Anyway, when, two years later, Melbourne finally resigned, the Queen quickly learnt to appreciate the great qualities of the " cold, odd man ", and gave him her complete confidence.

**The Bedchamber Question.**

The Queen's conversion to Peel was doubtless rendered quicker and easier by the fact that she no longer needed Melbourne's services as a private secretary, having found a secretary, and a husband, in Prince Albert of Saxe-Coburg-Gotha, whom in 1840 she had married. After the incident of 1839 the position of the Melbourne ministry became increasingly precarious. Parliament was dissolved in 1841; the ensuing election gave the " new Conservatives " a large majority; Melbourne finally resigned, and the Queen sent for Sir Robert Peel, who formed a Government destined to make history. Melbourne, before quitting office, warned the Queen that she must not repeat the blunder of 1839, and (indirectly) assured Peel that, if he were patient and considerate, the Queen would meet him in the same spirit. An accommodation was reached without difficulty. The great offices of the court, and the situations held in the royal Household by members of Parliament, were henceforward to

**Prince Albert.**

be included in the political arrangements made on a change of administration. The Mistress of the Robes was also to change with the ministry, but the ladies-in-waiting were to hold their appointments without regard to their political connexions.

**The Crown: Right of Consultation.**

Prince Albert and Sir Robert Peel fully appreciated each other, and to the policy of fiscal reform carried out by Peel the Prince gave consistent support, not least on the crucial question of the Corn Laws. The Queen was not less cordial in support of Peel, but she nevertheless continued her correspondence and intercourse with Melbourne. Baron Stockmar, who continued to act as a confidential adviser to the Queen and the Prince Consort, remonstrated against this practice as unconstitutional and unfair to Peel.[1] Melbourne was annoyed, and the letters now published show that he acted throughout "with scrupulous honour and delicacy, and tried to augment rather than undermine Peel's growing influence with the Queen and Prince". Nevertheless, Stockmar had raised a point of considerable constitutional significance. How far is a constitutional Sovereign entitled to seek or receive advice, on political matters, from any person other than her ministers? The question is evidently one of extreme delicacy, and cannot be answered dogmatically without reference to each particular case. In Lord Melbourne's case there is no evidence that he ever overstepped the rigid limits of constitutional discretion. At a much later date (1876) Mr. Gladstone, commenting upon the attacks made on Prince Albert on the eve of the Crimean War, wrote: "It was a matter of course that the Queen's husband should be more or less her political adviser. . . . We must go further. It does not seem easy to limit the Sovereign's right of taking friendly counsel, by any absolute rule, to the case of a husband. If it is the Queen's duty to form a judgment upon important proposals submitted to her by her ministers, she has an indisputable right to the use of all instruments which will enable her to discharge that duty with effect; subject always, and subject only, to the one

**Gladstone's Opinion.**

[1] *Q. V. L.*, I, pp. 415–64.

vital condition that they do not disturb the relation, on which the whole machinery of the Constitution hinges, between those ministers and the Crown. She cannot, therefore, as a rule, legitimately consult in private on political matters with the party in opposition to the Government of the day." [1]

This is evidently an opinion of high authority; but it remains an opinion, and includes limiting words. To the "rule" there may obviously be exceptions. Each case must be decided on its merits. In January, 1886, for example, the position in regard to Home Rule for Ireland was exceptionally difficult. The response of the new electorate, consulted in the autumn of 1885, was ambiguous. A Conservative Government was still in office, but was likely to be turned out as soon as Parliament met. The Liberal Party was hopelessly divided on the dominant question of the hour. Under these circumstances the Queen, distraught with anxiety, pressed Mr. (afterwards Viscount) Goschen to go down to Osborne for a personal consultation. Goschen was in a peculiarly independent position: he had served only in Liberal Cabinets, but had refused to join Mr. Gladstone in 1880, and on the Irish Question was strongly opposed to him. Nevertheless, he begged the Queen to excuse him on the ground that his visit would "expose the action of Your Majesty to much misconstruction and misrepresentation". The Queen demurred to his objections and quoted precedents against him, to such effect that he was fain to admit that "Your Majesty is constitutionally entitled to consult anyone on an occasion such as this in whom Your Majesty places confidence". Nevertheless, Goschen did not go to Osborne, but advised the Queen to send for Mr. Gladstone. "Anyone" went perhaps too far. Anson, on the contrary, seems to limit the right of consultation to peers, though perhaps too narrowly. "The Sovereign," he says, "has a right to demand, and any peer has a right to offer, counsel on matters which are of importance to the public welfare."

**The Queen and her Counsellors.**

Whether Privy Councillors have an equal right to "offer

[1] *Gleanings*, I, p. 73.

counsel" is doubtful; that the Sovereign has the right to seek it from them is not.

**The Crown Right of Dissolution.**

The correspondence between the Queen and ex-ministers raised another question even more difficult than that of consultation. Is the Sovereign entitled to insist on a dissolution of Parliament, and a consequent appeal to the electorate? The Queen had been contemplating such a step on her own responsibility in May, 1886, in order to prevent the passing of a Home Rule Bill. Lord Salisbury, when consulted, replied that "a dissolution, if resorted to, should take place on the advice of Mr. Gladstone, according to the usual practice, for the present House of Commons was summoned on Lord Salisbury's advice".[1] The Queen had not, in fact, long to wait, and she attained her end by less dangerous means. The House of Commons rejected Gladstone's Home Rule Bill on 8th June; Gladstone at once appealed to the country, and on his defeat made way for the Unionist Party.

**Situation in 1893.**

A similar though slightly varied situation arose in 1893. Gladstone, having been returned to power by a small and precarious majority in 1892, brought forward in 1893 his second edition of Home Rule. The Queen considered it a "foolish and terrible Bill", and consulted the Duke of Argyll, Lord Salisbury and the Duke of Devonshire as to the constitutional propriety and wisdom of her insisting on a dissolution, if, after its anticipated rejection by the House of Lords, Mr. Gladstone wished to introduce a third Bill. Lord Salisbury was of opinion that the Queen had an "undoubted right to do so", and that it might come to this; but agreed with the Duke of Devonshire that the necessity had not arisen. In the course of a memorandum which has become classical he gave his reasons. "A Dissolution by the Queen against the advice of her ministers would, of course, involve their resignation. Their party could hardly help going to the country as the opponents of the royal authority; or at least as the severe critics of the mode in which it had been exercised. No one can foresee what the

[1] *Q. V. L.*, 3rd Series, I, p. 117.

upshot of such a state of things would be. . . . But there must be *some* hazard that, in the end, such a step would injure the authority of the Queen." [1]

In the event it was Mr. Gladstone himself who was anxious, on the rejection of his Bill, for an immediate appeal to the country. Only the opposition of his own Cabinet prevented him. The old man would not brook opposition, and on 3rd March, 1894, resigned.

The Queen, entirely on her own initiative, replaced him by Lord Rosebery, but derived little comfort from his succession. Particularly was she perturbed by Rosebery's proposals in regard to the House of Lords. Again she toyed with the idea of a dissolution, and in great agitation wrote (25th October, 1894) to Lord Salisbury asking him a number of questions to which he unreservedly replied. He assured the Queen that she would be "entirely within her constitutional rights in demanding that the Cabinet" should announce no policy on the subject [of the House of Lords] which had not been previously submitted to and approved by her; and in requiring, if she thought fit, that the country should be consulted before a decision on so grave a matter is taken. In answer to another specific question whether "the Unionist Party [is] fit for a dissolution *now*", he replied: "As far as it is possible to judge, the Unionist Party is quite prepared for a dissolution and would be likely to fare well if one should now take place." He added: "Though he is very anxious to avoid even the appearance of obtruding his opinions upon Your Majesty it will always be his duty and his pleasure, as a former servant of Your Majesty and as a Privy Councillor, to answer any questions which you may think fit to put to him."

**Lord Salisbury's Opinion.**

That Lord Salisbury was constitutionally correct in his views about the respective rights of the Sovereign and Privy Councillors, and of the obligations of the latter, is hardly open to question; though it would obviously be convenient, if not essential, that the responsible minister should be at least informed of the Sovereign's intention to ask for, and

[1] *Q. V. L.*, II, pp. 282–99.

the Councillor's intention to tender, advice. If the minister objected it would be open to him to resign, and the Sovereign would then be confronted with the task of finding a minister willing to accept responsibility for the advice tendered.

As to a dissolution of Parliament without the consent of the ministry in office, the Queen thought it wise, before deciding on so strong a step, to consult Sir Henry James, as an ex-law officer, as to the proper procedure, and, as a shrewd politician, as to the probable result of an appeal to the electorate. Sir Henry gave his opinion that to demand an immediate dissolution would be premature and inadvisable. In that view the Duke of Devonshire, the Duke of Argyll and Mr. Chamberlain concurred. Lord Salisbury, also, in further correspondence agreed that an immediate dissolution was inexpedient, and shrewdly added: "At present opinion is so sluggish on the whole question [of the House of Lords] that people would be startled by the direct intervention of the Crown", which might have the unhappy result of stimulating interest in it.[1]

The Queen wisely followed this advice, which was more than justified by the event. Lord Rosebery himself advised a dissolution in 1895; he was soundly beaten, and for the next ten years the Unionists remained in power.

The question of dissolution emerged again under King George V; but further treatment of it must be deferred. After a long parenthesis we return to the situation in 1841.

**Dethronement of the Landowners.**

Peel's fiscal reforms completed the constitutional process begun by the Reform Act of 1832. By subordinating the interests of agriculture to those of industry and commerce they tended to dethrone the landowners and exalt the influence of the urban constituencies. But economic causes are even slower than political in operation. Not until the last decades of the century did agriculture and the agricultural interests meet the biting wind of adversity. In the meantime, the prosperity of the country at large increased amazingly. The Bank Charter Act, devised by Lord

[1] *Q. V. L.*, 3rd Series, II, pp. 441–9.

Overstone and passed into law by Peel (1844), made London the financial capital of the world, but accentuated the tendency already noticed. So did the final repeal of the Navigation Laws (1849). During the interval between the fall of Peel (1846) and Gladstone's accession to power (1868) the attention of the Government was, however, largely concentrated upon foreign affairs, and the direction of foreign policy was mainly in the hands of Lord Palmerston.

**The Queen and Lord Palmerston.**

Of all the leading statesmen of the reign Lord Palmerston was, with one exception, the least acceptable to the Queen. The Queen disliked his levity, and resented his neglect to consult her upon foreign affairs, which she regarded as her peculiar province. Lord Palmerston, though anxious to show all due respect to the Queen, of whose intelligence he had a high opinion, was genuinely unable to understand why a young wife and mother should want to interfere in such matters as long as there was an exceptionally capable minister at the Foreign Office! Consequently, he was remiss in taking her pleasure, and dilatory in sending her dispatches in time for her to master and approve their contents. Again and again she reproached him for his carelessness, and in 1850 addressed to him a formal memorandum defining his duty in relation to the Sovereign. Neglect to obey her directions would, she warned him, be considered "as failing in sincerity towards the Crown, and justly to be visited by the exercise of her constitutional right" to dismiss the recalcitrant minister.

**Dismissal of Palmerston.**

Matters came to a head in 1851. The Queen was deeply incensed when she learnt that the Foreign Secretary proposed to receive at his house Louis Kossuth, one of the leaders of the Hungarian insurrection of 1848. The Premier and the Cabinet supported the Queen, and Palmerston abandoned his intention. A few weeks later, he sinned once more by receiving a deputation of Radicals who, without protest from the Foreign Minister, described two friendly Sovereigns, the Emperors of Russia and Austria, as "odious and detestable assassins". So gross a breach of international good manners deeply annoyed the Queen, but the Premier, Lord John Russell, while not justifying his colleague, hesitated to dismiss him. But in December Palmerston, despite the Queen's orders that strict neutrality should be observed, expressed his approval of the *coup d'état* by which Louis Napoleon virtually destroyed the Constitution he had sworn to defend. The Queen's anger knew no bounds, and at her instance Lord John Russell plucked up courage to dismiss the offending minister, and the Queen insisted that he should never again be appointed to the Foreign Office. Nor was he.

**Ministerial Instability.**

Within a few weeks, however, Palmerston had his revenge by turning out Russell (20th February, 1852), who was succeeded by Lord Derby as Prime Minister, with Benjamin Disraeli as Chancellor of the Exchequer and leader in the Commons. To the latter's appointment the Queen at first demurred, but yielded to Lord Derby's insistence. The new Government had no majority, and when, after less than twelve months in office, they were defeated on Disraeli's budget, the Queen parted with them without regret. Especially did she resent the outgoing Premier's suggestion that she should consult Lord Lansdowne as to his successor. She contended that the responsibility of appointing a Prime Minister was hers. Her contention was justified. That prerogative does unquestionably belong to the Crown, as was demonstrated in 1885, in 1894 and in 1923. But it can be exercised only within narrow limits, and only if the Crown's nominee can command the support, with or without a dissolution, of the House of Commons.

**The Aberdeen Ministry.**

On Lord Derby's resignation in December, 1852, the Queen entrusted the formation of a Government to Lord Aberdeen, a Peelite, who formed a Coalition Cabinet of Peelites and Whigs. The Duke of Argyll, who was a member of it, declared that no Cabinet in which he ever sat "worked more smoothly or with less individual friction".[1] It has, however, been generally held responsible for allowing this country to drift into the Crimean War; it was defeated on

[1] *Autobiography*, I, p. 388.

Roebuck's famous motion for " a select committee to inquire into the condition of our army before Sebastopol "; and in February, 1855, gave place to a reconstructed ministry under Lord Palmerston.

**Palmerston's Ministry.**

Palmerston brought the Crimean War to a successful conclusion (1856), and the electorate, when consulted in 1857, affirmed its confidence in the Government and its chief. The feature of the election was, indeed, the rout of the Pacifists, John Bright being defeated in the free-trade stronghold of Manchester, and Cobden at Huddersfield.

**The Queen and the Mutiny.**

Hardly, however, had the new Parliament met before the Mutiny broke out in India (May, 1857). The Queen's feelings had been deeply moved by the sufferings of her soldiers in the Crimea, and she had been untiring in her efforts, with Florence Nightingale's help, to mitigate them. Nor had she neglected to stimulate her ministers to more vigorous prosecution of the war. She was even more deeply distressed by the outbreak of the Mutiny. During the anxious months that followed on the first news the Queen suffered, as her biographer has told us, " acute mental torture ". The Queen suspected that Palmerston and his Cabinet failed to realize the gravity of the crisis; she repeatedly warned them that the measures they adopted were quite inadequate to meet the emergency, and peremptorily insisted that large reinforcements under competent officers should be sent out. Nor did Palmerston improve matters by jocularly declaring that it was " fortunate for the Government that the Queen was not sitting on the opposition benches in the House of Commons ". The Sepoy rebellion was not stamped out until April, 1859, and by that time the Palmerston ministry had fallen. Lord Derby had again taken office, very unwillingly, without a majority, and after an appeal to the country in the spring of 1859 was defeated in the new House of Commons by a majority of 13.

**The Government of India Act.**

Lord Derby had, however, placed upon the statute book one measure of first-rate constitutional importance. The Mutiny had brought the dual system of government in India to an end. The Crown now assumed the direct government of British India; a Secretary of State, with a Council to assist him, replaced the old Board of Control and its President, and the Governor-General was transformed into a Viceroy. The process was completed when in 1876 the Queen, on the advice of Disraeli and with the sanction of Parliament, assumed the appropriate title of Empress of India. The assumption was bitterly criticized at the time, a famous pamphlet[1] depicted "*The Blot on the Queen's Head*", but at a great Durbar at Delhi (1st January, 1877) the Queen was proclaimed Empress, and saluted by over seventy ruling princes and chiefs as Shah-in-Shah Padishah, Monarch of Monarchs.

**The Queen and her Ministers**

To return. On the resignation of Lord Derby (1859), Lord Palmerston became, for the second time, Prime Minister, and retained office until his death (18th October, 1865), when his ministry was carried on by Earl Russell, with Gladstone as leader in the House of Commons. The Queen would gladly have avoided the necessity of an invidious choice, in 1859, between "the two tiresome old men", each of whom had been Prime Minister, and both of whom she disliked. Accordingly she had asked Lord Granville to form a government, but Russell's refusal to serve under him frustrated the plan, and the Queen reluctantly sent for Palmerston.

Not that she had been satisfied with the Conservatives. Lord Derby had, indeed, pleased her by drafting in peculiarly happy terms the Proclamation which she issued to her new subjects in India; but he had offended her by surrendering, "in several important points", the prerogatives of the Crown, notably in regard to the Indian Civil Service, to the right of declaring war and making peace, to the drafting of the Queen's Speech, and to the Queen's right of conceding or refusing a dissolution of Parliament. In May, 1858, when the defeat of the Government appeared to be imminent, Lord Derby asked the Queen's permission to announce her anticipated consent to a dissolution. To make such an announcement would, she held, be tantamount to a

[1] Still in my possession.

threat to Parliament, and as such unconstitutional. She was undeniably right. A minister has no right to ask for a hypothetical pledge from the Sovereign. The Queen consulted Lord Aberdeen on the larger issue already discussed, and he correctly answered that though a minister might properly threaten the House of Commons with a dissolution, he must not "join the Queen's name in it". To refuse to grant a dissolution was, he held, "one of the very few acts which the Queen of England could do without responsible advice at the moment"; but he strongly advised the Queen not, in the present instance, to exercise her right. When in 1859 Lord Derby did go to the country he was defeated.

During Palmerston's and Russell's second ministries public attention was mainly concentrated on foreign affairs —on the Italian War of Independence (1859), the Austro-Prussian war against Denmark (1865), the Prussian war against Austria (1866), and, above all, on the Civil War in America (1861–5). It was in the first year of the American war, and at a moment when relations between Great Britain and the United States were severely strained, that the Queen suffered the terrible bereavement that darkened all the rest of her days.

On 30th November, 1861, Russell sent to Windsor for the Queen's approval a dispatch which, if it had gone to Washington unamended, would almost certainly have led to war between the two great English-speaking nations. The English case as presented by Russell was, indeed, unanswerable; but it was provocatively stated, and the Prince Consort, though already a sick man, so amended the form, without impairing the substance, of the dispatch, as to offer to President Lincoln a way of honourable retreat from a false position. The President wisely took it, and on 9th January, 1862, the good news reached England that the war cloud had passed.

**Death of the Prince Consort.**

The Prince Consort did not live to see the happy issue of his tactful intervention. On 14th December, 1861, he died at Windsor. The Queen's anguish was indescribable, and her people, realizing at long last that the loss was theirs as well as hers, shared the Queen's sorrow, and extended to the desolate widow their genuine sympathy.

Not that the Prince had ever been really popular. Until the last weeks of his life the nation had never appreciated his worth, or realized the debt it owed to his wisdom, modesty and self-restraint. The Prince may not have understood all the niceties of the English Constitution; but no foreign consort could have understood them better, or done less to violate the spirit underlying them. With Peel and Cobden he was a convinced free trader, and not less devoted than John Bright to peace. His was the conception of the Great Exhibition of 1851, and nothing short of his enthusiasm could have carried the scheme through against the persistent hostility it encountered and the fantastic fears it evoked. It was not his fault if the Exhibition, having given a splendid advertisement to English trade, failed in its ulterior purpose of establishing international peace.[1]

After the Prince's death the nation learnt something of his character and aims; but, as time went on, and the "widow of Windsor" seemed obstinate in her determination to nurse her grief and remain immured in her retirement, grumblings were heard. Of all her ministers Gladstone, as she confessed, sympathized most fully with her in her grief. Nor was any minister of the reign a more fervent believer in the Monarchy as an institution, or more respectful towards the occupant of the throne. In later years his patience was sorely tried, but he never in public betrayed the loss of it, he consistently supported adequate parliamentary grants to the Queen's children, and if, after many years of continuous seclusion, he deemed it his duty to remonstrate with the Queen he did so in most considerate terms and solely in the interests of the Monarchy.

**The Queen's Unpopularity.**

Between 1864 and 1874 the Queen's personal popularity reached zero, and more than once it looked as though the throne itself were in danger. For two years after the Prince Consort's death his desolated widow never appeared in

[1] On this see Marriott: *Commonwealth or Anarchy* (1937), pp. 123–7.

public, and on 1st April, 1864, Delane, the all-powerful editor of *The Times*, in a leading article, referred in terms, not to be misunderstood, to those who " isolate themselves from the world and its duties ". On the 6th the Queen herself addressed to *The Times* (though, of course, anonymously) a spirited reply. She explicitly contradicted the rumour—itself Delane's invention—that she was about to resume the place in society which she occupied " before her great affliction ", and declared that she was devoting herself, to the utmost of her strength, to duties imposed upon the Sovereign, more important than participation in public ceremonials. Nevertheless, the intrepid Delane returned in December to the attack. " The living " (he reminded the Queen) " have their claims as well as the dead. . . . It is impossible for a recluse to occupy the British throne without a gradual weakening of that authority which the Sovereign has been accustomed to exert." He therefore begged the Queen not further to postpone her subjects' claims, and the performance of the duties of her high station, " to the indulgence of an unavailing grief ". Nor did *The Times* stand alone. On 28th September, 1865, *Punch*, portraying the Queen as the statue of Hermione, and Britannia as Paulina, in *The Winter's Tale*, adjured the Queen: " 'Tis time! Descend; Be stone no more."

A rebuke to the critics came from an unexpected quarter. At a Reform meeting in London in the autumn of 1866 a London member of some prominence in Parliament spoke slightingly of the Queen's seclusion. John Bright's immediate and eloquent rebuke to the ill-mannered and ill-natured critic was received with tumultuous enthusiasm: " I am not accustomed " (he said) " to stand up in defence of those who are possessors of crowns; but I could not sit here and hear that observation without a sensation of wonder and pain. I think there has been by many persons a great injustice done to the Queen in reference to her desolate and widowed position. And I venture to say this, that a woman—be she the Queen of a great realm, or be she the wife of one of your labouring men—who can keep alive in her heart a great sorrow for the lost object of her life and affection, is not at all wanting in a great and generous sympathy with you." It was finely said. But the Queen had already given ear to the appeals addressed to her. In February, 1866, she opened Parliament in person, and later on held courts at Buckingham Palace, reviewed the troops at Aldershot, attended the wedding of Princess Mary of Cambridge to the Duke of Teck (12th June), and herself gave away her daughter Princess Helena at her marriage (5th July) to Prince Christian of Schleswig-Holstein. She attended a Highland gathering at Braemar in September, opened new waterworks at Aberdeen in October, and, in November, visited Wolverhampton to unveil a statue of the Prince Consort.

**Grants to the Royal Family.**

Nevertheless, the voice of criticism was not hushed, and though the Queen prudently opened Parliament in person in February, 1871, the question of a dowry for the Princess Louise on her marriage to the Marquis of Lorne (1871) aroused much "very unpleasant cavilling"—the Queen's own words. Eventually, and largely through the influence of Mr. Gladstone, the House of Commons, with only three dissentients, voted the Princess a dowry of £30,000, together with an annuity of £6000. Considerably more formidable was the opposition in the same year (1871) to a grant to Prince Arthur (the Duke of Connaught) on attaining his majority. No fewer than fifty-three members voted to reduce the annuity from £15,000, as proposed by the Government, to £10,000, and eleven voted against any grant at all.

A good many people thought that a widowed Queen, living in semi-retirement, was well able to provide for her family out of the Civil List. Some years later Mr. Labouchere, a Radical politician of aristocratic birth, declared in *The Fortnightly Review* that "Nothing has conduced more to shake that decent respect for the living symbol of the State, which goes by the name of Royalty, than the ever-recurring rattle of the money-box". Meanwhile, there had appeared in 1871 a closely reasoned pamphlet "What Does She Do

With It?" declaring that the Queen had accumulated, by her savings on the Civil List, a very large private fortune.

**A Wave of Republicanism.**

That Republican sentiments were (perhaps under the influence of events in France) developing in this country was undeniable. The foremost spokesman of the small knot—it was very far short of a party—of republicans was Sir Charles Dilke, an extreme Radical, but with a first-hand knowledge of the Empire rare among the politicians of that day. In November, 1871, Dilke made at Newcastle a speech so definitely republican in tone as to cause serious perturbation to Mr. Gladstone, and to evoke from Dilke's friend, Mr. Joseph Chamberlain, a prediction which he did more than most men, by his colonial policy, to falsify: "The Republic must come, and at the rate at which we are moving it will come in our generation." On the other hand, a Republican demonstration organized in Hyde Park, earlier in the year, to express sympathy with the Paris Commune was a complete fiasco. Instead of the 100,000 expected by the promoters, only a handful—500–600 people—"of the lowest order" were present.[1] Nevertheless, early in 1872 Dilke moved for an inquiry into the Civil List. Gladstone seized the occasion to pass a warm eulogy upon the conduct of the Queen, and resisted the motion, which was supported only by Dilke, Auberon Herbert, Sir Wilfrid Lawson and Mr. George Anderson against a contemptuous and angry majority of 276.

**Illness and Recovery of the Prince of Wales.**

Dilke's motion could hardly have been more ill-timed. In the previous November the Prince of Wales had been struck down by a dangerous attack of typhoid fever. The progress of his illness, which at one time seemed likely to be fatal, was followed by the whole nation with profound sympathy and consternation. Joy was correspondingly great when the Prince's recovery was assured, and in February, 1872, the Queen with the Prince and Princess attended a Thanksgiving Service at St. Paul's. The boundless loyalty to the Throne then manifested, extinguished the last embers of Republicanism in England. Dilke and his handful of

[1] The Home Secretary to the Queen, *Q. V. L.*, Series II, II, p. 130.

associates became the objects even more of ridicule than of execration.[1]

Much criticism has lately been directed against Queen Victoria for her ingratitude towards Mr. Gladstone as a man and her "unconstitutional" treatment of him as a minister.[2] It has, moreover, been suggested that her deepening hostility to Gladstone and his policy was due in large measure to her rapidly maturing friendship with Disraeli. The facts are not in dispute, but the imputations are unfair and the deductions are inaccurate. Gladstone's policy was increasingly distasteful to the Queen, and from 1869 onwards there was a steady deterioration in the relations between the Crown and the minister. Nevertheless, on two crucial occasions the Queen rescued the minister from an embarrassing position, and by her experience and tact averted a constitutional crisis.

**The Queen and Mr. Gladstone.**

The first was in connexion with the Church of Ireland, which Gladstone, in 1869, proposed to disestablish and partially disendow. The Bill had passed the newly elected House of Commons by large majorities, but strong opposition to it was threatened in the House of Lords. The Queen's ecclesiastical creed was Erastian: she had a high sense of her position as "Head" of the Established Church, and heartily disliked a Bill which impinged upon it. Nevertheless, she accepted the verdict of the country, and persuaded Archbishop Tait—her own nominee to the see of Canterbury—to confer with Mr. Gladstone and facilitate the passage of the Bill through the House of Lords. Her intervention secured for the Bill a second reading, but the Lords insisted on committee amendments which Gladstone refused to concede. A deadlock seemed inevitable, and was resolved only by the patience and tact of the Queen. Gladstone was

**The Irish Church.**

[1] I vividly remember being taken as a child to a pantomime in Manchester and hearing in a topical song the refrain:

> Let republican Dilke
> Drink Salford skimmed milk—
> If ever I cease to love!

[2] In particular cf. H. (Viscount) Gladstone: *After Thirty Years* (1928); F. Hardie: *The Political Influence of Queen Victoria* (1861–1901) (1935).

unfeignedly grateful, and " strove in vain " to express to her " his relief, thankfulness and satisfaction ", not least for the undoubted signal blessing of an escape from a " formidable constitutional conflict ".

**Reform Bills of 1884 and 1885.**

A not less formidable conflict was threatened in the autumn of 1884. By this time the Queen was hardly on speaking terms with Mr. Gladstone, now for the second time Prime Minister. But she was not less the jealous guardian of the Constitution than she had been fifteen years earlier. A Bill for the enfranchisement of the agricultural labourers had passed the Commons, but the Lords not unreasonably demanded to be acquainted with the proposals for the redistribution of seats before they admitted 2,000,000 additional voters to the franchise. They accordingly passed (8th July) an amendment demanding " an entire scheme ".

Mr. Gladstone was obstinate; his supporters carried on, throughout the autumn, a noisy, if somewhat artificial agitation directed against the Peers, and when in October Parliament reassembled, the hope of a compromise seemed remote. But the Queen had never relaxed her efforts towards that end. She exerted all her influence alike on Mr. Gladstone and on Lord Salisbury, with the happy result that a compromise was reached, and the lines of the Redistribution Bill were agreed between the Government and the Opposition before the Franchise Bill became law.

Once again Mr. Gladstone was fain to tender his grateful thanks to the Queen for " the wise, gracious and steady influence which has so powerfully contributed to bring about this accommodation and to avert a serious crisis of affairs ".[1]

**Army Reform.**

To revert to Mr. Gladstone's first ministry. There were other matters besides the Church in Ireland on which the Queen and her minister were at variance. She was the " Head " of the army as well as of the Church, and cordially disliked Cardwell's " reforms "—in particular the abolition of the purchase of commissions. Nevertheless, she persuaded

[1] For further details of the two crises cf. Marriott: *Queen Victoria and Her Ministers*, p. 150.

her cousin, the Duke of Cambridge, not to obstruct them.[1] Moreover, she began to suspect Mr. Gladstone of indifference to the prestige of England among the Powers. She did not accept as tamely as her ministers the rebuff to British diplomacy involved in Russia's repudiation (1871) of the Black Sea clauses of the Treaty of Paris (1856),[2] and rated less highly than did Mr. Gladstone the moral significance of the Alabama arbitration. As usual, the Queen's sentiments were in unison with her people's, and when in 1874 the electorate preferred Disraeli to Gladstone the Queen gladly endorsed their preference.

**Disraeli's Ministry (1874–80).**

Long and bitter as had been the Queen's resentment against Disraeli for his attacks on Peel, she came to repose in him a confidence enjoyed by none of her ministers since Peel had (in 1846) resigned. That Disraeli flattered the Queen in terms too extravagantly Oriental for the taste of Englishmen is true; but his admiration for her character and judgment was sincere. Moreover, Disraeli was strong where Gladstone (as the Queen thought) had been weak. Alien though he was, he had an unbounded belief in the greatness of England and employed all his arts to restore and heighten her prestige. The brilliant coup by which Disraeli acquired a large measure of control over the Suez Canal (1875), as well as her proclamation as Empress of India (1876), gave the Queen unfeigned delight, and enhanced the esteem in which she held her minister. She was greatly pleased also by his firm resistance to Russian advance in the Balkans, by his unshrinking preparation for war, and the skill with which he averted its outbreak. She approved his support of Lord Lytton's "forward" policy on the North-West Frontier, and was plunged in despair when the country repudiated the policy of her favourite minister and compelled her to recall Mr. Gladstone to office (1880).

She did her utmost to avoid that cruel necessity. Mr. Gladstone had formally retired from the leadership of the Liberal Party in 1875. Consequently the Queen sent for

[1] On the details see Marriott: *England Since Waterloo*, pp. 428–31.

[2] Cf. Marriott: *The Eastern Question* (3rd Ed., 1924), p. 278; and Marriott: *England Since Waterloo* (10th Ed.), p. 426.

Lord Hartington, and on his refusal to form a government, for Lord Granville. In so doing she acted with perfect constitutional propriety. Lord Hartington led the Opposition in the House of Commons; Lord Granville led it in the Lords and was, moreover, Mr. Gladstone's successor in the leadership of the party. Both statesmen were, however, well aware that the result of the general election was in effect a plebiscite in favour of Gladstone, and each told the Queen that she had no alternative but to accept it.

**The Crown: Choice of Ministers.**

The Queen accepted it, but with an ill grace, and she has, in consequence, been severely criticized by the adulators of Mr. Gladstone. But it is undeniable that one of the few personal prerogatives left to the Sovereign is to select the Prime Minister. The field of choice is, evidently, very limited. Under some circumstances there is, indeed, no choice. Under others a real discretion remains to the Sovereign. In 1885, and again in 1886, Queen Victoria exercised it in favour of Lord Salisbury; in 1894 in favour of Lord Rosebery. In 1895 the Queen might have preferred the Duke of Devonshire to Lord Salisbury, and the latter might have been able to persuade his party to accept a nomination in accord with his own wishes.[1] In 1905 King Edward's appointment of Sir H. Campbell-Bannerman accorded with his own preference, but, had it been otherwise, a Liberal Cabinet might possibly have been formed under another Premier; or in the alternative Mr. Balfour might have been compelled to go to the country again as Prime Minister. What effect either course might have had on the results of the ensuing election it is impossible to surmise. In 1923 King George V might well have appointed Lord Curzon in succession to Mr. Bonar Law, and in 1924 might have sent for Mr. Asquith instead of Mr. Macdonald, or have insisted that Mr. Baldwin—or some other Conservative statesman—should attempt to form a Coalition. In 1937 the choice of Mr. Chamberlain to succeed Mr. Baldwin was cordially endorsed by Parliament, but the assumption,

[1] The main obstacle was the Duke himself. He had refused office in 1886 and 1887, but in 1895 accepted the Lord Presidency of the Council.

widely circulated, that there was no alternative was not perhaps warranted by the facts and was certainly disrespectful to the Crown. It is not within the rights or duties of an outgoing minister to proffer advice as to his successor, and the Queen sharply rebuked Lord Derby for even suggesting consultation on the matter.

Accounts as to what happened on the resignation of Mr. Asquith in December, 1916, are conflicting, and in the absence of authoritative information it is profitless to discuss whether King George V could have found, had he wished to, an alternative to Mr. Lloyd George.[1] But though the foregoing analysis is not exhaustive even for the period covered (1880–1937), it should suffice to establish the initial proposition that in the appointment of the Prime Minister the Sovereign has some voice, though the range of choice is never wide, and sometimes is non-existent.

There is, for obvious reasons, greater ambiguity as to the amount of influence which the Sovereign can exercise over appointments other than that of the Prime Minister. Over ecclesiastical patronage Queen Victoria kept a very tight hand, and she did not regard her headship of the army as a sinecure. Over the allocation of political offices she exercised considerable influence and insisted successfully both on inclusions and exclusions. She was especially careful about the appointment of the Foreign Secretary. In earlier days she preferred, on inadequate grounds, Lord Granville to Lord Clarendon, but by 1886 she had come to regard the former as weak and, greatly to Gladstone's distress, insisted that he should give place to Lord Rosebery. But for her personal regard for him Viscount (Sir R. A.) Cross might not have been included in the Cabinet of 1895; she certainly postponed the promotion of Dilke, and was reluctant to admit Chamberlain to the Cabinet in 1880, though she subsequently found him "very gentlemanly" and was much fascinated by his American wife. Labouchere she would

[1] Mr. Churchill (*Great Contemporaries*, pp. 149–50) holds that "the fullest and most authoritative account" is that given by Lord Beaverbrook: *Politicians and the War*, Vol. II, especially Chaps. XI–XXVI. On the whole I am inclined to agree.

never admit to any office under the Crown—naturally and wisely. Queen Victoria, being very human, had her prejudices, and sometimes allowed them to deflect her judgment, but surveying the reign as a whole it is impossible to doubt that, as a judge of character and perhaps of capacity, she was more shrewd than any of her ministers; she saved Disraeli from a blunder in regard to the Primacy, and wisely vetoed Lord Salisbury's nomination of Canon Liddon for the see of Oxford. She was deeply offended by the courageous candour of Dr. Randall Davidson in regard to *More Leaves from the Highlands*, but nevertheless she gave him her confidence in ever-increasing measure and insisted on his rapid promotion. Such magnanimity is rare among princes, and not common among lesser mortals.

To resume the sequence of events. The Queen's reluctance to accept Mr. Gladstone in 1880 was justified by the unfortunate history of his second administration. Ireland, South Africa, India, Egypt, the Sudan—it is a terrible catalogue of blunders and disasters. The Queen's ever-deepening mistrust of Mr. Gladstone was not due entirely, as filial piety and political partiality have suggested, to the malign influence of Lord Beaconsfield, who died in 1881, but to the Queen's conviction, rightly or wrongly held, that the honour and even the safety of England was imperilled by his pre-eminence. Gordon's death she attributed to Gladstone's procrastination, and neither she nor the country ever really forgave it.

**Home Rule.**

Then came, after the ambiguous election of 1885, Gladstone's "conversion" to Home Rule. Not even his unique powers of oratory could persuade the country to follow his lead in 1886, and the result was to put the Unionist Party into power and with one short interlude to keep them in power for the next twenty years. By a series of bold measures, the Unionists transferred the soil of Ireland from great proprietors to cultivating owners; they administered the law with firmness and impartiality, and after twenty years of "resolute government" handed Ireland over to their successors in a more peaceful and prosperous condition than it had known for centuries.[1] Meanwhile, Mr. Gladstone had become, to the Queen's chagrin, for the fourth time Prime Minister (1892), and had, with marvellous energy and endurance—he was then 84, very deaf and nearly blind—carried his second Home Rule Bill through the House of Commons. The election of 1895 proved, however, that the House of Lords, in rejecting the Bill, was more truly representative of the country than the small and precarious majority by which Gladstone had carried it in the Commons.

Gladstone resigned in 1894 and the Queen parted with him with cold courtesy. The old man was deeply pained, but was magnanimous enough to admit that in all this he found a "great sincerity". John Bright had long ago found the Queen the most absolutely honest person he ever met.

**Closing Years of the Reign.**

Meanwhile, the Victorian monarchy had entered upon an entirely new phase. The last fifteen years of the reign witnessed a remarkable revival, if not the birth, of the Imperial sentiment. The Imperial note was first clearly sounded at the celebration of the Queen's Jubilee in 1887, and still more loudly at the Diamond Jubilee of 1897. But British Imperialism was part of a larger movement. The era of *Welt-Politik* had arrived. The characteristics of that new era and the relations between the Monarchy and the Empire will demand more detailed examination in a later chapter.

Sixty years a Queen! The reign should have closed in 1897. The South African War broke out in 1899. Before it ended Queen Victoria was dead. The remnant of the reign was thus in one sense an anti-climax. Yet never had the Queen been in closer touch with her people than in the dark days of the war.[2] For the first time she made a real effort to win the love of her Irish subjects. She won it. But the effort cost the Queen her life. On 22nd January, 1901, ended the longest, perhaps the greatest reign in English History.

[1] This was not only admitted at the time by Mr. Bryce and Mr. Birrell, successively Chief Secretaries, but has been reaffirmed a generation later (1937) by Mr. Winston Churchill (*Great Contemporaries*, p. 254).

[2] Cf. a remarkable letter from Lord Rosebery to the Queen, *Q. V. L.*, Series III, Vol. III, p. 513.

## CHAPTER XXIV

# Monarchy and Democracy
# King Edward VII. The Advent of Labour

QUEEN VICTORIA was wont to insist that, though she remained to the end faithful to the Liberal traditions in which she was reared, she was not a Radical, still less a Democrat. Rather than be the "Queen of a democratic monarchy", she was resolved to abdicate.[1] Her resolution was never put to the test. Democracy did not come in her time. For the first half of her reign the Queen was served by ministers drawn, for the most part, from the Whig aristocracy, to whom the Hanoverian Sovereigns had long been accustomed. Not until 1868 did the new middle-class electorate created in 1832 begin to control the Executive Government. Thus a full generation elapsed before the results of the first Reform Act were completely manifested. It was about as long before the wage-earners enfranchised in 1867 and 1884 exercised an appreciable influence upon policy.

**The Advent of Democracy.**

If a specific date can be assigned to the advent of Democracy, it must be that of the general election of 1906. The Conservative Party, which had been in power for twenty years, was shattered; but though the Radicals numbered 377 in the new Parliament, the portent of the election was the return of no fewer than fifty-three "working men". Of these twenty-nine were nominees of the lately formed Labour Representation Committee and were pledged to act in Parliament as an independent party. The remaining twenty-four were returned as "Liberal-Labour" members

[1] *Q. V. L.*, 2nd Series, III, 166.

and accepted the Liberal Whip. A Socialist, in the person of Mr. John Burns, was for the first time admitted, as President of the Local Government Board, to the Cabinet. Within less than twenty years the Socialist Party was called upon to take office, though neither in 1924 nor at any subsequent time did it enjoy an absolute majority in the House of Commons.[1]

**Social Legislation.**

The presence in Parliament of more than fifty wage-earners inevitably gave a new character to legislation. Act after Act was passed which, if not actually socialistic, was undeniably designed to increase the comfort, and strengthen the security, of the poorer classes, at the expense of the more wealthy. Hitherto " social reform ", though not the monopoly of either party, had been mainly promoted by Conservatives, who were less devout worshippers than the Liberals at the shrine of Bentham. For half a century the Manchester School, with its strict adherence to the doctrine of *laissez-faire*, had been dominant in English politics. The only serious inroad upon the integrity of that doctrine was represented by the long series of Factory Acts. That humanitarian legislation was the work not of the Liberals, who so long monopolized office, but of Tory " Socialists "—of the type of Lord Shaftesbury, Michael Thomas Sadler, and Benjamin Disraeli.

Disraeli clearly apprehended the truth that his " leap in the dark " in 1867 portended something more than the advent of political democracy. Consequently, social reform occupied a prominent place in the programme which he put before the new electorate in the election of 1874. " Sanitas Sanitatum Omnia Sanitas " was the text of his election speeches. Opponents might deride his policy as one of " sewage and shoddy ", but the legislation of the Disraeli Parliament (1874–80) was inspired by the faith of the new Toryism. Such Acts as the *Settled Estates Act* (1875), the *Agricultural Holdings Act* (1875), the *Enclosure of Commons Act* (1875), and the *Contagious Diseases* (*Animals*) *Act* (1875) gave proof of its solicitude for the rural community; the

[1] Written in 1937.

*Artisans' Dwellings Act* (1875) and the *Factory and Workshops Act* (1878) were designed to increase the comfort and safety of the urban artisans; while the legislation of 1875–6 came to be regarded as the Magna Carta of Trade Unionism. Lord Salisbury's second ministry (1886–92) carried on the Disraelean tradition, though between 1892 and 1906 the work was interrupted by other preoccupations. But the great Liberal victory of 1906, the appointment of Mr. Lloyd George to the key-post of Chancellor of the Exchequer (1908), and, not least, the large representation of manual labour in Parliament noticeably quickened the pace of social legislation. The result may be measured by the rapid growth of public expenditure on what have come to be known as Social Services. In that category are now included Old Age, Widows and Orphans Pensions (non-contributory and contributory), War Pensions, National Health and Unemployment Insurance, Poor Relief (now designated as Public Assistance), Education, Housing and Slum Clearance, and a large number of miscellaneous benefits provided for women, children, blind persons and others. The total expenditure on such services has risen from about £36,000,000 in 1900 to £488,000,000 in 1934–5. Towards this total taxes and local rates contributed over £340,000,000, and the rest was made up from the contributions of employers and employees and some other miscellaneous sources. Expenditure on this scale evidently imposes a very heavy burden upon productive industry, upon which the whole of it must ultimately fall. So long as industry is expanding the burden can be borne; should it begin to contract, the burden may easily become intolerable.

**Edward VII.**

To resume the story of events. From 1906 onwards the Government of England may be accurately described as a Democratic Monarchy. But English Democracy has always been "parliamentary"; the English Monarchy continued to be "constitutional"; the Crown, itself a constituent element of Parliament, is advised by ministers selected from the parliamentary majority, though not elected directly by the constituencies. In fine, English Democracy is indirect.

The four Kings who since the death of Queen Victoria have occupied the throne have all been personally well equipped for the rôle they have been called upon to play. In his first speech to the Council, King Edward VII made an emphatic declaration on the position of the Monarchy. " I am fully determined," he said, " to be a constitutional Sovereign in the strictest sense of the word, and, as long as there is breath in my body, to work for the good and amelioration of my people."

To the pledge thus solemnly given the King was entirely faithful. King Edward owed little to his apprenticeship. From all participation in high politics his mother's mistrust or jealousy had rigidly excluded him.[1] But he was blessed with native shrewdness and tact; if he read little, he had a marvellous capacity for picking brains; he had seen more of the overseas Empire than any of his predecessors, and by frequent sojourns on the Continent he had made the personal acquaintance of nearly all the rulers and most of the leading statesmen in Europe. He had thus obtained a profound and first-hand knowledge of the main lines and even the by-paths of European diplomacy. Nor had he neglected such opportunities as fell to him of acquainting himself with the problems affecting the lives of the working classes at home. He took a warm personal interest in the work of the voluntary hospitals, and as a member of the Royal Commission on the Housing of the Poor had acquired an intimate knowledge of one of the most difficult problems arising from the recent and rapid urbanization of Great Britain. On that Commission the Prince had mingled freely with his colleagues, including two " Labour " representatives, Henry Broadhurst, an Oxfordshire stone-mason, and Joseph Arch, the champion of the agricultural labourers. With equal assiduity had the Prince devoted himself to the work of the Old Age Pensions Commission, though he tactfully with-

[1] On the relations of the Queen and the Prince cf. Bolitho: *Victoria: The Widow and Her Son* (1934).

drew from it when the question seemed likely to become a party one.

Edward as Pacificator.

Conscientiously as King Edward worked on such questions, his primary interest, like his mother's, was in foreign affairs. The nature and extent of the King's actual influence upon English foreign policy is, however, still a matter of controversy. Mr. (afterwards the Earl of) Balfour, writing in 1915 to Lord Lansdowne about the origins of the Anglo-French *Entente*, described the idea that King Edward was responsible for it as a foolish piece of gossip, and denied that the King ever " made an important suggestion of any sort on large questions of policy ". But Balfour's relations with King Edward were not cordial. Balfour habitually underrated the King's intelligence, and thought him tiresomely insistent on matters which to the minister seemed unimportant. On the other hand, the King had reason to complain that the Premier treated him " with scant courtesy ", and there is no doubt that Balfour was less careful of the royal prerogative than might have been expected from a Conservative Premier. As to King Edward's influence on foreign policy, Sir Edward Grey confirms Balfour. " The King," he wrote, " not only accepted the constitutional practice that policy must be that of his ministers, but he preferred that it should be so. He read all the important papers, and now and then a dispatch would come back with some short marginal comment approving of something contained in it; but comment of any sort was rare, and I do not remember criticism or suggestion." Such testimony is clearly irrefutable, as far as it goes. But while it proves that the King's practice was wholly " constitutional ", it does not prove that his influence on European politics was negligible. M. Maurois, regarding the matter from a more detached standpoint, puts it in perfect perspective: " He [Edward VII] left marks [on European politics] which were none the less real for being quite human and quite simple. He liked to be a welcome guest wherever he went, and to be on good terms with every one. He was cosmopolitan, devoid of racial prejudice, concerned for his popularity abroad as at home, always anxious to compose international quarrels. . . . A Sovereign, a great statesman, men who are momentary incarnations of a whole people can wield powers of swift healing, if they are living, natural, good-humoured men, able to impress foreign opinion by small symbolic touches. That was what happened in France in 1903 . . . it all seemed as if a general neurasthenia had been suddenly cured, and the Foreign Office recognized that this was due to the King, personally and alone." [1] The Anglo-French *Entente* was primarily the work of three men—Lord Lansdowne, M. Cambon and Lord Cromer—but Lord Lansdowne himself referred to the "powerful impulse" given to the good work by King Edward, and M. Poincaré, when paying an official visit, as President, to London, used with Gallic precision the same word: "Il n'est pas un de mes compatriotes qui ait oublié l'heureuse impulsion donnée en cette occasion [1903] décisive par sa majesté le roi Edouard VII à l'œuvre de concorde, qui lui a survécu." Impulsion is the exact word. Nor is there any doubt that King Edward was equally ready and anxious to play the part of peacemaker at Berlin, had the personality of his capricious nephew permitted it.

**The King and the Constitution.**

Not that King Edward's interests were limited to foreign affairs. He definitely refused to be *un roi fainéant*. Not only did he make it a rule to open Parliament in person, but insisted that the terms of the King's Speech should be submitted to him in ample time to allow of consideration and comment. He also required to be promptly and precisely informed on all matters under consideration by his ministers. He allowed the Prime Minister to delegate to the Home Secretary the duty of writing to the King a daily précis of the proceedings in Parliament, but he rebuked Mr. Balfour for undue brevity in reporting on the proceedings in the Cabinet, and requested that "as of old the length should run to four sides of a quarto sheet". His personal relations with Sir Henry Campbell-Bannerman were invariably cordial, but even to him he had frequently to complain

[1] *King Edward and His Times*, pp. 286–7.

of the meagreness of the information with which he was supplied. When, for instance, a Cabinet Committee was appointed (1907) to consider the question of the House of Lords, the King insisted that he should " be kept *au courant* with what goes on at the Committee, and further that he should be consulted before any recommendations are approved of by the Cabinet ".[1]

In a careful memorandum [2] dated 28th August, 1905, Lord Esher, who was the approved unofficial adviser of King Edward, contrasted the present procedure of ministers with that of their predecessors under Queen Victoria. Such casual conduct towards the Sovereign would " have been impossible even under ministers as headstrong as Palmerston, or as truculent as Lord John Russell ". Two things in particular astonished Lord Esher: the remissness of the present ministers in failing to keep the King informed and seeking his authority *before* action was taken; and their gross carelessness about the sanctity of the Privy Councillor's oath. From his close study of Queen Victoria's letters and other documents in the royal archives, Lord Esher reached the conclusion that the monarchical system as worked by Queen Victoria and her ministers was " of immense value to the State and to the people of this country ". That system he was naturally anxious should remain intact. An illustration is afforded by the circumstances attending the change of Government in December, 1905. Mr. Balfour's position had been rendered embarrassing by the emergence of the Tariff Reform controversy; the Parliament elected in 1900 was due to expire in 1906, but in December, 1905, Mr. Balfour decided not to dissolve but to resign. The King disapproved of a decision which was dictated by party tactics. Mr. Balfour, however, persisted, and the King sent, not without relief, for Sir Henry Campbell-Bannerman, acting, as was proper, entirely on his own initiative and responsibility.[3]

On this, as on other points of constitutional etiquette, King Edward was exceedingly punctilious, and in the

[1] Lee, II, p. 466. [2] Esher: *Journals*, II, 120 and 56. [3] Esher: *Journals*, II, p. 103.

discharge of the routine duties of his office he was far more industrious than is commonly supposed. He had his own views, too, on questions of patronage, ecclesiastical and civil. He refused to allow Lord Salisbury to appoint Dr. Edgar Jacob to the see of London, and Mr. Balfour to nominate an American citizen to the Regius Professorship of History at Cambridge. He was most anxious to see Lord Esher Secretary of State for War, and his wishes were frustrated only by Lord Esher's own refusal. That his intervention in such matters was invariably to the advantage of State or Church it were rash to affirm; but his knowledge of men was amazingly wide and his judgment was shrewd. Nor had he any personal or party interests to serve. On balance, therefore, his intervention was probably advantageous.

**The House of Lords Question.**

Whether his shrewdness and wisdom would have availed to solve the two most difficult problems of those pre-War years it is impossible to surmise. The Irish Question and the problem of the relations between Lords and Commons were part of the legacy bequeathed by him to his son.

On the question of the House of Lords trouble had been threatening ever since the Lords rejected Gladstone's second Home Rule Bill in 1893. In his last speech in Parliament the old statesman warned his party that the differences between the House of Lords and the House of Commons had created "a state of things of which we are compelled to say that in our judgment it cannot continue. . . . The issue which is raised . . . is a controversy which when once raised must go forward to an issue." Had he not been thwarted by his colleagues, the old man would have gone to the country on that issue at once. Many of his more ardent disciples regarded his farewell speech as a testament bequeathed to the Liberal Party which it was their pious duty to execute.

The opportunity did not come until the Liberal triumph in 1906. The issue was then forced by the Peers. Between 1906 and 1909 Bill after Bill was passed by immense majorities through the House of Commons, only to be rejected or emasculated by the Lords. Little wonder that the Liberals were exasperated beyond endurance. " It is plainly intolerable that a Second Chamber should, while one party in the State is in power, be its willing servant, and when that party has received unmistakable and emphatic condemnation by the country, be able to neutralize and thwart and distort the policy which the electors have shown they approve." So said Campbell-Bannerman in 1906. Mr. Lloyd George, who in 1908 insisted, to Mr. Asquith's embarrassment, on becoming his principal lieutenant, put the same point more picturesquely: " The House of Lords," he said, " is Mr. Balfour's poodle. It barks for him; it fetches and carries for him; it bites anyone that he sets it on to."

Mr. Lloyd George not only derided the Peers, but cunningly set a trap for them. He devised a budget in 1909 which, with all its parade, proved hopelessly unproductive of revenue, but was none the less alarming to the landed interest. Would the Lords permit it to pass into law? That the Lords would be within their legal rights in rejecting it was unquestionable; but the House of Commons had long since acquired an exclusive control over finance, and it was gravely doubted whether the Lords would be politically wise in exercising an almost obsolete legal right.

**Edward VII and the Peers.**

That doubt King Edward shared. He strongly disliked the budget and had, before its introduction, acutely criticized the proposals of the Government. Nevertheless, he held that for the Lords to reject it would be a tactical error, and he did his utmost to avert the crisis which he foresaw.[1] With Mr. Asquith's approval, and following the precedents set by Queen Victoria, the King consulted the Opposition leaders, Lord Lansdowne and Mr. Balfour, but to his great annoyance and chagrin he failed to persuade them to let the budget pass the Lords. On 30th November, 1909, the Lords rejected the Finance Bill by 350 votes to 75. Mr. Lloyd George was exultant: " We have got them at last." The House of Commons declared the action of the Lords

[1] Esher: *Journals*, II, p. 411.

to be " a breach of the Constitution and a usurpation of the rights of the Commons ". Parliament was immediately dissolved, and the Government asked the electorate to give them a mandate to curb the " veto " of the Lords.

The election was held in January, 1910, but the response of the constituencies was ambiguous. The Liberals, though they lost heavily, returned to Westminster 274 strong; the Conservatives numbered 273; the Labour representation was reduced to 41; the Irish Nationalists, with 82 votes, held the balance. Nor were the Irish members slow to take advantage of their commanding position. They disliked the budget, and let the Government know that they would help to carry it only on the strength of an explicit assurance that the Lords should be deprived of the power to veto a Home Rule Bill. So alarmed were some of the ministers by the " exorbitant demands " (the words are Asquith's) of the Nationalists, that they would have sought safety in immediate resignation. But alike against the cowardice of those colleagues and against the threats of the Irishmen Asquith stood firm. The Irish members, thereupon, gave way, voted for the budget, and were eventually rewarded by receiving their pound of flesh in the shape of the Parliament Act.

**The Cabinet and the Crown.**

So much for the Irish Nationalists. As to the negotiations between the ministers and the Sovereign there is some controversy. Had the Government, before the dissolution, obtained or sought for a " guarantee " from the King that he would, if necessary, coerce the House of Lords by the creation of Peers? On 1st December, 1909, Lord Esher, who was in close touch with members of the Cabinet, wrote to his son: " The Government propose to ask the King for authority to use his prerogative to create Peers in the event of their obtaining a majority at the election. But they want him to give his pledge *now*." To Lord Knollys, the King's private secretary, he deemed it his duty to write, on the same date, even more explicitly. " I saw Haldane yesterday, and he told me the following very grave facts. The Cabinet are discussing whether, instead of attempting to alter by Statute the relations between the two Houses of Parliament, they shall advise the King to place permanently in the hands of the Prime Minister of the day H. M.'s prerogative to create Peers. The only alternative, according to their views, is a Bill which they would introduce, coupled with a statement that the ministers had obtained from the Sovereign a promise to create a sufficient number of Peers to pass the measure." Lord Esher expressed the view that either alternative would be an outrage, and could not believe that responsible ministers would make such a request. If, however, they did, and, on the King's refusal, resigned before a dissolution, the King would be " supported by this country and all over the Empire ".[1]

Lord Esher's revelations seem somewhat at variance with Asquith's statement to the House (21st February) that he had not " received " or " asked for " any " guarantee ". That statement must be accepted; but mystery deepens. About the budget there was no further difficulty. By the end of April the Finance Bill had become law.

**The Parliament Bill.**

A month earlier Asquith had proposed the resolutions on which the Parliament Bill was subsequently based; they were carried, against the passionate and determined opposition of the Conservatives, on 14th April, and on the same night Asquith introduced his Bill. Money Bills, carefully defined, and certified as such by the Speaker, were not to be amended or rejected by the House of Lords; ordinary Bills, having passed the Commons in three successive sessions, and been thrice rejected by the Lords, were to become law on the declaration of the Royal Assent; and the possible duration of Parliaments was reduced from seven years to five. Should the Lords reject the Parliament Bill, the Government, so Asquith in menacing terms announced, would either resign or advise a dissolution. But they would not advise a dissolution " except under such conditions as will secure that in the new Parliament the judgment of the people as expressed in the election will be carried into law ". The meaning of the threat was unmistakable. The

[1] *Journals*, II, pp. 423–4.

King was to give a hypothetical promise to coerce the Second Chamber.

In March, 1910, King Edward had gone to Biarritz for the sake of his health, which was more precarious than the public were permitted to know. He returned on 27th April to find himself confronted by a political situation demanding the exercise of all his skill and patience. Unfortunately, those great qualities were no longer at the service of the State. On 6th May, to the consternation and grief of his people, King Edward suddenly passed away.

**Death of Edward VII.**

The nation was stunned, and recovered from the stroke of fate only to realize the immensity of its loss. "At a most anxious moment in the fortunes of the State, we had lost without warning or preparation, the Sovereign, whose ripe experience, trained sagacity, equitable judgment and unvarying consideration counted for so much." Mr. Asquith's words expressed the sentiment of the whole nation. The loss was literally irreparable. Whether, had his life been spared, King Edward could have found a solution of the dilemma other than that embodied in the Parliament Bill it is vain to speculate. It is certain that he would have spared no effort to avert so momentous a change in the balance of the Constitution. With kingly pomp, "with an Empire's lamentation", "to the noise of the mourning of a mighty nation", King Edward was, on 20th May, borne to his grave.

**His Funeral.**

Little did the world guess that King Edward's funeral was to mark the passing of an era in history. In the great procession were no fewer than eight foreign Kings. The German Emperor was there, his heart momentarily but sincerely softened towards the uncle he hated, and genuinely sympathetic towards the cousin whom he could not but love. His Balkan ally Ferdinand of Bulgaria was there also, while the Hapsburg Empire was represented by the ill-fated Archduke Franz Ferdinand. With them were the Kings of the Belgians, of Denmark, Norway, and Greece, of Portugal and Spain. The funeral of King Edward was Europe's spectacular farewell to the monarchical order.

For his own subjects it was a more intimate occasion—an affectionate tribute to a great King and a lovable man. *Son métier était Roi.* He was pre-eminently a kingly King. Sir William Harcourt, who was no courtier, declared that Edward VII was the greatest King of England since William the Conqueror. Had he said since Henry VIII none would have gainsaid him. King Edward was intensely human. A red-hot Radical remarked after his first meeting with him: "That is the greatest man that ever I had speech of." Nor, as he came to know him better, did he ever change his opinion. "King Edward had," said Sir Edward Grey, "a rare, if not a unique, power of combining bonhomie and dignity." The monarchs who rode behind his coffin symbolized his position in the European polity; the mourning multitudes who thronged the streets of his capital, bore witness to his place in the hearts of his people.

## CHAPTER XXV

# The Constitution under King George V
# The Crown and the People

A GREAT Monarch was dead; the Monarchy lived. All eyes in Europe and in the Empire were turned on King George V. Mr. Asquith came away from his first audience with the new King " deeply moved by his modesty and good sense ". Modesty was, indeed, the key-note of King George's character; but if mistrustful of his own powers, he devoted them, with undeviating loyalty and ceaseless industry, to the service of his country.

**King George V.**

Though nearly forty-five, the new King's apprenticeship to the craft of Kingship had been, as compared with his father's, brief. He had, indeed, travelled widely in the Empire, but he was, relatively, little known to his subjects at home. Nor was the heritage to which he succeeded an easy one. The European atmosphere was heavily charged with explosive elements; at home there was profound unrest in the ranks of manual labour, civil war threatened in Ireland, and at Westminster there was the prospect of a conflict more bitter than any that had occurred since 1688 if not since 1640.

So grave, indeed, was the situation that the political leaders on both sides, sobered by the sudden death of King Edward, sought a peace by negotiation. " Then the nation," said Mr. Asquith, " witnessed an incident unparalleled in the annals of party warfare. The two combatant forces already in battle array, piled their arms, while the leaders on both sides retired for private conference."

**The Constitutional Conference.**

Mr. Asquith and Mr. Balfour, each supported by three leading colleagues, sat in private conference from 17th June until the following November. While the conference was in progress Mr. Lloyd George actually approached Mr. Balfour with a proposal for the formation of a coalition or "national" Government. The proposal came to nothing, but it was none the less indicative of the serious view of the situation, abroad and at home, taken by responsible statesmen. The conference itself reached a considerable measure of agreement, but not sufficient to avert its ultimate breakdown, which was communicated to the King by the Premier on 11th November.

**The King and the Crisis.**

The King was gravely perturbed; he refused to contemplate the coercion of the House of Lords until the Parliament Bill had been submitted to the Second Chamber, and the electorate had had the opportunity of pronouncing judgment upon it. Accordingly the Parliament Bill was introduced into the House of Lords, but the Peers refused to read it a second time until alternative proposals of their own for a drastic reconstruction of the Second Chamber had received consideration. As for a dissolution of Parliament, the Asquith Government refused to advise the King to dissolve unless the King would undertake, "in the event of the policy of the Government being approved by an adequate majority in the new House of Commons", to use his prerogative (if the need arose) to swamp the House of Lords.[1] That the King assented to the demands of his ministers with undisguised and "legitimate reluctance" was subsequently admitted by Lord Crewe, who with Mr. Asquith was alone present at the decisive interviews with the King.[2] Asquith, when challenged, simply said that the King "felt that he had no alternative but to assent to the advice of the Cabinet".[3]

Meanwhile, the general election of December, 1910, had resulted in "no change". Between Liberals and Unionists it was a tie (272 each), Labour won one seat

[1] For a full account of the events connected with the passing of the Parliament Act see Marriott: *Second Chambers* (revised ed., Oxford, 1927), Chap. XII; and Spender and Asquith: *Life of Asquith*, Chaps. XXII–XXVI.

[2] *House of Lords Debates*, 8th August, 1911, p. 836.

[3] House of Commons, 7th August, 1911.

(42), and the Irish Nationalists two. The Irish remained masters of the situation.

The Parliament Bill was reintroduced in February, passed its second reading in March by 368 to 243, and its third before the end of May. On 22nd May the Lords gave a second reading to Lord Lansdowne's admirable Bill for the reconstruction of the Second Chamber. But the sands had run out. The Liberals and their Irish allies were resolved to push through their own scheme. A large section of the Lords were prepared to die in the last ditch rather than accept it. But the "Hedgers" prevailed against the "Ditchers", and in August the Parliament Bill became law.

**The Parliament Act (1911).**

The Irish Nationalists thereupon demanded their pound of flesh, as did the English and Welsh Nonconformists. A Bill for the Disestablishment and Disendowment of the English Church in Wales was passed through the House of Commons and rejected in the Lords in the session of 1912–3. It then came under the operation of the Parliament Act, and, having been passed (without amendment) through the Commons and rejected by the Lords in the sessions of 1913 and 1914, it received the Royal Assent on 18th September, 1914. But the country was then at war, consequently the operation of the Act was, by agreement, suspended until the end of the War, and ultimately became law, together with a separate amending Bill, on 31st March, 1920.

**The Church in Wales.**

A Home Rule Bill for Ireland was introduced into the House of Commons in April, 1912. It passed through that House in three successive sessions, 1912, 1913 and 1914. In each session it was rejected by the Lords, but received the Royal Assent under the terms of the Parliament Act on 18th September.

**Irish Home Rule.**

Before the Royal Assent was given much had happened in England, in Ireland and in Europe. The governing fact of the situation was that the Ulster Protestants had in 1912 made a Solemn Covenant that under no circumstances would they recognize or submit to a Home Rule Parliament in Dublin. The Covenant was signed not only by loyal Ulstermen, but also by a large body of British

**The Ulster Covenant.**

Unionists. A Volunteer Force was raised in Ulster, and Mr. Bonar Law, who in 1910 had succeeded Mr. Balfour as the leader of the Unionist Party, made on its behalf a momentous declaration. "I can imagine," he said, "no length of resistance to which Ulster will go in which I shall not be ready to support her."

The country was, in July, 1914, nearer to civil war than at any time since 1642. The King, like all his loyal subjects throughout the Empire, was profoundly perturbed at the prospect. All through the year 1913 he had laboured assiduously for peace; he had summoned the Unionist leaders in the autumn to Balmoral and had attempted to effect a compromise between them and the Cabinet. The effort was vain.

The King's position was thus rendered exceedingly difficult. His Prime Minister reminded him of his personal irresponsibility and of the constitutional responsibility of his ministers.[1] But the circumstances were without precedent since the monarchy had become "constitutional". Direct appeals were made to the King to intervene, and by an exercise of the prerogative submit the issue to the electorate. Once again the question was raised of the King's constitutional right to force a dissolution upon reluctant ministers, or, in the alternative, to dismiss the ministers who resisted the exercise of that prerogative. Mr. Asquith, as in duty bound, pointed out the risk to which the throne might be exposed. But Mr. Balfour was at one with Lord Lansdowne and Mr. Bonar Law in holding that the King would be acting within his rights, and was supported in that view by lawyers so eminent as Sir William Anson and Mr. Dicey. Nor had Balfour the least misgivings as to the outcome of a conflict between the King and party politicians should such a conflict unhappily arise. "You forget," he said in conversation with Lord Esher, "the changed circumstances since 1832. During the latter half of Queen Victoria's reign and more than ever now, Great Britain means the

[1] Cf. two elaborate and important memoranda drawn up by Asquith in September, 1913.

British Empire. Our people oversea do not care a rush for Asquith or me. They hardly know our names. For them the symbol of the Empire is the King. Hands laid on the Sovereign would mean the disruption of the Empire." Mr. Balfour spoke the simple truth.[1]

**Ulster.**

The Ulster Protestants, under an intrepid leader Sir Edward Carson, were, meanwhile, preparing for the worst. Arms were imported in large quantities—and not only into Ulster. Southern Ireland was arming too. Would the Cabinet dare to use the Forces of the Crown to suppress rebellion in North or South? Could they rely upon the Services for that dirty work? The question had never been asked since 1642; but it was raised in an acute form when, in March, 1914, certain officers, stationed at the Curragh, from a misunderstanding of orders, preferred to be dismissed the Service rather than march against Ulster.

Strenuous efforts were made to avert an explosion. The Government brought in a Bill to allow any Ulster county to vote itself out of Home Rule for six years. It passed the House of Commons, but the Lords transformed it into a Bill to exclude the whole of Ulster without any time limit. In that form it went back to the Commons on 14th July—a fortnight after the murder of the Archduke Franz Ferdinand at Serajevo.

On 21st July, Asquith, urged thereto by the King, announced (in a letter to Mr. Balfour) that the King had consented, "should the necessity arise", to create Peers in sufficient numbers to ensure the passage of the Bill.[2]

**The King's Efforts for Peace.**

The King then made another effort to bridge the narrowing but still menacing gulf between parties. He summoned a conference of eight leaders—two ministers, two British Unionists, two Ulstermen, two Irish Nationalists—to Buckingham Palace. They met under the chairmanship of the Speaker on 21st July. The King opened the proceedings with a short but solemn address; but to no purpose. On

[1] Esher: *Journals*, II, 421. The conversation actually took place in November, 1909; but Mr. Balfour's words were at least as appropriate to the situation in 1914 as to that in 1909.

[2] Fitzroy: *Memoirs*, p. 460.

24th July the breakdown of negotiations was announced to Parliament. On that same day news of Austria's ultimatum to Serbia reached England. Asquith and Bonar Law agreed that "under conditions of gravity almost unparalleled" domestic controversies must be postponed. Nevertheless, as we have seen, the Royal Assent was given to the Home Rule Bill (18th September), though its operation, like that of the Welsh Church Bill, was suspended until the end of the War.

**Ireland and the War.**

On the outbreak of the War, Ulster flung itself into the struggle against the common enemy. Southern Ireland, exasperated by the German violation of Catholic Belgium, seemed, at first, disposed to do likewise; but Catholic Ireland was mishandled by the English War Office; the disloyal section gradually gained the ascendant, intrigued with Germany, and, relying upon the promised assistance of England's enemies, raised, in April, 1916, the standard of rebellion. The rebellion was suppressed, though not without considerable loss of life and much damage to property in Dublin, and after a delusive lull due to war-time prosperity, the National movement in Ireland passed under the control of out-and-out Republicans. They were perfectly candid: "Our nationalism is not founded on grievances. We are opposed not to English misgovernment, but to English government in Ireland." A Provisional Government was set up in Dublin (January, 1919), and during the next twelve months Southern Ireland was in the grip of terrorism.

**Irish Rebellion (1916).**

**Home Rule Act (1920).**

What was to be done with the Act of 1914, still on the Statute Book? The official end of the War would, if Parliament had taken no action, have brought it into operation in 1920. Accordingly, in that year the Act of 1914 was repealed and was replaced by the Act "for the Better Government of Ireland". A united Ireland was contemplated, but partition was for the moment accepted. There were to be single-chamber Parliaments at Belfast and Dublin, with Executives responsible thereto, and each Parliament was to contribute twenty members to an All-Ireland Council which, it was hoped, would develop into an All-Ireland Parliament. Ireland was to continue to be represented in the Imperial Parliament. Neither Northern nor Southern Ireland liked the Act, but six Ulster counties, however reluctantly, accepted it, and have worked it with success.

**The King and Ireland.**

Despite the condition of Southern Ireland, the King was resolved to make yet another effort to heal, by the royal touch, the sores of that unhappy land, and in June, 1921, accompanied by the Queen, he visited Belfast, and on the 22nd opened the Northern Parliament. No more touching speech was ever delivered by a Sovereign to his subjects. Giving expression to his whole-hearted love for Ireland, the King appealed to all Irishmen, of all creeds, " to stretch out the hand of forbearance and conciliation, to forgive and forget, and to join in making for the land which they love a new era of peace, contentment and good will ".

The omens were none too favourable. Southern Ireland had derisively rejected the Act of 1920, and instead of working it, had carried on an unceasing campaign of murder and outrage. Nearly 400 police were murdered, and English soldiers gave their lives in support of a Government unworthy of their devotion. Nevertheless, the rebellion would, at whatever cost, have been in time suppressed. But England was war weary. The King's touching appeal could not be disregarded; negotiations were opened for peace, and, though deadlock seemed more than once to have been reached, an agreement—ominously described as a Treaty—was at midnight on 6th December, 1921, concluded. Ireland was to remain in the Empire on the same footing as Canada, under the style of the Irish Free State; but six Ulster counties were to have the right to contract out of it. Within the prescribed month after the enactment of the Free State Constitution, Ulster exercised that right. Ulster still remains, therefore, in a curiously anomalous position, under the Act of 1920. But the definition of the frontier between Ulster and the Free State proved a difficult task which was not accomplished until 1925. Meanwhile, a Bill implementing the treaty was passed (March, 1922)

**The Irish Treaty (1922).**

by the Imperial Parliament, not without a strong though ineffective protest from a minority of Unionists. "Most of the majority were miserable and all the minority were furious." Such is Mr. Churchill's grim comment.[1] The forebodings of the minority have been justified.

For ten years Southern Ireland was under the leadership of Mr. Cosgrave, and it looked as though the treaty might have brought reconciliation. That hope, however, was dissipated by the success at the election of 1932 of Mr. de Valera, who embarked on a policy involving (as it seemed) the repudiation of the treaty and the ultimate establishment of a Republic in Ireland.

The growth of the Republican Party in the South only served to bind the Ulster counties more and more closely to Great Britain. Nor will Great Britain, under any circumstances that can be foreseen, consent to betray the loyalists of the North. Yet in both parts of partitioned Ireland there remains a feeling of uncertainty and unrest.

Nor is that feeling confined to Ireland. With the antecedents, the course, and the sequelæ of the World War this narrative cannot be concerned. Something must, however, be said of the reactions of the War upon the British Constitution. Among these the most important was the effect produced upon the relations between Great Britain and the Dominions. But a discussion of this topic must be deferred to the next chapter. Of other reactions, not the least important was that upon the position of the electorate, the legislature, and the executive—parliamentary and departmental.

**Adult Suffrage.**

The War gave a great impulse to the movement in favour of adult suffrage. After the War it was conceded in two stages. For half a century at least the advocates of woman suffrage had kept that question before the country. As far back as 1867 J. S. Mill moved an amendment for the inclusion of women in the Reform Bill of that year. It was rejected; but from that time onwards Bills were periodically introduced into Parliament to effect the same object. Not,

[1] *World Crisis Aftermath*, p. 320.

however, until after 1905 did the question of woman suffrage become a live political issue. Between 1905 and 1914 a persistent and at times violent agitation was carried on in the country, but the tactics of the militant suffragettes undoubtedly tended to alienate public opinion and to delay the triumph of the cause they had at heart.

The War gave to women an opportunity which they splendidly redeemed. In the face of their self-sacrificing and patriotic services, there could no longer be any question about their admission to the franchise. By the Reform Act of 1918 adult suffrage was adopted for males, and the franchise was extended to all women (not legally incapacitated) of thirty years of age, who were entitled to be registered as local government electors in respect of the occupation of land or premises, and to the wives of men so entitled. The first register compiled under the Act contained no fewer than 8,856,493 women as against nearly 13,000,000 men. A later Act of the same year made women eligible for election to Parliament, and in 1919 Viscountess Astor was elected as member for Plymouth, and in 1921 Mrs. Wintringham for Louth—in both cases in the place of their respective husbands.

In 1928 the Equal Franchise Act completed the process begun in 1832. It placed women in exactly the same position as men as regards both parliamentary and local government elections. As a result, the electorate was at once brought up to the vast total of 28,850,776. Of these no fewer than 15,195,199 were women, but the number of women returned to Parliament has as yet been comparatively small.[1]

The Post-War Parliament.

In the composition and aspect of both Houses of Parliament there has been since the War a marked change. The House of Lords has increased in membership from 622 (in 1910) to 770 (in 1937). The new Peers include not only soldiers, sailors and others who were properly rewarded for War services, but a large number of ex-ministers, a still larger number of eminent financiers, industrialists, newspaper proprietors, and a small number of Labour politicians.

[1] Written in 1937, when there were nine women in the House.

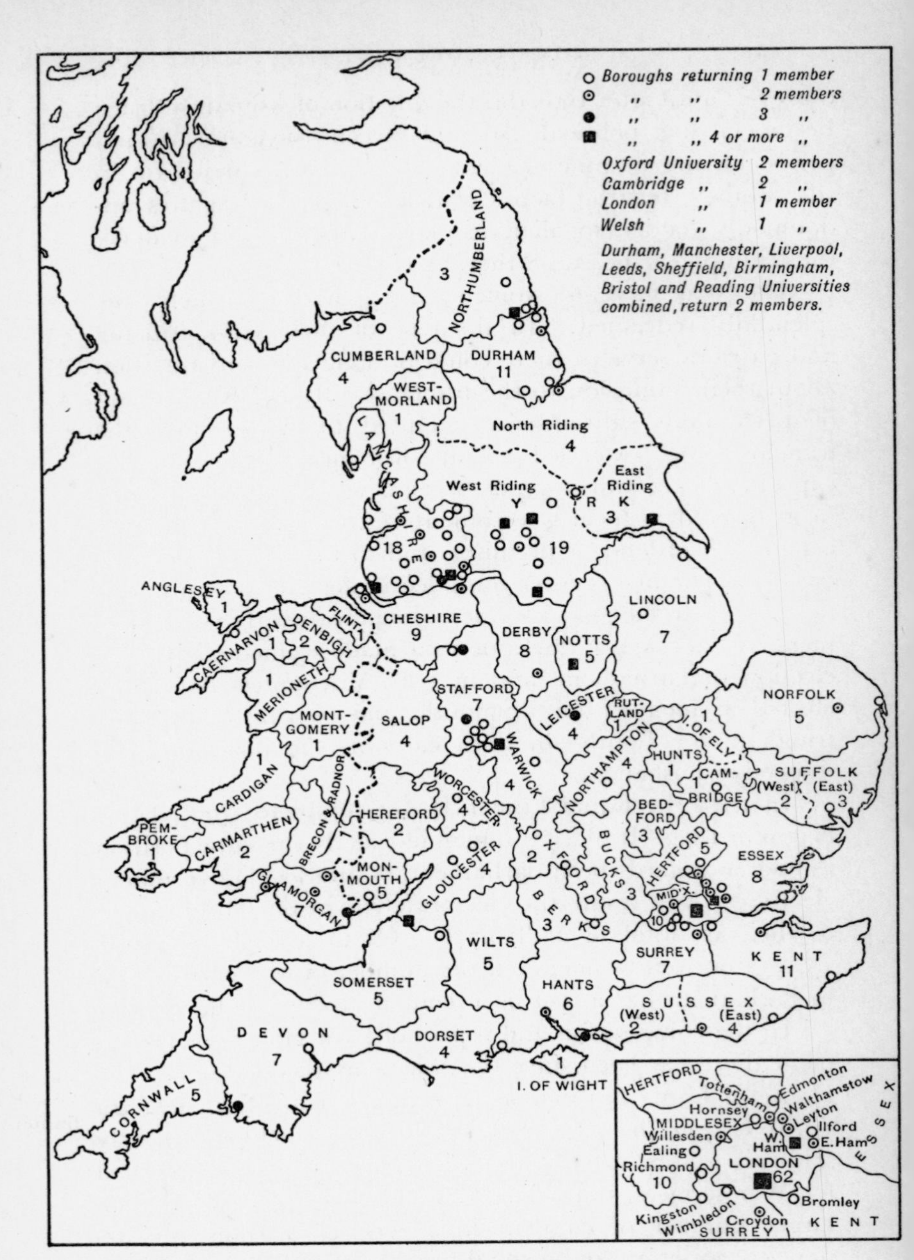


PARLIAMENTARY REPRESENTATION, 1937

No Irish representative Peers have been elected since 1920, and that element of the House will gradually disappear. The actual work of the House is done, and exceedingly well done, by about one hundred Peers, most of whom have served an apprenticeship in the House of Commons.

The House of Commons also has been transformed. The Irish Nationalists have gone; a few women have come in; the Liberal Party, having been undermined by the coalition of 1918–22, is now almost extinct, and since 1924 the Socialists have replaced them as His Majesty's Opposition and have twice, though never with a majority behind them, formed a Government. But they have much to learn before they can be regarded as efficient either in office or opposition, with the result that, in respect of debates, the Second Chamber is incomparably superior to the First. Nevertheless, the House of Commons, though it has evidently ceased to be "the best club in London", does an immense amount of work, the value of which is not adequately appreciated.

**Social and Economic Legislation.**

Since the conclusion of peace, its legislative activities have been largely concentrated upon the task of rebuilding, on better and sounder foundations, the economic and social structure which the War shattered. The "harvest of victory" proved disappointing to those who anticipated that peace would bring in its train prosperity and tranquillity. For two years after the conclusion of the Armistice trade was stimulated by an outburst of extravagance. Despite the fact that some 4,000,000 men were demobilized, the amount of unemployment was negligible. But by the end of 1920 the stimulus was exhausted, and the nation began to exhibit all the symptoms of what Mr. Lloyd George appropriately described as "the fever of anæmia". Unemployment, labour unrest, bitter industrial conflicts, strikes and lock-outs, threats of "direct action" met by the conferment upon the Executive of "emergency powers"—these things fill the pages of post-War history; but the details must be sought elsewhere. Unrest culminated in the General Strike of 1926. The prompt suppression of incipient revolution proved the mettle of the nation. Not less was it proved by the absence of violence on both sides, and of vindictiveness on the part of the victors. But another trial of a different sort awaited a sore stricken people. The financial and economic crisis of 1931 again put to the test the courage and resourcefulness of the British nation. To that test also it has superbly reacted.

**Bureaucracy.**

Through these troublous times the country owed a considerable debt to the excellence of its public administration and the loyalty of its public servants. The multiplication of administrative departments and the enormous expansions of their staffs have been, since the outbreak of the War, and still more since the conclusion of peace, the subject of severe animadversion. The War demanded much improvisation. Improvisation involved extravagance and waste. One " department " after another was set up to meet fresh needs. Many of these have happily disappeared; of those that survive the most important are the Ministries of Labour, Pensions, Transport, and Agriculture. Against the danger to liberty involved in the growth of bureaucracy, and in the growing practice of substituting legislation by Departmental Orders for parliamentary statutes, much has been urged, and justly.[1] But the English Civil Service, if swollen in size out of recognition, remains a model of efficiency, devotion and incorruptibility.

**The Parliamentary Executive.**

War-time experiments were not confined to the " permanent " Executive. During the War, Parliament was necessarily compelled, if not to abdicate its functions, at least to concede more and more power to the Executive. But the old Cabinet system proved quite unequal to the task suddenly thrust upon it. Mr. Lloyd George insisted that the War could not be successfully carried on by a " Sanhedrin ", and on becoming Prime Minister in December, 1916, he appointed a War Cabinet or Directory of five (subsequently seven) members who were to devote themselves to the conduct of the War. Of the members of the

[1] See Lord Hewart: *The New Despotism* (1929); F. J. Port: *Administrative Law* (1929); Marriott: *The Crisis of English Liberty* (Oxford, 1930); *Report of Committee on Ministers' Powers* (Cmd. 4060, 1932); C. T. Carr: *Delegated Legislation* (1921); C. K. Allen: *Bureaucracy Triumphant* (Oxford, 1931).

Directory only one, the Chancellor of the Exchequer, retained any departmental duties. The other departmental ministers were summoned to the Cabinet only when the affairs of their several departments were under discussion. The experiment was brought to an end in October, 1919, when the old Cabinet system was restored.

But with an important amendment. The procedure of the Cabinet, in pre-War days, was almost incredibly haphazard. There was no settled order of business, no agenda, no minutes, and the only record of business done was that contained in the Prime Minister's letter to the Sovereign.

**The Cabinet Secretariat.**

The War necessitated more business-like methods. A Cabinet Secretariat was set up, and, with the Committee of Imperial Defence out of which it developed, had by 1922 a staff of 98 persons. The staff has now been greatly reduced, but the Secretariat remains a permanent adjunct of the Cabinet. The Cabinet now has its agenda prepared, after consultation with ministers, by its secretary, who attends all meetings, and takes and circulates the minutes. But the minutes are as brief as possible: they record only decisions, and avoid, as a rule, reference to discussions or to individual opinions. Ministers are required to return the minutes after perusal. In fine, everything is done, consistent with more business-like procedure, to maintain the old traditions of Cabinet secrecy and solidarity.

**Imperial War Cabinet.**

Another interesting War-time innovation has unhappily not survived. One of the first acts of Mr. Lloyd George in 1917 was to invite ministers from the Dominions to take their places side by side with English ministers in an Imperial War Cabinet. The invitation was accepted, and so successful was the experiment in 1917 that it was repeated in 1918, and in 1919 the Imperial Cabinet took its place in the Peace Conference at Paris as the British Empire Delegation. It had been resolved in 1917 that the new machinery should be retained in perpetuity. But after the Peace Conference it was suddenly and inexplicably scrapped.

The abandonment of the experiment of an Imperial Cabinet threw into still bolder relief the position of the

The Monarchy.

Crown, and not only in relation to the overseas Empire. Of all British institutions the one which emerged from the War with most clearly and definitely enhanced prestige and significance was the Monarchy. The War naturally brought the King and Queen into closer relationship with their people than ever before; in every form of national service they took the lead; they gave to the nation an unforgettable example of ceaseless industry, of unfaltering courage and quiet confidence, of rigid economy and stern self-denial. But there was more in it than this. The wonderful demonstrations before the palace on Armistice Day testified to something more than a people's loyalty and affection. They proved that the nation had come to realize, more clearly perhaps than ever before, that in the Monarchy, at once hereditary and constitutional, it possessed both a symbol of national unity and a guarantee of political stability.

Preceding paragraphs have illustrated the steadying influence exercised by the King at dangerous crises in national affairs. It was exercised again and again during the difficult years that followed the conclusion of peace, and never more notably than in the financial and political crisis of 1931.

Crisis of 1931.

A Socialist Government had for the second time come into office in 1929, only to encounter the full force of the " economic blizzard " that was sweeping through the world. International trade was completely dislocated; confidence was destroyed; credit collapsed; the universe was threatened with irretrievable ruin.

Even in England a grave situation arose. Unemployment rose rapidly towards the 3,000,000 mark; the deficit on the Unemployment Fund had by 1931 reached the appalling total of £115,000,000. " I say with all the seriousness I can command that the national position is grave." So Mr. Snowden, the Socialist Chancellor of the Exchequer, had said in February. It was far graver by 31st July, when an Economy Committee set up under the chairmanship of Sir George May issued its Report. The Report was a veritable bombshell. Even England was heading for bankruptcy. Foreigners took alarm: called in their loans; withdrew their gold. The Prime Minister had gone to Scotland on his holiday, but on 11th August was recalled to confer with the Cabinet and the bankers. On 19th August the Cabinet sat for nine hours and agreed on certain economies. Next day the Opposition leaders, Conservative and Liberal, were called into consultation. The Opposition leaders regarded the Cabinet proposals as inadequate, but the Socialist rank and file refused to consider economies at all.

**The King and the Nation.**

The King had, of course, been kept continuously informed of the development of the crisis. On Sunday, 23rd August, he hurriedly returned to London from Balmoral. Mr. Baldwin returned on the same day from Aix. With a sense of profound relief and gratitude, the nation learnt that the King had personally assumed control of a dangerous situation. The Socialist Government resigned on the 24th, and the King entrusted Mr. Macdonald with the formation of an emergency Cabinet. It consisted of four Socialists, four Conservatives and two Liberals. The majority of the Socialist ex-ministers went into opposition and carried with them almost the whole of their party. But they were in a minority in the House of Commons, which on 8th September endorsed the drastic proposals of Snowden's supplementary budget. A month later Parliament was dissolved, and the electorate returned no fewer than 554 members (out of 615) pledged to support the National Government. The Opposition Socialists numbered only 52, and lost practically all their leaders.[1]

In effect, though not in form, it was the King who had appealed to the nation. The nation responded loyally, enthusiastically, and wisely. England was saved.

[1] The whole story of the crisis is told in great detail and with intimate knowledge by Lord Snowden, *Autobiography*, Chaps. LXXI–LXXXIII, and from a different angle by Mr. Clynes: *Memoirs*, Vol. II, Chaps. XV–XVI.

## CHAPTER XXVI

# The Crown and the Empire

"This Realm of England is an Empire,
and so hath been accepted in the world."
*Act in Restraint of Appeals* (1533).

"THE importance of the Crown in our Constitution is not a diminishing but an increasing factor. It increases and must increase with the development of those free self-governing communities beyond the sea, who are constitutionally linked to us through the person of the Sovereign, the living symbol of Imperial Unity." So spake Mr. Balfour, on the death of Queen Victoria, in 1901.

**Mr. Balfour and General Smuts.**

"How are you going to provide for the future government of this Commonwealth? . . . There are two potent factors that you must rely upon for the future. The first is your hereditary Kingship. . . . You cannot make a republic of the British Commonwealth of Nations." Those were the words of General Smuts, speaking in the Royal Gallery of the House of Lords on 15th May, 1917.

Mr. Balfour's words had in them something of prophecy—a prophecy which, in form, he himself did more than any other man to fulfil by drafting the Report of 1926. What General Smuts said was recognized as true in 1917. In 1937 it has become a truism, emphasized with indisputable authority by one of the leaders of the Socialist Party. "I am," wrote Mr. Clynes, "no supporter of the fulsome adulation of monarchs." No one would suspect him of it. "During the crisis (i.e. in December, 1936) the voices of certain extremist members were raised vociferously demanding the abolition of the Crown in favour of a Republic. These voices were merely those of troubled souls crying in the wilderness and hoping against hope to be noticed. They represent neither British Labour and thought nor the Parliamentary Labour Party. So long as the Throne remains loyal to the Constitution, British Labour remains loyal to the Throne." And for that loyalty Mr. Clynes gives two conclusive reasons. The first is that the Labour Party does not wish to commit suicide. "If it came to a clash between the Labour Party and the Throne or between the King and any Party, the Party would be doomed to defeat. . . . That is one reason why the Trade Unions and the Labour Party have always displayed loyalty towards the Throne." There is another.

"The British Commonwealth of Nations is not a musical comedy State like Monte Carlo. It has a population of some four hundred and sixty-five millions. Think of trying to elect a President for such a multitude, not for England, but for an Empire whose coloured millions outnumber Britain's peoples by six to one! At present the King's hands hold together one of the greatest factors for peace—the friendly alliance of the British Empire. Remove those hands from their work and the structure would fall to pieces in five years." [1] Truistic in 1937, those words would in 1837 have been regarded as grotesque. They could not, indeed, have found utterance. The formal contrast between the situation in 1837 and that in 1937 is sufficiently pointed by the difference in the form of the Coronation Oaths taken respectively by Queen Victoria and King George VI. Queen Victoria merely pledged herself to govern, according to law and custom, "This kingdom of England and the Dominions thereto belonging". King George VI is the King of self-governing Dominions. He solemnly promised and swore "to govern the people of Great Britain, Ireland, Canada, Australia, New Zealand and the Union of South Africa, of [his] Possessions and the Territories to any of them belonging or pertaining, and of [his] Empire of India, according to their respective laws and customs". Such change has a century wrought. The Crown is

**1837–1937.**

[1] Clynes: *Memoirs*, II, 239.

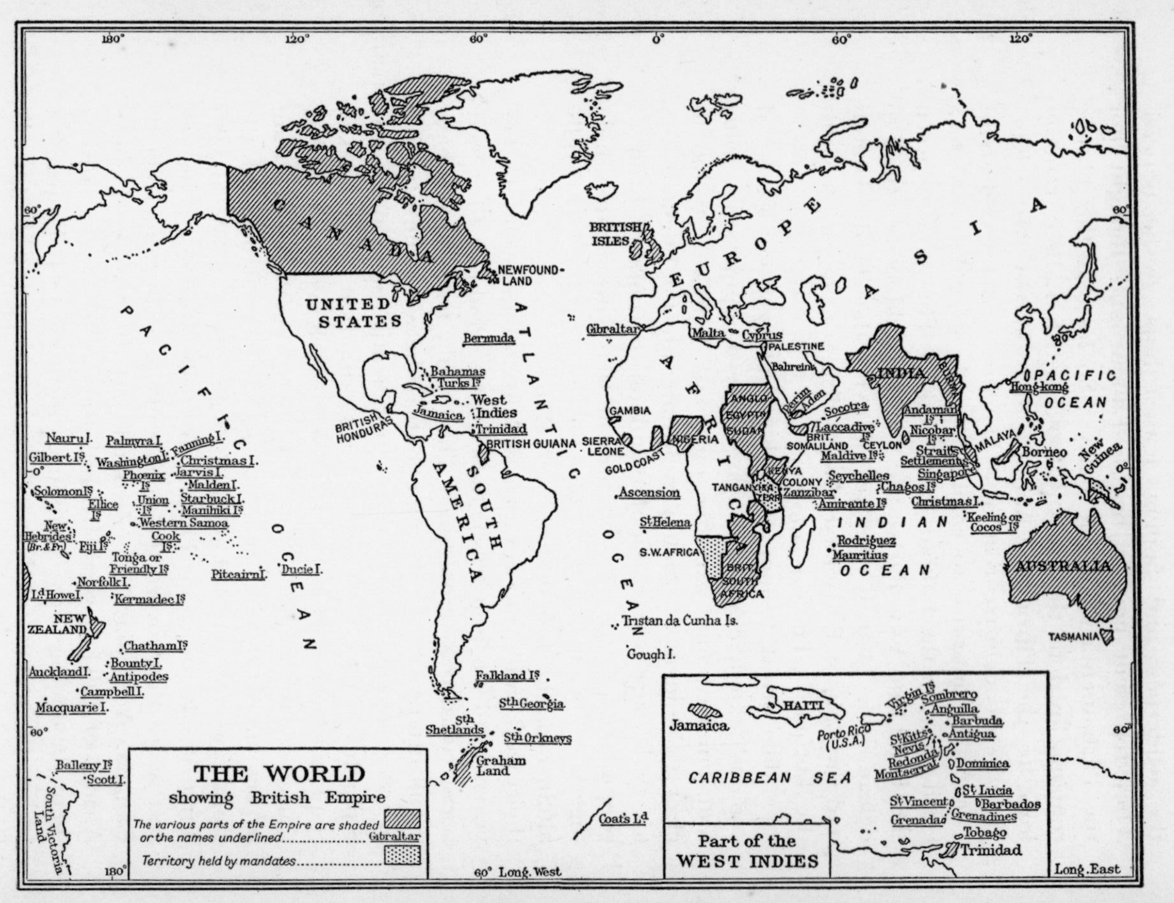


BRITISH EMPIRE, 1937

not merely the strongest link in the chain of Empire, but as between the self-governing Dominions the sole remaining link.

**The Crown and Overseas Enterprise.**

From earliest days the Crown has stood in a special relation to the Colonial Empire, but not until the seventeenth century was its Sovereignty established in any land overseas. The Tudors had, however, prepared the way for future developments. Both by legislation and administration Henry VII laid the foundations of that mercantile system under which, until the nineteenth century, English trade flourished and expanded.

By the Navigation Acts of 1485 and 1489 aliens were forbidden to import into England wines from Bordeaux and woad from Toulouse. Thus was the policy of Richard II carried a stage further towards its complete adoption under the Commonwealth and Charles II. There are traces, also, of a conscious policy in regard to currency: the export of gold and silver was restricted, and merchants were required to bring home in payment for exported wool and cloth a certain proportion of bullion.

Henry VIII was not less anxious than his predecessor to further the interests of the new middle classes and to widen the basis of national prosperity. He extended his royal patronage to voyages of discovery, encouraged merchant shipping, and laid the foundations of a permanent navy.

There was a set-back under Edward VI and Mary, but the accession of Queen Elizabeth, her repudiation of Papal supremacy, and her hostility to the monopolizing policy of Spain, gave an immense impulse to maritime activity. That activity was due to the initiative of adventurous individuals, but only the Crown could authorize the settlement of Englishmen overseas. The Charter of the East India Company (1600), and the Virginia Charters of 1606–12, were granted by the Crown. Even the Pilgrim Fathers, with all their independence, executed a document—the *Mayflower Compact*—acknowledging their allegiance to King James I, and the much more important Puritan settlement in Massachusetts was made under Charter from Charles I.

The Commonwealth was no less insistent than the Monarchy on a recognition of its authority by English settlers overseas. But Charles II was the first English King to define colonial policy and, as already indicated, to devise machinery for the regular administration of the overseas possessions of the Crown.[1] James II was almost equally interested in naval administration and colonial policy.

William III was, as we have seen, primarily a continental statesman, but the prolonged duel with France, in which his policy involved his island kingdom, had extra-European repercussions of the highest significance. So far as the first British Empire was the product of conquest—as opposed to simple settlement—it was mainly built up by the wars between Great Britain and the Bourbon Powers of France and Spain, and under the terms of the treaties which severally concluded these wars between 1713 and 1763. The Treaty of Paris (1763), as already disclosed, marked the zenith of the first Colonial Empire.

**The Great Schism.**

Paradoxically, it led almost immediately to its disruption. The victories won in the Seven Years' War, the expulsion of the French from Canada and of the Spaniards from Florida dispelled all the immediate dangers which, from 1740 to 1760, had threatened the British colonies. All restraint upon their westward expansion was removed by the defeat of the French plan for connecting, by a chain of forts, the great Canadian lakes with the valley of the Mississippi and the French colony of Louisiana. The policy of George Grenville and his successors supplied the colonists with a grievance, and, thanks to the victories of Wolfe and Amherst, Hawke and Boscawen, they were in a position without risk to themselves to exploit them.

The disputes about commercial policy and taxation were mishandled on both sides, but the constitutional point essentially at issue has been curiously obscured.

What those small communities, each with its own repre-

[1] See *supra*, Chap. XVII.

sentative Legislature, resented was the authority claimed by the Imperial Parliament. The theory to which they had long and tenaciously adhered was that each colony was united to Great Britain solely through the Crown. "Our allegiance is due to the natural body alone of the King, not to the publick body." So ran a resolution passed in the time of Charles II by the Assembly of Massachusetts. And that doctrine the colonists in America, like the colonists in Ireland, firmly held. It applied, however, only to internal government. The right of the Imperial Parliament to control external affairs, and in particular to regulate overseas trade, was never, before the outbreak of the rebellion, questioned in theory, though it was consistently evaded in practice. It was, indeed, the profits of the smuggling trade which had brought such prosperity to the merchants of Massachusetts.

**The Colonies and the Crown.**

But wherever the responsibility for the schism lay, the result was to shatter the first Colonial Empire. From its ashes there quickly arose a second. A large body of Empire Loyalists, men and women who disdained to live under the Stars and Stripes, trekked over the American border and laid the foundations of a British Canada, side by side with the Canada conquered from France. The natural refusal of the Carolinas to receive English convicts led to the establishment (1788) of a convict settlement on the great continent lately rediscovered by Captain Cook. Botany Bay was the nidus of New South Wales, the germ of the Commonwealth of Australia. Cape Colony was one of the few conquests retained by Great Britain after the close of the Napoleonic wars.

**The Disruption of the First Colonial Empire.**

So a second White Empire came into being, but during the first half of the nineteenth century no one supposed that it would remain under the sovereignty of the British Crown.

**The Second.**

All these new Possessions were at first placed under military government. In 1791, however, Pitt took the first step towards colonial self-government by conferring representative institutions upon the two Canadas. But this failed

**The Evolution of Self-government.**

to bring contentment or tranquillity to either colony, and in 1837 both were in revolt.

The rebellions were without difficulty suppressed, but the Melbourne Government sent out Lord Durham to report on the whole situation. The outcome of Durham's mission was the famous *Report* which bears his name, the union of the two Canadas, and the gradual concession of Responsible Government.

Canada showed the way to the rest of the Colonial Empire. Between 1840 and 1900 Responsible Government was conceded by successive stages to all the greater colonies.

The Manchester School.

During the first half of that period the Manchester School—whatever the party in power—dominated English politics. Their cardinal doctrine of *laissez-faire* was applied all round: not least to colonial policy. The almost universal expectation—the avowed hope—was that self-government would prepare the colonies for independence.

But in the 'seventies there came an astounding change in public sentiment. Under the influence of newly born national ambitions, of the industrialization and urbanization of Europe, of scientific inventions that annihilated space and time, a new era dawned. Europe was expanding; the globe was shrinking; *welt-politik* emerged. A scramble ensued among the countries of Western Europe for the acquisition of tropical dependencies. In the ultimate partition the largest share went to Great Britain and Germany.

The New Imperialism.

The British colonies, notably in the Pacific, believed themselves to be menaced by the proximity of European neighbours, particularly by the French in the New Hebrides and the Germans in New Guinea. They appealed to the Imperial Government to dispel the menace, but Whitehall was slow to move, and the Colonial Governments for the first time realized the paradox of their constitutional position.

Colonial Conferences.

Completely autonomous as regards internal government, they were subject, in respect of external relations, to the autocratic control of Whitehall and Westminster. Nor did the autocracy seem to them efficient. It was too susceptible to pressure from European neighbours, and too careless of colonial sentiment. These feelings found eloquent expression in the first Colonial Conference of 1887. The public at home were ready by 1887 to heed colonial grievances as they had never heeded them before. The philosophy of the Manchester School was at a discount. During the last fifteen years of Queen Victoria's reign, the separatist doctrines which had so long inspired colonial policy were submerged by a wave of ardent Imperialism. The new Imperialism found its focus and symbol in the Crown.

The greatest of the Victorian Laureates was an ardent Imperialist, and, particularly in his later years, emphasized the importance of that symbol:

> The loyal to their Crown
> Are loyal to their own fair sons who love
> Our ocean Empire with her boundless home
> For ever broadening England, and her Throne
> In one vast orient, and one isle, one isle
> That knows not her own greatness.
> If she knows and dreads it we are fallen.

Events were to prove, in the first decades of the twentieth century, that she knew it as never before had she known it, and that she did not dread it.

**Royal Visits.**

To the revolution in sentiment the Crown itself made an important contribution. King Edward VII was the first Prince of Wales to visit Canada and India. His sons saw a great deal of the Overseas Empire as midshipmen, and in the first year of King Edward's reign the Duke of York, his heir apparent, went out to Australia to open the first Parliament of the Commonwealth in the King's name. Before returning home the Duke with his Duchess visited New Zealand, South Africa and Canada. Royal princesses played their parts as wives of Governors-General in Canada and South Africa. King George V, as Prince of Wales, made with his consort a tour in India in the winter of 1905–6, and as King-Emperor attended, at Delhi, with the Queen-Empress the great Coronation Durbar in December, 1911. The Duke of Connaught represented the Sovereign at the inauguration of the new Constitution in India (1921), and in the autumn of the same year, on the urgent appeal of ministers, but contrary to the wishes of the Queen, the Prince of Wales was sent off to India in the hope of counteracting disruptive influences.

The Prince's first mission as the "Ambassador of Empire" had, in fact, been made to Canada in 1919. It was a toilsome tour undertaken to convey the thanks of the English people to their Canadian brothers for their superb contribution to the victory so lately won in Europe. The Prince fell in love with the people and the country, and by purchasing a ranch at Calgary, established himself as a citizen of the great Dominion. Before he returned home he crossed the border and captivated the Americans, as his grandfather had done some sixty years before.

The young "ambassador" was allowed little respite, for in 1920 he went to New Zealand and Australia, and, returning by the Panama Canal, visited British Guiana and the West Indies. Of the Australian visit it has been admirably said by Mr. Bolitho: "The Prince of Wales gave Australia a new light upon royalty, but he also gave many people in the South a new conception of the English aristocracy. . . . Upon his example Australia revised its opinion of the ruling classes of England, and the people of the Antipodes saw, through him, that the Monarchy stood for the perpetuity of national life, and not for the transient phases of its political existence." The tour in India followed in 1921, and before he came home he had seen Ceylon, Malaya and Japan. In 1925 the Prince made a journey of 35,000 miles, in the course of which he completed his tour of the great Dominions by a tour in South Africa and Rhodesia. He also visited Saint Helena and the Argentine, and crossed and recrossed the Andes. Nor was that the end of his travels—but the tale of them becomes almost catalogic.

Yet the catalogue has profound political significance. Under Queen Victoria the Crown was an Institution wrapped in mystery. King Edward VII, without loss of dignity, dissipated something of the mystery. King George V and

Queen Mary went in and out among their people without sacrificing anything of the deep respect due to the office they represented, and, aided by the magic of science, made all the peoples of the Empire one, bound together by common devotion to the " Head of the Family ".

None the less, the reign of King George V was more critical for the Empire than any reign since that of George III.

The centripetal movement discernible in the last years of the Victorian era had been checked partly by the revelation of England's weakness in the South African War, and partly by Chamberlain's failure to convert England to Imperial Preference. The atmosphere of the Imperial Conferences of 1907 and 1911 was, moreover, ungenial. In 1907 Mr. Deakin, Premier of the Commonwealth, complained of the " indifferent attitude of statesmen in this country to British interests in the Pacific ", and confessed to " an exasperated feeling thus created in Australia ". The Conference of 1911, though unsatisfactory as regards constitutional development, was important for the opportunity given to Sir Edward Grey to reveal to the statesmen of the Empire, of course confidentially, the intensely critical state of the European situation. That revelation, full and frank, undoubtedly contributed to the instantaneous apprehension of the crisis when it came in 1914.

**The Empire and the War.**

In August, 1914, the declaration of war against Germany, though made on the sole responsibility of the British Cabinet, technically involved the whole Empire. The active participation of the Dominions in the War was, however, entirely voluntary and spontaneous. At war they were, whether they liked it or not; but not a man or a shilling were they legally compelled to contribute.[1]

**Constitutional Relations.**

The position was not satisfactory and was resented; especially by Canada, which was more remote from any of the areas of war, and perhaps less directly concerned in its issue, than the other Dominions. No Dominion, however, decided more promptly on active participation, or made a

[1] On the whole question see Marriott: *The Mechanism of the Modern State*, I, Chaps. XI, XII.

more splendid contribution to the final victory. Nevertheless, Canada was under no illusion about the lamentable deficiencies in the machinery of Imperial co-operation. "It is impossible to believe," said Sir Robert Borden, "that the existing status, so far as it concerns the control of foreign policy and extra-Imperial relations, can remain as it is to-day." A remedy was found in the Imperial War Cabinet (1917) already mentioned.[1] Though the experiment seemed to many to be full of promise, it did not survive the Peace Conference, where colonial nationalism was clamant for recognition. Recognition could not, in view of the war efforts of the Dominions, be refused. Separate representation was conceded to them not only at the Peace Conference but on the League of Nations. The centrifugal tendencies manifested at Paris were accentuated at a Conference of the Prime Ministers of the Empire in 1921. That Conference banged and bolted the door against Imperial Federalism.

**Centrifugal Tendencies.**

The attitude then taken up by the Dominions was accentuated by the course of post-War diplomacy. At the Washington Conference, which met in 1922 to deal with the naval situation in the Far East, Mr. Balfour represented (at General Smuts's request) South Africa as well as the United Kingdom, but the other Dominions and India were separately represented, and also (as at Paris) formed part of the British Empire Delegation. To the decisions then reached the Empire as a whole assented. The Chanak crisis (1922), on the contrary, revealed a rift in Imperial unity, though New Zealand and Australia announced their readiness to co-operate with the Imperial Government in whatever action might be deemed necessary. Fortunately the promptitude and tact of Sir Charles Harington, the Allied Commander-in-Chief at Constantinople, averted the necessity.[2] To the Lausanne Conference (1923), which arranged terms of peace with the Turkish Republic, Dominion repre-

[1] *Supra*, p. 369.

[2] For further details cf. Marriott: *Modern England* (Methuen, 1934), pp. 428 and 461.

sentatives were not invited. Whether their exclusion was due (as was supposed) to pressure exerted upon the British Government by France, or to some other cause, it was deeply regrettable. It had a swift reaction upon British diplomacy. The Treaty of Locarno expressly provided that its terms should impose no obligations upon any of the Dominions or upon India unless their several Governments signified their acceptance thereof. That exemption does not, however, resolve the problem of "legal belligerency", should circumstances unhappily raise it.

**Treaty-making.**

Of not less crucial significance were the circumstances attendant upon the conclusion, between Canada and the United States, of a treaty designed to protect the halibut fisheries (1923). The Canadian Government refused to allow the British ambassador at Washington to participate in the treaty, and an awkward corner was turned only by the issue of full powers by the King to the Canadian plenipotentiary.[1]

The Treaty-making power of the Dominions was the most important political question under discussion at the Imperial Economic Conference of 1923. Further concessions were there made to the doctrine of Colonial Nationalism, though steps were taken, by closer economic co-operation, to counteract the tendency towards Constitutional separatism.

**The Imperial Conference of 1926.**

In the whole series of Imperial Conferences none was so important as that of 1926. The Report of that Conference contained a passage, drafted by the Earl of Balfour, which has already become classical. "Nothing would be gained," it ran, "by attempting to lay down a Constitution for the British Empire." Nevertheless, it proceeded to define the "position and mutual relation" of "Great Britain and the Dominions. . . . They are autonomous communities within the British Empire, equal in status, in no way subordinate one to another in any aspect of their domestic or external affairs, though united by a common allegiance to the Crown and freely associated as members of the British

[1] On the Halibut Treaty, cf. Cmd. 2377; Keith: *Responsible Government in the Dominions*, pp. 897 f.; and Marriott: *Empire Foreign Policy*, *ap. Fortnightly Review* (May, 1923).

Commonwealth of Nations. . . . Equality of status, so far as Britain and the Dominions are concerned, is thus the root principle governing our Imperial relations. But the principles of equality and similarity appropriate to *status* do not universally extend to functions. Here we require something more than immutable dogmas." This Report has been acclaimed as the masterpiece of a modern Athanasius. The recommendations of the Conference of 1926 were elaborated by a committee of expert lawyers and permanent officials (1929), and were embodied in the *Statute of Westminster* (1931).[1] The King was henceforward to be the sole link between the several Dominions of the British Commonwealth. The Governors-General were to be his personal representatives, appointed by him on the recommendation no longer of the Imperial Government, but of the respective Dominion Governments; nor were they to be any longer the official channel of communication, which in future was to be direct between Government and Government. The King was in future to be advised by ministers responsible to half a dozen different Legislatures, and to act on advice which might, as between one Dominion and another, be flatly contradictory. The " Crown " was eliminated from the constitutional machinery of the Empire; the " King " was suffered to survive. In legislation, the supremacy of an Imperial Parliament was repudiated. The Imperial Parliament became, in fact and in name, the Parliament at Westminster, as the ministers became merely " His Majesty's Government in the United Kingdom ". The *Statute of Westminster* further emphasizes the tenuity of the constitutional links. The Preamble states " that any alteration in the law touching the succession to the Throne or the Royal Style and Titles shall hereafter require the assent as well of the Parliaments of all the Dominions as of the Parliament of the United Kingdom ". Preambles are of doubtful validity, but Section 4 explicitly says: " No Act of the United Kingdom passed after the

**The Statute of Westminster (1931).**

[1] For Conference of 1926, see Cmd. 2768 and 2769; of 1929, see Cmd. 3479 and generally Marriott: *Modern England*, pp. 465–70.

commencement of this Act shall extend, or be deemed to extend, to a Dominion as part of the law of that Dominion, unless it is expressly declared in that Act that that Dominion has requested, and consented to, the enactment thereof."

Neither the Commonwealth of Australia[1] or New Zealand have ever ratified the Statute of Westminster, but it is, of course, binding upon the Parliaments that have enacted it, and has been tacitly accepted by the others.

Old-fashioned Constitutionalists are naturally aghast at the rapidity of the post-War development, but the crucial question evidently was: if a crisis came, would the sole surviving link of Empire hold?

**The Crisis of 1936.**

A crisis came in December, 1936. The link, though slender, held. An effort had meanwhile been made in the previous decade to counteract the weakening of the constitutional links by strengthening those of inter-Imperial trade.

**Imperial Preference.**

The Conferences of 1917 and 1918 had reaffirmed the principle of Imperial Preference. By the Finance Act of 1919 it was incorporated in the fiscal system of Great Britain, and was further applied in the *Safeguarding of Industries Act* of 1921. An Imperial Economic Conference was specially called in 1923 to promote Imperial co-operation in matters of trade and finance, and to stimulate, as contemplated in the *Empire Settlement Act* (1922), the slackening process of migration. The Socialist Government of 1924 repealed all the Preferences and even the mildly protective duties imposed in 1915 by Mr. McKenna; but the Baldwin Government which was in power from 1924 to 1929 restored the McKenna duties, and extended the range of Preference and Safeguarding. There was a set-back when the Socialists returned to office in 1929, but the financial crisis of 1931 impressed most serious people with the gravity of the situation, and in 1932 Mr. Neville Chamberlain, as Chancellor of the Exchequer in a National Administration, was able to carry through a fiscal revolution comparable in comprehensiveness with that effected by Peel in the 'forties of the preceding century.

[1] Australia is reluctantly doing so in 1937.

The way was thus cleared for the Economic Conference which met at Ottawa in 1933. That Conference resulted in a series of agreements which, though falling far short of the highest expectations, have certainly done something to stimulate inter-Imperial trade.

There was a steady recovery in trade after 1933, and in 1935 the nation could give itself up to a joyous and grateful celebration of the Jubilee of King George V and Queen Mary. All the greater, however, was the shock to the nation when the King died, after a very brief illness, in January, 1936. King George, greatly loved and deeply mourned, was succeeded by his eldest son, who for twenty-five years had as Prince of Wales endeared himself to his future subjects as no Prince of Wales had ever done before. Not least was he beloved in the Overseas Empire, of which he had a first-hand knowledge unprecedented in the history of the English monarchy. Auspicious, then, in a remarkable degree, was the opening of the reign of Edward VIII.

**Edward VIII.**

Plans were already maturing for giving to his coronation a special Imperial significance, when the high hopes entertained of the new King were suddenly dashed by the news that he contemplated a marriage which seemed to his people to be incongruous, and which his ministers could not approve. Every effort was made to shake the King's resolution, but they availed nothing. By the King's wish Mr. Baldwin consulted the Dominion Premiers as well as the Opposition leaders at home, and it quickly became clear that the whole Empire was virtually unanimous in preferring the distressful alternative of abdication to any expedient for facilitating the King's marriage to the lady of his choice. The King on his part was adamant, and on 10th December, after a week of tense public anxiety, King Edward executed a formal Instrument of Abdication renouncing the throne for himself and his descendants. The King's message announcing his decision was presented to Parliament on the same afternoon at an hour chosen to make possible a simultaneous announcement in the other Parliaments of the Empire; a Bill to give effect to it was immediately intro-

**Abdication.**

duced. The Preamble to the Bill contained clauses that will henceforth be reproduced in every History of England:

"Whereas His Majesty . . . has been pleased to declare that he is irrevocably determined to renounce the Throne for Himself and His Descendants . . . and has signified His desire that effect thereto should be given immediately:

"And whereas, following upon the communication to His Dominions of His Majesty's said declaration and desire, the Dominion of Canada pursuant to the provisions of section four of the Statute of Westminster, 1931, has requested and consented to the enactment of this Act, and the Commonwealth of Australia, the Dominion of New Zealand and the Union of South Africa have assented thereto:

"Be it therefore enacted, &c."

The variation of phrase in the reference to Canada and the other Dominions will not escape notice.

On Friday, 11th December, the Bill of Abdication passed through all its stages, and the King, having given his assent to it, ceased to reign, and his brother, hitherto known as the Duke of York, succeeded to the throne. On 12th December the Duke was proclaimed King as George VI. At ten o'clock on the previous evening the ex-King had broadcast a farewell message to his peoples, and directly afterwards had in silence and secrecy left the country.

The hearts of his peoples were deeply moved by the tragedy enacted before their eyes. But, distraught with grief, they were not dismayed. Rather were they heartened by the grave dignity and quiet efficiency with which all the leading actors in this tragedy had played their parts—not least the Prime Minister of the United Kingdom and the statesmen of all parties throughout the Empire. Deep was the sympathy felt for the Queen-Mother, so lately widowed, and now so grievously disappointed in her first-born. Particularly cordial was the welcome extended to the new King and Queen, suddenly called upon, and under circumstances deeply distressing, to assume a terrible and unexpected load of responsibility. Yet the dominant note was one of thankful pride that a crisis so grave had been surmounted, with no breach of constitutional continuity and without any disturbance of public order. Nor will students of Politics fail to reflect, and if sympathetic towards Great Britain to rejoice, that from its first practical test the *Statute of Westminster* had emerged triumphantly. The abdication of a King who had earned unprecedented popularity in his Overseas Dominions might well have shaken the Empire to its foundations. It evoked, on the contrary, a wonderful manifestation of Imperial unity, and of loyalty to the wearer of the Imperial Crown. "The Throne is greater than the King." That, as a leading Review well put it, was "the central lesson of the crisis, and a lesson expounded no less surely by the response of the people of the Dominions than by that of the people of Great Britain."[1] The sentiment was general, but nowhere was it more emphatically or more eloquently expressed than in the Federal Parliament of Canada by the Minister of Justice, Mr. Lapointe:

**The Golden Link of Empire.**

"I desire to say to-day that the British Throne is the cement, the bond that unites all of us, and if it should disappear and be replaced by some other form, I am afraid that the end of the British Empire would be in sight and that Canada would soon not be part of the British Commonwealth of Nations. That is the great and the consoling lesson which comes to us as an outcome of all these troubles. . . . But we are proud to say at the end that the action which has been taken, the sentiments which have been expressed, the feeling of all British citizens throughout the world, have been such that we have demonstrated not only to every one in our own Dominions but to all the world the granite strength of the British Constitution, enshrined as it is in the British Throne."[2]

With the strength of granite the British Constitution combines the flexibility of rubber: it can resist shocks; it can also absorb them. Parliamentary Monarchy was a great experiment when first tried in the insular State. That the system could ever be adapted to a World-Empire is

[1] *Round Table* for March, 1937, p. 254. [2] *Round Table*, p. 368.

an idea which would have staggered the imagination of the Pyms and the Walpoles, or even the Pitts and the Peels. That it has been so adapted, that it has resisted a terrible shock, and has survived a grave crisis, is conclusive testimony to the political genius of the British race.

# APPENDIX

## SOME USEFUL BOOKS

This list must not be taken as a formal bibliography, for which students may refer to Methuen's *History of England* (ed. Oman), *The Cambridge Mediæval History*, and *The Cambridge Modern History*, which contain full and critical Bibliographies. This is only a comparatively short list of useful books. A few other books are mentioned, *in loco*, in the notes.

### A. *Textbooks covering most of the period*

Sir C. Oman (ed.): *History of England*, 8 vols. (Methuen, 1910–34.)
G. M. Trevelyan: *History of England* (n.e.). (1938.)
D. J. Medley: *Constitutional History*. (1913.)
T. P. Taswell-Langmead: *English Constitutional History* (n.e.). (1919.)
J. A. R. Marriott: *English Political Institutions* (revised ed.). (Clar. Press, 1938.)
J. R. Green: *Short History of the English People*. (1874.)
C. R. L. Fletcher: *History of England*, 4 vols.
R. von Gneist: *History of the English Parliament* (800–1887). (1889.)

### B. *Books I and II*, 43–1485

W. Stubbs: *Constitutional History*, 3 vols. (Clar. Press, 1880.)
—— *Select Charters*. (Clar. Press, 1895.)
—— *Lectures on Mediæval and Modern History*. (Clar. Press, 1886.)
—— *Prefaces to the Rolls Series* (ed. Hassall). (1902.)
(But reference should be made, by preference, to Stubbs's and other *Prefaces* to the many volumes in the *Rolls Series*.)
J. Rhys: *Keltic Britain*. (1904.)
R. G. Collingwood: *Roman Britain*. (1932.)
F. J. Haverfield: *The Romanization of Roman Britain*. (1923.)
—— *Roman Occupation of Britain*. (1924.)
T. R. Holmes: *Ancient Britain*. (1907.)
W. Scarth: *Roman Britain*.
Sir C. Oman: *England Before the Norman Conquest*. (1910.)
Sir J. H. Ramsay: *The Foundations of England*, 2 vols. (1898.)
C. Plummer (ed.): *Two of the Saxon Chronicles*, 707–1001. (Clar. Press, 1892–9.)
—— Bede's *Ecclesiastical History*. (1896.)
W. Bright: *Early English Church History*. (Clar. Press, 1878.)

J. R. Green: *Making of England.* (1882.)
J. R. Lightfoot: *Leaders of the Northern Church.* (1890.)
F. W. Maitland: *Township and Borough.* (Camb., 1898.)
—— *The Constitutional History of England.* (Camb., 1908.)
—— *Domesday and Beyond.* (Camb., 1897.)
C. Petit Dutaillis: *Studies Supplementary to Stubbs.* (Manchester, 1908.)
J. M. Kemble: *The Saxons in England.* (1849.)
Asser: *Life of Alfred.* (Bohn.)
H. M. Chadwick: *Studies on Anglo-Saxon Institutions.* (1905.)
—— *The Origins of the English Nation.* (1907.)
J. R. Green: *The Conquest of England.* (1883.)
F. Pollock and F. W. Maitland: *History of English Law.* (1895.)
J. H. Round: *Feudal England.* (1895.)
F. Seebohm: *The English Village Community.* (1883.)
P. Vinogradoff: *Growth of the Manor.* (1905.)
—— *Villenage in England.* (Clar. Press, 1892.)
E. A. Freeman: *Norman Conquest*, 6 vols. (Clar. Press, 1867–9.)
R. W. Church: *Anselm.* (1870.)
K. Norgate: *England under the Angevin Kings*, 2 vols. (1887.)
H. W. C. Davis: *England under the Normans and Angevins.* (1905.)
W. S. McKechnie: *Magna Carta.* (1913.)
W. R. W. Stephens: *The English Church*, 1066–1272. (1901.)
J. H. Round: *Geoffrey de Mandeville* (for Stephen's reign). (1892.)
H. Gee and W. J. Hardy (ed.): *Documents Illustrative of English Church History* (314–1689). (1896.)
E. C. Lodge and G. A. Thornton (ed.): *English Constitutional Documents* (1307–1485). (Camb., ? )
A. F. Pollard: *The Evolution of Parliament.* (1920.)
C. H. McIlwain: *High Court of Parliament.* (1910).
F. W. Maitland (ed.): *Memoranda de Parliamento.* (*Rolls Series*, 1893.)
J. F. Baldwin: *King's Council in the Middle Ages.* (1893.)
F. S. Stevenson: *Grosseteste.* (1899.)
Pauli: *Simon de Montfort* (trans. Goodwin). (1876.)
Bémont: *S. de Montfort.* (Paris, 1884.)
T. F. Tout: *Longman's Political History of England* (1216–1377). (1905.)
—— *Chapters in the Administrative History of Mediæval England*, 5 vols. (1920–30.)
Sir C. Oman: *Longman's Political History of England* (1377–1485) (1904.)
B. Wilkinson: *The Chancery under Edward III.* (Manchester, 1929.)
G. M. Trevelyan: *England in the Age of Wyclif.* (1900.)
Sir James Ramsay: *Lancaster and York.* (1892.)
J. H. Wylie: *Henry IV*, 4 vols. (1884–98.)
—— *England under Henry V*, 3 vols. (1914.)
T. F. Plucknett: *The Lancastrian Constitution ap. Tudor Studies* (ed. Seton-Watson). (1924.)

J. Gairdner: *History of Richard III.* (1898.)
S. B. Chrimes: *English Constitutional Ideas in the Fifteenth Century.* (Camb., 1936.)
M. V. Clarke: *Mediæval Representation and Consent.* (1936.)

C. *Book III.* (*a*) *Sixteenth Century*

G. W. Prothero: *Statutes and Documents.* (1894.)
J. R. Tanner: *Tudor Constitutional Documents.* (Camb., 1922.)
Sneyd (ed.): *The Italian Relation of England about* 1500. (Camden Soc., 1847.)
K. Pickthorn: *Early Tudor Government*, 2 vols. (Camb., 1934.)
J. Gairdner: *Letters and Papers of Richard III and Henry VII.* (*Rolls Series.*)
—— *English Church in the Sixteenth Century.* (1902.)
F. Bacon: *History of Henry VII.* (1621.)
W. Busch: *England under the Tudors* (Eng. trans. Todd). (1895.)
H. Hallam: *Constitutional History of England*, 3 vols. (1827.)
H. A. L. Fisher: *Longman's Political History of England* (1485–1547). (1906.)
Brewer and Gairdner (ed.): *Letters and Papers, Foreign and Domestic.* (1862.)
J. S. Brewer: *Reign of Henry VIII*, 2 vols. (1884.)
A. F. Pollard: *Longman's Political History*, 1547–1603. (1910.)
—— *Henry VIII.* (1905.)
—— *Wolsey.* (1929.)
—— *Protector Somerset.*
—— *Life of Cranmer.* (1904.)
J. A. Froude: *History of England* (1529–1588), 12 vols. (1856–70.)
J. B. Black: *The Reign of Elizabeth.* (Oxford, 1936.)
E. S. Beesley: *Elizabeth.* (1892.)
Sir Thomas Smith: *De Republica Anglorum* (1583) (ed. Alston). (1906.)
W. Lambarde: *Eirenarcha.* (1581.)
—— *Archeion.* (1591.)
Lord E. Percy: *Privy Council under the Tudors.* (1908.)
D. Gladish: *The Tudor Privy Council.* (1915.)
Tawney and Power (ed.): *Tudor Economic Documents*, 3 vols. (1924.)

(*b*) *Seventeenth Century*

G. W. Prothero (ed.): *Statutes and Documents* (1625). (1894.)
S. R. Gardiner (ed.): *Constitutional Documents* (1625–1660). (1889.)
Sir C. Grant Robertson (ed.): *Statutes, Cases and Documents from* 1660. (1930.)
D. Oswald Dykes (ed.): *Source Book of Constitutional History* (1660–1927). (1930.)
T. Carlyle: *Letters and Speeches of O. Cromwell*, 5 vols. (1871.)

Sir C. H. Firth: *Scotland and the Commonwealth.* (1894.)
—— *Scotland and the Protectorate.* (1898.)
—— *Cromwell.* (1900.)
—— *The Last Years of the Protectorate*, 2 vols. (1909.)
—— *The House of Lords during the Civil War.* (1910.)
J. A. R. Marriott: *The Crisis of English Liberty.* (Clar. Press, 1930.)
S. R. Gardiner: *History of England* (1603–1649), 14 vols. (1883–6.)
—— *The Commonwealth and the Protectorate*, 4 vols. (1903.)
L. von Ranke: *History of England*, 6 vols. (trans.). (1875.)
G. M. Trevelyan: *England under the Stuarts.* (1904.)
J. R. Tanner: *English Constitutional Conflicts of the XVIIth Century.* (Camb., 1928.)
J. A. R. Marriott: *Life and Times of Lord Falkland.* (1907.)
Lady Burghclere: *Life of Strafford*, 2 vols. (1931.)
J. Morley: *Oliver Cromwell.* (1900.)
W. D. Christie: *Life of Shaftesbury*, 2 vols. (1871.)
A. Bryant: *Charles II.*
North: *The Lives of the Norths*, 3 vols. (1890.)
H. D. Traill: *William III.*
D. Ogg: *England in the Reign of Charles II*, 2 vols. (Clar. Press, 1934.)
G. N. Clark: *The Later Stuarts.* (Clar. Press, 1934.)
Lord Macaulay: *History of England*, 5 vols. (1849–61.)
G. M. Trevelyan: *England under Queen Anne*, 3 vols. (1930–4.)
K. G. Feiling: *History of the Tory Party* (1640–1714). (1924.)
E. R. Turner: *The Privy Council*, 2 vols. (1927.)

D. *Book IV* (1714–1936)

F. A. Ogg: *English Government and Politics.* (1929.)
L. B. Namier: *The Structure of Politics at the Accession of George III*, 2 vols. (1929.)
Sir C. Grant Robertson: *England under the Hanoverians.* (1911.)
F. S. Oliver: *The Endless Adventure*, 3 vols. (1930–5.)
J. A. R. Marriott: *England Since Waterloo* (10th ed., 1930.)
—— *Modern England* (1934.)
E. Halévy: *A History of the English People*, 3 vols. (trans.). (1927–34.)
R. H. Gretton: *A Modern History of the English People.* (1912–29.)
H. Paul: *A History of Modern England*, 5 vols. (1904.)
J. A. R. Marriott: *Queen Victoria and Her Ministers.* (1933.)
Sir T. Erskine May: *Constitutional History of England*, 3 vols. (1878.)
Sir W. Anson: *Law and Custom of the Constitution*, 3 vols. (1907–35.)
W. Bagehot: *The English Constitution.* (1867, n.e. 1913.)
E. Boutmy: *Development of the English Constitution* (trans.). (1891.)
A. V. Dicey: *Law of the Constitution.* (1885–1915.)

Sir Sidney Low: *The Governance of England.* (1914.)
J. A. R. Marriott: *Mechanism of the Modern State*, 2 vols. (Clar. Press, 1927.)
Alpheus Todd: *Parliamentary Government of England*, 2 vols. (1867–9.)
R. Muir: *National Self-Government.* (1918.)
W. E. Hearn: *Government of England.* (1867.)
R. von Gneist: *The English Constitution*, 2 vols. (1886.)
E. and A. Porritt: *The Unreformed House of Commons.* (1903.)
G. L. Dickinson: *The Development of Parliament in the Nineteenth* Century. (1895.)
J. R. M. Butler: *The Passing of the Great Reform Bill.* (1914.)
M. T. Blauvelt: *The Development of Cabinet Government in England.* (1902.)
J. Morley: *Walpole* (for the Cabinet).
W. E. Gladstone: *Gleanings of Past Years*, Vol. I. (1898.)
W. Ivor Jennings: *Cabinet Government.* (Camb., 1936.)
A. S. Turberville: *The House of Lords in the Eighteenth Century.* (Clar. Press, 1927.)
J. A. R. Marriott: *Second Chambers.* (Clar. Press, 1927.)
W. S. McKechnie: *The Reform of the House of Lords.* (Glasgow, 1909.)
—— *The New Democracy and the Constitution.* (1912.)
R. H. Gretton: *The King's Government.* (1913.)
Lord Haldane and others: *The Development of the Civil Service.* (1922.)
Lord Hewart: *The New Despotism.* (1929.)
C. K. Allen: *Bureaucracy Triumphant.* (1931.)
J. A. Williamson: *British Expansion*, 2 vols. (1930.)
A. E. Zimmern: *The Third British Empire.* (Clar. Press, 1934.)
K. C. Wheare: *The Statute of Westminster.* (Clar. Press, 1938.)

*Contemporary Memoirs, &c.*

Lord John Hervey: *Memoirs of Reign of George II*, 3 vols.
Taylor and Pringle (ed.): *Chatham Correspondence*, 4 vols.
Lord John Russell (ed.): *Correspondence of Fourth Duke of Bedford*, 4 vols.
W. J. Smith (ed.): *Grenville Papers*, 4 vols.
Lord Holland (ed.): *Walpole's Memoirs of Reign of George II*, 3 vols.
—— *Memoirs of the Whig Party*, 2 vols. (1852–4.)
—— *Further Memoirs of the Whig Party.* (1905.)
Duke of Buckingham: *Court and Cabinets of George III*, 4 vols. (1853.)
—— *Court of England during the Regency*, 2 vols. (1856.)
—— *Court of George IV*, 2 vols. (1859.)
*Diary and Correspondence of Charles Abbott, Lord Colchester.* (1861.)
G. Pellew: *Life and Correspondence of Henry Addington, Viscount Sidmouth*, 3 vols. (1847.)

A. G. Stapleton (ed.): *Correspondence of George Canning*, 2 vols. (1887.)

Lord Londonderry (ed.): *Memoirs and Correspondence of Viscount Castlereagh*, 12 vols. (1848–53.)

Sir H. Maxwell (ed.): *The Creevey Papers*, 2 vols. (1894.)

L. J. Jennings (ed.): *The Croker Papers*, 3 vols. (1884.)

C. C. F. Greville: *Journals*. (1874, &c.)

A. C. Benson, Lord Esher, and G. E. Buckle (ed.): *Letters of Queen Victoria*. (1907–32.)

M. V. Brett (ed.): *Journals and Letters of Reginald Viscount Esher*, 4 vols. (1934–8.)

(The two last-mentioned works are invaluable for the reigns of Queen Victoria, Edward VII, and George V.)

*Biographies*

Lives of *Walpole* (by J. Morley and Stirling Taylor); *Stanhope* (by Basil Williams); *Lord Chatham* (by B. Williams); *C. J. Fox* (by Sir G. O. Trevelyan); *William Pitt* (by Lord Rosebery and J. Holland Rose); *Castlereagh* (by J. A. R. Marriott); *Sir Francis Burdett* (by M. W. Patterson); *Canning* (by J. A. R. Marriott and H. Temperley); *S. Perceval* (by S. Walpole); *Francis Place* (by Graham Wallas); *W. Cobbett* (by E. I. Carlyle); *Lord Grey of the Reform Bill* (by G. M. Trevelyan); *Sir Robert Peel* (by Miss Ramsay); *Palmerston* (by H. C. F. Bell); *Lord John Russell* (by S. Walpole); *Disraeli* (by Monypenny and Buckle); *Gladstone* (by J. Morley); *Lord Randolph Churchill* (by W. Churchill); *Lord Salisbury* (by Lady Gwendolen Cecil); *Lord Rosebery* (by Lord Crewe); *Joseph Chamberlain* (by J. L. Garvin); *Sir H. Campbell-Bannerman* (by J. A. Spender); *H. H. Asquith* (by Spender and C. Asquith); *A. J. Balfour* (by Mrs. Dugdale); *Queen Victoria* (by Sidney Lee); *Edward VII* (by S. Lee and A. Maurois); *George V* (by Sir G. Arthur).

(Out of a great mass of Memoirs and Biographies I have selected only those of men who played a prominent part in shaping the Constitution since 1714.)

*Books of Reference*

Among many, perhaps the most useful in the present connexion are *The Dictionary of National Biography* and *The Encyclopædia Britannica* (eleventh ed., with Supplements).

The *student* is recommended to take as the basis of his studies the Collections of Documents edited by Stubbs, Miss Lodge, Tanner, Prothero, Robertson, Dykes, and Gee and Hardy (for Church History).

# INDEX